LILLIAN ROXON:
MOTHER OF ROCK

LILLIAN ROXON:
MOTHER OF ROCK

ROBERT MILLIKEN

THUNDER'S MOUTH PRESS
NEW YORK

LILLIAN ROXON
MOTHER OF ROCK

Published by
Thunder's Mouth Press
An Imprint of Avalon Publishing Group Inc.
245 West 17th St., 11th Floor
New York, NY 10011

AVALON
publishing group incorporated

Library of Congress Cataloging-in-Publication Data is available.

ISBN 1-56025-671-0

9 8 7 6 5 4 3 2 1

Book design by Black Inc.
Printed in Canada on recycled paper
Distributed by Publishers Group West

Contents

On any person who desires such queer prizes, New York will bestow the gift of loneliness and the gift of privacy. It is this largess that accounts for the presence within the city's walls of a considerable section of the population; for the residents of Manhattan are to a large extent strangers who have pulled up stakes somewhere and come to town, seeking sanctuary or fulfillment or some greater or lesser grail. The capacity to make such dubious gifts is a mysterious quality of New York. It can destroy an individual or it can fulfill him, depending a good deal on luck. No one should come to New York to live unless he is willing to be lucky.

– E.B. White, *Here is New York*

You have to understand that rock stars are like avocados. When that moment of supreme and perfect ripeness comes, it is almost by definition doomed.

– Lillian Roxon

Prologue

Lillian Roxon once wrote about Dorothy Parker, the New York writer, wit and journalist: "Young, devastatingly attractive, devastatingly witty, she came to epitomise the giddy twenties when life was a laugh, and a well-turned quip was even more admired than a well-turned ankle, though it helped if you could produce both." Substitute the sixties for the twenties and she could have been writing about herself.

She came out of the fifties, one of the wittiest young women Australia produced from that dour decade, to inhabit the New York of the sixties, the decade of the Beatles, the Rolling Stones, Bob Dylan, Vietnam, the Kennedys, sex, drugs and rock and roll, a decade that seemed to be in a state of permanent revolution against the social and cultural rules that hitherto had governed Western societies. Her milieu was the famous round table at Max's Kansas City, the Manhattan bar and restaurant through which everyone who was anyone in the sixties passed. From that milieu she wrote, in 1969, *Lillian Roxon's Rock Encyclopedia*, the world's first encyclopedia of rock music and the book that made her a New York celebrity.

Like Dorothy Parker, who presided over another famous round table at the Algonquin Hotel forty years earlier, Lillian Roxon was someone of whom many stories have survived about what she said and what she did. Some of them happened, some of them might have happened. And if they didn't happen, they still found their way into the realm of myth and legend. When Sir Frank Packer, the legendary Australian newspaper tycoon, tried to lure Lillian away from the *Sydney Morning Herald*, did she really reply that she would require not just a very large salary but the entire senior class of a top Sydney private boys school in a *cage*?

Craig McGregor, the Australian writer, wrote of her in the *New York Times*: "Like Oscar Wilde, what she writes is but a pale imitation of what she says." Karin Berg, the New York feminist writer, says: "Lillian was more loving than Dorothy Parker. She had the wit of Parker but she wasn't so vicious. She was one of the few people I met who would be talking all the time but who you wanted to hear." Mary Cantwell, the managing editor of *Mademoiselle* magazine in New York, introduced Lillian to her readers as "the kind of human being you want to talk with for hours because the talk's all a lovely combination of a good brain, a heart and a soul." (Lillian's column for *Mademoiselle* was called "The Intelligent Woman's Guide to Sex".) Danny Goldberg, the president and chief executive of Mercury Records in New York, says: "She had an elevated notion of rock and roll as culture, a notion that was ahead of its time." Germaine Greer, who dedicated her momentous book on feminism, *The Female Eunuch*, to Lillian, says: "I admired her but she disliked me and did not bother to hide it."

I met Lillian Roxon for the first and only time at the end of 1972, when I was a young journalist working in London. She was visiting from New York writing about the British glam rock group Slade, and I went to meet her at the Portobello Hotel, a boutique hotel in Notting Hill favoured by the rock crowd. The triumph of *Lillian Roxon's Rock Encyclopedia*, which cemented her status as the unrivalled queen of the New York rock scene, was behind her. So was her feud with Germaine Greer and her friendship with Linda Eastman, the rock photographer with whom Lillian had worked the sixties rock scene in New York, who had married Paul McCartney and simultaneously turned her back on Lillian, her best friend.

Lillian was then forty and at a crucial turning point in her life. Her love affair with rock and roll and the people who made it was undiminished. But asthma had started to ravage her health, the drugs she took to control it had caused her to put on weight, and the glamorous woman I had expected to meet was actually insecure. She started by apologising for the way she looked, even though the facial beauty for which she was renowned, the flawless skin, ravishing smile and sparkling eyes, still shone through.

Then she talked without interruption for the next two hours, entertaining me, shocking me and making me laugh. She told scandalous stories about this one and that one, and even about herself. She also talked about her problems with editors, her asthma and her mother, three principal preoccupations of her life, even though Mrs Roxon, caricatured as an interfering Jewish mother, was long since dead. I remember little of what she said about her, except the line with which she abruptly closed that part of her monologue: "Well, now she's up in heaven making God's life a misery."

A few months after our meeting, Lillian was dead, a victim not of the drugs and the lifestyle that killed so many of those she wrote about but of asthma and its overwhelming impact on her constitution. Yet when I went to New York twenty-five years later, I was amazed to discover how much Lillian Roxon still inhabited the city in the minds of the movers and shakers of rock's golden era. She was being written about as the mother of rock and roll journalism, America's doyenne of rock critics, the late, beloved rock duchess, and talked about as the world's first pop journalist, the one who translated sixties culture, art, fashion and music in a popular way ahead even of Tom Wolfe.

The world that Lillian Roxon inhabited is now part of history, the world of the Pink Elephant, the Lincoln Inn and Jamison Street, of Max's Kansas City and The Scene. And the people who inhabited those places with her are now part of history, too, dispersed into a world of myths and legends that now seems so far away it is often hard to imagine that it ever existed.

ALASSIO, 1930s

Chapter 1 Where Hemingway Walked

It was the Year of the Monkey, 1932, when Liliana Ropschitz was born. According to Chinese astrology, those born in this year will be charismatic and social. Liliana turned out to be both, especially social. She grew up to be one of New York's and Sydney's most social animals, and both a star-maker and a star herself.

Liliana came from Alassio, on the Italian Riviera. In the 1930s, Alassio was quite detached from America, Australia, the Orient, indeed from the world in general, and this was a large part of its charm. It was a playground for rich English and American visitors, Charlie Chaplin and Ernest Hemingway among them: a sun-drenched town of stone and terracotta villas, palm trees, gardens, laneways and squares, stepping down a hillside to a long, sandy beach curving around the Mediterranean, about halfway between Nice and Genoa.

Liliana's parents, Izydor and Rosa, had settled in Alassio in 1926. As a newly qualified doctor, Izydor made a comfortable living there and the family's house was typical of Alassio's well-to-do. Iron gates opened into a garden dominated by tall palm trees, and marble front steps led into spacious rooms with sunny wrought-iron balconies. Here Liliana spent the first six years of her life.

Like all centres of happy childhoods, the place gripped her imagination for the rest of her life. Years later, shortly after arriving in New York to start a new life there, Lillian (as she had become) wrote to her mother in Australia to report a "very strange experience". She had gone to New York University to see a film, *Our Children Are Watching Us*, made by the Italian director Vittorio de Sica. The film's story was seen through the eyes of a four-year-old child. "But this is not the important part," Lillian wrote:

That part is that about half the film takes place in Alassio, and was actually filmed there. I recognised the island and the mountain at one end of the beach and the palm trees and the railway station and the little cabins and those funny boats with chairs on them and the water. And it all came back to me in the strangest way, as if I was suddenly only four years old myself. The film was made in 1942 during the Fascist regime, but not so far away from 1938 when we left. I can tell you it was a strange experience to see it half as the child in the film saw it, and my own memories, and half through my own adult eyes so that suddenly I saw Alassio as you must have seen it – with all those so-called "sophisticated" people and the men and the old, old women. As you know [de Sica] is a genius at showing life as it is, even then so early in his career. At one stage the child is learning to swim and the water is, of course, smooth but small waves come in his face and frighten him. Can you imagine what it meant seeing that? I am quite shaken by all this.

The child senses danger in an otherwise innocent setting and something sinister always shadowed the Ropschitz's idyllic life in Alassio. Anti-Semitism had driven Izydor and Rosa there in the first place and it eventually drove them out, to the other side of the world.

Izydor and Rosa were Polish, from Lvov, a magnificent old city and the historical crossroads of the eastern Galicia region of middle Europe. Izydor was born there in 1895 into a family of ten children. His parents had a gem business.

Although Lvov always remained a centre of Polish culture, ownership of the city was liable to change regularly. When Izydor and Rosa were young, it was controlled by Austria. Later, when the Russians occupied Lvov during World War I, the Ropschitzes fled to Vienna, which offered more stable business prospects than their home town. They were escaping, too, from the anti-Semitism that pervaded Catholic Poland long before the Nazi occupation. Izydor wanted to be a doctor but many Polish universities imposed enrolment quotas on Jews, and some excluded them altogether.

Izydor and Rosa were married in Vienna and, in May 1922, Rosa returned to Lvov from Vienna for the birth of their first child, Emanuele, later Milo. Meanwhile Izydor enrolled in medicine at the University of Padua, then Italy's leading medical school and one of the most outstanding in Europe. He graduated with a diploma in medicine and surgery in 1925, by which time he had fallen in love with Italy and its lifestyle. Fifty years before the age of mass tourism, Alassio was a world of its own, at the height of its charm. Izydor and Rosa moved there in June the following year.

When Milo was ten, Lillian arrived. She was born on 1 February 1932 in Savona, a port city between Alassio and Genoa. She was a plump baby, with lots of dark hair, and she quickly grew into an attractive child with a lively, intelligent, animated face, an open smile and a forthright manner. From the start she did not depend on others to make fun for her; rather she stamped her own authority on whatever she was doing. She was a child in charge of herself.

Lillian spent her first four years frolicking on the beach at Alassio with her mother, her older brother and their nanny while her father attended to his well-heeled patients. There were visits to Vienna and family holidays to Zakopane, a resort town nestled in a valley of the Taris mountains in southern Poland, on the border with Czechoslovakia. When she was five, her parents enrolled her in a Jewish school in Genoa, less than an hour's train journey along the Mediterranean coast.

Travelling with her family between Italy, Poland and Vienna in prewar Europe planted in Lillian the seeds of a sophistication that made her stand out later in Australia and America, an instinctive worldliness that some of those around her associated with European culture. Yet her background was something she rarely discussed. In both Australia and America, she did what most successful immigrants have always done: she started again.

In Alassio, too, her later prickly relationship with her parents, particularly her mother, began. The family were close, although from all accounts Izydor and Rosa's marriage was not happy. Izydor was a dapper man, astute, practical and intelligent. He had all the qualities a successful immigrant needed. He liked to gamble, on roulette in Europe and racehorses in Australia, and he was prepared to gamble on his family's future in a faraway country at a time when everything was collapsing around the Jews of Europe. Izydor was also an excellent storyteller, a quality Lillian inherited. But he was also something of a dictator to his children, keeping them in their places even as young adults.

Rosa's intelligence was equal to her husband's, but she suffered the fate of most women of her generation in having little outlet for her talents outside the family circle. Family photographs chart a steady downturn in her mood. As a young woman among family and friends in Lvov, Vienna and Zakopane after World War I, laughing, stylishly dressed and attractive, she looks happy. Walking along the beach in Alassio in the thirties in a smart black swimming costume, arm in arm with her handsome teenage son, Milo, she looks animated. By the time of her arrival in Australia, Rosa's expression had become downcast and she wore this look for the rest of her life. She had already moved from Lvov to Vienna to Alassio to Britain to Australia, with demanding language changes along the way. Perhaps Australia was one move too many.

Her gloominess also stemmed from the inevitable disappointments consequent on a Jewish mother's focus on her children. Successful as they all became, when the children later grew up and moved away, Rosa was left with little to sustain her. Lillian, her only daughter, was the embodiment of this motherly disappointment, especially as it was she who moved the furthest of all physically from her mother. For Rosa, Australia was the end of the line; for Lillian, it was just the start. The mother who had lived through the best and worst of times in Europe, who had seen Jewish families betrayed to their killers by those whom they thought they could trust, told her young daughter in Australia never to trust anyone, not even your neighbour.

But Lillian ignored this advice. Her rebelliousness in this and other respects left Rosa completely perplexed. She always hoped for a conventional mother–daughter relationship, including steering Lillian towards marriage with a nice Jewish man. But Lillian was never conventional, and their relationship was forever turbulent. "My daughter is a *mostro* [monster]!" Rosa would complain in Sydney, mixing her strange blend of English and Italian. After her mother's death, Lillian analysed Rosa's predicament: "My ... mother was not Sadie Portnoy's sister, her cousin maybe, and the embodiment of a middle-aged European Candide totally bewildered by the unadorned earthiness and directness of Australian life. Vienna it wasn't."

Chapter 2 Getting Out

In February 1936, Izydor took Rosa to Genoa for the birth of their third and last child, Jacob, later Jack. The baby's arrival brought joy to the family, and they might well have expected to carry on their idyllic life in Alassio untouched by the stormy events unfolding elsewhere in Europe. But eight months later something closer to home sealed their fate. In October 1936, Italy's dictator, Benito Mussolini, formed an alliance with Adolf Hitler, the Axis, which linked Italy and Germany in a so-called "Pact of Steel".

The formal alliance between the two fascist states meant that what the German government was doing to its Jewish population could eventually be repeated in Italy. After 1933, when Hitler and the Nazi Party came to power, life for Germany's 500,000 Jews had grown steadily worse. By 1935, thousands of Jewish doctors, lawyers, journalists, academics and artists had been barred from working. In September 1935, Hitler had enacted the Nuremberg Laws, which effectively excluded Jews from further participation in German life.

In March 1938, Germany annexed Austria. Vienna's Jews, including Izydor's parents, sisters, cousins, aunts and uncles, were stripped of their citizenship and rights to work. The Nazis started arresting Jews and sending them to Dachau and Buchenwald, the first of the concentration camps. And on the night of 9 November 1938, "Kristallnacht", Hitler unleashed an extraordinary wave of violence throughout Germany which saw thousands of Jews arrested or killed, homes destroyed and almost 2,000 synagogues smashed and set on fire.

During the first half of the thirties, a false sense of security lulled Alassio and the rest of the Mediterranean; life retained a timeless quality. Unlike German Nazism, Italian Fascism had no fanatical commitment to anti-Semitism, and Jews were not hounded. But the Axis of 1936 shattered all this. Italy now had a role to play in Germany's mounting campaign against European Jewry.

In the month following "Kristallnacht", the Italian government ordered the Ropschitz family out of the country because they were Jewish. Their fate was recorded by J. S. Hutcheon, a barrister in Brisbane, who wrote to the Medical Board of Queensland in 1940 supporting Izydor's application to be registered as a doctor: "In 1938 my wife's cousin, who is a retired cotton broker of Manchester, England, and who has for many years been in the habit of spending several months annually at Alassio in Italy, wrote to me telling me that Dr Ropschitz had been ordered by the Italian government to leave Italy – as being of Jewish nationality – and asking me to assist his application to the Federal Government to be permitted to come to Australia."

At first Izydor considered moving his practice along the Mediterranean coast just inside the French border, hoping his patients would follow. But this proved impractical. So, on 10 December 1938, accompanied by sixteen-year-old Milo, he left by train for London to plan the family's flight to a new world. Rosa, Lillian and Jack followed soon afterwards.

*

In September 1938, Izydor had obtained a Polish passport through the Polish consul-general in London – a valuable asset, as it made him not an "enemy alien" but an ally of Britain and Australia when war finally broke out. By contrast, those Jews who held Austrian and German passports and fled to Britain were placed in internment camps on suspicion of being Nazi fifth-columnists – as was the case with Izydor's seventeen-year-old Viennese cousin Fritz, later Fred, and his father, Sigmund, who joined the Ropschitzes in London. (Their imprisonment did not last; in late 1940, young Fred Ropschitz joined the British army to help fight the enemy he had been suspected of helping.)

In London, Izydor applied to enter the United States and Australia. The US, with a tight system of immigrant quotas, was pretty much a lost cause. Australia was a gamble but offered two big advantages: it was a long way from the conflicts of Europe and it was warm and sunny, like the life they had left behind in Alassio. At this time Australia had no immigration or consular offices in Europe; the application for an

Australian Landing Permit had to be sent to Canberra and took months to come through. But finally, on 21 July 1939, the permit arrived. Izydor was free to take his family to Australia.

They were lucky. It was hard for European Jews to enter Australia before World War II, and even harder afterwards. Australia in the 1930s had no immigration department and no immigration policy apart from one cardinal rule: to keep Australia white and British. Australia had just seven and a half million people, 97 per cent of British stock. It was an insular country, often deeply suspicious and resentful of any-one and anything foreign, especially of anyone who could take jobs or introduce "ethnic" elements into the culture.

Ezra Norton, proprietor of *Truth*, a popular tabloid newspaper, voiced the prevailing suspicion:

> We do not want Jewish refugees! Not because we do not sympathise
> with their plight; but because we cannot possibly allow them to under-
> mine our life and economic fabric. As a racial unit they are a menace
> to our nationhood and standards. As an inflow of migrants, they are
> a menace to employment ... It is a problem of self-preservation.

This attitude was effectively the official attitude, too. At an interna-tional conference on refugees in July 1938, T. W. White, Australia's Minister for Trade and Customs, announced that Australia was not pre-pared to compromise the essential British character of its population: "It will no doubt be appreciated that as we have no racial problem, we are not desirous of importing one."

But even faraway fortress Australia could not stay indifferent to the horrors that were unfolding in Europe. From the mid-thirties, Australia and other rich countries came under increasing international pressure to accept refugees. In December 1938, as the Ropschitzes left Italy, Australia announced it would accept 15,000 refugees over the next three years. This quota was never filled: when war broke out nine months later, refugee migration to Australia almost stopped. Those who arrived were not always treated well. In 1940, as the Nazi jugger-naut rolled across Europe, Australia agreed to take 2,542 of Britain's interned refugees. They arrived in September 1940 on the ship *Dunera* after a voyage from hell, during which they were beaten and abused by their British guards, only to be marched straight into camps at Hay,

New South Wales and Tatura, Victoria when they landed. Those who stayed in Australia went on to capture a niche in Australian history as the "Dunera boys", a group of outcasts who eventually triumphed in their new land.

Like the Dunera boys, the Ropschitzes were members of a small, isolated group of pioneers: continental, non-Christian, multilingual "foreigners" who spoke heavily accented English. As such, they encountered few welcoming hands across the water. Suzanne Rutland, a historian of Jewish immigration to Australia, has noted how the refugees who arrived just before World War II received a "hostile reception" from Jews and non-Jews alike. Australia's anglicised Jews saw the newcomers as a threat to their high social status; the non-Jews simply saw them as foreigners. Both reactions were "typical of an isolated and parochial community".

While waiting for a Landing Permit, Izydor applied for and obtained registration by the General Medical Council in Britain. This did not necessarily allow him to practise as a doctor in Britain at that time, but it did qualify him to work as a surgeon on a British ship leaving for Australia, the *S.S. Tyndareus*, of the Blue Funnel Line.

In early July 1940, the family assembled on the cargo-ship's deck. The photographs that record their departure also hint at the emerging family dynamics. Izydor and Rosa are divided, he looking dashing, she looking anxious with eighteen-year-old Milo on her arm. Rosa's carefree smile of Alassio has gone; her mouth is turned down, her face seemingly worried at what lies ahead. Eight-year-old Lillian, dressed in an overcoat and beret, has eyes and a face full of confidence and expectation at the adventure awaiting her.

The *Tyndareus* sailed in a convoy escorted by Royal Navy destroyers. One night the family woke to the sound of an explosion and rushed up on deck to see the sky lit by flames from one of the other ships that had been hit by a German U-boat. When they reached the coast of southern Africa, the destroyers peeled off and the *Tyndareus* continued safely to land in Melbourne on 13 August.

Izydor had gambled and won. Skilfully and fairly painlessly, he had got his wife and children out. They had escaped the worst of fates in Europe. When the war ended in May 1945, one-fifth of Poland's population, about six million people, including almost the entire Jewish population of three million, had been killed. Some of the worst Nazi atrocities happened in Lvov, the Ropschitz home town, where only about 3 per cent of the city's 100,000 Jews were estimated to have survived. Izydor's parents, Moritz and Sophie, both died in the Holocaust, as did three of his five sisters.

For Lillian's parents, Australia represented the main freedom that mattered to their generation: physical survival. But for Lillian herself, Australia was just the first step in a lifelong quest for a wider personal and cultural freedom.

BRISBANE, 1940s

Chapter 3 New Land

Once the *Tyndareus* was safely docked in Melbourne, the Ropschitz family prepared to move north, straight to Brisbane. In fact, Melbourne would have been a more logical place for them to stay. In the forties, enclaves of continental Europeanness were confined largely to Melbourne and Sydney and these were the cities where most pre-war Jewish refugees settled.

But there were barriers to foreign doctors working in both cities. Australia's medical profession lobbied to stop refugee doctors from being allowed to practise, appealing to what historian Suzanne Rutland describes as "Australian nationalism and xenophobia to protect the self-interests of the medical establishment". In both Melbourne and Sydney, Izydor would have to spend up to five years re-qualifying before he could work. For once, Queensland was more liberal than the southern states. It accepted foreign doctors with British registration automatically, as well as graduates from a select list of European medical schools including the University of Padua. Izydor qualified on both counts and had written ahead from London to the Medical Board of Queensland applying for registration. Now that they were on Australian soil, he bundled his wife and three children and their luggage on to a train for the two-day journey to Brisbane, capital of Australia's Deep North.

Their first home was a flat in Moray Street, New Farm, a pleasant suburb on a small peninsula jutting into the Brisbane River near the city centre. On 14 November 1940, the medical board approved Izydor's application, after the Commonwealth Investigation Branch, the forerunner counter-espionage body of the Australian Security Intelligence Organisation, gave him a security clearance.

Those who did get through Australia's tough immigration barriers in the 1940s found themselves in a country that was suspicious of, even hostile towards, non-British accents and names. No sooner had boats carrying displaced people tied up at the docks than officials from the Australian Jewish Welfare Society were on hand to issue the bewildered disembarking passengers with written instructions on how to conduct themselves in their new land: "Modulate your voices. Do not make yourself conspicuous anywhere by walking with a group of persons all of whom are loudly speaking in a foreign language ..."

It was a bizarre irony that the Jews of Europe had fled from a continent where their brethren were being forced underground if they wanted to survive to one where they were being told to make themselves inconspicuous if they wanted to get on. It fell to the Ropschitzes, like others, to reinvent themselves for their new land. Eight-year-old Lillian, she told her friends years later, did the reinventing. Soon after settling into New Farm, Izydor, Rosa, Lillian, Milo and Jack went on a family outing to a beach near Brisbane where they talked about adopting a more "Australian" name. Glancing at the rocks, Lillian started thinking aloud about how she could blend this simple word with the name they had, then added a melodious suffix and came up with Roxon. Her parents approved. On 27 November 1940, Izydor swore by deed poll, "on behalf of my heirs and issue", to "absolutely renounce and abandon" the name Ropschitz and assume the name Roxon. Izydor became Isadore and Rosa became Rose.

As they became Roxons, Lillian and her brothers also ineluctably became Australians. With the new name came a new way of life and the disappearance of any surviving traces of an Italian accent. For their parents, the finality of abandoning their European identity was harder to bear. Within two years, Isadore changed his name again by deed poll to Roxon-Ropschitz, the name under which he practised as a doctor in Brisbane. His family did not follow suit. What must he and Rose have felt about their bolt-hole from the Holocaust? Relief, certainly, but also despair.

*

Brisbane in the 1940s was a semi-tropical, insular city of 345,000 overwhelmingly Anglo-Celtic people, a city of trams, rambling weatherboard houses, frangipani trees and solid, low-rise commercial buildings.

"Keg parties" were a popular social activity, and cultural diversity and adventurism were barely tolerated. The *Courier-Mail*, the city's main newspaper, dismissed the first exhibition in Brisbane of paintings by the young Sidney Nolan in 1948 as "monstrous daubings". The paper also described Picasso and Matisse as "disciples of the cult of ugliness". The hero of *Johnno*, David Malouf's novel of Brisbane of the forties, remembered it as a "world so settled, so rich in routine and ritual, that it seemed impossible then that it should ever suffer disruption".

But a year after the Roxons arrived, it was disrupted dramatically. Japan bombed Pearl Harbor on 6 December 1941, catapulting the United States into World War II. Singapore fell two months later; Darwin, on Australia's northern coastline, was bombed four days after that; and Broome, on the north-east coast, was hit two weeks after Darwin. Australians, especially Queenslanders, suddenly felt the possibility of imminent Japanese invasion.

Brisbane became the operational front line in the Pacific war. General Douglas MacArthur, Supreme Commander of Allied Forces in the southwest Pacific, took up residence in Brisbane in July 1942, living at Lennon's Hotel. From his headquarters in the AMP building in Queen Street, he directed the war against Japan. Here was another irony: the Roxons had escaped Hitler only to land in a faraway place where the war was being fought in the oceans and islands just up north.

The war brought Brisbane to life. There were sandbags in the streets, brownouts (a lesser form of blackout), rationing of petrol, butter and tea and the wholesale transformation of routine and ritual. Orchestral concerts, then one of Brisbane's few forms of high culture, switched their performances from Saturday evenings to Saturday afternoons in case Brisbane was bombed at night (defying logic that the bombs could just as easily rain down in the afternoon).

Brisbane was soon crawling with American troops whose very presence precipitated a challenge to the city's manners, customs and sexual mores, which had barely changed since Edwardian times. By August 1942, there were 99,000 American military personnel based in Australia, two-thirds of them located in and around Brisbane. They were better paid and, on the whole, better turned out than their Australian counterparts. They mesmerised Brisbane's young women.

The Americans brought jazz, swing and a new way of dancing. Segregated from the central city and confined to the south side of the

Brisbane River, the black American troops turned an old building there into a jazz club, the Washington Carver Club, named after a distinguished black American, George Washington Carver. The painter Donald Friend, then an official war artist with the Australian Infantry Forces, described the breaking down of old inhibitions at a dance at the Brisbane Town Hall: "The band was good, Yankee and very hot. I remember how Queensland danced a little while ago: waltzes, two-steps, the Pride of Erin and all those Victorian affairs. Now they jitterbug at terrific speed, kicking, belly-wobbling, bum-popping, tapping, whirling insanely like people possessed by devils ... They seemed drugged, while their bodies (bedwracked, easy) pulsed erotic contortions to the rhythm."

All this was not lost on Lillian. Though not yet in her adolescent years, she was fascinated by the influx of this modern, overtly sexual American popular culture. She set out to track it down as an observer, the way she would do on a grander scale years later. Hotel rooms in Brisbane during the war were scarce, and the park at New Farm became a nightly hangout for the American troops and their girlfriends. Anna Lewensohn (later Muir), a school friend of Lillian's who also became close to her mother, recalls: "It was well known that New Farm park was a favourite mating spot for American soldiers. The bushes were known to be shaking every night. So who was it who conducted me to New Farm park? Lilly. She took me on a tour of the park at night. Sometimes we'd go for walks at night, playing make-believe games and entertaining ourselves with ridiculous scenarios along the way. It was quite safe to do that in Brisbane then."

At the park all the girls saw were legs, "a lot of legs". Some of the women called to them to go home where they belonged. "Quite right," says Anna. "We were invading their privacy. But it wasn't very private. Well, that's war. Tomorrow the men were going off to the islands. They might be dead."

Chapter 4 Toowoomba

In late 1941 the Roxons moved to Toowoomba, a town on the plateaus west of Brisbane, where Isadore became a resident medical officer at the local hospital. As a newly arrived foreign doctor, he was obliged to fulfil wartime needs for medical services and this inland town was just the first of several such postings. Toowoomba became the centre of a big Allied military base and an evacuation place for coastal children whose families feared invasion from the sea or air at any minute.

Before their move to Toowoomba, the Roxons had made contact with other evacuees from Europe whom the war had landed in Queensland. Lillian's mother became friendly with Rose Jofeh, a Jewish woman who had been evacuated by the British from the Baltic States after the Soviet occupation in June 1940.

Mrs Jofeh, as everyone knew her, lived in Four Oaks, a private hotel in South Brisbane facing Musgrave Park, where her fellow residents included Barbara Patterson (the future writer Barbara Blackman) and her mother. Mrs Jofeh was a large woman "whose corpulence was of almost liquid immensity" according to Barbara Blackman – as a girl, one of her duties was to help this colossal figure into her corsets. Mrs Jofeh saw in Lillian and Barbara two bright girls and introduced them; they soon became lasting friends. Barbara was three years older than Lillian and already suffering from poor eyesight. She recalls that Lillian "was wonderfully observant of people. As a child I loved going about with her because she was such a wonderful describer of things to me."

Mrs Jofeh also moved to Toowoomba in 1941 to be close to two of her fellow evacuees, Mrs Louie Green and her young son, Louis. When Louis's mother fell ill with an infection, Mrs Jofeh recommended Isadore. It happened to be Lillian's tenth birthday, 1 February 1942, when Louis's mother visited the surgery in the Roxon house. While his mother was being treated, Louis was ushered into another room where Lillian was holding her birthday party with some other little girls. Although Louis was two years older than Lillian, the younger girl managed to shock the shy, older boy at this, their first meeting. Almost sixty years later, Louis Green recalls: "Lillian immediately suggested we play postman's knock or something like that. I think she decided that having a boy there would spark the whole thing up. Even at that age Lillian was fairly overwhelming. I demurred. Eventually things settled down."

Lillian had already formed the strong character and outspoken personality that became her hallmark as an adult. "She was spirited, lively, good company and very witty," Louis Green says. "She was very interesting to talk to, very intelligent and very provocative. And she was tremendously good at involving people in her life." When the Greens and the Roxons moved back to Brisbane, Louis and Lillian stayed friends during their adolescence among a group of bright students that Brisbane produced during the forties, but which the city could not hold.

*

The Roxons moved from Toowoomba back to Brisbane in late 1942 and settled again in New Farm, this time at 1 Sydney Street, where they stayed for the rest of their time in that city. The house was a rambling, weatherboard "Queenslander", standing on stilts above the ground, with generously spaced rooms. Mrs Jofeh, also returned from Toowoomba, was a regular visitor there. So was the Gradwell family who lived a couple of streets away. The Gradwells were true Queenslanders, but they were also Christadelphians, members of a small Christian sect who sympathised with the Jews and saw them as the Chosen People. As such, they were drawn to the Roxons; it did not seem to matter that they were not observant Jews. For her part, Rose Roxon, starved of stimulating conversation in her new home, was happy to find an opportunity for it with the Gradwells.

A short block down from the Roxons' house, Sydney Street ended and hit the Brisbane River. The war had come to the end of their street, pulsating with noise and action. American warships and troop barges tied up at New Farm Wharf. Shipyards directly across the river worked around the clock making corvette escort vessels for the Royal Australian Navy. Seaplanes took off and landed along the river. Lillian's younger brother, Jack, and Harry Gradwell, both aged seven, made adventurous forays on to the warships where the crews, unrestrained by onshore rationing, offered them food treats.

June Gradwell, Harry's sister, became friends with Lillian. In most respects they were each other's antithesis: June, the girl who was at home in Brisbane suburbia, and Lillian, the one who was already destined to break free of it. Yet the two women corresponded for the rest of Lillian's life. Over the next twenty years, as Lillian became a friend of the stars, June gave her faithfully written accounts of a daily life that rarely changed. From Sydney in the fifties, Lillian wrote June frank, anguished accounts of her boyfriend problems in the bohemian world of the Push, to which June replied with down-to-earth advice. From New York in the sixties, by then a prominent name in Australian magazines, Lillian posted June gifts of scarfs, perfume and parcels of magazines. When June wrote asking Lillian if she would write to a co-worker, an eighteen-year-old youth who was "quite a fan of yours and would be thrilled to receive a letter from you about New York, men's fashions, people you meet", Lillian wrote to the boy. It was a measure of Lillian's generosity but also, perhaps, of how the conventional, anchored world that June Gradwell never left remained one of Lillian's unconscious reference points. June signed her letters to Lillian "your friend always"; and she was.

Chapter 5 School Years

Isadore led something of an itinerant war, moving back and forth between Brisbane and country towns that needed doctors. After Too-woomba, he spent some time in Woodford, north of Brisbane, and then in Quilpie, a hot, dusty outback town about 1,000 kilometres west of Brisbane on the edge of Australia's central desert, where he stayed for almost two years until the war ended. It was a long way from Alassio.

Rose and their three children stayed for the most part in New Farm. Lillian had gone to local schools in Brisbane and Toowoomba, but in 1944, when she was twelve, her parents sent her to St Hilda's, an Anglican girls' boarding school at Southport on the coast, to begin her secondary schooling. Today, St Hilda's is an oasis of elegant brick and wooden buildings, picket fences and sprawling grounds amid a tangle of concrete towers and traffic. But in 1944, when Queensland's Gold Coast consisted of a string of quiet seaside towns, St Hilda's was a semi-rural school where the daughters of Queensland's professional and pastoral families received a well-rounded, if conventional, education. With Isadore absent in Quilpie and Lillian already showing signs of the rebelliousness that would worry her parents for the rest of their days, St Hilda's reputation for discipline clinched the decision to send her there.

She shone academically. In 1945, when she was thirteen and still in the junior school, she won the Hodson Cup for English and the Barnes Cup for Languages, two prizes usually won by girls from the senior grades. The same year, the school magazine published what was probably her first work. The article showed imagination and a tight, journalistic style. In it she transported herself back one hundred years to converse with a family in "the land of dreams", then woke in a disturbed state, rather like Dorothy in *The Wizard of Oz*, with her mother standing over her. She gave her mother a subversive line of dialogue: "I really don't know why they teach you so much Latin and Geometry! It makes you sleepy."

Lillian wrote to her father in Quilpie, sending him accounts of life at St Hilda's and poems she had written. In one undated letter, she wrote: "Dear Daddy, We went to see 'The Great Dictator'. It was very good. You see Chaplin plays 2 roles in the film, one as a poor barber who at wartime is a soldier. He is a Jew and he saves Commander Schultz's life and he goes back to his shop in the Ghetto. The Germans come and paint on his windows the word Jew. Later he is mistaken for the Dictator. You see Chaplin plays the part of the Dictator. Kisses, Lilly. P.S. How do you like my drawings? It is my birthday today."

The war in Europe ended on 8 May 1945 and the Pacific war ended dramatically with the atomic bombings of Hiroshima and Nagasaki three months later. Lillian was at St Hilda's, her mother and brothers were in New Farm, and Isadore was still in exile in Quilpie. A few years later, Lillian told her friends in Sydney that her father had celebrated VE Day and his release from wartime duties in Queensland's wild west by riding a horse down Quilpie's main street calling: "Europe is free, and so by God am I!" Myth or not, it was the sort of thing her father, with his flair for spontaneity and a talent for telling a good story, might have done. He returned to Brisbane and opened professional rooms in Queen Street in the city.

Lillian herself returned to Brisbane at the end of 1946, telling some of her friends she had been expelled from St Hilda's. It seemed a curious outcome after her achievements there, and the reasons for her expulsion varied in the telling: that she had worn a brassiere, breaking a strict rule that girls were not to wear any garment under their navy-blue pleated tunics that would show off their figures; that she had hurled a hairbrush in a rage at a schoolmistress; and that she had been caught stealing biscuits. There is no record of her expulsion for these or any other reasons. Yet all of these incidents could well have happened, and if they did Lillian knew how to turn them into a good story.

In this she took after her father. Through the prism of Lillian's friends' memories of their Brisbane adolescences, an image emerges of Isadore as a dapper, energetic, outgoing man with a flair for telling stories that people wanted to hear. Some of his stories involved the intrigues of pre-war Europe, of how people had outsmarted the authorities by getting money out of Germany and Italy. Rose appears in the same memories as a more withdrawn figure, although intelligent and supportive of those who sought her help. Isadore still had his life as a doctor, but Rose was marooned in a suburb of a semi-tropical city that could not have been further from her cultural roots. Rose compensated for the distance between her and Isadore by focussing on her children, but the children would soon start leaving one by one. Milo, ten years older than Lillian, was already embarked on a university career in Sydney.

Lillian's dark hair, pigtails and school uniform gave her the appearance of any other adolescent girl of the mid-forties. But her flawless skin, captivating smile and self-assurance gave her the manner of someone considerably older. "She wasn't like any other teenager I'd ever met," Anna Lewensohn remembers. "She was very young but appeared to be very much in command of herself, and she seemed to be distracting attention from herself by telling amusing and rather shocking stories." The stories could have been a distraction from her weight, which would be a principal preoccupation throughout her life. She was plump rather than fat, but for a small person this was enough to cause anxiety. Lillian told Louis Green in 1948 that her favourite line from *Hamlet* was: "Oh! That this too too solid flesh would melt/ Thaw, and resolve itself into a dew."

Her plumpness became a source of tension with her father. Although Isadore and Lillian shared characteristics in common, Isadore was also an austere figure who kept his family in line. He nagged Lillian about her weight and sometimes humiliated her over it; and he was not averse to punishing his children with the strap. For her part, Lillian performed for her friends what Barbara Blackman describes as "wonderful, diabolical imitations" of her parents and their middle European accents. Her stories about her father usually involved his humiliations of her. "No porridge for my fat daughter!" she reported him commanding a waiter when Lillian and her father were once having breakfast at a hotel. "If you could see yourself from behind you wouldn't go out," he allegedly told her after she had dressed up for her first schoolgirl date in Brisbane.

*

In early 1947, Lillian started her last two years of secondary education at Brisbane State High, an academic school that attracted bright students. State High was an exception in the limited Queensland state education system of the forties. Its curriculum was conservative, but it had a tradition of non-conformity that suited Lillian better than St Hilda's. In years to come, the school's cultural influence would extend well beyond Queensland. Other graduates in the 1940s included Barbara Blackman, Roger Covell, a future professor of music at the University of New South Wales and fellow correspondent of Lillian's for the *Sydney Morning Herald*, Keith McWatters, a future professor of French at the University of Liverpool in Britain, Louis Green, a future historian at Monash University, Melbourne, and Charles Osborne, a future arts administrator in Britain and prolific author of books on opera, music and art.

Lillian was fifteen when she arrived at State High. If Rose and Isadore thought the academic demands of State High after the discipline of St Hilda's might settle her down, they were mistaken. Her fellow State High students remember her as a rebel who irritated some teachers by questioning them at a time when pupils, especially girls, did not do this. Grace Garlick, the 1948 girl's captain, a friend of Lillian's and a member of the girls' debating team with her, recalls:

> Somebody like Lillian had never hit the place. She seemed to be full of sex and wisdom and boys talk. I would have thought it was all talk, but she seemed to have an awareness so well ahead of her time.
>
> She was the Germaine Greer of the classroom. She would have been much more fun, I think, than Germaine Greer at the same age because she was so completely uninhibited. I wasn't even much aware of Germaine years later because I felt we'd already had it all. It was the start of womanhood. She was irresistible, the most attractive, the brightest of us all. No wonder the teachers didn't know how to deal with it.

The Latin mistress declined to deal with it. Grace remembers her resorting to a standing order before each lesson: "Lillian Roxon! Outside please!" Lillian would spend the Latin lessons sitting on the veranda. Grace and her friends found Lillian's questioning "enormously attractive"; she was "impossible to contain".

Lillian's diary for the first half of 1948 records her matter-of-fact responses to these classroom expulsions. They were not confined to Latin. "Got kicked out of Latin for a 'vulgar display'," she wrote on 11 May. Eight days later: "Got kicked out of Latin class. Wrote poems." On 16 June: "Went to school. Disgusted. Kicked out of Fr. and maths. Went to town. Bought brown slacks. Saw Danny Kaye in 'Wonder Man'. Rang Grace."

*

During her State High school years, when she was fifteen and sixteen, Lillian held her first teenage parties. She planned them enthusiastically, especially the guest lists. Louis Green, a regular guest, remembers that, "She had a tendency to bring beautiful girls in as a sort of lure to attract men to the parties." The parties usually ended at an early hour when Isadore would appear from another part of the house and tell Lillian's guests it was time to go home. Another regular was Rhyl Sorensen, a young music teacher who became a close friend. Through their interests in music, art and literature, Lillian and Rhyl were drawn to two bright boys from State High, Keith McWatters and Peter Munro. The four went with Roger Covell to orchestral concerts at the Brisbane Town Hall. They wrote frequently to each other to arrange social outings, in an era when there were mail deliveries twice a day and on weekends.

Rhyl recalls: "There was so much old culture in Lillian's veins. She had all that Jewish inheritance that made her background richer and more knowing. But for all her sophistication, we were innocents abroad in Brisbane then. We were just loving friends and very fond of each other." In her diary, Lillian wrote of one of these outings with Rhyl, Peter Munro and Keith McWatters: "A rather exciting thing happened. Peter kissed me. Peter, my platonic lover. We went for a walk, held hands, switched men at which both R and K sulked. Found this a little foolish."

For all Lillian's unorthodoxy, post-war adolescents in middle-class Australia still conformed to strict mores that frowned on teenage drinking and sexual experimentation. Recreational drugs did not exist. Adolescents followed established conventions of dress and manners and showed due deference to the authority of parents. But that was soon to change: "teenagers" as a word and an idea appeared in the 1940s. Soon after the war, popular magazines hit on teenagers as a new marketing target. *Woman,* a national magazine published by Associated Newspapers in Sydney, later to become *Woman's Day,* started running a page-three feature called "Teen-age World", featuring "Teen-agers of the Week", complete with pictures.

Lillian got herself into this column. On 24 May 1948, Lillian Roxon, sixteen, student of "New Farm, Q", smiled from the page beneath a white hat, listed her favourite record as Chopin's Waltz in C Sharp Minor, her favourite hobby as photography, her favourite film star as Humphrey Bogart, her pet aversion as "having nothing to do" and her ideal man as, "Not necessarily handsome, but must have good teeth, nice eyes and a sense of humour". Twenty years later, the teenage world would explode into something called youth culture on a scale no one in 1948 could have imagined, and Lillian would be one of its chief reporters.

But in 1948, her ideal man was Peter Munro. Peter was both brilliant and beautiful-looking. He wanted to become an actor, and acted in everything at State High and in Shakespearean and other plays performed by the Twelfth Night Theatre, an amateur company in Brisbane. Peter and Lillian were each other's match intellectually. Lillian told Louis Green that Peter was the first man she was ever in love with. They formed a crush on each other which could well have developed into something more lasting if fate had not intervened. A few years after leaving State High, Peter Munro was dead. A tumour of the pancreas killed him at the age of twenty-two. His tragic death was something of an omen. Peter was the first of three brilliant young men of his generation who became central figures in Lillian's life, all of whom would die young.

Chapter 6 The Pink Elephant Crowd

Beneath the city at war, and the city of rigid social attitudes and conventions, another scene was stirring in Brisbane. From the mid-forties,
a small group of young artistic rebels reacted against a cultural establishment that frowned on modernism in art and literature and tended
to look down on new Australian writing and painting.

The group launched its own magazines and staged its own exhibitions in a bid to find a voice for youth in the post-war world. Most of
its members were older than Lillian Roxon, but during her last two years
in Brisbane she gravitated to this group whose principal movers and
shakers came from State High School itself.

Already Brisbane had given birth to *Meanjin*, a literary magazine
launched by Clem Christesen in 1940 which took its title from the
Aboriginal name for Brisbane. Now came *Barjai*, a magazine for poets,
critics and all subversive young writers who were prepared to take the literary agenda forward. *Barjai* (also Aboriginal, for meeting place) was
started by three students at State High, Barrie Reid, Laurie Collinson and
Cecel Knopke. At first they produced it clandestinely from the school,
but its venue became the wider world. Soon after its launch in 1943, it
declared itself a magazine not just for senior students but "a magazine
for Youth", and *Barjai* groups sprouted in Sydney, Melbourne and
Adelaide. It borrowed a motto from *Eureka*, the magazine of the Eureka
Youth League: "Tomorrow belongs to youth and youth intend to have
their say in what sort of tomorrow it will be."

Over *Barjai*'s five-year life, the people known as the "*Barjai* group"
held Sunday meetings in the Lyceum, a women's club in Queen Street,
Brisbane where the magazine's editors and contributors, nearly all
aged under twenty, read their works. Older outsiders, some already

distinguished and most destined to be so, came in to read theirs, including the novelist Thea Astley and Judith Wright, who read her first book of unpublished poems at a *Barjai* meeting.

Two years after *Barjai* started, a group of young Brisbane artists formed a collective called the Miya Studio as an outlet for the sorts of modern works spurned by the Brisbane art establishment centred on the Royal Queensland Art Society. Miya and *Barjai* had members in common and the two groups formed a loose coalition against the constraints of traditional high culture. Laurie Collinson and Cecel Knopke were among the artists who co-founded Miya in late 1945, after Collinson had written, in a provocative foreword to a catalogue for an exhibition by the Art Society's Younger Artists' Group: "Queensland art today is practically sterile." The Miya modernists found little support in their city. The *Courier-Mail* heaped derision on their 1947 exhibition at Finney's Gallery, dismissing it as "Brisbane's Little Chelsea peddling its brave imitations of Picasso, Matisse and other disciples of the cult of ugliness". The paper declared: "Malformations of the human body are the subject of our pity, but some members of the Miya Studio have set out to glorify these atrocities and (sublime insult) actually affix a price to their efforts."

Lillian Roxon was not a Miya artist; the last *Barjai* magazine, with Barbara Blackman as editor, appeared in 1947, the year Lillian returned to Brisbane to start at State High. But, schoolgirl though she still was, Lillian became a part of this slightly older group outside the school boundaries, whose waywardness and championing of youth culture clicked with her own sense of who she was. She attended readings at the Lyceum Club and hung out with the *Barjai*–Miya crowd at the Pink Elephant, post-war Brisbane's only late-night cafe. In their own ways, the *Barjai*–Miya crowd at once reflected and gave a kick-start to Lillian's enthusiasm for the fabulous world of pop culture that she took on twenty years later. And wayward they certainly were, at least for their time and place.

Barrie Reid and Laurie Collinson were both gay, which put them as much on the fringe of forties Brisbane as did their literary rebelliousness. In fact, Collinson scored a trifecta in being an outsider: "Jewish, homosexual and Communist", as Barbara Blackman described him. "As pale and consumptive as a poet should look". Reid was a charismatic figure, good-looking and regarded as the best of the *Barjai* poets. T. S. Eliot and Dylan Thomas were his literary yardsticks. He stepped out for a time with the beautiful, young Diane Cilento (later a noted actress, and daughter of Sir Raphael Cilento, a leading Queensland medical figure), before becoming more closely identified with Brisbane's gay bohemia.

Barrie Reid formed a partnership with Charles Osborne, another State High graduate, who had an intimidatingly broad grasp of music, art, poetry and drama. Osborne acted on the stage, directed plays and met every outstanding musician and orchestral conductor who passed through Brisbane during the war years. Osborne regarded himself as entirely divorced from mainstream Brisbane: in an era when beer and rum were the city's staple social drinks, he once boasted, "At fifteen I drank only wine." With money provided by their parents, Reid and Osborne adventurously opened a bookshop in the heart of Brisbane called the Ballad Bookshop in 1947 when they were both aged around twenty. They imported books in languages other than English, as well as titles outside the usual run of stock with which British publishers swamped Australia; they specialised in books on music, art and politics.

Sidney Nolan visited the Ballad Bookshop in 1947 on his way north to produce his Fraser Island paintings. When he exhibited them at the Moreton Galleries in Brisbane the following year, the *Courier-Mail* lambasted him for his "blatant extremism" and his "deliberate maltreatment of so much useful and hard-to-come-by building material" (Nolan's works were on masonite, in short supply after the war). Judith Wright sprang to Nolan's defence in a letter to the paper castigating its "hysterical and ill-balanced attack" as a "display [of] provincialism which is a disgrace to Brisbane's standards of judgment". Nolan returned to the Ballad Bookshop to paint and exhibit other works.

Cecel Knopke, another core *Barjai*–Miya figure, had an outward eccentricity that Lillian mischievously spent long sessions cultivating. Osborne recalls: "Cecel had a very colourful manner, particularly for Brisbane in those days. He dressed rather flamboyantly, sort of a mid-twentieth century equivalent of what Oscar Wilde would have worn fifty years earlier. And he spoke in a very deliberate way, as though he were carefully weighing every word. He just affected this deliberate way of speaking. Lillian thought that was funny. She used to encourage him to say things and tell long stories just so she could listen to this funny way of speaking. I remember saying, 'Lillian, behave!' when she'd encourage Cecel to go off on some long monologue."

Peter Porter, who grew up in Brisbane during the war years before leaving for London to become a distinguished poet, wrote about what he called the "Intellectual Brisbane" of that time almost thirty years after its young participants had all dispersed:

> I was just the right age to have partaken of this strangely anachronistic literary ganging-up, but years in Toowoomba and my own diffidence kept me from joining Barrie Reid, Charles Osborne, Barbara Patterson [Blackman], Laurie Collinson, Laurie Hope, Cecel Knopke and the rest. I did meet Louis Green at my South Brisbane boarding house but I doubt that he knew that I wrote poetry. Louis (now a historian at Monash) was very exotic and the once or twice I met Charles Osborne I found him dauntingly sophisticated.
>
> Charles was always a man of great courage, and he led the way in defying Brisbane's puritanism and philistinism ... All this group dared to practise a mixture of left-wing politics and high camp at a time when such notions were dangerous. They believed not only in art but in the calling of the artist. I have always preferred to practise art behind a front of bourgeois respectability – it's less time-wasting – but I never forgot the example of the Barjai Group ... I am sorry that I was too shy to seek them out in the late forties. It might have made my life in Brisbane less lonely.

The Ballad Bookshop, in Adelaide Street, became as much a meeting place as a bookshop. But the more colourful place where the *Barjai* crowd gathered was the Pink Elephant Coffee Lounge a couple of blocks away. Frank Mitchell, an enterprising young man from down south, opened the Pink Elephant after drifting around post-war Brisbane accompanied by the artist Donald Friend and finding nowhere to have a coffee after business hours. Mitchell teamed up with another enterprising drifter, Philippa McLaney, to run the cafe and give Brisbane its only venue in the way of a cultural salon. Mainstream Brisbane quickly labelled the Pink Elephant raffish, even though it did little more than serve coffee and toasted sandwiches until well after midnight. Barbara Blackman's spinster aunt warned her not to go there for fear of meeting "unwholesome characters". The ever-lurking Brisbane police wrongly suspected the Pink Elephant of dealing in sly grog and raided the place.

The cafe was in a semi-basement. Blackouts still happened and it was often lit just with candles, which heightened the bohemian ambience. Charles Osborne recalls: "Everybody in literary, theatrical and artistic Brisbane, such as we were, went there at night. It was the only place to go. And there was no real gay scene in Brisbane then, although the Pink Elephant had a gay element to it. Certainly I think it was used as a kind of pick-up place, but much more discreetly than the only other pick-up place in town which was a public lavatory surrounded by Moreton Bay fig trees at the bottom of Wharf Street on the way to the Pink Elephant."

Having somehow managed to convince her parents that she was attending something "legitimate", Lillian joined her friend Barbara Blackman and the other "unwholesome characters" for nights at the Pink Elephant, where she struck Osborne as "certainly out of the ordinary for a schoolgirl. She seemed much older than her age and very precocious. She just seemed very bright and very knowledgeable. She particularly liked Barrie Reid's poetry." The Pink Elephant became the first of her salons, a teenage version of the more intense bohemian and counterculture cauldrons at the Lincoln Inn coffee shop in Sydney and Max's Kansas City nightclub in New York.

Osborne had a knack for persuading eminent artistic visitors to Brisbane to go to the Pink Elephant. During the 1948 Old Vic theatre company tour by Laurence Olivier and Vivien Leigh, according to an account by Barbara Blackman, "Charles gave [Olivier] in the Pink Elephant his scatological essay on *Hamlet* entitled 'The Two Queens' and won him as much by this as by his almost direct translation of Leigh into male form."

Lillian was at the Pink Elephant the night Osborne held a small party there for his twenty-first birthday in November 1948. She was sixteen. His guests included four dancers from Ballet Rambert, a touring British company for which Osborne had been working as an occasional rehearsal pianist. One of the dancers, John Gilpin, a year older than Lillian, brought fireworks which he started exploding in the street outside the Pink Elephant as the party moved into high spirits. The police were soon on the scene to investigate this shattering of the silent Brisbane night. Lillian's reaction to the melee showed signs of the budding journalist in her, keen to let a good story unfold. Osborne recalls the night:

After a few minutes a police car turned up. I suppose someone should have gone out to rescue John, but we didn't. I remember Lillian saying, "No, don't go out, don't go out. Let's just see what happens." What happened was that two policemen got out of the car and said to John Gilpin, "You can't let off fireworks in the street. It's just not allowed." And he, typical ballet dancer, said as we all shuddered: "I don't think you know who I am. I'm John Gilpin of the Ballet Rambert!" They said, "I don't give a stuff who you are." At that point Barrie Reid went out and calmed the police down and said we were having a birthday party, and the police were nice and said don't let him do it any more. When Barrie came back, Lillian reproached him: "Barrie you should have waited. They might have arrested him."

*

Lillian's last year in Brisbane was drawing to a close. And in late 1948, Brisbane itself was returning to its comfortable staidness. The Americans had gone. Already, the bright young things from the *Barjai*–Miya crowd were making plans to follow them out. By the early 1950s, the three nodes of rebellious cultural life in Brisbane, the *Barjai* meetings, the Ballad Bookshop and the Pink Elephant cafe, had all gone. Barbara Patterson married Charles Blackman, a young artist visiting from Sydney, and the couple moved to Melbourne where Australian art was then focused. Barrie Reid and Charles Osborne moved together to Melbourne in 1951, the first stage of Osborne's permanent departure for London. "By this time," Osborne wrote later, "I cordially loathed my native town and hoped never to see it again." He did, of course, and wrote about his youth in forties Brisbane with barely disguised fondness thirty-five years later in his memoir, *Giving It Away*. Barrie Reid (as Barrett Reid) became a figure among the Heide group of avant-garde painters and writers.

Lillian had made her own plans to move to Sydney once she had matriculated from State High at the end of 1948. Milo had preceded her and enrolled in philosophy at the University of Sydney. He wrote back glowingly of the city and encouraged Lillian to follow him. To both of them, Sydney represented freedom from their parents and a wider, more diverse world. Her parents seem to have accepted her decision as inevitable. Rose was already talking to her of the need to find a good husband after she left home. On 2 May 1948, Lillian recorded in her diary: "Had long talk with Mum re. Sydney, my future husband and what not."

Most sixteen-year-old girls at this time were thinking of future husbands, but Lillian was not among them. She was thinking of adventure, of new friends and breaking into journalism. And she was leaving a city that, in many ways, never left her; reacting against its restraints and restrictions helped to shape her attitudes and her pursuit of the unconventional for the rest of her life. Brisbane in the forties produced a tension in young people with any imagination or artistic aspiration that allowed little middle ground between conforming to its conservatism or rejecting it completely. For its exotic youth, those such as Lillian Roxon and Barrie Reid, conforming was never an option.

*

On 1 February 1949, Lillian celebrated her seventeenth birthday. Mrs Jofeh had her to lunch. June Gradwell gave her a farewell gift of writing paper. In the evening, Keith McWatters called to take her to a performance of Beethoven's *Pastoral Symphony*. Rose had gone ahead to Sydney to find accommodation for her daughter, leaving Lillian with Isadore and her younger brother, Jack. On 28 February, Lillian did the rounds of the Gradwells and other local families to say goodbye. Next day, Isadore drove her to the railway station to catch the 11 a.m. train to Sydney. Rhyl and Peter Munro saw her off "amid tears, kisses etc.", Lillian recorded in her diary. A lady on the train later told her that she "knew it wasn't yer brother because of the way ya kissed him". Lillian did not put these Brisbane friendships behind her. Two days after arriving in Sydney, she wrote back to Rhyl: "To my bosom friend and boon companion of my middle adolescence, with gratitude for the pleasant company she offered me, and in memory of happy days, from her ever affectionate friend, Lillian."

She did not sleep on the overnight journey south, her mind racing ahead to the new life awaiting her. Milo met the train in Sydney on 2 March and took her to join Rose at a boarding house in Bondi run by a Mrs Watt. After tea, she went for a walk with other girls from the house, then made her first diary entry for Sydney: "Boys tried to pick us up." She had arrived in the big smoke.

Lillian Roxon aged five in early 1937.

Lillian with her mother Rose and brothers Milo and baby Jack at the family's home in Alassio on the Italian Riviera, 1937.

Lillian on the beach in Alassio in about 1937.

On holiday with Rose and Milo in the mountains
at Zakopane in Poland, 1936 or 1937.

Escaping Hitler: Isadore, Jack, Lillian, Rose and Milo assemble on deck of the *S.S. Tyndareus* for their voyage to Australia, July 1940.

Lillian's father, Isadore Roxon-Ropschitz, late 1930s to early 1940s.

Rose Roxon in Brisbane, 1940s.

Lillian aged thirteen with prize cups for English and Languages won in 1945 at St Hilda's School, Southport, Queensland.

Lillian aged seventeen visiting the campus of the University of Queensland in Brisbane, 1949.

Lillian with friends, Sydney 1950s.

Lillian in Sydney, mid-1950s.

Windsor House (left) in Jamison Street, Sydney, where
Lillian lived from 1951 to 1955 during her student days.

Neil C. Hope (Sope) at the
University of Sydney, 1946.

Lillian (left) in the 1950s with her Push friends Margaret Elliott (later Fink) and Ruth Biegler (right), taken by Lillian's brother, Jack Roxon.

Lil & Dad (S.S. Himalaya) 1954.

Farewelling Isadore on the *Himalaya* in Sydney for his last visit to Europe.

Where's the party? Lillian and Ross Poole ready for a fancy dress party, Sydney 1957 or 1958.

On her way to America in 1959, Lillian stopped in Honolulu to interview Elvis Presley's manager, Colonel Tom Parker (right), and impresario Lee Gordon. "I Met the Colonel Who Counts Elvis's Money" was how *Weekend* headed her story.

The following week she was in Hollywood interviewing Rock Hudson.

Lillian interviewing Peter Finch for *Woman's Day*.

Lillian interviewing Richard Burton on location in Mexico for *Night of the Iguana*, 1963.

SYDNEY, 1950s

Chapter 7 Where's the Party?

When Lillian Roxon arrived at the University of Sydney for the first time on 3 March 1949, a month after she turned seventeen, she was overcome by an "acute inferiority complex when I saw how smart the girls there were". It was not how she struck the bright young men and women of her new city. They can remember her to this day.

Aviva Cantor (later Layton) first saw Lillian at Manning House where, before long, Lillian held court in the women's union cafe, always amid laughter. "Lilly was talking and everyone was terribly interested because the subject was who were virgins and who weren't and when they were not going to be virgins. I can remember what she was wearing: some sort of coat, and thick, plastic cherries at her neck. It sounds hideous but in those days they were the thing: red and yellow plastic cherries. I went that afternoon to David Jones to buy plastic cherries because I wanted to look like her."

Ruth Biegler, fresh from being dux of Sydney Girls High School, also met Lillian at Manning House where Ruth had gone to seek the secure company of girls she'd known at school. "We were all very innocent. With her rather cruel wit, Lillian made one feel like an inexperienced little girl, which is what I and my friends were. She could show off and frighten us with her wickedness."

Two years later Margaret Elliott (later Fink) encountered Lillian at a party in Ocean Avenue, Double Bay, one of the smartest addresses in Sydney: "She bustled up to me and I remember her brown and white gingham dress. I was struck by her phenomenal beauty. She was nineteen with a most strikingly beautiful face, one of the most beautiful faces I've ever seen. Her pale eyes were extraordinary. The gentlest, flawless, olive complexion with just a blush on those fantastic cheeks which weren't too round. There was a refinement in her face that didn't appear in her body. And under the eyes, the most wonderful faint, mauve shadow. Her mother had very dark shadows under her eyes, so she would have inherited that. Marvellous teeth, fabulous smile, perfect nose, dreadful hair."

The three women, all from Sydney Girls High School, became Lillian's lifelong friends. In the restlessness of their youth, they gravitated together towards a self-styled group of socially, intellectually and sexually adventurous young people known later as the Push.

Lillian, Sydney and the Push were predestined to collide. Ever since her fledgling appearance in *Woman* magazine at the age of fourteen, she had wanted to be a journalist and had applied unsuccessfully for cadetships after she left school. She wrote twenty-five years later: "When I wasn't able to get even a copy girl's job, despite my then three-year-old career as a published writer, I went to the university, a nice place to hang out and meet boys." When Lillian arrived there, the University of Sydney was in a ferment of excitement and ideas, aided by the influx of ex-soldiers under the Commonwealth Reconstruction and Training Scheme who were hungry for new thinking and keen to put the older order behind them.

The Push had taken its initial inspiration from the radical thinking of John Anderson, a charismatic figure who was the university's Challis Professor of Philosophy. Lillian was better prepared for this new life than many. Milo Roxon had written to his sister in Brisbane about the exciting and romantic life that awaited her down south, and when she arrived she quickly found her way to the corner of the quadrangle outside the Philosophy Room where much of the excitement was happening.

"She absolutely stood out," says Gustav Nossal, a contemporary of Lillian's at Sydney University, and later (as Sir Gustav) one of Australia's most eminent immunologists. "She swilled around with a very interesting crowd of people who were fairly strong followers of John Anderson. They were aggressively atheistic when most students were very good boys and girls. And they projected an image of sexiness and sexuality when everyone else was sex-starved and scared of sex, or at least of knocking up a girl or getting knocked up if you were a girl. There was no Pill and attitudes were very different then. They looked fairly liberated."

*

At the end of Lillian's first year in Sydney, the conservative Liberal-Country Party coalition, headed by Robert Menzies, came to power. In the popular imagination – and not altogether unfairly – the fifties has come to stand for dullness and social conformity. Menzies personified the fifties in Australia, much as Dwight Eisenhower, the popular war-hero-turned-president, did in America. The Menzies era was also the start of a long age of economic prosperity. Menzies opened up a consumer economy and made big public investments in higher education. All this was shadowed by the Cold War and the fear that a third world war could break out at any time, destroying the new life of middle-class affluence hard won from two decades of Depression and conflict.

The Sydney in which Lillian arrived was a city of 1.5 million people, bigger than the Brisbane she had left behind, certainly more raffish, but still overlaid with a legacy of Edwardian primness. Its centre had changed little since the 1920s, the streets lined with sandstone buildings and drawn over with tram wires. From its harbour and bustling wharves, wool, wheat, beef, lamb and butter – then Australia's lifeblood – were shipped to the world. The city centre's life came from its theatres, cinemas, pubs and grand hotels, but there was little distinctively Australian about the public culture. When Tennessee Williams's *A Streetcar Named Desire* was performed in Australia in 1950, its cast were billed as "brilliant overseas artists". Such artists dominated commercial theatre, leaving Australian actors to eke out livings on radio – or leave the country.

Sydney's newspapers devoted many pages to reporting the latest arrivals from and departures for "overseas", and to announcing who was lunching, dining or dancing with whom at Prince's and Romano's, the city's two society nightclubs. Together with the dining rooms of the Australia, Metropole and Ushers hotels and the charming Belvedere in Kings Cross, these were the smart places to be seen in fifties Sydney. Pubs closed at 6 p.m. Nothing opened on Sundays. Censorship of books and films was commonplace.

Women had a strong presence in fifties Australia, but they were largely confined to running families and managing households. Men were the breadwinners and women who chose to make independent professional or personal lives were a rare breed. *Woman's Day* was one of the most influential magazines in expressing the values of middle-class Australia. In November 1950 it published an article, "How to Get a Husband" by Cora Carlisle, which encouraged women to focus on one goal only:

> You may have told yourself that you want a career, that you want to express yourself, that you never want to degenerate into a dowdy housewife whose world consists of menus and baby napkins. Now is the time to get rid of such self-deceptions. They may have satisfied you in the past, but now they should not. For a true fulfilment of yourself, you want permanence in your relationship, the security of a home and the protection of one man. No substitute for marriage exists to establish a girl's position in the cosmic scheme of life ... So, sharpen your wits and face the fact that you – and you alone – must ensnare your prey.

*

For adventurous young adults seeking a freer life of the mind and the body, there was plenty about prevailing attitudes to react against and reject. The Push's origins lay in the Freethought Society co-founded by John Anderson at Sydney University in the thirties. The Scottish-born Anderson encouraged his followers to question authority in all its forms, especially that of church and state, at a time when such authority was rarely, if ever, questioned. Strongly influenced by Freud, Anderson regarded sexual freedom as a condition of political freedom. Freedom from authority included the need to be free of what he called "sexual repression" and "fear of sexuality". He wrote: "Freedom in love is the condition of other freedoms."

By the time Lillian arrived in Sydney, Andersonianism, as it was known, had had its heyday. It wasn't that Anderson's followers had abandoned his ideas; more that they thought Anderson himself had grown too conservative. By 1951 the Freethought Society was fading, and out of it grew a new group now called the Libertarian Society or the Sydney Libertarians, and later known as the Push. Some called themselves Realists, others Pluralists; but all opposed authoritarianism, whether it meant the church, Stalinism, censorship, wowserism or state restrictions on drinking hours and sexual relations.

They created their own alternative salons to the accepted "smart" venues. An early hangout was the Lincoln Inn Coffee Lounge where artists, actors, journalists, students, musicians, poets and bohemians of all kinds rubbed shoulders. The Lincoln was located in a downstairs room in a Dickensian building in Rowe Street, a charming lane of small shops that linked Pitt and Castlereagh Streets along one side of the Australia Hotel near Martin Place. The Lincoln's walls served as a rotating exhibition space for artists such as John Olsen and Rosaleen Norton, a notorious woman of fifties Sydney who ran a witch's coven in Kings Cross.

Soon after she arrived in Sydney, Lillian became a Lincoln identity. Tony Delano, recently discharged from the navy and then training as a photographer under the Commonwealth Reconstruction and Training Scheme (which he soon abandoned to join *Truth* as a journalist), remembers the Lincoln:

> There were overlapping circles at the Lincoln, some intellectuals, some Andersonian students, a few musicians and painters—John Olsen, Charles Blackwell—and a lot of free-thinking, free-floating layabouts who had a curiosity about life, which a lot of middle-class Australians then, by and large, did not.
>
> It was underground, dim and dark. On bright days a shaft of light would come down the stairs. I have a vivid recollection of Lillian walking down illuminated by it. She had a beautiful face, a marvellous golden complexion. She was wearing quite a short dress for the period in very summery, bright colours. She looked very exotic.

When the Lincoln closed in 1952, the crowd moved to Repins, a more commercial coffee shop upstairs in King Street. "A bunch of science fiction fans used to go to Repins," Lillian later wrote. "They used to talk about how one day man would go to the moon and we would laugh at them, we girls would. The poets didn't laugh. Everyone knows poets can see the future. Or rather everyone can see the future, but only poets recognise it."

In the fifties, central Sydney had a pub on almost every corner. These were not the most graceful places: their tiled walls and floors had to withstand being hosed out at the end of each day when the slops from the frantic "six o'clock swill" left them awash with beer and sometimes worse. But they were small and intimate; and, where the Push gathered in the saloon bars, one step up from the public bars, the drinking, smoking and talking were loud and intense. The Push organised a series of these pubs as their own: first the Tudor Hotel in Phillip Street, then the Assembly Hotel a few doors away and later the Royal George Hotel in Sussex Street.

The pubs, the Lincoln and Repins were central to Push life. Telephones were still expensive and took forever to install. Calling into the pub was the most assured way of seeing your friends and, even more important, of finding out where the scene was moving later. "Where's the party?" was a familiar, almost desperate cry as the clock approached six, especially on Friday nights when the weekend parties were set up.

As the scene broadened from the university to the city, so did the various groups with whom the Libertarians intersected. There were left-wing groups, Trotskyists, right-wing Catholic Labor people and young, entrepreneurial Liberal Party figures such as Gordon Barton, a future newspaper and transport tycoon. There were devotees of George Orwell's defence of freedom against authoritarian ideologies. And there were poets such as Harry Hooton, Lex Banning and other literary figures. Hooton was an anarchist in his forties who projected an aura to the younger crowd.

Lillian's friend Margaret Fink (as she later became) was a strikingly beautiful eighteen-year-old art student at East Sydney Technical College when she met and was captivated by Hooton. She left home to live in Kings Cross with a man twenty-five years her senior. Margaret's life with Hooton was interrupted by an affair with Barry Humphries, then a fledgling actor at the Phillip Street Theatre but never a Push person. It was a sign of the prudish times that Margaret and Barry were once asked to leave the Australia Hotel after the staff disapproved of their kissing in the foyer.

In the Lincoln's leather-bound folio, in which its habitués sketched drawings and wrote thoughts, Hooton inscribed a line of verse that captured his outlook: "No matter how angry we may become, we must always remember that there is ONE side to every argument – our own side, the right side, the outside." Lillian later wrote of Harry Hooton: "Harry looked like Henry Fonda and was years ahead of his time, as we all found out too late after he died. As he was dying he wrote a book of poems called 'It's Great to be Alive' and I always think about that when I'm down and remember to be grateful for small mercies."

For all the Push's emphasis on sexual equality, its two most prominent figures were both men – Darcy Waters and Roelof Smilde, both handsome and charismatic, and both bright dropouts from Sydney University. Some children from war refugee families were drawn to the Push; Roelof was one of them. Unlike Lillian, Ruth Biegler and others, Roelof was not Jewish, but his parents in Holland had decided that Europe was no place to raise children and got out just before the Nazis overran their country. Roelof was eight when his family landed in Australia in 1939, a year ahead of the Roxons. He went on to be captain of North Sydney Boys High School, one of Sydney's top schools, and arrived at the university in 1948.

Even though Roelof's and Lillian's lives connected often during the fifties, he only learned that Lillian had landed in Australia in circumstances that mirrored his own when I told him this almost fifty years later. "I wish I'd known that about Lillian," he replied. "We might have swapped notes a bit more."

Push people like Roelof, Lillian and Ruth never talked about their recent shared backgrounds – of parents gambling on death or survival, tyranny or freedom for their children. Instead they seemed to set out to divorce themselves from their parents' worlds and to define themselves through the freedoms they could help to create in this new land.

Sometimes, though, the freedoms turned out to be not all they had seemed from the distance of Europe: "The society I grew up in as a teenager in Australia in the 1940s was very restrictive and conventional," says Smilde. "I felt its restrictions quite keenly. When I was a teenager there were no cigarettes, no alcohol and no sex. Not for me and not for anybody I knew at school. We were nearly all pure and all purely repressed. If you were what they called a deviant, if you spoke out, you were regarded as a psychological problem. When I got caught up with the Philosophy group at Sydney University, all of a sudden here was a way of interpreting the society I was in. There was constant discussion and debate. And it was helped by a wave of returned soldiers, cynical and disillusioned with war."

What distinguished the Libertarians from the few others who criticised the fifties political and social order was that the Libertarian Push set out to *live* their definition of freedom, not just to argue about it. And live it they did, or did their best to. Many of the bright men like Roelof and Darcy turned their backs on careers. Such anti-careerism was a badge of honour in the Push. It was a hallmark of true opposition to authority and to the expectations of authority figures like parents, teachers, churches, employers and governments. When the men worked they took casual jobs as tram conductors and wharf labourers. They made and lost money at card games and at the races, which they took very seriously indeed.

Other conventions were simply disregarded. In the Push pubs, they insisted that women be allowed to drink with men in the public and saloon bars at a time when women were confined behind the frosted-glass doors of the "Ladies Parlours". If the publicans did not agree, they moved to another pub.

Push people believed in sexual emancipation, although many myths surround the true extent of promiscuity. Sexual freedom has been part of life for so long now that it is hard for anyone below the age of thirty-five to fathom how unenlightened fifties attitudes were to sex. For women the rules for conduct were particularly repressive. So for Push men to encourage Push women to be predatory about their sexual partners, in a way that only men had ever been allowed to be, flew in the face of everything.

Not all of the women were. And, of course, the emancipation had its downsides. The Libertarians prided themselves on their opposition to romanticism and sentimentality, which meant love affairs were not meant to last and people were not meant to feel jealousy or pain if their lovers decided to move on to someone else. And if women became pregnant, they were expected to arrange their own abortions at a time when this was illegal, dangerous and beset with trauma (although the men did agree to pay the exorbitant "fees" by whipping around the hat in the pub or at the races). Some feminists have since dismissed Libertarian men: they were not really liberated at all, just male chauvinists like the average Australian bloke. Did they not, after all, get a laugh out of naming some Push women after champion racehorses such as French Deal and Redcraze?

But the Push did not see it that way. By and large they were bright young people from conventional middle-class homes and good schools, drawn together by the promise and excitement of connecting with a crowd that offered an alternative to authoritarianism and to the conformity of Menzies' Australia; of meeting poets, artists, anarchists and philosophers; of fraternising with like-minded misfits in pubs and coffee shops, going to parties and exploring sexual relationships. The only criterion for acceptance was whether you were prepared to be open about yourself and to question the prevailing values and conventions. If conventional society regarded the Libertarians as a bunch of sexually immoral ratbags, the Libertarians believed their own codes of morality, truth and loyalty to each other were more honest than the hypocrisy that surrounded conventional morality. They were not interested in changing society, more in understanding it and living their own versions of it.

Like the so-called Beat Generation that flourished in America around the same time, and in reaction to the same sort of stifling middle-class conformity, the Push were pioneers of what became the counterculture in the 1960s. But unlike the Beats, who produced writers such as Allen Ginsberg, William Burroughs and Jack Kerouac, who set out to influence the society they had rejected by publishing books and poems that offered an alternative vision of American life, the Push at the time remained largely an inward-looking group.

In later years some became painters and musicians, Margaret Fink produced *My Brilliant Career*, one of Australian cinema's new wave landmarks, and several Push people figured in the dramatic, successful campaign in the seventies to stop developers destroying Victoria Street, one of old Sydney's grand precincts. And two former Push women, Lillian Roxon and Germaine Greer, produced groundbreaking international books on themes that sprang out of their Push periods – youth culture and women's liberation – well after they had moved on from their Push roots.

Chapter 8 Lillian and the Libertarians

If the Push stood out from the rest of Sydney, then Lillian Roxon stood out from the rest of the Push. She enrolled in Arts at the University of Sydney in 1949, soon after she turned seventeen, and took the next five years to complete a degree that should have taken three. Bohemian life and new friends in this boisterous new city were often more alluring than the university. She quickly became a star figure on the campus and in town. Everyone knew her, or knew of her, and she seemed to know everyone. Yet she managed to achieve her star status in the Push on her own terms, often flying in the face of everything the rest of the Push stood for.

She did not define herself through the earnest pub discussions of Andersonian philosophy and of the writers and thinkers at the centre of Libertarian arguments: Karl Marx, Leon Trotsky, Arthur Koestler, Karl Popper, Wilhelm Reich and Sigmund Freud. (There was a Push myth that Lillian's Viennese Jewish doctor father had studied psychoanalysis under Freud. This was not so: Isadore held a diploma in medicine and surgery from the University of Vienna but never practised psychiatry, although Lillian's uncle, Dzuinek, did.)

If anything, Lillian found this theoretical side of the Push rather tiresome, a bit of a joke. In this she was at one with Neil C. Hope, a young man who was also drawn to the Push by its people more than by its philosophical arguments. Neil Hope called himself "Sope", and it was as Sope that everyone knew him.

Sope was four years older than Lillian. He was born into a Christian Science family in Perth, Western Australia and went to school in Canberra, where he excelled in English. During his last year at Canberra High School, Sope and another student, Mel Woods, were said to have invented a language complete with its own grammar. Lillian's first year at the university was Sope's last, when he qualified as a teacher.

Lillian and Sope became great friends, never lovers. Some believe Sope had an unrequited sexual passion for Lillian, which might explain some of their famous rows. They had a lot in common. Both were short people with remarkable smiles that gave them great presence, yet both were forever self-conscious about their looks. Both had extraordinary wit and ability with language and knew how to use these skills, often without mercy. No one and nothing was sacred; they drew their identities from their power to paint verbal pictures of people and situations, to exaggerate and to create myths. Whatever shortcomings they felt about their physical appearances – Lillian with her fluctuating weight, Sope with his height – they both had absolute confidence in their verbal command over others.

Lillian and Sope both wrote novels that drew on the world they observed in Sydney in the fifties. The novels remained unpublished after each writer met with sudden death. Looking back, their friends wonder if Lillian and Sope had been rehearsing their novels at Push gatherings, striking sparks off people who crossed their paths. This was a time – before television, and when film meant only Hollywood – when every ambitious, creative young person wanted to write a novel, in the way everyone forty years later wants to be a movie star, a director or a screenwriter.

In Sope's novel the narrator is Sam, a Sope-like figure, and one of the women characters, Lola, resembles Lillian. Here is how Sam describes his relationship with Lola:

Marvellous Lola! I adored her. I loved her round, pneumatic curves, her golden skin, huge slash of a mouth and fine, slightly almond-shaped eyes. The sheer unfashionableness of her figure exhilarated me; voluptuous, firmly bulging, dynamically active in an epoch when women's shapes should be slim and sporty, healthy and outdoor, in our vast suburban continent. It was delicious to hear Lola on herself, merciless, side-splitting self-mockery, done no doubt to anticipate criticism by going one better. Lola herself christened her oval melon-heavy breasts Happy and Gloomy, explaining that one nipple drooped, the other perked. Lola aired her troubles with her rubbery, bole-like upper thighs, unable to scissor together, so she said, without searing friction. Lola invented phrases like: cold-slice elephantine buttocks; sausage-belt fingers; pin-cushion hands; plasticine spare tyres; "You've absolutely no neck, my dear"; and a thousand other variations with Rabelaisian fecundity …

What were my feelings towards Lola? Since I liked to think of myself as a male edition of Lola, the affection could easily have been explained as projected identification, loving myself in her. Certainly, what we had in common was a mutual passion for gossip, a weakness for exhibitionism, an undying streak of adolescent vulgarity. I would like to add that we both liked sex but two considerations stop me here. One is that Lola is female, attractive and predatory whereas I am donkeyishly male, ugly (unless you call prematurely pot-bellied, pustular and red-haired beautiful) and almost pathologically timid with women unless beyond the consciousness barrier of advanced inebriation.

So, to put it flatly, she certainly got a lot more grinds than I ever had. And the second factor is that both Lola and myself got a greater kick talking about it than actually doing it. Once we got used to this idea, we comforted ourselves by reflecting how fatal a sense of humour or of the grotesque or even a happy vein of ribaldry proves to the ultimate enjoyment of the two-backed beast. Mind you, Lola and I had never slept together – goodness me no! – and were both frightened of doing so, on my part, at least, for the mordant act she would make of it at Push parties and the like.

But I often indulged in a virile rape scene, Lola as victim and myself as protagonist, in the eventuality that she should, by some miraculous chance, be rendered permanently mute. Nor did she object to my frigidity in the slightest degree, unless you were so thin-skinned as to count assiduously fostered rumours that I was camp, impotent, castrated or of miniscule proportions genitally as calculated spite. Finally, Lola and I were fond of negroes, homosexuals, misfits and lamedogs, and the one major note of cacophonous discord in the symphony of our friendship was her taste in men, a recurring theme in my life during those days, a theme almost as obsessional as my mission to save Ryan from Valerie. I am incapable of self-analysis and the reader can interpret my feelings and motives, but the thought of that alluring young woman with this desiccated human computer made me lie awake at night, sore with indignation.

Years later, when she read the manuscript of Sope's novel after he died, Lillian wrote from New York to her mother in Australia: "It's not me he portrays, just the person he thought I was or would have liked me to be – a female version of himself." But Lillian and Sope were at one in seeing the Push as a network of people before anything else, linked by their non-conformism. This is how Sope saw it through Sam's eyes:

> Arguments bored me stiff ... The Push was not a repository of dedicated thinkers drawn to its vortex by an inexorable logic. It was an atmosphere, congenial to like temperaments, a refuge, a fireplace and a home. Anyone mingling with us because of reasoned conviction stood suspect. It was a union of outsiders, a haven for non-conformists, free-lovers, perverts, impotent husbands, unsatisfied wives, failed first-year students, unemployed bookies' clerks, ex-members of the Committee for the Re-invigoration of Communard Ideals, unwanted homosexuals, coloureds, foreigners, nymphomaniacs, austere ascetics, flat-earthers, cranks, prostitutes, pimps, clamouring virgins, unfrocked bank clerks, dismissed elementary school teachers, drug addicts, the bored, the living dead, the unsuccessful punter and the lonely, the seeker after sensation, the ratbag, the pathologically innocent, the exalted, quacks, ex-convicts, the rejected, the unaccepted, and it included people like me who just happened to feel at home in the Push like converts do in Rome and Miller did in Maroussi.

Lillian felt at home there, but it was an ambivalent relationship nonetheless. She refused to be typecast or to identify with any prevailing Push ethos. She was particularly sceptical of its anti-careerism since she had already set her sights on a career in journalism, something she played down in Push circles. For Lillian all the groups that intersected with the Push were social oil, and she circulated among them using the networking skills which later helped her make a hit in New York. Glen Hamilton, a friend of Lillian's from the university who later moved into journalism himself, says: "There was a huge mixture of people, and Lillian had a finger in every pie. I don't think there was anyone like her. She was a remarkable networker. She was marvellous at maintaining contacts assiduously and with care. I still don't know to this day whether Lillian was doing a university degree or not. I think she was. She did Arts? You were never aware of that being part of her interest!"

Lillian wrote her own novel about Sydney several years later in New York. By then, immersed as she was in the explosion of rock and youth culture in the America of the sixties, it would have been easy to let the smaller world of Sydney in the fifties recede. Yet these formative years held an unshakeable grip on her imagination. The 350-page manuscript is with her papers in the Mitchell Library, Sydney.

But possibly more interesting than the novel is a fifteen-page essay that accompanies it. The essay is about the manners and mores of a city still hemmed in by social restrictions. Its approach mirrors her approach to the rock revolution years later when she looked beyond the details of the music itself to the people and the social movements around it.

In her essay, Lillian describes the "where's the party?" syndrome and the vagaries of male–female relations in fifties Australia:

No phone was nice. No one had a phone then. People dropped by or met each other at five in the pub. You could always find someone in Repins from three on, and later at five in the pub. The pubs closed at six, after which you'd all go and have a meal at an Italian place called Florentino's [in Elizabeth Street] where, really and honestly, a three-course meal cost 25 cents. Soup, spaghetti and later six or so square inches of minced animal flesh with some grated lettuce, and some kind of groats. Small servings, you filled up on bread. Everyone went, sitting in twos and fours and sometimes at big tables.

Girls always paid for themselves. If a man was seen paying for a girl it was assumed he was from out of town, or worse. It wasn't called Men's Liberation or anything, but it was considered unmanly for a man to pay out like that. If the girl paid for him from time to time that was all right. That meant her man had lost his all at the races that day (the dogs, the horses, the trots) and that she was being womanly and supportive.

Only a man from out of town or an outsider would waste good gambling money on such a pointless gesture as paying for a girl's meal. Australians are shocking gamblers and the boys of my young girlhood gambled then as they gamble now and always will gamble, so solemnly studying the form on Wednesdays, playing boards (cards) on Thursday to raise a bank for Friday when the dogs run and Saturday for the horse races and Saturday night for the trots.

No one ever won, not really. The usual pattern was to take a cab or four-wheeler to the track and come home on Shank's pony, that is walk. If anyone won, all that meant was that the evening's meal was at the Tai Ping or Gravas, the fish cafe, instead of the Hasty Tasty [a legendary fast food cafe in Kings Cross], where the steaks were suspected of being more equine than bovine. Coffee was brown-coloured boiled milk, but American servicemen remember it fondly as the place Sydney's ugliest but most uncomplicated prostitutes used to hang out.

I don't know where the pretty, complicated ones hang out, but I do know that when Sharon, a rather homey drag queen, offered some tourists French love they didn't know what she was talking about, and when she explained a little they asked in a puzzled manner exactly what it was she proposed to suck, and when she explained that, too, they seemed even more puzzled and said, "Yes, but why would you want to do that?" So she explained that too and they drew back horrified. "Oh, no," they said, "We wouldn't want anything like that."

Australians, I think they've changed, were very Victorian a few years ago and referred to anything outside intercourse in the conventional, or missionary, position as "the fancy stuff". Australians disliked fancy stuff in bed and thought it unmanly. Here is what else they thought unmanly then – foreign food, especially Czech and Hungarian, bright colours, longish haircuts and well-ironed shirts. One man, jealous of his masculinity, found a special way of crushing his shirts each day so he wouldn't look ironed. He wore, to his credit, a freshly crushed shirt every time I saw him.

What Australians found particularly unmanly was any act of attention of chivalry to a woman. To open a door for a woman was to proclaim to the world your effeminacy. To speak to one at a party, before the beer had run out that is, was an open admission of homosexuality. When the beer had run out, that was different. Then it was all right for a friendly arm to fall carelessly and patiently on the waiting shoulder.

You didn't court your girl, you didn't woo her. You just kind of casually made sure she'd be where you were when the beer ran out and then, you – put the hard word on her. I told that to someone here [in America] and they said, "Do you mean pit the hard wood on her?" That version made more sense.

*

In the fifties sexual freedom was still a taboo subject, fraught with risks and fears. Contraception was awkward and risky, confined largely to the use of diaphragms and spermicides. Condoms were rarely used – in the words of one Push man, they were considered "very working class and vulgar. They were just too awful." So in Push circles, where men tended to regard contraception as the woman's responsibility, women who wanted to be sexually free had to take enormous chances. Choosing to become a single mother was simply not an option.

In the background essay to her novel, Lillian evokes a Sydney summer of the fifties:

In Australia, you see, the seasons are reversed from America. The summer romance season coincides with the Christmas party season – the two high romance, high fertility seasons of the year happen at once. Anyone who wasn't pregnant by February wasn't a real woman. It got so that if you weren't you'd pretend to be, to save face. I suppose things have changed since the Pill, but I bet they haven't changed that much. What you always did on New Year's Eve, because it was so hot, is take a swim on a deserted beach with your date and then stay and watch the sun come up. Some summers every night was New Year's Eve.

You always knew who was pregnant because there was only one way to raise the money to pay back the people who'd so kindly lent it, and that was to work as a waitress. There was only one place to work as a waitress and that was called King Street Repins. They had starched, flesh pink cotton uniforms and a matching headpiece that sat like a tiara on the head. Wearing those uniforms was the way God punished you for the lovely things you did in the moonlight at Chinaman's Beach or Nielsen Park or Redleaf.

Working there was no punishment because everyone went there anyway to drink black coffee and eat cinnamon toast, and on a good day you could find Lex Banning, the poet, who was spastic and beautiful and died the other day which saddened me because one of his most beautiful poems was an epitaph for a girl called Tanya who died of an abortion, as they sometimes did.

Lillian was instinctively a journalist, and she observed a world that was full of restrictions for women. She never suggests in either the essay or the novel that the story is her own or that of any of the people she was closely involved with in her Sydney years. Rather, the novel was "mainly about a young girl's discovery that, when the cards are down, she is nothing but a fancy incubator and hatching machine for perpetuating her race".

Her characters, rather than being based on particular people, are "composites". They are embroiled in their own personal dramas that reflect aspects of Sydney's Libertarian world of the fifties. The men disdain contraception, and when women, such as Camilla, the novel's main character, get pregnant they turn to a reliable abortionist, a qualified doctor called Hennessy who conducts his illegal operations from rooms in the best part of town, mixes in the top rungs of Sydney society and is seen every Saturday at the races.

Mechanically he pulled a chart from a drawer. "You see this?" he said, and you knew he'd said it a million times before. "This is the cervix or neck of the womb. We put the needle here at twelve o'clock and again here at three and six." He was drawing the hours on it as if it were a watch face. "You feel nothing."

Camilla let out a big pent up breath. In the same voice, Hennessy continued: "Sixty quid. Five pound notes. In a plain envelope. Bring a sanitary belt and pads and don't eat the night before. OK?"

Camilla thought of her tiny guest with a heart that beat, limbs, brains and even sex, and trembled.

Two weeks later she returned.

For an abortionist, and a well known one, Hennessy made the black tie and society dinner circuit in a big way. He was said to be a man with big underworld connections and great personal charm.

In fact, as he advanced on her with the hypodermic syringe he was positively jolly. "This is the first time for you, isn't it?" he said pleasantly, showing teeth that rumour said he had gone to Hollywood to have capped. "You'll find it won't hurt more than the needle you get at the dentist. Besides, the womb doesn't have any nerves."

A long needle of pain shot into Camilla's body. "Ah," she cried … There were three more of the needles. Camilla thought she would faint.

"For God's sake keep quiet," hissed the nurse. "I didn't expect it to hurt," said Camilla. "You could have warned me."

Now he was Society Jack again. "It's all over my dear. Get dressed and let's go."

She tottered weakly to her feet, dizzy with pain and relief. "He said get dressed," said the nurse. "Get a move on."

In Sydney during Lillian's time, abortion was a risky business not just for the women who resorted to it but for the doctors who practised it. Doctors who terminated unwanted pregnancies risked exposure by the police and ruin, so their patients were usually pushed out the door soon after it was over. A Push friend of Lillian's describes her own experience:

> They were qualified doctors we went to, but it was not just the Push that knew. Everyone in Sydney knew. They presumably paid off the police the way prostitutes paid off the vice squad. One was particularly notorious. He did it without anaesthetics. When he got the money it went immediately on horses. That's where the abortion money went, on the races.
>
> Two had rooms in Macquarie Street, but they operated from premises that were like a little private hospital tucked away in Bondi. There was a nurse who got you ready. "Have you got Doctor's money, dear?" You handed it over in the envelope, in cash of course. None of us had cheque accounts in those days and credit cards hadn't been invented. The money was usually obtained by a whip-around in the pubs.
>
> As soon as you came out of the anaesthetic you got a cup of tea. You were pushed out about an hour afterwards. I remember staggering out and promptly being sick in some shop doorway.

*

Lillian's novel and essay focusses less on the Push and more on the problems of a young woman setting out to lead an independent life in the Sydney of the fifties: the conflicts of balancing the need for intimacy with men with the pursuit of a career in a world dominated by them. But the Push as a group or movement barely features at all.

The Push provided her with some of her most lasting female friendships: Margaret Fink, Ruth Biegler, Aviva Layton and Judy Smith. The men and their attitudes offered less enduring satisfaction and ultimately she was impatient to break free. Years later, Lillian looked back on the Push when she wrote from New York to John Moses, a friend and colleague in Sydney:

> Since you took the trouble of writing about it, I did want to say something about the Push. Look John, they WERE dreary and sordid. They used to bore me terribly, which comes out very strongly in my book which really does pass over them. They are still collectively dreary and sordid. I was out ("monogamous" they used to say in disgust), but not to Sope who saw me as a bright, orange Venus flytrap who swallowed little boys whole. What *he* secretly wanted to do, no doubt. The Push, like any other group, had some individually nice people and I am grateful to it not just for bringing me together with them but, because it still continues to function, for keeping me in touch with them.

Chapter 9 Jamison Street

Lillian Roxon's most colourful residence during her Sydney years was an early nineteenth-century colonial house in Jamison Street that had survived in the heart of the city to become a haven of forties bohemian life. On her way there she had to run the gauntlet of various landladies at a time when a post-war housing shortage made rooming houses the only affordable accommodation for most young people. Few flats had been built in Sydney since the thirties, most tenants were protected by rent control laws, and property owners demanded an unrecorded cash payment of "key money" for those rare places that became available. So for students there was little alternative to the world of rooming houses with strict rules enforced by censorious landladies. "I can still recite the names of my old landladies," Lillian wrote from New York almost twenty years later. "Mrs Curtis, Mrs Allan, Mrs Riley, Mrs Finnair." Tony Delano recalls the post-war austerity that constricted the living conditions of most young people. His own Commonwealth retraining scheme living allowance was £3 ($6) a week.

> Many lived in student rookeries around Glebe, near the university, or in Darlinghurst and Kings Cross. The rooms were cold, primitive, dismal. Bathrooms were shared between three and four of them. Hot water came from chip heaters. Everyone was hungry. The food you could get or afford was pretty ghastly. People would regard toasted cheese or mince on toast as a treat. And the landladies were ferocious. The slightest sign of sexual activity and you'd be thrown out.

The University of Sydney was then a close-knit world of fewer than 10,000 students, a fraction of its present population. The quadrangle, bound by the university's original sandstone buildings, was the lunch-time turf of the Arts and Architecture students. Lillian soon became the queen of the corner of the quadrangle where students gathered near the frangipani tree outside the Philosophy Room. She sat on the benches holding court with her friends and quizzing strollers-by who took her interest. Sometimes she would startle them if she felt they needed taking down a peg. "Hey, Sophie," one former student remembers Lillian calling to her across the lunch-time crowd. "Are you still a virgin?"

Her other social centre was *Honi Soit*, the student newspaper whose pages reflected an intellectually exciting time at the university with a mixture of student satire, articles by Freethinkers and their critics, and pieces on world affairs by ex-World War II soldiers-turned-students. To earn extra money beyond the allowance from her parents, Lillian took a part-time job as a life model for art students at East Sydney Technical College. It was different from the waitressing and shop assistant jobs most other female students took.

Lillian's last stop before Jamison Street was a rooming house in North Sydney, a rambling building on the corner of Berry Street and the Pacific Highway that still bore a sign, "Braitlings Piano Works", from the days when it had housed a piano factory. Lillian's narrow upstairs room had two single beds, a wardrobe and a gas ring. Water came from a tap in the courtyard. A fellow lodger was Ross Parish, a shy economics student from the university and intellectual Freethinker who later became a distinguished economist.

In August 1949, Barbara Blackman and some of her old Brisbane friends visited. Barbara Blackman remembers Lillian introducing her to life modelling: "Lilly had this gorgeous body. She'd put on her cor-duroys and a big sweater and off she'd go to the art school. She was the first woman I knew who wore corduroy pants. She said, 'Students in Sydney dress like this.' Then one day she came back and told me, 'I'm not going tomorrow so I've booked you in.'"

The art school in Darlinghurst, the Mitchell Library in Macquarie Street, the university, the Lincoln coffee shop and Kings Cross: these were their day-and-night worlds. The city was a small place then, easy to navigate. Kings Cross was still Australia's only pocket of genuine bohemia, not yet ruined by hard drugs, a place of elegant coffee shops such as the Arabian and the Kashmir, flower shops and restaurants where even the straightest middle-class people would go to end their evenings in the hope of nothing more wicked than catching a glimpse of a transvestite.

*

Having established her Sydney parameters, Lillian turned her attention to a question that had preoccupied her. She had written to Barbara Blackman in Brisbane on the subject: "They were long letters talking about the necessity for and process of losing one's virginity. She asked me to be her mentor in all that." Now, on turning eighteen and starting her second academic year in early 1950, she met the man with whom she decided to form her first long-term relationship after she had made the crucial transition. George Clarke, a second-year architecture student three weeks younger than Lillian, had also arrived at the university in 1949. He was handsome with dark, wavy hair and sharp eyes, although, he recalls, "far less worldly than she". Clarke came from Sydney Grammar, one of Sydney's leading private boys schools. His studio opened on to the quadrangle close to the Philosophy Room, but he spent his first year absorbed in his studies and Orwell, Koestler, Anderson and other writers. Early in his second year, Clarke decided to branch out and join the crowd in the quad.

"I became aware of Lillian's remarkable presence walking through the quad talking, laughing, smiling, being the centre of attention," he recalls. "She had a rich wit. She embraced all of life's ironies and charms. She spent her time at the university cultivating personalities, spotting each person's and group's follies and foibles."

Clarke joined the Sydney University Dramatic Society (SUDS) and became a habitué of its club room located in Gould's Private Hotel in George Street. Lillian introduced him to the Lincoln in Rowe Street where he was impressed by talk of life and art, painting and sculpture, literature and poetry, politics and sex. Clarke recalls:

We met over coffee. I learned that Lillian was majoring in psychology, and was a celebrity in the *Honi Soit* and among the philosophy and psychology crowds. She appreciated the relative innocence of architecture students. She cultivated my acquaintance, and it didn't take her long to decide that I was interesting yet safe, virginal, wooable and winnable.

Lillian carefully planned, organised and executed her safe escape from virginity and transition to serial monogamy. One day we were sitting in the stalls at a SUDS rehearsal. Lillian was instructing me, making arrangements, telling me she had everything organised. She was totally consumed when I met her with the need to lose her virginity. This was a problem to be addressed and overcome. Part of the advantage of being in the avant-garde with the philosophy crowd was that people quoted Freud as saying sexual repression was authoritarian. Sexual experimentation was regarded as good. Freud was very fashionable then. He was all the talk. And Lillian was knowledgeable in pop Freudian banter.

Their friendship was consummated in the North Sydney rooming house. About 11 p.m. that same night after this "astonishing event", there was a knock on the door, Clarke recalls. It was Darcy Waters, the tall, blond, charismatic "prince" of the Push. Waters apparently had called to check out Lillian's young man. An early Freethought devotee and Libertarian co-founder, Waters sat on one of the beds and began to explore Clarke's philosophical credentials by grilling him on the question of whether beauty is absolute or relative. According to Clarke, Waters asked him to imagine a Gothic cathedral from England or France built today in Sydney. Would it still be beautiful? Clarke replied that it would not because real beauty would have to spring from the material, climate and environment that created it and could not be duplicated. Waters then turned to Lillian and declared, "Jesus, Lil. This boyfriend of yours is a fuckin' relativist!"

Clarke recalls: "I was a little chagrined. But it didn't upset Lillian. She regarded all of life as a great adventure. She wasn't an ideologue. She loved social drama and human comedy." The whole experience for both of them was part of the freeing up of attitudes that university life represented in these post-war years:

In March 1949 the university gave to seventeen-year-olds like Lillian and me an explosive shock of liberation, exposure to wide worlds of ideas and possibilities in all fields, of which sex was only one – in a way that no one today can comprehend because, since the late fifties, youth have been indoctrinated with the need to "express themselves". In those now far-off days of Depression and post-war austerity,

Australian suburban schoolchildren who moved to university were
suddenly thrown in at the deep end. To Andersonians the university was an undefiled enclave of academic freedom. Our socratic-style
dialogues in the quad, the Lincoln, the Tudor and above all at Push
parties were ends in themselves. The unexamined life was not worth
living. That's why Darcy came that momentous night to conduct a
socratic-style dialogue with me.

Lillian's "happy release from that wretched condition", as she
described the state of virginity in her novel, lifted a burden from her
mind, one she was keen to see her women friends liberated from as
well. Twenty years before feminism and sexual liberation reached full
flower, Lillian was something of a pioneer and an example to her
Libertarian friends.

Lillian's relationship with Clarke continued for almost two years
until January 1952 when, as he puts it, "she decided it was time for both
of us to move on". She bought a book of love poems, *Donne to Dryden*,
from the Penguin Bookshop in Hosking Place, wrote inside it "For all
lovers ..." and gave it to Clarke. She sometimes quoted one of her
favourite verses from this book of Cavalier poets to her women friends
at the university. It was from Robert Herrick's "To the Virgins, to make
much of Time":

> *Gather ye Rose-buds while ye may:*
> *Old Time is still a-flying:*
> *And this same flower that smiles today,*
> *To morrow will be dying.*

Perhaps it reflected her own extraordinarily energetic assault on life,
and prefigured her untimely exhaustion of it.

*

In the first months of their relationship Lillian and George Clarke kept
separate lodgings, she in North Sydney, he at home with his widowed
mother. Then, in early 1951, Lillian landed herself a room in Jamison
Street in the middle of central Sydney, where they moved in together.
It was in the attic of Windsor House, a two-storey sandstone residence
that had survived, miraculously, for more than a hundred years.

People still lived in the centre of Sydney then, although it was becoming rather unfashionable at a time when the suburban dream of house and garden was fast taking root in the Australian imagination. There were small buildings, linked by laneways, where artisans and shopkeepers lived cheek by jowl. Jamison Street was one such quarter. It was bound by George Street, the city's spine, on the east side, and Clarence Street on the west, both streets tumbling down a few blocks to the Rocks, the disreputable heart of colonial Sydney and still in the fifties a tough residential area, not the pristine tourist zone it later became.

Lillian's brother, Milo, had also lived in Windsor House. It had close connections with the philosophy crowd from the university, who held earnest discussions and great parties in its rooms, parties which sailors on the town from ships docked at nearby Circular Quay would sometimes wander into looking for women. By the late forties, Jamison Street had become something of a bohemian centre in a bohemian part of town. The rooms of the Poetry Society, run by Imogen Whyse, were in lower George Street. Another old building nearby, once a sailors' home, was used as artists' studios and known as Buggery Barn apparently because, in 1940s Sydney, anyone who was an artist was assumed to be gay. A block away in lower Pitt Street was the New Theatre and the Studio of Realist Art, an outlet for exhibitions with socialist themes.

The attic that Lillian and Clarke shared consisted of a bed-sitting room with an alcove containing a small stove. The only light and air came through two attic skylights which propped open in the sloping roof. There were no power points, so power came from a chord plugged into the light socket and looped around the room to service lamps; an immersion element was used to heat water. The bathroom was in a yard at the back. Looking back on the Jamison Street accommodation, Clarke recalls that: "The Andersonians, and then Lillian and I, valued it for its rarity – a rentable room that gave freedom and privacy to come and go without surveillance or censoriousness, and was affordable. The non-suburban location was romantic in its unconventionality. It had no snob value [although] it was what later came to be called a 'heritage' building."

*

For a young woman of Lillian's age and background, to live with a lover was to go against the conventions of middle-class morality. It meant pretending to landladies that the relationship was "legal" and playing a constant cat-and-mouse game with parents who might visit unexpectedly. But Jamison Street stayed firmly in Lillian's imagination for the rest of her life. Her novel is set in a "ten-room residential city building" that seems to be modelled on Windsor House. Her essay on the novel's background describes the house and young people living unconventional lives in Sydney at that time:

> It had once been glorious, an old ship's surgeon had owned it. Now it was beautiful but a blight on a busy little street that housed a Red Cross gift shop, a Qantas terminal and an army and navy disposals store that did a roaring business in khaki digger hats from the second world war.
>
> The dust on the window sills was outside dust, hard and gritty. On cold nights it would move on to mantelpieces and dressers and book shelves for warmth and comfort.
>
> The walls were crumbling slowly and systematically, so it was hard to know where they ended and the real dust began. The space above the ceilings was inhabited entirely by rats. As they moved around in their rat games, something that looked like pepper sifted through the joins between the boards. I never wanted to think about what kind of dust it was but I was always glad the rats didn't live above the kitchen.
>
> Here and there on the floor the dust had won and what had once been a floorboard was now a hole you had to be careful not to walk through because there was no knowing where it was going to take you, maybe to hell and back.
>
> This house of dust and rats and linoleum that rotted in a sort of inanimate sympathy with its surroundings was to be the setting for my story.

Like the residents, the landlady was different from the norm:

> One room at the front was kept vacant so the landlady could keep her bowling uniforms in it. Bowling in Australia is quite different from the game in America. It is played outdoor on green lawns by ladies, usually middle-aged, in neat, white uniforms (not starched white but soft and creamy), white shoes, white stockings and squashy white hats.

The landlady did not live on the premises, which was thought to be a huge advantage since she was not there to police the halls or learn which unauthorised person was using the bathroom after midnight, a sure giveaway of sexual mischief. No, the landlady only came in on Saturdays to collect rents and change into her bowling outfit. Sometimes she would stay long enough to hear complaints from two elderly sisters who lived on the first floor. The complaints had mainly to do with the noise of my quarrels.

In the book the landlady gets deeply upset because a character paints his room black and answers the telephone naked. In real life, all he had to do to shake her up was paint his ceiling black.

The men's bathroom had no doors, which shouldn't have mattered to me except that the ladies' bathroom did have a door and a lock and the key was not always available as it was kept in the custody of the two old ladies. The ladies' bathroom was a real bathroom, that is it had a tub in it. I should explain here that the building with nine tenants had only two bathrooms, one for each sex, that both were outside in the dusty yard and that only one had washing facilities, the only one in the house.

The washing facilities consisted of a rusted tub always filled with brackish water and a coat of verdigris. I always called the tub Dorian Gray because its carbuncles and boils seemed to suppurate. You did not bathe in it; you stood on a rubber mat and showered. I would have had a bath at a friend's place, except that my friends lived in their own dusty houses too. Dusty houses were all there were then.

In the dusty houses you were at the landladies' mercy. No typewriters after eight. No radios after seven. No visitors of the opposite sex ever. There was a downstairs lounge for entertaining them. If your guest of the opposite sex could make that bathroom without encountering the landlady well and good. If not, out. Eviction. In the end it became easier to move in together as man and wife just for the sake of bathroom privileges. Nobody looked, nobody checked, but our consciences were guilty in those unliberated days and we always made sure to add a glass engagement ring to our Woolworths ring, a nice little modest one as befitted a nice modest little bride.

It's so nice to see those double nameplates on American mailboxes. People keep them on even after they've stopped living together and are actually married. In Australia it simply wasn't possible, and God help you if your parents came to visit and one of the tenants said, "She isn't in, but her husband is." Oh boy, did we dread that.

*

Lillian and Clarke's relationship flourished. They took the train to Brisbane where Lillian introduced Clarke to her parents. He found Rose a "highly strung Yiddish mother" and Isadore a "crusty father": "They were traditional, professional central Europeans concerned for their daughter."

While Lillian focussed more deeply on the people in her life, Clarke's interests diverged into social, political and environmental issues. In Australia in the early fifties the big political issue was the Communist Party. During 1950–51, Menzies tried to ban the Communist Party of Australia, dividing the country in a bitter campaign that involved some members of the Push.

Legislation to outlaw the Communist Party passed through parliament in October 1950. But five months later the High Court ruled that the legislation contravened the Constitution. After his election win in April 1951, Menzies announced he would hold a referendum to amend the Constitution to overturn the High Court's ruling.

By and large, Push people preferred discussions at parties and pubs to political activism, but a few were so outraged by Menzies' plan that they took up the cause for the referendum's "No" campaign. For Clarke and other anti-authoritarians including the future businessman Gordon Barton, the issue was civil liberties: the attempt by Menzies to use authoritarian methods to fight an authoritarian movement. Clarke attended a crowded lunch-time meeting on the referendum at the Wallace Theatre at Sydney University, where the legendary Labor-turned-Liberal figure Billy Hughes, then eighty-one and still in parliament, spoke in support of the government. From the back of the theatre, Clarke shouted out a question: "Should we use the methods of communists to fight communism?" Clarke recalls: "Hughes had an ear trumpet. He called back, 'What? What? I can't hear you.' He ignored my question." The "No" case narrowly won the referendum, after opinion polls had predicted an overwhelming "Yes" victory.

Lillian was not a regular foot soldier in the referendum campaign, and she and Clarke drifted apart. Their relationship finally came to an abrupt end one evening in early 1952 when Clarke and a friend, Kevin Borland, were setting up a design exhibition in the Ironworkers' Union building in George Street near Jamison Street. Clarke invited his friend back to Jamison Street for refreshments. They walked up the stairs to the attic where Clarke opened the door to find Lillian in the company of a young man.

There was a split-second's awkward silence, then introductions were made. "Although I was very brave and sophisticated about it that night, I suffered the normal pains of a supplanted lover," Clarke recalls. "I went through a period of feeling sorry for myself, until I discovered the joys of being an active young man and embarked on adventures of my own." When he had recovered, he inscribed and gave to Lillian a copy of Dostoevsky's *The Brothers Karamazov*. Twenty years later, in New York, Lillian gave it back to him for safe-keeping. The inscription reads: "To my dearest sister Lillian in remembrance of (and to the future of) our brothers: from George, 20th March 1952". Clarke moved into a wooden former school room in the suburb of Randwick, where he set up a studio and held memorable parties attended by the Push and art and architecture crowds. He went on to have a distinguished career in environmental planning in Australia and overseas.

Lillian's new boyfriend was David Ivison, a younger psychology student who later lived at Jamison Street. In the background essay to her novel, Lillian leaves her own succinct account of this dramatic moment in all their lives: "I lived in this house with two men. One from the age of eighteen to twenty, the other from the age of twenty to twenty-two. It was a smooth enough transition. One came home one day and found me entertaining the other in a dressing gown of coral rayon (perhaps there was some cotton in it) with a black design. Frankly it looked suspicious and frankly he was right. Well, you don't leave a nineteen-year-old girl alone night after night and then look astonished when she's found consolation."

Chapter 10 Zell

In January 1953, David Malouf called at Jamison Street for the first time to meet Lillian Roxon. Malouf, later to become one of Australia's most outstanding novelists, was then a shy eighteen-year-old student from Brisbane visiting Sydney to research his university thesis. Sheltered and shockable, Malouf was a sitting target for Lillian, the older woman, who set out to show this youth from her old home town what the world was really about.

He had been sent to Lillian by another student, Zell Rabin, with whom Malouf the previous year had co-edited *Semper Floreat*, the student newspaper at the University of Queensland. Lillian and Rabin had met in Sydney when they were both nineteen, and became lovers. They shared much in background, good looks, temperament and ambition. And Rabin had the sort of charisma that knocked women sideways.

When David Malouf first met Lillian in early 1953, her affair with Rabin was already over, although in another sense it never really ended. For the rest of their lives they maintained a friendship that Lillian described as "one of those peculiar intertwining of destinies"; almost until his own untimely death in 1966, Rabin wrote Lillian long, confidential letters pouring out his problems.

After checking into the Balfour Hotel in Sydney, Malouf called at Jamison Street to introduce himself. Lillian greeted him warmly as a friend of Zell's and introduced him in turn to some Push friends. It turned out that the Maloufs and the Roxons had a connection in Brisbane: one of Malouf's aunts was the next-door neighbour of Lillian's parents in New Farm. Lillian instantly took command of the situation and announced, "David, before we go any further, there's something we'd like you to do."

She handed the uncomfortable young man a 630-page textbook with a dark blue hardcover and gold lettering across its spine. It was called *Sexual Anomalies and Perversions: Physical and Psychological Development, Diagnosis and Treatment*. The author was Dr Magnus Hirschfeld, a nineteenth-century German pioneer sexologist. Well before their time, Hirschfeld and his followers argued that society's conception of normal sexual behaviour was prejudiced and hypocritical, and that sexual practices then labelled perverted and abnormal were more widespread than most were prepared to acknowledge.

When Malouf opened *Sexual Anomalies and Perversions*, his eyes came to rest on an eight-page table of contents that covered such topics as "The Psychological Basis of Sexuality", "The Eternal Child", "Hypereroticism", "Masturbation and Self-Love", "Hermaphroditism", "Androgyny", "Transvestism", "Forms of Homosexuality", "Feminine Homosexuality", "Sadomasochism" "Necrophilia", "Fetishism", "Exhibitionism" and "Scopophilia".

Lillian then handed Malouf strips of paper and said: "Read this book and put the bits of paper in the places that excite you. We want to know everything about you." Lillian was setting a test for the teenager. How would he react? Would he keep his cool and do as he was bidden, exploring a sexual underworld that these uninhibited people were opening before him? Or would he, as many a teenager of his day might, feel intimidated and flee in terror? Malouf kept his cool. Recalling this event years later, Malouf says: "It was all in public and I was kind of terribly embarrassed, as I was meant to be. Lillian was partly playing a game with me. But I also thought this was the most perverse and sophisticated thing I'd ever heard."

It was the openness of it all in a society that placed so many restrictions on sex that left the young man flabbergasted. The people of the Push – upfront, independent women like Lillian, the openly gay, the sexually liberated (or seemingly so) – were not part of the Australian story where Malouf grew up. Yet here they were, living characters in Sydney. "It was quite clear they couldn't have given a stuff one way or the other which pages in Dr Hirschfeld's book you got excited about. They just wanted to know. It didn't matter to them what you did. But it was to be public and everybody was to be in on it. That's what shocked me more than anything else."

Malouf passed Lillian's test and she adopted him as a friend. During the rest of his time in Sydney he returned to Jamison Street, where there always seemed to be a party. He noticed that the men at these gatherings would sometimes relieve themselves by standing on a chair in front of the windows that pushed out from the attic apartment's sloped roof and urinating into the gutters below. None of the lavatories downstairs was considered "safe", he was told, because you never knew if prostitutes from around the area had been using them. Lillian told Malouf she would walk all the way up George Street and Broadway to the lavatories at Sydney University rather than use those at Jamison Street. It might have been another of her myths; it was more likely that the men were too lazy to walk downstairs to the lavatories in the yard out the back.

When Malouf went home to straitlaced Brisbane, the liberated sexual world of Sydney and his exposure to Dr Hirschfeld's book kept playing on his mind: "I felt confused." To open up about it, he decided to consult none other than Lillian's father, Dr Isadore Roxon-Ropshchitz. In this he might have been influenced by the apocryphal story that Isadore had studied psychology under Freud. "I went to see him and said I thought I was very, very confused. He sent me off to write an account, about as frank as I was willing to be, of whatever life I'd been living up to that delicate age of eighteen. I went away and wrote about ten single-space typed pages. I didn't know I had enough experience beyond that."

Malouf left his account with Isadore. When he returned, Isadore told him he had nothing to worry about, "that within his version of what normal functioning was, I was doing perfectly okay". Isadore then fell silent for a few seconds. Then he suggested it might be a good idea if Malouf got married. After another short silence he looked at the young man and asked, "Would you marry my daughter?" It was a measure of how much Lillian's parents were already worried about settling her down that Isadore was prepared to propose this. And a compliment that they considered this bright young man worthy of their daughter. Malouf's response was polite but non-committal. When he related the story to Lillian they both had a great laugh.

Malouf returned to his studies at the University of Queensland and whenever Lillian went north to visit her parents she sought out his company. On his visits to the Roxons in New Farm, he was struck by a sense that Lillian's parents lived largely separate lives. Isadore had his own world outside the house and seemed secure in himself, if aloof. But without any working life of her own, Rose seemed trapped in an isolated, alien suburban world that offered little, if any, support for her inquiring mind. Together with her limited grasp of English, her isolation seemed to exacerbate the feelings of insecurity she had brought to Australia as a Jewish woman in flight from the persecutions of Europe.

The marriage proposition was never mentioned again. But on one of Malouf's visits to New Farm, Rose's frustrations about her life poured out in a slightly unnerving way. It was soon after the execution in June 1953 of Julius and Ethel Rosenberg, the American Jewish couple found guilty – wrongly, many then believed – of conspiring to sell atomic secrets to the Soviet Union. Lillian had invited a visiting American student, Aaron Wildawski, home for dinner. Malouf recalls: "Lillian's mother was scrupulously polite to him, but very cold. In the kitchen she banged around muttering to herself. Finally, wringing a tea towel in her hands, like the neck of a chicken, she came in, stood behind the American boy's chair and said in her heavy European accent, 'And vot about the Rosenbergs?'" This was apparently Rose the liberal but pessimistic outsider, for whom betrayal and insecurity was the Jewish fate, even in the world's safest havens.

Malouf and Lillian both left Australia in 1959 to pursue careers on the other side of the world – he in Britain, she in America. But Lillian Roxon's world in Sydney in the early fifties, and her place in it, left a lasting impression on Malouf. To the future novelist, Lillian defied the conventional fifties view that independent women did not exist at that time. She represented the sort of woman who emerged more openly twenty years later; one who created her own identity in a way that, up to then, only men could expect to. And it was not until Malouf met Lillian's middle European parents in Brisbane that he realised how adroitly she had done it. "Lillian had made herself very much part of the Australian world," he says.

She seemed utterly to fit into that world and to feel very powerful in it. She was really in flight from everything her parents represented: Jewishness, the distrust of everything that went with that, the feeling that there was a kind of burden on you that restricted you. She told me she had to resist her parents' suggestion to her that neighbours could look like friends but you couldn't really trust that; a time could come when they could turn against you. Lillian set herself out defiantly to ignore that kind of notion.

She was a woman who simply didn't accept any kind of restriction that either men or other women thought there was in your being a woman. She saw herself as being absolutely free, as someone who could make her own life in any way she wanted. We wouldn't have called women like Lillian feminists then. Did they know such a word existed? They existed.

A lot of women in the Push world were very docile objects of the men's aggressive sexuality. They set themselves up as that. Lillian was never one of them. She said to herself, "I will be as aggressively and actively sexual as any man can be, if it suits me." There was no limitation on your freedom if you wanted to grab it. And it involved a kind of game, that people think is also a later kind of thing, of fiddling around on the edges of relationships with women.

In those days at Jamison Street there was always a girl around, an extraordinarily beautiful blonde girl who was a swimmer and who wore dresses with no backs in them. She would lie down with this wonderful, muscular back. Lillian would rub her hands up and down her back and say, "I just know what makes women so attractive to men." That again was my first encounter with that kind of world. It was a kind of role that Lillian wanted people to believe she could choose for herself if that's what she wanted to do.

Lillian represented Sydney. That very lucky, fearless kind of experimentation with everything, whether it was thoughts or style. It belonged to Sydney. If you came from a place like Brisbane you were just bowled over by the sophistication and the glitter and the wit and the goldenness of all those people. But there was also something about that world that used people up very quickly. It was a place where people were brilliant at the age of twenty-three or twenty-four. But hardly a single one of them ever came to anything.

*

Zell Rabin, like Lillian Roxon, was one who did come to something. They were born within a month of each other in the heart of Europe, and both were destined for lives in journalism. Rabin's grounding equipped him for a meteoric rise at a time when equally talented women such as Lillian were obliged to find a more circuitous path into mainstream journalism. Zell Rabin became one of Rupert Murdoch's earliest newspaper editors, and probably his most prized one. "He's atomic," Murdoch boasted at the time; forty years later he still describes Rabin as the best editor he ever hired.

Rabin was never part of the Sydney Push. He was too restless, energetic and ambitious for the endless hours of partying, pub-crawling and earnest discussions of Andersonian philosophy. And too ruthless. In the newspaper world, he had one ethical rule: if it was a good story it was a good story. David Malouf believes Rabin's approach had something to do with his origins: "It just seemed a kind of European thing. Australians were extraordinarily innocent then, at a time before there was any big European influence which might have introduced us to a world of bigger moral complexities."

Rabin was born Zalmenas Rabinavicius in Lithuania in March 1932, and fled the rise of Nazism with his family when he was six in circumstances similar to the Roxons. They reached Sydney in February 1939 and settled in Mosman on the North Shore. Zell spoke four languages when he arrived – German, Lithuanian, Russian and Yiddish – but quickly adapted to English with a broad Australian accent.

His father, Alexander, was a pharmacist, but Australia did not recognise his qualifications so the family moved around Sydney while he tried first farming, then bought an industrial chemical business. Zell went to four schools before finishing his secondary education at Sydney Boys High School, one of Sydney's best.

He came to despise the country of his birth – principally because of the collaboration of some Lithuanians with the Nazis who invaded in 1941 and murdered 165,000 Lithuanian Jews – and became a lifelong supporter of Israel. While still at school Zell tried unsuccessfully to persuade his father to let him join the Israeli army fighting for the foundation of the new state in 1948. His sister, Milly, remembers their father telling him: "Look, all the refugees from Europe are going to Israel. They don't need you. Get yourself a profession. Become an electrician, a plumber – anything that you can add to this country." Along with this immigrant sense of opportunity went a Jewish sense of burden that mirrored Rose Roxon's. When Zell told his father he planned to go into journalism, Alexander replied: "But how many editors are there? And on top of that, you're Jewish." It was an attitude his children found hard to deal with.

He found his way into journalism at the University of Queensland where he went to study physical education, that being the only institution then offering this course. Rabin later qualified as a physical education teacher but never practised; he also studied commerce. By April 1951, Rabin had joined *Semper Floreat*, the student newspaper that turned out to be an unlikely but excellent proving ground for the rough-and-tumble world of journalism that Rupert Murdoch would involve him in a decade later.

Semper Floreat was then at war with Brisbane's establishment press, chiefly the morning *Courier-Mail*. Its editor was John Quinlem, a bright student who had suffered discrimination by the Queensland education authorities. Quinlem won a teaching scholarship to the university only to have it withdrawn, according to an account published in the *Courier-Mail*, when the mandarins discovered he was of Chinese descent, although an Australian citizen. The Queensland Teachers Union supported this stand when one of its officials told the paper: "You couldn't have a full-blooded Chinese or Aborigine teaching."

Quinlem did not take his rejection easily and used his editorship of *Semper Floreat* to attack the establishment. One such attack was a front-page piece – accompanied by a picture of Quinlem, Rabin and other staff – decrying the shortcomings of the mainstream press. The article described the *Courier-Mail* as a newspaper "controlled by a monopoly-minded press mogul from Melbourne, adept at distorting the facts and little more than a megaphone for the Liberal Party."

The mogul was Sir Keith Murdoch, Rupert's father. Three weeks later, the *Courier-Mail* terminated its arrangement of lending photographic blocks to *Semper Floreat*. The student paper responded in outrage: "We may grovel in slime, but we would not wish to drag the Murdoch chain down through it ... Though spanked we are in no way cowed."

At the end of 1951 Rabin was appointed editor of *Semper* for the following year, then went home to Sydney to enjoy the summer holidays. Through Quinlem's introduction it was then that he met Lillian. Rabin already had a reputation as a great charmer of women. That summer of 1952 his youthful looks – blond hair, sleepy blue eyes and athletic features – were in full bloom. Quinlem recalls: "Zell came at women like a bulldozer. Lillian told me he presented himself to her as someone who was confident that no woman could resist his charms. And Lillian certainly wasn't able to resist him." Their mutual friend Aviva Layton, a former high school girlfriend of Rabin's and a Push friend of Lillian's, says: "She was absolutely bananas about him."

Lillian's diary for early 1952 indicates they spent much time together. Rabin took her home to meet his parents in Bondi, where she joined the family on Friday nights for their Sabbath observance with candles and wine. "My mother thought she was a delight," says Milly. "Our parents knew Zell was a rascal with women and they wanted him to settle down as quickly as possible. That wasn't to be." Their time together as a couple was intense but short. Rabin's return to Brisbane and Lillian's sense of independence in her own Sydney world probably doomed anything more lasting. Yet they shared enough – in age, Jewishness, European roots and professional destiny – to form a bond that linked them for the rest of their lives.

Returning to Brisbane as editor in early 1952, Rabin oversaw a re-design of *Semper Floreat* to give it a more racy, tabloid look, with head-lines, pictures and artwork that grabbed attention. Sex got prominent treatment alongside politics. Rabin appointed David Malouf co-editor in August. And the war with the *Courier-Mail* continued unabated. When *Semper Floreat* closed the year with its "Oscars and Awards for 1952", its dismissal of the *Courier-Mail* was more crushing than any-thing so far. To that paper, it awarded "The Senator Joseph McCarthy Oscar for Eternal Vigilance", with the citation: "The Champion of the oppressor, the Destroyer of justice and fair play, the Advocate of lies, prejudice and deceit, the Master of intrigue and corruption, the Apostle of sensationalism, distortion and political bias, the Disciple of tyranny, authoritarianism, reaction, conservatism and Big Business – ladies and gents, at great expense, we give you our colleague of dubious parentage – the Yellow Press. The award is for Redphobia and false accusations directed against *Semper Floreat* throughout the year."

Rabin's parting shot at the enemy of the metropolitan press had a finality about it, so Malouf was taken aback at Rabin's news a few weeks later. Rabin had just completed his final exams for his diploma in phys-ical education when, according to Malouf, he announced: "I'm going to work for the *Courier-Mail*. They've offered me a cadetship."

"Zell, how could you?" Malouf replied. "Everything the *Courier-Mail* stands for you've spent this year attacking."

"Well?"

So Zell Rabin got his first job in mainstream journalism with the *Courier-Mail*. He had already laid the groundwork with casual Saturday sports reporting for the paper while still studying. Its editors were apparently impressed enough by his drive, tenacity and opportunism to turn a blind eye to the attacks emanating from the student organ. Little did Sir Keith Murdoch know that the new cadet with the troublesome reputation would one day be a linchpin in his son's quest for a global media empire.

Grace Garlick, Lillian's old friend from State High School, had won a cadetship on the *Courier-Mail* when she left school in 1949, the only woman in her year's intake. She remembers when Zell Rabin joined the paper. "He was little and fair and pale and attractive and aesthetic-looking. A powerful sort of paleness. He made more of an impression than anybody from the university. We were all very aware of Zell the iconoclast. It seemed a bit of a shame when he came to work at the *Courier-Mail*, as though it was going to restrict this free spirit to some degree of conformity. But the cadetship would have been too hard for him to resist. They were glad to have him."

*

As Rabin started work on the Brisbane daily in early 1953, Lillian was contributing to student journalism as a prelude to her own career. She had already written for *Honi Soit*, the University of Sydney student newspaper, and in 1953, under Edmund Campion as editor, she wrote a gossip column called "Postman's Knock" which she signed "The Postmistress" and used shamelessly to report the goings-on of her friends. Zell Rabin featured in her first column on 19 March 1953. At the age of twenty-one, Rabin had become engaged to a young woman in Sydney; it did not last. If she was pained by the engagement, Lillian disguised her feelings by roasting her former boyfriend:

In Memoriam: Gone but not forgotten ... Zell Rabin, 21, live wire editor of Brisbane's *Semper Floreat* in 1952 – engaged. Ten thousand women in Melbourne, Sydney and Brisbane are mourning his loss. To add insult to injury, the "lucky" girl is one of OUR freshettes. How about sending one down in return, Brisbane? R.I.P.

*

The *Courier-Mail* became Rabin's springboard to the more competitive world of Sydney newspapers. After a year at the Brisbane paper he wrote to Milly, who was in her last year at Sydney Girls High School, asking her to scout for possible openings. The Sydney evening paper the *Sun* expressed interest. Rabin's news editor at the *Courier-Mail* wrote asking the *Sun* not to take him, "as the young man has high potential". So the *Sun* took him.

Rabin rose quickly through the *Sun's* ranks. After two years, the editors sent him to a coveted post reporting America and the world from the paper's New York bureau. The year was 1956, a big year for Lillian Roxon too. The university, the Push and Jamison Street were about to give way to a new life in the rumbustious world of Sydney tabloid journalism, before her own move to New York where she and Zell Rabin would reconnect, not always harmoniously.

Chapter 11 The World of *Weekend*

When he was shopping one day in January 1957 in the Fortitude Valley district of Brisbane, David Malouf ran into Lillian Roxon's mother, Rose. She seemed nervous and agitated. "Oh, David, I'm so sorry I've run into you. I'd hoped I'd come to the valley and not see anyone I knew."

"Why is that, Mrs Roxon?"

"It's Lillian."

"What about her?"

"Something so shameful I can't tell you."

Malouf thought he knew everything there was to know about Lillian by now, so he coaxed her mother.

"Oh, I can't look you in the face and tell you, David."

"I'm sure you can."

"Well, you mustn't tell anyone in Brisbane, but that Lillian ... she is working for WEEKEND!"

Weekend was a weekly tabloid magazine published in Sydney that specialised in scandal and shock. Frank Packer, the newspaper tycoon who owned the Sydney *Daily Telegraph*, had launched *Weekend* on a whim in 1954. On a visit to London that year, he heard a rumour that the British publishers of *Reveille*, a racy weekly tabloid, were planning an Australian edition. *Weekend* was Packer's response to freeze them out of the market. He recruited as editor Donald Horne, then a journalist in Packer's London bureau. Horne was thirty-two. He agreed to Packer's offer to return to Australia and edit *Weekend* for six months, after which he planned to resume a career in London. Packer installed Horne on an expense account in the Australia Hotel, a few blocks down Castlereagh Street from the magazine's office at the headquarters of Packer's company, Australian Consolidated Press. Horne never returned to Britain. He went on to become one of Australia's most prominent editors and prolific authors, best known for coining the description of Australia as "the lucky country" through his 1964 book of that title.

Horne once described editing *Weekend* as "a bit like directing a B-grade movie". Its first issue displayed a long-legged cover girl with three headings splashed around her: "I Married the World's Strongest Woman", "How to Recognise the Face of Your Ideal Mate" and "Bushranger Cut off Their Heads". Horne welcomed readers to that first issue with the message: "There is nothing dreary – or dirty – in *Weekend*. You can read it from cover to cover – and ENJOY every word." Packer set Horne a national circulation target of 500,000 copies. Horne wrote years later that, "I was ... held together (if by anything) by a belief that *Weekend*, a publication that, when I thought about it honestly – which was not often – gave me psychosomatic pains, should sell half a million copies."

By the time Lillian Roxon found her way on to the staff of *Weekend* in January 1957, the magazine was approaching the height of its commercial, if not its editorial, fortunes. It was a brilliant tabloid product of its day, pushing the barriers between good and bad taste, knocking at the walls of sexual prudery – and a lively milieu for an aspiring journalist to cut her teeth. Lillian arrived at *Weekend* by a circuitous route.

*

She finally finished her degree in 1954 and graduated from the University of Sydney on 29 April 1955, a Bachelor of Arts with majors in English and Philosophy. She had taken two extra years to complete her three-year degree. Most students then could not afford such an indulgence: if they failed a year they lost the bursary or teaching scholarship on which they depended.

Lillian later wrote that "being there was ever so much more rewarding than working". The problem in mid-fifties Australia was not getting a job but getting the job you wanted. Women still had limited access to journalism as a career. A handful of women had come through the war years with distinction and were names to be reckoned with, but they were the exceptions. For the most part women had to settle for reporting the "society" or "women's" pages. The weightier sides of journalism – politics, the law, crime, sport, business and general news – were all reported by men.

She found a job in the advertising department of McDowell's, a Sydney department store, and her savings financed a voyage of reconnaissance to New York. A few days before she left in January 1956, her father Isadore died in Brisbane from leukaemia, aged sixty. Whatever psychological ties Lillian felt her father maintained over her were now transferred to her mother, who came to focus more and more on her daughter's welfare.

Lillian stayed away for eight months, the visit cementing her decision that New York was where she would eventually return for good. In this respect she was a trail-blazer. Most young Australians still chose London as their world city, but New York's restlessness, energy and open attitudes were natural magnets for her own. It was as if this was to be her ultimate destination in the diaspora that had begun back in Alassio. Roxon relatives lived in Locust Hill Avenue, Yonkers in New York, and she started out staying with them. By May she had fallen out with her aunt in Yonkers and moved to West 10th Street in the heart of Greenwich Village.

The year 1956 also saw Elvis Presley explode on to the scene. But while rock and roll was being born, folk music was still very much a musical force; during her visit Lillian explored some of the networks she would establish on a larger scale ten years later. After her *Rock Encyclopedia* was published, she talked about this 1956 visit to the *Herald*, an American newspaper, in 1971:

> I first came to the United States in 1956 on a visit and I was engaged
> to the president of the Australian folklore society. I looked up all the
> folk people here. I lived with Patty Clancy of the Clancy Brothers
> and his first wife Betty. Living with them I met everybody including
> Woodie Guthrie. That was the year of the big folk revival so I was in
> on all that. I've said this a thousand times but it's true, I was attracted
> by the lifestyle. When I first came to the United States people were
> very uptight and then after England and the music, everybody
> changed.

Lillian's reference to being engaged is curious. Glen Hamilton was then president of the Australian folklore society and a friend from the Push with whom Lillian shared an interest in folk music. He says they were never engaged: "Engaged and fiancé were not Push words or

Lillian words. If she'd said in Sydney she was engaged to Glen Hamilton people would have fallen about laughing." He believes the word probably found its way into Lillian's interview as a shorthand description for American readers of a close friendship.

Before Lillian returned to Sydney in August, Zell Rabin, now living in New York as the Sydney *Sun's* correspondent, gave her a farewell party. After she arrived home, the Australian Security Intelligence Organisation (ASIO) opened two files on her. According to ASIO in 2001, the files – which have never been fully released – relate to a letter Lillian wrote from New York to someone "of interest" to ASIO at the time. This caused Lillian to come to ASIO's attention. But the letter, according to ASIO, is now lost.

The mystery of Lillian's letter written to an unknown friend and intercepted by ASIO is another example of how Australia's intelligence service spent much energy in the fifties and sixties securing the state from the threat of subversive types, real or imagined – most of them imagined.

*

The Sydney to which Lillian returned in August 1956 seemed to be marking time. The buzz was in Melbourne, its rival city down south, with the Olympic Games set to open there in three months' time. The newspapers were focussed on the crisis over Egypt's nationalisation of the Suez Canal, with Menzies attending talks in London and making an embarrassing foray into world affairs by taking on the role of the mother country's envoy to Egypt.

But Sydney was starting to change, albeit gradually. The city of low-rise sandstone and wood buildings, whose streets were linked by lanes and courts laid out in the nineteenth century, was coming under the sights of property developers who wanted to pull down the old buildings and replace them with towers. An early casualty was the old Jamison Street house where Lillian had lived before she left the university. By the mid-fifties Windsor House and its neighbour Jamison House were targets for demolition. The site became a car park for almost twenty years.

Before she left for America, Lillian's parents had rented a flat in an art deco building at 31 South Avenue, Double Bay in Sydney's eastern suburbs. It was to be a base for the family in Sydney, but Lillian always

suspected that it was also a way for Rose to keep a closer eye on her
daughter when she visited from Brisbane. Lillian's move to Double Bay
on her return from New York was part of a psychological transition as
well. She was starting to cut a figure in Sydney beyond the Push world
represented by her Jamison Street days. A few months after her return,
a Sydney gossip column reported: "Vivacious Lillian Roxon, of Double
Bay, was seen wining and dining at Caprice, last week, with handsome
visiting American, Dr Milton K. Stein. Lillian first met Dr Stein when
she was holidaying in New York last year."

In the background essay to her novel, Lillian describes this transition: "Eventually in the book and in real life I moved away from the
dusty house to a place with its own bath. There's a move away from the
bohemians and their horses and card games to a richer world of lobster
dinners beside the waters of the harbour, elegant parties where food is
served, holidays spent not hitchhiking on the highways but driving
and sleeping in motels (and somehow, despite the bull ants, not as
much fun)."

But her Push friends remained the core of her social life, and the
South Avenue flat was the scene of many parties over the next three
years. The Push itself was changing, too. Sope (Neil Hope), now an
English teacher, had introduced young blood into the Push circle in
the form of John Roberts, Ian Bedford and Ross Poole, three of his former students at North Sydney Boys High School. Sope had recognised
their academic talents, spent time training them in the art of passing
examinations and encouraged them to read Graham Greene, Ernest
Hemingway, D. H. Lawrence and other authors outside the school
curriculum.

Lillian was still in New York when Roberts, Bedford and Poole, as the
Push people referred to them, started appearing at Push gatherings during their first year out of school. Ross Poole, a good-looking eighteen-
year-old fighting the constraints of parental authority on Sydney's
conservative North Shore, found the Push an "intoxicating escape".
Ross was charmed by Lillian's accounts of life in New York, her funny
stories about a Jewish man called Mr Zimmerman who she said had
pursued her there, and her use of New York terminology like "cold
water walk-up". She left no doubt in Ross's mind that returning to
New York was her project; the only issue was when, and under what
conditions.

Lillian was twenty-four when she met Ross, six years her junior. They began a relationship that lasted for the next two years. Lillian sometimes joked about her relations with men by declaring that, as far as she was concerned, men reached their peak at the age of nineteen and after that went rapidly downhill. Ross Poole was an intelligent young man who appealed to Lillian's sense of adventure, and she a slightly older woman of the world who appealed to his. But these differences did create friction in their relationship.

And, as Ross was just discovering his passport to freedom through the Push, Lillian was finding the freedom the Push represented had its limits. Ross Poole says: "She was interested in becoming a journalist, in mixing with journalists. She was in love with movement, with being at the centre of things and writing about them. I don't think she ever cared very much about the part of the Push that I became attracted to later: the political ideas, the anarchism, its relationship with left-wing politics. I don't think Lillian would have been capable of not creating a world around her in which she could function and flourish. The Push was ceasing to be that world. For me the Libertarian Push was freedom. For Lillian it wasn't offering the kinds of things she was going to get in New York."

When she returned from her New York visit she was hired by Anthony Hordern's, a department store that covered an entire city block and traded under the motto, "While I Live I Grow". "I lasted as a copywriter exactly one day but was allowed to stay on as head of publicity which was considered a very crummy job," she wrote later. Then came her break into journalism. "Barbara Broadbent (now Mrs Jack Pollard) told me she was leaving a job on Donald Horne's then new *Weekend* magazine and would I like it? *Weekend* was then still done in newsprint, like *Reveille*, and it was appalling with stories like 'Nude starlet swallows live toad' and 'Vicar posed as mermaid'. But working for Donald Horne meant having a ringside seat at the most spectacular show in town, so goodbye while-I-live-I-grow."

*

Lillian joined the staff of *Weekend* on 10 January 1957. Donald Horne had managed to convince Frank Packer to give the magazine expanded editorial space on the fifth floor of the *Daily Telegraph* building in Castlereagh Street. The building had barely changed since Packer had taken it over two decades earlier. The cramped newsrooms were straight from an old Hollywood movie, lined with dark wood, filled with smoke and clattering with typewriters.

Horne was an incongruous figure for a magazine such as *Weekend*. He looked, and was, intellectual. He went to work in suits cut in England, his rather thin hair combed straight back, his eyes framed in severe, dark spectacles, his mouth set seriously. When Lillian walked into his office to be interviewed, she had an instant impact on him: "I can see her the day she came for a job. She was there at the other end of the table with that beautiful skin of hers, smiling away. I hired her on the spot because I loved the way she talked."

Lillian had landed herself in the most colourful location of an otherwise bland journalistic scene in 1957. When she joined *Weekend* it had recently ditched its earlier cheap newspaper appearance and had switched to a rotogravure printing technique that made it look more like a magazine. Just over a month after she joined the staff, *Weekend* cracked the 500,000 circulation target Packer and Horne had set, something it was never to achieve again.

Horne's formula for the magazine's success was to play on the themes of the fifties – a clear definition of sexual roles, with marriage as the ultimate life achievement for women – but also to titillate readers by questioning these norms. The in-house habit, according to Horne, was to "write the poster heading first, and then the story". The magazine's formula for the commercial exploitation of sex was quite straightforward, he later wrote: "Visually, it was a matter of choosing two or three photos each week of female breasts arranged so that they projected the concept of *breast*. Verbally, it was a matter of ensuring that the words 'nude' and 'sex' occurred in two or three headings each week, and thereby projected the concept of *sex*."

Guy Morrison, a reporter and designer on Horne's staff, remembers being despatched to Melbourne with a photographer to do an article on Trappist monks: "We spent a lot of time choosing the page one picture. I think Donald had probably already decided he wasn't going to use the monks on page one at all because that wouldn't sell any copies. The cover headline was 'Secrets of the Silent Monks'. But the cover picture was a rather depraved-looking young woman in a flimsy dress sitting at the edge of the surf. The sea had washed around her thighs and washed her dress up. I got a very sad telephone call from the head of the monastery saying thank you for the article, but then deploring the cover."

The Australian stories often took second place to news and gossip about American celebrities of the day: Elvis Presley, Elizabeth Taylor, Eddie Fisher, Debbie Reynolds, Ricky Nelson, Tommy Sands, Fabian, Tab Hunter. There were articles about Hitler by "his sister, Paula Hitler"; on "Why Wives Are Unfaithful"; "Did My Mother Kill My Wife?"; "My 10 Ways To Deal with Men", by Joan Collins; "Brigitte Bardot's Phoney Honeymoon"; "The Things the Queen Hates about Us"; "The Real Reason Tab Hunter Hasn't Married"; "Elvis Presley says, 'I'm Not Going to Marry an Australian Girl'"; "Is Australia Becoming a Woman's Country?"; and "Why Queensland Will Become a Second Hollywood".

In November 1957, the authorities in Queensland tried to ban *Weekend* and *Crowd*, a short-lived competitor launched by the rival Fairfax group. Horne and Clyde Packer, Frank's elder son, fought the injunction in the courts and won. As Peter Coleman, a colleague of Horne's, later remarked, in the battle over freedom of speech *Weekend* became an unlikely ally of James Joyce and Vladimir Nabokov, both of whose works were also then banned in Australia.

The *Weekend* staff was composed mainly of men, among them Steve Dunleavy, Pat Burgess and Larry Boys, all big names in later years. Lillian became one of Horne's favourites, if not his most favoured reporter. He found her "ambitious, dedicated and determined to succeed". It helped that she had not had any formal training in journalism: Horne tried to recruit talented young people from outside the conventional cadetship training system for a magazine that required imagination in its writers as much as rigid adherence to the facts.

He was a tough editor. His sackings, as he put it, were "notorious". From staff conferences that sometimes happened on Sundays at Horne's flat in Kirribilli, on the north side of Sydney Harbour, some survivors recall an unspoken social gradation in which Lillian and Horne tended to regard themselves above the rest of the fray. In his memoirs, Horne writes: "As when I was a student, I was still ready to chair discussion groups on the subject of who or what I really was, but mostly this subject now had to be discussed by Horne himself, sitting on his own case. The only person who might join me was Lillian Roxon, a former member of 'the Push' (or was she still a member? We kept most of our lives from each other). In the testing business of 'earning a living' she had been writing advertising copy for a department store of declining prof-itability, and when she asked for a job, and I gave her one, it was the acknowledged sense of parody in what we were doing that made work-ing on *Weekend* a kind of liberation. We would speak to each other in half-meanings."

Lillian became a chief reporter and section editor. And if the bizarre story-lines that satisfied *Weekend*'s readers were not always available in real life, Lillian recruited some of her Push friends to pose as eccentric Sydney characters who could become the stories. These were journalis-tic "acts of parody" pushed to extremes. Sope was used under a pseu-donym as a man who had built his own coffin; he was pictured sitting up inside it in Kinsella's, a funeral parlour in Taylor Square. For another story he was Sam Craddock, a clerk from Paddington and a reformed drunk, who had his face made into a poster with the message "Stop! Don't Drink" plastered across it, which he would drop on to floors of Sydney pubs in a campaign to warn people off drink. The story ran under the heading "The Face on the Bar-Room Floor". Sydney has always been a city that likes to believe its own legends, so these blatant exercises in delusion were perhaps not far from the city's own ethos. Their merging of fact and fiction provided set pieces for both Lillian and Sope in their unpublished novels of Sydney in the fifties.

*

Horne was very serious about making *Weekend* a market leader. Between July and September 1957, he produced eleven weekly bul-letins for his staff, each up to twelve pages long, saying what was wrong with the previous issue and how they could make the next one better. These bulletins were also detailed critiques of and guides to the practice of popular journalism that could stand any newspaper or mag-azine in good stead. *Weekend* was lucky to have them. Horne wrote of the rules for writing good blocklines, of employing every trick and stunt of presentation and display, and of the need to make every story a "swiftly moving whole" with not one wasted word. He praised the handling of short features such as "Set Himself on Fire for Love", "Slept 300 Nights", "Run Over by His Own Car" and "Killed by His Clothes", and roasted others for being "subbed into senselessness". He advised his staff of the need for a consistent editorial policy: "Just as your fear can be transmitted instinctively to an animal, uncertainty of editorial policy can transfer itself somehow to readers; it is better to stick to even a dubious policy than to have no policy at all, or to try out a different policy every week. Certainly, nothing is worse than too much chopping and changing (as distinguished from well controlled contrast and surprise)." And, "There is a moment of truth for every journalist when he must forget what he meant to do and evaluate what the readers are going to see of his work. It's usually a rather chilling moment, but a really necessary one."

When she left Australia for the United States two years later, Lillian took copies of these bulletins and kept them with her in New York until she died. She told Horne years later that on nights when she could not sleep in Manhattan she sometimes re-read her old *Weekend* bulletins, to "reassure myself that life can seem orderly".

*

In 1958 *Weekend* started to tone down its salacious side, display fewer breasts and run more stories on beauty, cooking and home decorating. This was partly a response to the settlement of the Queensland bid to ban it, partly a recognition of the new consumer market popular magazines were starting to chase. Lillian edited a section that focused on mind, body and health and, for a while, wrote the Harriett Kaye agony column. Judy Smith, a prominent Push figure – whose husband Howard masqueraded as a goldfish-swallowing waiter for one of Lillian's earlier stories – recalls how effortlessly Lillian had transformed her life out of the Push: "She was accused by the serious Libertarians of being a lightweight because she wasn't earnest and ponderous. But she took journalism very seriously. She was prolific. She put words on to a page the way a painter paints a picture. They went straight there with a quick, verbal brilliance and nothing was ever changed."

In February 1958, while still editing *Weekend*, Horne started editing the *Observer*, a quality fortnightly magazine that Frank Packer launched and after which Horne had long hankered. (When Packer bought the *Bulletin*, a legendary literary magazine, three years later, he merged the *Observer* into it and made Horne editor.) The *Observer* was, in Horne's words, "radically conservative" – liberal for its day on social issues such as censorship, women's rights, Aborigines and homosexual law reform but, deferring to its proprietor, conservative on politics. Clyde Packer was the executive in charge and he gave Horne his head to hire writers on art, theatre and film such as Robert Hughes, Barry Humphries and Bruce Beresford.

Peter Coleman and the *Observer*'s other heavyweight writers on politics, business and culture were surprised when Horne assigned Lillian Roxon, his star reporter from the downmarket *Weekend*, to write a lead story for the *Observer*'s arts pages on Liberace, the flamboyant American showman who sang, played the piano and pranced across stages covered in jewellery and outrageous costumes. Lillian went to meet Liberace in Sydney and wrote the story in a style that was to become her hallmark well before such an approach was accepted in Australian newspapers. She put herself into the story as much as the people she was writing about. It ran in the *Observer*, under the by-line "By a Staff Correspondent", on 8 March 1958:

A small group of my colleagues were already waiting patiently outside Liberace's hotel when I arrived (punctual to the minute) for my exclusive interview. Liberace, it seemed, was late. He had been held up at the Royal Garden Party. His publicity woman explained that I would have to wait my turn with all the others. They had been promised exclusive interviews too. There was a young man from a morning paper looking nonchalant, a dapper type from a women's magazine stroking his moustache anxiously and a man from a radio station hugging a tape recorder. Some photographers huddled together in a corner, probably wondering if there was anything to drink. There wasn't.

While we waited Liberace's very worried publicity woman hovered about us and an American woman, arrogant and unfriendly in a white dress, kept looking at us with suspicion. She turned out to be Liberace's sister, Mrs Anne Liberace Farrell, who was afraid the Press were going to do her brother out of his sleep. By the time Liberace got there, several hours late, we were all ready to hate him. Hadn't Cassandra, columnist of the London *Daily Mirror* called him a "deadly, winking, sniggering, mincing heap of mother love"? We were all ready to make mincemeat of this pompadoured sissy.

Then a black hire car pulled up and Liberace walked up to us smiling, calling us each by our name after the introductions. Our mouths fell open. In one minute flat, with all those odds against him, the man had charmed us silly, and there wasn't a single old lady of any age among us ...

So it was that when the bombshell was dropped, none of us really cared. "I'm sorry," he told us suddenly with a winning smile, "but I never give exclusive interviews. Life is too short and I just haven't the time." You can't blame the man for not wanting to spend the rest of the evening talking to newspapermen. If Liberace is publicity hungry, he definitely did not show it then when he risked offending the Press.

The gentlemanly reporter from the ladies' magazine beckoned his photographer and walked out on principle. We stayed. The questions started. I wondered just what people would ask. I was a bit nervous remembering the answer he had given to an English reporter who asked him, "Do you lead a normal sex life?" Liberace's smile had not wavered as he replied quietly, "Yes, do you?"

She concluded her piece:

As I went out the door Liberace flashed me another marvellous smile and his sister squeezed out an acid grin. Out of the presence I stopped to think. Was he after all odious? Had he hypnotised me? No, he is charming and pleasant. He is not effeminate. He is fond of his mother. He is unhappy about some of the publicity he gets. What can he do about it? Nothing. The publicity has not hurt his career and he likes being a success.

But it makes me wonder about Elvis Presley and Jayne Mansfield. Are they sweet unspoilt kids too? Nothing would surprise me after meeting Liberace.

Some at the *Observer* disapproved of Lillian's piece. As far as they were concerned, if the *Observer* was to run anything at all on a figure such as Liberace it should be to ridicule him, not to be surprised and charmed by him. But they bowed to instructions from Horne, who wanted to lighten up the arts pages and broaden their appeal.

*

Towards the end of 1958, Lillian's relationship with Ross Poole came to an end. She went to Melbourne for a work assignment and Ross followed her. They joined a friend and his family for a weekend's camping at Wye River on the south coast of Victoria. There was drinking at a local pub and in the evening at the camp site. Lillian was never much of a drinker and she did not join in. When Ross woke the next morning, Lillian was gone; she had got up and hitchhiked back to Melbourne in the middle of the night. She and Ross returned to Sydney separately and when they met there again, Ross recalls, Lillian told him their friend had made a pass at her, that she had had enough and just wanted to get out.

Ross and Lillian stayed friends, nevertheless. When Horne later offered Ross work at *Weekend*, Lillian approved. It was a strange assignment that lasted three weeks. Ross was that rare figure: a Push person who starred as himself, not as a fictional character, in the pages of *Weekend*. It was a typical but effective example of *Weekend*'s gimmicky brand of journalism. Horne made Ross the centre of a lead story on 16 May 1959 about a man whom *Weekend* had confined to spending a week in a room by himself in order to test the impact of isolation on humans. Ross's cell was a tiny bedroom in the King's Head Hotel, just around the corner from *Weekend*'s offices. He was allowed one book, Dostoevsky's *Crime and Punishment*, and three meals a day brought to him by a *Weekend* photographer with whom he was allowed to exchange just ten words. A condition of the story was that Ross was twenty when he went in and twenty-one when he came out: he was to pass his twenty-first birthday alone in his bedroom cell.

Consisting of Ross's diary, the opinions of a Sydney psychiatrist and plenty of pictures of a winsome-looking Ross Poole, the feature played out over the following three issues and ended with a picture of Ross released from his agony, laughing, drinking champagne and surrounded by showgirls in Kings Cross. But it was not the making of Ross Poole, the journalist. "It was an opportunity I don't think I took seriously." He went on to have a career as an academic philosopher.

*

"Memo: Miss Roxon. I have arranged for you to have a telephone conversation with Miss Jayne Mansfield. Will you see me about this straightaway, please?"

Jayne Mansfield was a Hollywood bombshell whose platinum hair, hourglass figure, plunging neckline and tight-fitting clothes symbolised the fifties image of female sexuality. She appeared frequently in the pages of *Weekend*, along with Brigitte Bardot and Sabrina, a British version of Mansfield. When Lillian received this command from Horne on 10 April 1959, she was already planning her move to America later in the year. *Weekend* had been good to her and she had been good to *Weekend*. But she had exhausted it and Sydney – her work was starting to go round in circles. In a cover story on 11 April she had tried to set up a cat fight between Sabrina and Jayne Mansfield when she interviewed Sabrina in Sydney. Now she was expected to do the same thing again when she talked to Jayne Mansfield by radio telephone in Hollywood. And that is how the story appeared on 2 May, taking a quote as its headline: "Sabrina? Never Heard of Her!"

Sope had made his own escape two years earlier when he sailed out of Sydney for Italy. He echoed his farewell lunch with Lillian in the form of a similar encounter in his novel between the characters Sam and Lola in an Italian restaurant in Woolloomooloo:

All our squabbles were forgotten. It was a sad little meal.

"Sam, I'm going to miss you. And to think if I hadn't played that coffin trick on you, I might have watched you become a headmaster. Now I'm watching you sail away to freedom."

"But all by myself, Lola. That's the pity of it. I need a few trusty fans. Like you."

"Background people," she said.

"Yair, background people. They're an essential part of the act. Giving cues for the applause. I'm no showground spruiker for myself."

"Me. I find Sydney – or I will now – I'll find it a bit of a backwater."

"Why not go to America, Lola? New York must be longing for a girl like you."

"I've been doing a bit of thinking on those lines myself ..."

*

Weekend was starting to reflect the new world of teenagers and the advent of rock and roll, and it ran a series on "The Teenage Revolution". The first wave of Australian pop singers was getting noticed. On 4 July *Weekend* started a regular column by Johnny O'Keefe, Australia's biggest rock and roll star at the time. O'Keefe and other early Australian rockers like Col Joye, Johnny Reb, the Delltones and Johnny Devlin had struggled to find an audience in their home country until Lee Gordon, an impresario, had given them their first real exposure by booking them as supporting acts to the so-called "Big Shows" of American stars he toured in Australia. By mid-1959, they were ready to take off.

That same year, another person slipped into Sydney who was also preparing to take off and who would become a volatile presence in Lillian's life a decade later. In 1959, Germaine Greer was a star English student at the University of Melbourne and already a prominent figure on campus. She was seven years younger than Lillian. Towards the end of 1959, Germaine visited Sydney and gravitated to the Royal George Hotel where she fell in among the Push crowd. She met Roelof Smilde, one of the Push's leading men. "We got to talking and liked each other," says Smilde. "She asked me, 'Would it be all right if I came back to Sydney?' I wasn't quite sure what she meant by that. I said, 'Yeah. Sure.' We weren't involved. Just talked and liked each other's company. So she did come back to Sydney and then we did get involved."

Germaine did her Master of Arts degree at the University of Sydney in the early sixties and lived with Roelof Smilde for two-and-a-half years in the old servants quarters of a nineteenth-century mansion in Glebe, near the university. Her Sydney milieu was the same as Lillian's, the Push. But, like Lillian, she ultimately found it too stifling and left to become a star in a bigger world. "I thought she was terrific," says Smilde. "She wanted to do everything. She wanted to act, sing, dance, write, recite poetry. She found our society, the Push, too restrictive. And we were pretty limited. She was raring to go. She wanted to go overseas and test the water all over the place. It was inevitable that we'd split up." Lillian and Germaine missed each other in Sydney by a few months in 1959, but there would be plenty of fireworks when they did meet in New York nine years later.

*

Frank Packer received a knighthood in June. He was in London when it was announced, and the Queen Mother conferred it on him at Buckingham Palace on 7 July. When the chief-of-staff at the *Daily Telegraph* in Sydney sent a telegram of congratulations on behalf of the staff, Sir Frank cabled back that it was much appreciated by himself and "Missus Packer". Around this time, Horne locked horns with the *Telegraph* over the paper's attempt to poach Lillian from his staff. In August, Horne wrote Sir Frank a memo seeking his intervention to stop the *Telegraph* from taking her. "The facts about Miss Roxon are as follows: Miss Roxon came on to the 'Weekend' staff about two and a half years ago and was trained by me. She was responsive and has for some time past been one of the most valuable members of the 'Weekend' staff."

If anyone should now offer Miss Roxon a rise, he argued, it should be *Weekend*, not the *Telegraph*: "The implications of any other action are that we shall be training staff to bring out 'Weekend' who can then better themselves going to the 'Daily Telegraph'." He suggested offering Lillian a "considerable rise" to stay with *Weekend*. If Sir Frank was not convinced by his memo, "may I see you before Miss Roxon does because the points of staff discipline involved are important?"

Lillian resolved the dispute herself by leaving for America the next month. She stayed loyal to Horne and continued writing for *Weekend* from Hollywood for a few months before she moved on to New York, her home for the rest of her life.

In Lillian's novel her heroine, Camilla, follows a similar path. After breaking up with her boyfriend and surveying the rest of her crowd, who seem to be either disappearing into marriage or not going anywhere very much, she suddenly decides to leave Sydney for London. Max Fowler, Camilla's editor at *Quick* magazine, tries to keep her, promising her that she could be editing the magazine one day if she plays her cards right. During her final weeks in Sydney, Camilla become romantically involved with Max. In the background essay to her novel, Lillian explains the editor figure:

> He was fifty-seven and inspired by a lot of people, including the late Ian Fleming and the distinguished *New York Times* reporter Harrison Salisbury. I worked for many years in the *New York Times* building and I often had Harrison Salisbury riding in the elevator with me. Clifton Daniel too, but he didn't fit into the book. I chose a 57-year-old hero because I have never been in love with a man more than two years older than me, and the idea of a much older man was very exciting. I wanted someone outwardly austere and controlled because it was going to be as much fun getting into his head in a novel as it would be in real life.

As she prepared to leave for New York, Lillian wrote to her mother in Brisbane: "I suppose the decision came as a shock to you even if you

ARE in favor of it! Still, since it was a hard decision to make, I am now sticking to it and everything (except me) seems to be under control." Her gossip column appeared in *Weekend* right up to her departure. On 29 August 1959 she was writing about the impending tour of Australia by Johnny Ray, a fifties crooner. A week later she was on her way, at the age of twenty-seven, to a new country and a new decade. Soon afterwards, Donald Horne wrote a cover piece in the *Observer* farewelling the 1950s, which he described as "ten years that did not shake the world". But all that would soon change.

On her way across the Pacific, Lillian stopped in Honolulu at the Hawaiian Village Hotel where she interviewed for *Weekend* one of the biggest names in show business, Colonel Tom Parker, Elvis Presley's manager, and the impresario Lee Gordon who was then trying to bring Elvis to Australia. Plump and balding, the colonel held a cigar; the money manager and the young reporter held each other's businesslike gazes. And years later, when she was the rock writer for New York's biggest selling paper, the *Sunday News*, Lillian looked back on this moment to give her readers an insight into the Elvis phenomenon. It was in June 1972 when Elvis was about to give a concert at Madison Square Garden:

For the benefit of you younger ones, I have to explain that Colonel Tom Parker, Elvis's manager, did not get himself or his client where either of them are today by trusting people. He does, however, have a high regard for efficiency. Nothing will go wrong with Elvis's concert next weekend. Nothing ever does. The houses will be packed. The sound will be superb. Every seat will be paid for, even Bob Dylan's. And although all kinds of friends and admirers will be there, those fantastic front seats everyone always wants will be filled with the real fans, the ones who stood in line all night to get first pick ...

I met the colonel once a long time ago in Hawaii ... and what I remember most about that meeting, poor unsophisticated kid that I was, was the colonel patiently explaining to me what a snow job was. I now know that the colonel is the king of the snow jobs, that is, he is a master illusionist who will always keep Elvis rich, elusive and a head or two taller than anyone even daring to compete with him. If you see a sort of chubby man with eyes like bright marbles and a misleadingly paternal smile, rush to get his autograph. There aren't too many celebrities bigger than Elvis around these days, but Colonel Tom Parker is still one of them.

Sydney and *Weekend* had been excellent preparation for the task Lillian had now set herself. Like Germaine Greer, her Australian background had equipped her with the self-confidence to take on the world. And like Colonel Tom Parker, as she headed towards a life of chronicling rock and roll, the "real fans" – her readers – would always come first.

Mirror meets Mr. Kennedy

A meeting with President Kennedy at the White House, 1961. Zell Rabin (left) with his new boss at the Sydney *Daily Mirror*, Rupert Murdoch (right).

Lillian (left) with fellow correspondents Don Riseborough and Margaret Jones in the *Sydney Morning Herald* New York bureau, mid-1960s.

The Easybeats on tour in America in 1967. Lillian credited the Easybeats, the first Australian rock group to break into the American charts, with sparking her interest in rock music.

The Sydney Morning Herald

One Hundred and Fortieth Year of Publication

28 PAGES & TV Guide

Friday, A

SUN: To
MOON:
2.04 p.m.
High 6.1
p.m. (3ft
(1ft 5in)

ges:

THERE IS A TIDE IN THE AFFAIRS OF WOMEN

ut

ay. — The oil
w likely to be
ny judgment
he industry's

nonwealth Arbi-
ssion today sent
tiations on the

tions are being conducted
in the main courtroom
in the Commission build-
ing in Little Bourke
Street.
   The instruction to the
parties to resume negotia-
tions is unprecedented in
the recent history of the
Commission.
   When earlier negotia-
tions before Commis-
sioner E. J. Clarkson
broke down last month, it
appeared that several im-
portant policies of the

Ships'

This is the hardest
piece I have ever had
to write in my life.
   I am supposed to be
telling what happened
when 25,000 women

New York, Thursday:
LILLIAN ROXON
cables a biased report

upsets me that even as I
write this I know that the
men editors and sub-edi-
tors handling this story
will probably choose to
delete this particular par-

Now

Lillian's report of the historic women's march down Fifth Avenue in New York in August, 1970 got front-page (and unorthodox) treatment in the *Sydney Morning Herald.*

Germaine Greer in 1969, the year she wrote
The Female Eunuch, with its dedication to Lillian.
The picture is from the alternative paper *Suck*,
in which Germaine featured during her late
sixties counterculture period as the columnist
"Earth Rose".

The apartment building at 221 East
21st Street, opposite the 13th Precinct
police headquarters, where Lillian
lived from 1963 until her death.

For her photo in *Mug Shots*, a book on the top 200 people in America's "alternate culture", Lillian chose a t-shirt with an old Australian theme.

Lillian Roxon with Lester Bangs: two legendary rock writers who both died young. Bangs was a character in *Almost Famous*, Cameron Crowe's 2001 film set in the 1970s rock scene.

Paul and Linda McCartney, from a
Christmas card Linda sent to Lillian
in 1972.

Lillian (front left) with New
York rock-writer friends:
Danny Goldberg (left),
Richard and Lisa Robinson,
and the Australian writer
Richard Neville (right).
With Cherry Vanilla, actress
and David Bowie's publicist,
at back, around 1972.

Lillian (centre) with writer
and guitarist Lenny Kaye
and Lisa Robinson at one of
Lisa's soirées for New York
rock writers, 1971.

Max's Kansas City bar and restaurant, the "epicentre" of New York's rock and art underground in the sixties and early seventies, where Lillian held court.

Lillian launching the *Rock Encyclopedia* at Max's Kansas City, late 1969.

The first edition of *Lillian Roxon's Rock Encyclopedia*, published in New York by Grosset and Dunlap, 1969.

Danny Fields (centre) with singer Lou Reed (right) and Jim Jacobs, manager of Joan Baez (front), at Max's Kansas City.

Lillian outside Bill Graham's famous New York rock venue, the Fillmore East, promoting *Rock Encyclopedia* for a *Newsweek* interview.

A poster promoting Lillian's rock talk show, which was syndicated to 250 radio stations in America in 1971.

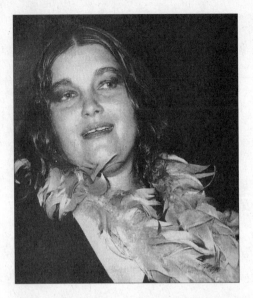

Lillian was suffering from asthma and the impact of cortisone treatment when her friend Danny Fields took this, the last picture of her, at Max's Kansas City two days before she died.

Lee Childers

Lillian Roxon: Energy, enthusiasm and an infectious joy

Lillian Roxon, Journalist-Author Of 'Rock Encyclopedia,' Dies at 41

Rolling Stone's tribute to Lillian, by her colleague Loraine Alterman with picture by Leee Childers, ran to a full page.

NEW YORK, 1960s

Chapter 12 From Kennedy to the Beatles

It was her old friend Zell Rabin who gave Lillian her first job in New York. While she was freelancing for *Weekend* in Hollywood, her first stop in America, Rabin became New York bureau chief of the Sydney *Daily Mirror*. "He knew he could get me cheap and fast and that, because I was a girl, he could intimidate me," Lillian wrote later. "We finished up intimidating each other and after a year I left."

She left the *Daily Mirror* bureau but stayed in New York for the rest of her life. The decade that was about to unfold would see political assassinations, the civil rights movement, the backlash against the Vietnam war, the explosion of rock music and a revolution in youth attitudes to sex, drugs, fashion and almost everything else. Little of this was foreseeable in 1960: the changes built strongly from the middle of the decade. But when Lillian arrived in New York in late 1959, the long, quiescent Eisenhower era was already drawing to a close.

She reported her early impressions in letters to her mother Rose. In March 1960 New York was covered by heavy snow which had "muffled the sounds of the city so that New York is overnight a ghost town". Above it all hung the Cold War: "What with Nelson Rockefeller, whom I liked before this, agitating for atomic shelters (I suppose it's just another money-making business), and the sirens being tested here once a month, there is a terrible feeling that we are on the brink of atomic warfare. Earthquakes, plane crashes, fallout, cancer. The Americans are real fear merchants." Rabin had given her a new novel, *Level 7*, by the British writer Mordecai Roshwald. It was written in the form of a diary by a "pushbutton officer" confined to living in an underground bunker from which atomic warfare would be fought. The author dedicated the novel "To Dwight and Nikita" – Eisenhower and Khrushchev. "To me it's a more honest and therefore much more upsetting book than *On the Beach*," Lillian told her mother. "Zell said he couldn't sleep."

Of American social mores, she wrote: "One of the problems of the American way of life is that very few men and women are just friends. Most American women spend all the time and energy on their looks because, by the 'date' system, it is absolutely vital to make a good first impression. How a woman can marry a man she only knows from a series of 'dates' is more than I can understand. He doesn't know her and ten to one she has pulled a confidence trick on him and he has never found her out. Still, I love to go out and see places and meet people. What else can I do? On Friday night I am dating a psychologist from Columbia University. I have an interview with Eartha Kitt, the singer, at 10.30 that night at the famous Latin Quarter nightclub, so if I don't like him I always have the excuse that I have to work after dinner."

She gossiped with her mother concerning the impending marriage of Princess Margaret to the photographer Antony Armstrong-Jones: "It's funny what you wrote about Princess Margaret ... Some people suspect she is pregnant to someone else and that all this was arranged quickly. In any case the homosexual fraternity is triumphant. 'It's been a wonderful year for US,' they're saying. 'All we need is for that dear Noel Coward to marry the Queen Mother, Robert Helpmann to marry the Duchess of Kent!!'"

Lillian found an apartment in Sullivan Street, near Bleecker Street, in west Greenwich Village. An early visitor was Marion Hallwood, an old friend from the Push who was studying in New York. They explored the city's bohemian hangouts, including the White Horse Tavern on Hudson Street in the West Village where poets, jazz people and folk singers gathered. It was there that Lillian introduced Marion to Tom, Paddy and Liam Clancy of the Clancy Brothers, an Irish-American folk singing group whom she had first met on her 1956 visit. The folk scene was still booming and the Clancy Brothers with it. For a time each Australian girl claimed a Clancy brother as her boyfriend: Lillian Tom and Marion Paddy. "Lillian wasn't interested so much in the old, classical jazz scene," Marion says. "Even then she was more interested in the young up-and-coming musos." (Years later Lillian gave the Clancy Brothers five non-committal lines in her *Rock Encyclopedia*.)

Another figure they befriended was Delmore Schwartz, a distinguished New York poet and critic who had inherited from Dylan

Thomas the role of the White Horse Tavern's house poet. As a visiting professor at Syracuse University, Schwartz also became a friend and mentor to Lou Reed, later lead singer with the influential rock group the Velvet Underground. Schwartz had a dazzling intellect but had already begun a decline into alcoholism when the two Australian women knew him in late 1959 and early 1960. His talent as a talker captivated them: he was once recorded talking for eight hours straight. But it was Lillian's hot-and-cold friendship with Zell Rabin that Marion remembers most from this time: "She had a very ambivalent, prickly relationship with him. I used to hear about Zell endlessly."

*

Life in the *Mirror* office at 1475 Broadway was tense. "The cold weather and Zell being difficult again has put a damper on my normal high spirits," Lillian reported to Rose. "When I fight with Zell my work is impossible and depressing. I suppose he is going through some depression himself. He manages to transmit it to me."

Rabin's life was turbulent. During his first stint in New York he had been a prolific correspondent for the Sydney *Sun* and the *Sydney Morning Herald*. He had married an American woman, only to be divorced in Mexico a year later. On his way back to Australia in 1959 he travelled through Africa to report on nascent nationalist movements there.

Rabin had no sooner returned to Sydney than his employers, the Fairfax group, sent him back to New York as bureau chief of the *Daily Mirror*, the evening tabloid rival to the *Sun* in Sydney. For a time Fairfax owned both evening papers, controlling the *Mirror* through a trust designed to disguise this state of affairs. But in 1960, soon after Lillian joined its New York bureau, the *Mirror* was about to change hands again and Rabin's career was about to take off.

Rupert Murdoch had arrived in Sydney from Adelaide hungry for a big city daily newspaper. The *Mirror* was it. Fairfax sold the paper to Murdoch for less than £2 million, believing the out of town "boy publisher" posed no real threat. Murdoch set out to reverse the status quo and turn the *Mirror* into Australia's biggest selling newspaper. Soon after he bought it in 1960, he went to New York to examine his bureau there and, some believed, to fire Rabin and install his own man. Whatever Murdoch's intentions, Rabin charmed him. There was only a year in age between them: Rabin was twenty-eight, Murdoch twenty-nine.

Murdoch quickly saw in Rabin his chief weapon to lead the assault on his rival Sydney publishers. Murdoch says: "He was very young, very experienced, a good writer with a clearly superior intelligence and he knew what newspapers were about and what newspaper wars were about." Rabin arranged a visit to Cuba, where Fidel Castro had recently come to power, and in September 1960 the two men flew to Havana.

*

Lillian, meanwhile, departed for London. Apart from the tensions with Rabin, the *Mirror* job offered limited prospects beyond reporting celebrity and fashion news; so, after a year establishing herself in New York, she left the job. In London she worked in the *Sydney Morning Herald*'s Fleet Street bureau for a few weeks filling a summer vacancy. The bureau then employed eighteen journalists. "Not too much tension ... no bullying and my work seems to get done pretty effortlessly," she wrote to Rose. Then she visited Paris, reconnecting with the European culture of her childhood. "What I loved best was the discovery of European culture, architecture, manners, outlook, way of life, attitude etc. This can't be described in words but it was a TREMENDOUSLY exciting thing for me ... Of course my values have been greatly shaken by seeing France and comparing it with America. Greatly shaken. The other thing I wanted to tell you is the sudden shock with which I realised that Paris was occupied during the war. I saw the notices 'here fell so-and-so defending the country' all over the place. How easy the war was for Americans and Australians!"

She returned to New York in October, just in time for the election the following month of John F. Kennedy. The arrival in the White House of the youngest man ever to become president, and his wife Jacqueline, opened a decade when youth, glamour and celebrity would become media obsessions.

Lillian launched herself back into New York with a party. It was one of her classic exercises in networking. She wrote triumphantly to Rose: "My party was a fantastic, undreamed of success. I really feel I have ARRIVED in New York. There must have been 100 people who covered a wide cross section of types. I asked everyone I knew, told them they could bring anyone they wanted. One girl almost spoiled it by bringing 20 people, but really it was OK. Four beatniks gatecrashed but they were so young and picturesque I let them stay. Zell came and said it was a good party. Libby Jones, who is America's No. 3 stripper, came – with husband. I had two new authors – Gael Greene, a reporter on the *New York Post*, and Bill Manville, who is a famous columnist. I had three psychiatrists, a couple of doctors, two lawyers (one white, one black), about six psychologists, Eddie the singer who was there, but not the actor who was working. Delmore Schwartz, who is America's greatest living poet came (he's about 50), there were dozens of beautiful girls. Everyone brought their own drink. Everyone danced. No one got drunk. The party ended at 6 am. Among the guests were some of my new neighbours – a Negro model, two painters, a South African, an English couple, an actor, two Negro singers, the lawyers, a social worker, a Belgian couple ... I am cheerful and optimistic and 100% glad I left the *Mirror*."

Within days of her return from London a letter arrived from Donald Horne seeking to entice her back to work in Sydney. Sir Frank Packer had recently bought the *Bulletin*, a famous but then moribund literary and current affairs weekly. This meant Horne was now managing editor of five publications: *Weekend, Woman's Mirror*, the *Bulletin*, the *Observer* and *Wild Cat Monthly*, a business journal. He had big plans to revive the *Bulletin* as a quality news magazine, aiming at sales of 100,000 copies a week. Then came his offer to Lillian: "I would like you to come back here and be my special assistant helping me run all these publications." He offered her a salary of £40 a week and "the usual garnishes of executive status – carpets, secretary and all that stuff".

While Horne's letter was on its way to her, Lillian wrote to her mother: "I am a little down at the moment because I had a letter from a friend telling me Horne has plans to FORCE me to come back to Australia by 'freezing' me out of New York. I wrote to him and explained that this is ridiculous, and that Australia doesn't pay so much money that I need him ... Do you know he had the cheek to ask someone, 'Has Lillian run out of money yet?'" She had continued sending freelance work to *Weekend* and other Consolidated Press magazines including the *Australian Women's Weekly*, whose veteran editor Esme Fenston had also offered her a job back in Sydney.

She turned both offers down. "I wrote this week to Donald Horne and told him I was not interested in his 40 pound job and carpet on the floor," she told Rose. "I am not interested in leaving America so there is no question of it." Horne persisted, saying that he would keep the job open for her until March and that to work with him on reviving the

Bulletin would be to work on "this year's greatest experiment in Australian journalism". He also reported that, on hearing of Lillian's proposed job as Horne's "personal assistant", Sir Frank had "raised his eyebrows. He did ask me about it with an old-fashioned look."

But nothing Horne could offer would persuade her: New York was Lillian's new home for life. "New York is hot and exhausting, a sort of huge Brisbane, but I don't mind," she told Rose. "I love it with a tireless and quite uncritical devotion."

*

A month after her return from London Lillian moved to a new apartment at 402 East 11th St on the Lower East Side. She later wrote of this: "I returned to New York with no job, very little money and for about two years managed to survive only because I had found a flat that cost less than 60 cents a day. People who visited me there (Michael Baume and others) will remember why it was so cheap – the hall was being used as a urinal by passers-by." Baume, a contemporary from Sydney University and colleague from the *Observer*, recalls that the flat indeed had few frills: its bath was in the kitchen. But Lillian, even in these early days, "already seemed to know everyone in New York". Reporting to her mother on her new flat, Lillian was less dramatic: "It's really a very nice and cheerful place ... It means a tremendous amount to me that my rent is only $22. That's why I don't mind that I have to fix the place up a little." In any case, the Lower East Side was the New York of her dreams, "so far away from the big brassy New York. It's like being in Europe or in a small town. Half the population speaks Yiddish. Moving in slowly are the Spaniards, the Poles, the new poor. You can eat pizza or potato knishes or blintzes or arroz con pollo ... That's why I'd like you to come over here so you can see that there is so much more to New York than the empty uptown life, the money grubbing, the neurosis."

During 1961 and 1962, Lillian set about establishing herself as a freelance journalist. She wrote for a syndication agency in Britain that sold her pieces to Israel and elsewhere, for the *News of the World* in London, and for anyone else who would take her work. What pleased her more than the money, she told Rose, was the independence her skills gave her: "It's the knowledge that I can earn it effortlessly – well without the strain and effort needed when I worked for Zell or Horne."

Horne continued to commission her work, including a 6,000 word series on Frank Sinatra. She felt "cheated" by the fee, but when Consolidated Press resold the series in America and she received an extra $300 she stopped complaining. She told her mother: "It's being printed in the American version of *Weekend*, a dreadful magazine called the *National Inquirer*, a sort of trade magazine for sex fiends (like *Weekend*). Ugh. As you see slowly, slowly things start to look up ... you see, I have been working on everyone, writing, talking, contacting."

In March 1961, Lindsay Clinch, New York bureau chief of the *Sydney Morning Herald*, offered her a staff job there, but the company's management in Sydney vetoed it. "[They] said no more women on the staff," Lillian told Rose. "Old-fashioned, aren't they? It's not just me, it's the whole principle that women are useless luxuries on a newspaper."

Then, in September, the Indonesian Consulate offered her a job as a researcher and speechwriter for three months until the end of the General Assembly session at the United Nations. She wrote to Rose: "For the first time in my life my 'major' in political science at Sydney University has meant something."

They were terribly impressed. They feel Australians have a lot of "sympathy" (in the Italian sense) with Indonesia. Now I tell myself it is probably an act of God that nothing could be a better antidote for Americans than the tranquil calm and honesty of the Indonesians. (I find it so difficult to "sell" myself to Americans because I am basically not a phony person. The Asians are not impressed by false sophistication.) The job is going fine. Luxurious office. Generals and ambassadors walking in and out dripping with medals. I wrote the Consul General's speech last week on Indonesia's economic problems. I knew nothing about them then but I certainly do now.

The only drawback was having to start at nine in the morning and make a forty-minute bus commute from 11th Street up First Avenue to 68th Street, followed by another bus trip to the consulate's office on Fifth Avenue. She was saved from all this just two weeks after starting when *TV Times*, the Australian Broadcasting Commission's magazine, took her on as an accredited correspondent. This gave her a foreign journalist's visa and for the moment solved the problem of her US immigration status, until now insecure. "I suppose the Indonesians will be terribly offended. But I don't ever want to be restricted to a 9–5 job, 50 weeks a year. Especially when I can make more money and still be free to wake up when I like and travel when and where I please." She left the consulate and freelanced from home again.

*

Her love life was complicated. On 29 January 1961, she wrote to her mother: "On Wednesday ... I am 29. I always thought I'd like to have a child before I was 30 so now if I want to achieve that ambition I'll have to act quickly – three months to go. Perhaps it will be easier if I set the date for 31. I must confess I feel nothing but happiness at being 29. I have no lines. I am in perfect health ... I can't speak for the future but up till now I'm glad I didn't marry. I know now I couldn't possibly have been happy. I would have been restless and caged."

There seemed to be no shortage of suitors, and she provided her mother with a running, if sanitised, commentary. One was "a very strange, silent person": "He is 29, very good looking and very intelligent. He has a lot of beautiful girls interested in him but he always gives the impression he is looking for something else. I think (I am sure) I scare him to death but he turned up the other night at a place where I often go and he admitted he was looking for me. Encouraged by a positive move on his part I have started trying to talk to him. The trouble with these bloody Americans is that even if they are nice, they are so neurotic you don't really consider them potential husband material."

But there were "a million complications" with the romance: "It seems a lot easier to back out now before anyone gets hurt. Just to tell you what a big thing it is, Zell just saw us talking at a party and he said immediately, 'What IS this? What's been going on here?' I talked it over with Zell without saying too much and Zell is the same as me, evenly split. The most revealing thing Zell said was, 'He's too much like me.' On top of all that he's Catholic, a bad Catholic but still ... So I think I'll forget it."

By April she was seeing a "Negro lawyer", an unusual relationship given the gulf then between black and white America. For most white middle-class women, a relationship with a black man, even an educated one, was impossible. The civil rights movement was two years away, and the replacement of the term Negro by African-American still twenty years in the future. Lillian's reports of her relationship with her unnamed man reflect the racial climate: "I had an interesting experience last Friday night. My Negro lawyer took me to his university reunion dance. I was the only white girl among 500 people. It reminded me of nothing more than a typical Jewish dance (funny how similar the minorities are everywhere). The same atmosphere exactly. Everyone was pretty nice – only when they found out I was not an American. The feeling against white Americans is very strong."

By June the relationship was petering out. "He's a really wonderful person but, as they say, the problem is bigger than both of us." One night they sat in a coffee shop for five hours. "He told me he was (and is) afraid of getting serious about me. Even as we sat, he went for a moment to get cigarettes and a completely normal person came to the table and said to me 'Nigger Lover'. This in so-called integrated New York. I was furious, but my friend just laughed. He said he's used to it. Anyway we are now friends."

Zell Rabin was a constant figure on the scene. He continued to see Lillian as a stable point in his life, though their time as lovers had passed. In April 1961, Rabin covered for the *Mirror* the trial in Jerusalem of Adolph Eichmann, the Nazi war criminal, and later flew to Cuba to report on the Bay of Pigs fiasco. Lillian welcomed him back to New York in early June with a dinner party at her apartment. "I had one of the most beautiful table settings with flowers and candles that I've ever seen anywhere," she told Rose. "He was very impressed. I must say he behaved nicely, so nicely in fact that one of my guests said he was the nicest man there. She also said: 'I watched him all night and he never stops looking at you, he follows you with his eyes.' Yes, there is I suppose some sort of bond in spite of our hostilities. I have known him since I was 19 and that's a long time."

She also invited her two recent boyfriends – "the Catholic boy that I liked so much and the Negro" – both of whom knew Rabin, and asked them to bring girls. "Everything would have been OK except that when the girls they brought wanted to leave they took the girls to the bus stop and came back. I finished up with half a dozen men on my hands … I hadn't seen any of them for a long time and they all wanted to stay and talk. Both Zell and the Negro boy came beautifully dressed – as a tribute to me."

*

Much of Lillian's life during her early years in New York is chronicled in correspondence with her mother in Sydney. There were two Rose Roxons. Lillian often caricatured her mother to others as her most exasperating problem, a domineering Jewish mother. But the letters reveal another side to their relationship. Rose was Lillian's emotional anchor during the years when she was fighting to establish herself as a single professional woman in a tough city. She shared with her mother her perennial worries about her weight, her sagas with diets, her battles to control her "compulsive eating". She swapped notes with Rose on Gayelord Hauser, the popular American nutrition king. In July 1961, for instance, she reported that her weight was down from a combination of diet, massage and emotional discipline: "Calm, no tension. To achieve this I've had to become abnormally detached from life ... This deadly calm is out of character for a Roxon."

Four months later she wrote that she was doing well and recalled her father's humiliations of her as a child: "My weight is marvellous. I have speeded it up now (no nerves, no tension) and I'm already well under nine stone. It's intoxicating. Why couldn't this happen years ago? Everything is approach. You see how Daddy used to nag me. It had the opposite effect on me. These things must come from within, from peace of mind." She told Rose that "all his [Isadore's] anger was really against himself. I didn't realise before what a lonely and unhappy man he really was and how this affected all his family."

She had recently met an astrologer who forecast that 4 February 1962 would be a day of disaster for America: "It's in the stars. She is undisturbed about this. All I can say is that if I thought I had to die on February 4th, I could face it with courage but by God, I would stop dieting. I would spend my last weeks on this earth putting away as many cheese blintzes, as much Italian gelato, as many slices of pizza as my stomach would hold. I'll be very bitter indeed if I don't get advance notice. Can you imagine going to heaven with three hard-boiled eggs and a bowl of salad in your stomach?"

Rose was sixty-two when Lillian went to New York. She had seven more years to live. Now alone, she moved from Brisbane to the inner Sydney suburb of Neutral Bay to be closer to her two sons, both embarked on academic careers. But she seemed to cling emotionally to her absent daughter in New York. Lillian's unconventional life perplexed her. Rose wanted her married and settled, and poured out her worries for Lillian's welfare, admonishing her for not answering questions: "Your letters are my heart's food, but you are different now – never mind." They wrote to each other in a weekly dialogue that was provocative, unwittingly or not, on both sides.

Depending on her mood towards her daughter, Rose started her letters "Dear Lilly", "My Golden Sunshine" or "Mamina mia dolce". She talked of her own pessimism – "one brings it into the world as one brings black or blue eyes" – but believed that, "after my 35 years of unhappy marriage I think myself that I am a strong character". Despite her own experience of marriage, Rose cautioned Lillian against a life spent alone: "You will take courage to marry some day, at least I hope so. One doesn't grow younger and better looking and to be alone is a curse, a very sad one, believe me I know what I write." She missed Lillian: "I am so far all right but I suffer from loneliness and longing. How I envy each mother who can see and visit her daughter when she wants it. For me it is denied. Why? Why?"

If such letters were intended to make Lillian feel guilty, her response was characteristically strong-willed: she challenged her mother's view of her independence with a feminist analysis of it – one that began subversively on her mother's level by arguing that work was a way to meet men, then crept up to argue for independence as a value in itself.

> Your insistence that work and marriage are incompatible irritates me because it is wrong. Don't you realise that through my work I meet dozens of charming and cultivated people too? I interview doctors, professors, scientists etc and I make some good friends. At the moment I am dating Joel Pomerantz who is the press officer for Grossingers. He's 32, tall, dark, good looking, Jewish, charming, successful, knows everyone in town etc ... It also helps that I am a foreign correspondent – I mean it makes people realise they are not meeting an idiot. So to say that being a journalist is not compatible with meeting eligible men is ridiculous. Should I stop work? It's true some jobs eat you up more than others and that it has been hard for me here, but I can't complain that I haven't made all my best social contacts through my work because I have ...
>
> But when you say the job makes me old and tired – you forget one thing, not working and boredom can also kill that vitality. This is a

country where women have exciting jobs, marry, have families and still manage to look and act young and vital. This is one thing you have to admire the American women for. After all Eleanor Roosevelt is only one of many fine, well adjusted, intelligent women in this country. I am sure that a woman with your brains and understanding, had you lived here, would have made a career of politics or social work or something AND had children as well. This is why you can't understand it because you were never fortunate enough to have the opportunity to use your intelligence and humane feelings to their fullest in some suitable work.

I am sure if you had worked too that it would have been easier for you to bear the problem of your unhappy marriage. Never say marriage versus career. You can and should have both and balance them. You don't have to lecture me about children – of course I will have a family. For God's sake I know I am not 20 but not for a minute do I want to be. I have much more to offer someone now. I don't expect to be young and fresh at 30 but I hope I will be healthy and attractive. If you had something in your life you would still be a beautiful woman now and you are 64. You know this – all that is missing from your face is that spark of gaiety. Sometimes when you go out I see it and I think my God, how wonderful she looks and it makes me feel good that when I am 64 I will still be attractive and look good like my mother ... Now don't be silly. Please be realistic. It is ridiculous for us to argue when we both agree. I agree 100% with you about marriage. Please don't worry about it or mention it. You don't need to warn me about anything. I know what I am doing and you know that. I hope you will understand what I'm saying once and for all and stop nagging me.

Too often, the lonely mother marooned in Sydney tested her daughter's patience. "Your letter brought roars of amusement from my friends," Lillian responded on one occasion to Rose's niggling questions. "I roared with laughter at your story that I was a Beatnik. First of all Beatniks had not been invented when I was at Uni!! ... All this seems so far away! I've always been outspoken and a little flamboyant. I still like to *startle* people out of their complacency. I suppose this is what made me a 'legend'." And sometimes Lillian's sarcasm became white hot anger:

I have just got your letter and I am SHOCKED on two counts. One, that you still haven't sent my parcel. You surely knew there was urgency for those things ... Of course I still have my beautiful flat. Do you think I am insane?? I would not let that go. Sometimes it horrifies me that there can be constant misunderstanding in letters ... Secondly, I am shocked and very upset that you keep expecting me NOT to write. I really don't understand you. Why shouldn't I write? Yes, I am getting plenty of sleep. I've stayed home every night since I've been back and gone to bed early. Last night I dropped in at a farewell party for an old friend, Charley Rotschild, who's going to Australia for two weeks to manage the folk singer Odetta on her tour. He'll be in Sydney a couple of days and promised he would phone you ...

I don't know what you mean by "there is in your interesting life too moments that you can write about". I've been writing about anything interesting in my life for the last five years. If it's interesting, you'll hear about it. When you are in an office, eight to ten hours a day, life is not always brilliantly interesting ... Anyway, do me a personal favor. For Godssake stop talking about my not writing when you know I am the best correspondent ever. Please, I beg you, no unpleasantness in letters. You KNOW I write.

Lillian summed up her attitude towards her mother's gloomy outlook on life when Rose made a trip back to Italy in September 1962. She wrote to Margaret Elliott, now married to Leon Fink: "My mother writes ecstatically of Italy, but since nothing is ever perfect for her, her health is not good. Poor thing, she was badly thrown by the bliss of Italy. She can't cope with happiness so it's just as well she suddenly stopped feeling good. I hope I never lose my capacity for being happy."

*

By the end of 1961, Rupert Murdoch was back in New York. Zell Rabin had scored another coup by arranging an audience for his boss with President Kennedy. Murdoch was still unknown in America but this was the start of the long climb to power and influence that would culminate in control of the world's biggest media conglomerate. At 5 p.m. on 1 December, Murdoch and Rabin were in the Oval Office with Kennedy for a half-hour, off-the-record talk. According to George Munster, one of

Murdoch's biographers, Murdoch nevertheless instantly filed a story to Sydney which was killed only after intervention from the White House itself. The *Sunday Mirror* ran only a picture of the three men with an extended caption.

It was also the start of Rabin's meteoric career with Rupert Murdoch. A few months later, Murdoch offered Rabin the editorship of the *Sunday Mirror*. Indeed, Rabin became the model for the many editors Murdoch later appointed to his empire of newspapers in Australia, Britain and America – one who, on Murdoch's own account, was rarely equalled and never bettered.

During a stopover in Fiji on his way back to Sydney in March 1962, Rabin married his second wife, Regina, also American. She was twenty-six, he had just turned thirty. But in Sydney the marriage did not go smoothly. Regina found Rabin's 24-hour devotion to newspapers hard to take. Ron Saw, who became a star writer on the *Mirror* under Rabin, later wrote: "He brooded and snapped and crackled at everyone from the copy boys to Rupert Murdoch. All he talked about, all he ever wanted to talk about – to the point of driving his friends mad – was newspapers. He ran himself ragged." Regina eventually left and took their son to America.

Within a year Murdoch appointed Rabin editor of the *Daily Mirror*. Its circulation still lagged almost 20,000 copies behind the rival *Sun*. Murdoch remembers the challenge of grabbing a new market for the *Mirror* partly in terms of Australia's Protestant-versus-Irish Catholic sectarian divisions of the time: "We were nationalistic, always anti-Menzies. The Catholic side of the population, which didn't have a paper, could identify with that. To be disrespectful to the sense of Empire and Britain fitted the youthfulness, the cheekiness and the readership, [which was] not the North Shore, not the old Fairfax Anglican crowd."

The *Mirror*'s liberal leanings also suited Rabin's New York Jewish ethos and his flair for giving big world and political stories as much prominence as a local murder, rape or sex scandal. The formula worked. The *Mirror* pushed the *Sun*, and the circulations of both evening tabloids went up, the *Mirror*'s by more than the *Sun*'s. From being Sydney's third and fourth newspapers, behind its two morning papers, they became first and second.

*

While Zell Rabin was helping Rupert Murdoch to launch his career as a global media tycoon, Lillian at last found a secure berth in New York working for Rabin's rival, the Sydney *Sun*. Before Lindsay Clinch returned to Sydney at the end of 1961, he brought in Lillian as a part-time reporter in the Fairfax bureau to replace his wife, Sally Baker. During the 1960s, Australian newspaper companies maintained big bureaus in New York and London through which most world news was filtered back to Australia. Lillian began to write a weekly column for the *Sun*'s women's pages in 1962 and also contributed to its sister papers, the *Sydney Morning Herald* and the *Sun-Herald*. Her stories ran under a nom-de-plume, "Kay Warner", or were attributed to "a special correspondent". *TV Times* ran her as "Gillian Yorke". Newspaper managements were still wary of giving women too much kudos or star status.

"I am slowly beginning to feel I am getting somewhere," she wrote to Rose. "And it is miraculous how by talking and discussing you can see how many things I (and everyone else) have been blind about. The best analogy I can think of is my fear of dogs in Toowoomba when I avoided whole streets because of this one dog. I feel I am going through life avoiding many streets, some ugly and some beautiful, because of something I'm afraid of."

In 1963, when she was thirty-one, Lillian joined the bureau's staff full-time. She wrote later: "I understand that I was the first female person to be taken on for a full-time job in that office since its beginning. It was revolutionary but I think it happened only because I was there." She continued working for the *Sydney Morning Herald* bureau for the rest of her life.

When she started the job she moved to a new apartment at 227 East 21st Street near Gramercy Park. It was her last move, her home for the next ten years. The small, one-bedroom apartment was in an unprepossessing three-storey walk-up building covered at the front by a green fire escape. Perhaps its biggest asset was the neighbour directly opposite: the 13th Precinct Station headquarters of the New York Police Department. Police cars and vans crowded the street day and night. "Of course it often happens that places close to the police are robbed," she told Rose. "But anyway it's a safeguard."

One of her first scoops came soon after she joined the *Herald* bureau and it helped to establish her in *Woman's Day*, the popular weekly

magazine that Fairfax controlled. The story was also a launching pad
for the Roxon style, which drew readers into her confidence and put
Lillian at the centre of the story with her subjects.

The previous year the world's press had been mesmerised by the
romance of Elizabeth Taylor and Richard Burton during the making of
Cleopatra in Rome. Their affair, and Taylor's one million dollar fee, then
the highest ever paid to a movie star, gave the film more publicity than
it deserved. Taylor was still married to the crooner Eddie Fisher, but it
was Burton's estranged wife, Sybil, whom the press pursued for interviews, with singular lack of success. In May 1963, while working on the
story for *Woman's Day* in New York, Lillian encountered Sybil Burton in
bizarre circumstances.

She had gone to interview Philip Burton, the former teacher from
Wales whose surname Richard Burton had taken when he chose acting as
his career. Philip Burton ran a drama and voice school in lower Manhattan that, according to Lillian, catered for "pony-tailed girls with theatrical aspirations and muscular, earnest young men". As Lillian waited for
her meeting with Philip Burton, a "striking blonde walked purposefully
to the reception desk". It was Sybil Burton. Lillian wrote in her story:

> I knew then why Richard Burton has hesitated for so long. It must be
> hard to let such a woman go, even for an enchantress.
>
> "Mrs Burton," I said, pushing my way past the pony tails and the
> drama notices. "I'd like to speak to you for a minute."
>
> She turned a wary face toward me and asked who I was. I told her.
> Her face closed up. "I'm sorry," she said with immense politeness. "I
> just don't talk to the Press."
>
> I smiled at her in return, and started to say that the Press – some
> of it at least – was on her side. "We know what you've been going
> through ..." I began.
>
> She seemed to hesitate. For a moment her lips trembled as she
> fought for control. Then she looked at me speculatively, as she some-
> times must have looked at Liz.
>
> "Do you?" she said, and her voice was suddenly very bitter.
>
> She swept into Philip Burton's office, leaving the echo of her
> words heavy on the air.
>
> To me, a woman of about the same age, that bitterly sad "Do
> you?" conjured up a clear, unmistakable vision of the misery and

pain Sybil Burton has suffered since Elizabeth Taylor first beckoned Richard Burton away from his family.

Lillian had got just two words from Sybil Burton: "Do you?" But they were more than anyone else had got, and they were the peg for an article that spun out over three pages complete with pictures and a phantomly pregnant headline, "Sybil Burton's Side of the Liz Taylor Affair".

Five months later, *Woman's Day* sent Lillian to Mexico for her first foreign assignment, a story on the making of *Night of the Iguana*, directed by John Huston, written by Tennessee Williams and starring Richard Burton, Ava Gardner and Deborah Kerr. Elizabeth Taylor, not in the cast, was in close attendance on the set. Lillian flew to the location at Puerto Vallarta, a remote seaside town on the west coast, where she received the sort of access to stars undreamed of today. She wrote an account to her mother:

Unlike Jack I have no gift for lyrical description, so I cannot tell you what a wonderful week I have just spent. From the minute I stepped off the plane I was in love with Mexico. After America you are immediately struck by the warmth of the people, their friendliness. I travelled down with a *Look* photographer. Puerto Vallarta is so remote it cannot be reached by road, but only by one rickety plane that flies people and supplies in daily.

The view and especially the sunsets just knocked me out. In many ways it looks like Italy – mountains and green seas and that hot, bright sun. It also looks like the Pacific. The houses are very Spanish in architecture. The people are incredibly poor but very clean. I didn't dare eat the food except for one night and was sick next day.

I lived in a luxurious hotel, got up each morning early to get to the film set which could be reached only by taxi, dugout canoe, launch and jeep in that order. During the whole five days I was there I was constantly with the people I had to write about – Richard Burton, Elizabeth Taylor, Deborah Kerr and her husband, Sue Lyon, Ava Gardner and director John Huston. Basically they are people like anyone else, inflated by publicity and sometimes actually believing their own publicity.

Taylor, of course, is not the monster she's painted, but simply a troubled girl who has lived her life under the disadvantage of being a film star. She adores her children, talks of giving up films. She seemed to spend all her time talking about pregnancy and children's diseases. Kerr is basically a hausfrau. They were all easy to get on with and since it was 100 degrees heat and full of insects and everyone was bored and restless this was really something.

I got on very well with Huston and also with Emilio Fernandez, who is a famous Mexican director and is an associate on the film. Emilio is the one who always carries a gun, but I think it's just for the publicity. I also met Budd Schulberg down there. He's the man who wrote *On the Waterfront*. He asked me out to dinner one night but it was the night I was feeling sick so I didn't go. I went back on the plane with Emilio as far as Guadalajara and he also asked me out, but my office wanted me back that night.

To her old friend Ross Poole in Sydney, Lillian wrote a more earthy account:

I am writing this in the hot Mexican sun, totally surrounded by cloud-capped mountains, tropical rainforests, aquamarine seas and Richard Burton. E. Taylor and A. Gardner are also here, so I don't have the field to myself. As I write this he's standing about three feet away carrying on like Larry Boys [an old *Weekend* colleague, also Welsh] which he always does and which, as far as I'm concerned, takes away all the magic.

The sexpot on the set, Lillian-wise, is John Huston, six foot something, snowy haired, nudging 60 and still making passes at young girls with quite deserved success.

We are doing the hotel scene on top of a high mountain in a god-forsaken, mosquito-ridden place called Mismaloya. A Gardner is a smasher, all sex appeal and oomph. Swears like a trooper. So does Liz, who reminds me of R.L.D. Ralph's little Daphne [a reference to a Push friend]. This is because she has a very prissy, affected voice. Otherwise she's a good bloke.

*

Rose had been a running critic of Lillian's work in *Woman's Day*. She could not understand why her daughter had to "use your intelligence on those stupid Hollywood idiotic stories". She wrote urging her to "rebel till they will give you more decent work, where your intelligence, ability to write, will show ... I think it is worthwhile to take a risk and rebel if not you will never progress."

Gradually she offered small praise after Lillian's writing in *Woman's Day* attracted notice and the magazine used a picture of Lillian with her by-line. "Yesterday somebody told me 'your daughter must be a clever person, I read her article in *Woman's Day*,'" Rose wrote in May 1963. "Naturally I bought at once *Woman's Day* and for the first time I have been pleasantly surprised." A year later, she congratulated Lillian on an article about Jacqueline Kennedy and another about Elizabeth Taylor. "You will win the hearts of thousands of women. Yes, you advance thank God." Lillian replied: "That was very nice of you to write me a special letter about Mrs K. Yes, it's true, I can always write with deep sympathy and understanding about any woman be it Mrs K. or Sybil Burton or even Liz Taylor. I wish I understood men as well."

In July 1964, Lillian wrote to reassure her mother after she was caught up in race riots in upstate New York as America's civil rights campaign erupted. She had driven to Rochester with a friend, Pat Clinton. "We were astounded to find we had driven straight into a riot which was making world headlines. Pat's father, who is the Deputy Fire Chief, wouldn't let either of us out of the house. Actually the rioting was confined to the Negro areas. Then there was a curfew and by law we had to stay home. The city is now under martial law and we left last night before the curfew. I naturally cabled a story from there. I will be doing another one for the *Herald* leader page. So you see it's not always film stars and drug addicts." The *Sun* had butchered one of her pieces: "The whole point is that New Yorkers are barely touched by the riots – the more's the pity – and that the tensions are not big ones for the average person but small pinpricks. It was these small pinpricks they removed from my story since they took the dramatic impact out ... So please take care and don't worry. The articles are over-dramatised because that's the way newspapers are."

Two months later terrible news came from Italy. Neil Hope, Sope of the Push and Lillian's old sparring partner, had been killed in a motor scooter accident near Turin. He was thirty-six. Sope and two friends had taken a liner from Sydney to Italy in 1957 and settled in Turin where they started an English school. His wife, Mary, had given birth to their son in May 1964, four months before his death. Their daughter was born eight months after the accident. A star of Lillian's youth had been extinguished with brutal suddenness. For the first time, life for this generation of freedom-seekers seemed finite. Ruth Biegler, another Push friend then living in London, wrote with the news:

> Unfortunately it's all too true ... It seems strange and wrong that such a shattering event should be encompassed in so few words, but there's little else I can tell you.
>
> I suppose you, knowing Sope even longer than I did, must feel exactly the same way as I do. It's as if part of my life has just disintegrated – that part in which all my ideas and attitudes and tastes and prejudices were formed, and now I don't know where to turn. His death is so difficult to accept because wherever one goes, whatever one reads, whatever one laughs over or thinks about, has some association with him and stirs some memory. One just can't get away from it. Ultimately I suppose the justification for any life might lie in how deeply it colours the lives of others and so all this grief and these constant reminders might have some purpose.

*

When Lillian joined the *Sydney Morning Herald* bureau, it was located at the epicentre of New York journalistic life, the *New York Times* building facing Times Square on 43rd Street. Later it moved into the old Paramount building next door, home of the famous Paramount Theatre in the forties and fifties. The staff of up to seven journalists worked in two shifts, the second ending at two in the morning. From the mid-sixties these journalists included Margaret Jones, Derryn Hinch, Don Riseborough, Peter Michelmore and Maurice Adams.

Riseborough arrived from Toronto in 1964 to a New York introduction from Lillian. She took him to Harlem, then a violent area that people were advised to circumvent. "As a woman she was fearless in the sixties," Riseborough recalls. "She knew what her life was all about, she knew the city and how to deal with it. As a young, single woman that was pretty progressive. This was before women's lib. Lillian already lived it."

Margaret Jones arrived the following year, to a hot summer drought and another of Lillian's guided tours. Lillian took her new colleague to

Harlem to see "nodding" addicts who had just had a successful heroin
fix and to a disco, both quite novel experiences then. The two women
went to a lecture by Timothy Leary, the sixties counterculture guru, who
talked on the subject "Turning On Without Drugs" using as a prop a
recording of a woman in the throes of orgasm. As the recording continued unabated, Lillian turned to Jones and said, "Do women really
carry on like that?"

Margaret Jones had her own distinguished career with the *Herald*,
moving from New York to become the paper's first full-time Washington correspondent in 1966 and later its first Peking correspondent.
Physically and temperamentally Margaret Jones and Lillian Roxon
were different, and these two talented women in the New York bureau
sometimes seemed to others like two sopranos sharing the same stage.
Both were on the cusp of a gradual movement of women journalists in
the mid-sixties out of the social pages into the news and features pages.

The emergence of both women as star writers on the *Herald* was due
in large measure to the encouragement of John Douglas Pringle, who
took over as the paper's editor for the second time on 1 June 1965.
When Pringle rejoined it, the *Herald* was a respectable but stodgy, old-
fashioned paper losing readers. Pringle set out to meet the competition
by overseeing a cleaner design of the *Herald*'s pages and by broadening
its content. His liberal views sat oddly with those of the conservative
Fairfax board, particularly over the Vietnam war. In his memoirs Pringle
recalled how, in his search for talent, "I was able to tap a rich and completely unexploited resource by using women journalists. I begged, borrowed and stole such brilliant women writers as Margaret Jones, Helen
Frizell, Sandra Jobson and the brilliant if wayward Lillian Roxon."

Zell Rabin kept Lillian informed about the Sydney newspaper scene,
including the war he and Murdoch at the *Mirror* were now within sight
of winning. In June 1965 he wrote:

> I'm sure your new editor will brighten your work but his real prob-
> lem is the SMH's falling circulation. They are in big trouble as their
> readers are literally dying. A better and brighter *Herald*, with much
> more attention to typography, will certainly improve the paper but
> I doubt whether it will get them circulation. The *Mirror* v. *Sun* war is
> as intense as ever but we have made real progress in the past two
> months. Couple of weeks ago we were only 800 away from them and

the margin today averages a few thousand. This time last year it was around 18,000. We're right up them and I don't mind taking most of the credit for it. The *Mirror* comes out of my guts every day, certainly not my head, and you'll have to forgive an old pal when he has a vulgar brag. If we had mechanical parity with them (loading dock, trucks, automated publishing room etc) we'd catch them and pass them strongly within a year.

As you can see I'm still thoroughly obsessed with newspapers. There is nothing else in my life and I often wonder whether it's worth it and why I should waste my best years here. The only comfort is the knowledge that I've learned the business backwards and could approach any newspaper job with confidence. I still think that I should have a crack at New York but wonder if I'd ever get the opportunity that I have here. I worry about being lost and forgotten down in Sydney and there is that terrible feeling that once you can do it, i.e., edit a paper, you should move on and try something new. I'd give a limb to get my hands on the *New York Post* – Christ, you could do something with that paper. If and when we ever catch the *Sun* I'll certainly piss off as there will be no need to stay. I like to work for underdog papers, trying to catch strong rivals ... it's the Jew in me.

Five months later, in December, Rabin wrote to Lillian: "We are working very hard and so close to the *Sun* it doesn't matter. I think we'll pass them next year which would be a tremendous lift for me and a good time to get out of this lousy business. I miss you!"

Part of Rabin's gathering disenchantment stemmed from feeling left out of the most exciting event in Australian journalism. The previous year Rupert Murdoch had launched the *Australian*, the country's first national daily broadsheet and a natural competitor to the *Sydney Morning Herald*. The *Australian* was fresh, liberal, daring and progressive, a formula designed to attract a new generation of readers.

Murdoch now acknowledges: "I went to Canberra to start the *Australian*, feeling the *Mirror* was in safe hands. It turned out afterwards, and I didn't realise it at the time, Zell was pretty hurt, I think, that I hadn't made him editor of the *Australian*, that I hadn't taken him on this new adventure. He was certainly pretty critical ..."

In his June letter to Lillian, Rabin announced his impending arrival in New York. His young son was now living in America with Rabin's estranged wife. "Hello Doll," he began. "Yes, I will be in New York around mid-July for a combined business and holiday trip. I don't want anyone to know about this so you must not mention a word of it. I've got a lot of problems too and when I see you I'll explain everything and you will appreciate my plea for complete secrecy. I may need a great deal of help from you."

Lillian had been agonising about her own life's direction. Should she go back to Australia, even temporarily, or return to Europe? She sometimes felt frustrated in the *Herald* bureau, even though she had more scope there than at the *Mirror*, and harboured ambitions to work for an American paper (*McCalls* magazine had shown interest in her pieces from Mexico). The *New York Times* talked to her about a job but it came to nothing because of difficulties about her immigration status: either she would have to marry an American or the *Times* would have to convince the authorities that Lillian Roxon had skills no American citizen could match.

Rabin now counselled her about these dilemmas: "All your doubts about Sydney are correct. Our Town's appeal is a negative one really and the things that are attractive here are the quiet and security as opposed to the madness of New York. I think the real compromise for a civilised mind like yourself would be Europe or one of the more advanced Latin American countries, but then NY is a town which you should use to become a writer. I hope you are still aiming for the American magazines – there's a big future for you there."

He concluded: "I don't take much notice of any rumours about you – I simply believe them *all*. It will be good to see you and I'll ring you as soon as I hit Manhattan. And remember ... shhhhhhssshhhhh. Love, Zell."

Lillian later wrote to a friend an account of their meeting in New York: "Zell has been in town. He rang me up one Sunday drunk and kept asking me if I loved him. He looked very embarrassed about it next day. We had dinner (he's really not a very interesting person for tete a tetes though probably a first rate catalyst in a larger gathering), and I kept asking him with quiet desperation 'What am I going to do about my life?' and he kept asking ME with quieter desperation, 'What am I going to do about my wife?'"

*

John Moses took over as *Herald* bureau chief the year Lillian joined the staff. Moses was a respected journalist who had started his career in an unconventional way, joining the *Sun* in Sydney as a music critic. In New York, he and Lillian became friends and corresponded for a time after Moses returned to Sydney in late 1964. In their different ways, John Moses and Zell Rabin were the two most important men in Lillian's life at this time. Her relationship with Rabin was always tempestuous, like with like. In Moses she seemed to find a father figure on whose intellect and authority she could rely. In the way that she was intrigued by the Harrison Salisbury figure in her novel and by John Huston in Puerto Vallarta, something in Lillian seems to have sought a replacement for her unsatisfactory relationship with her father. Beneath her outward bravado and self-control, she was often insecure. From Moses she sought and received reassurance about herself and her talents.

When Moses left New York, Lillian wrote to Rose, who had been ill:

I asked my boss, John Moses, to give Jack a ring and find out if you were still in hospital ... I must say I was quite heartbroken when he left. I don't shed tears very easily but I certainly shed them at his departure. He was very good to me not just in the office but personally. I always felt, although he is married and with a family, that I could phone him any time of the day or night if anything was wrong. When one of our reporters was in hospital, he personally drove all over Connecticut and New Jersey and Pennsylvania trying to find extra blood so there would be enough in case anything went wrong in the operation (the reporter had an unusual blood group which is very rare). So you see from that the sort of man he is. I could give you not a hundred but a thousand instances of his kindness and understanding and intelligence and I can assure you that if I ever met a man like this who was single there would be NO DOUBT about getting married because he has most of the qualities I am looking for in a man.

On his return Moses wrote to Lillian his impression of Sydney in 1964: "It's the lack of any real tension and dynamism in the place that worries me, after New York ... Nobody bloody cares, much, about anything."

Lillian visited Sydney in early 1965, the last time she would see her mother. When she returned to New York she wrote to Moses airing her frustrations about her work and the resistance to her ideas she had encountered. Some of the editors in Sydney, she felt, wanted standard stuff on movie stars and nothing more.

> You must know by now about my wafer thin streak of advanced para-
> noia ... If I sound rather desperate for this friendship at the moment
> it's because the past few weeks have been very difficult. I have felt
> myself becoming part of New York in a way I never wanted to again.
> It's almost as if I had never been to Sydney, as if you were just another
> shadowy figure ... There was a stage when I felt as if I was drowning
> and that when I reached for your hand it wasn't there. This is ... a lot
> to do with the fact that in some way you've been around since 1963
> and that I suppose I have become in some way dependent on your
> friendship ... Zell Rabin once told me he was the best friend I'd ever
> have. I was terribly insulted.

Moses replied telling her to stop worrying about conspiracies or feeling rejected by her superiors because she might have offended them: "The shifts and changes and decisions made in newspapers are too complex for this – the whole bloody business is so dicey ... You're a good writer: how many times do I have to tell you. Right? I know you must feel ter-ribly isolated within the office itself – you'll always feel this simply because your life is different, your attitudes are different. Above all you're a realist. You know what you can do. Do it your way, and force them to accept it."

*

In May 1965, soon after Lillian's Sydney visit, Rose's health rapidly declined and she went into hospital. Her letters stopped arriving. Lillian found herself staring at a gulf in her life and wrote trying to coax her mother back to health:

> You know when you hear from someone every week regularly for six
> years almost, you take it for granted. Now I find I miss your letters
> very much and am looking forward to hearing even two or three
> words from you. It's not the news or the words but the contact.

Remember I am very far away and that even if it's not easy for me to show feelings I do feel isolated and cut off here.

I cannot think of you at 69 as old. You know yourself that your mind is in almost first class condition and that your physical weakness is, let's hope, temporary. Do me a favor and think hard about how the next 10, 15, 20 (why not) years can be made not only comfortable but pleasant for you. If you feel it would be good for your morale to see more of me then I can arrange (and I mean this, I promise you) to make an annual visit home of four to six weeks holiday. I made a big mistake with my last visit and I am the first to admit it. I returned exhausted having achieved very little.

If I could get married tomorrow and present you with a grandchild I would because I KNOW this would immediately make you feel better. Remember the palm reader. Only 15 months to go and three children in the next five years after that [Lillian had visited a palm reader who had predicted motherhood in her mid-thirties].

Please be of good cheer. If that monster Sir Winston Churchill and Cardinal Mannix and Archbishop Duhig [both Australian Catholic clerics] can keep going till they're 90 I am sure with your good record you can make the grade. Read Gayelord Hauser again. And know that I am thinking of you and wishing you a speedy recovery.

Rose never recovered. Lillian's brother Jack cabled Alan Dobbyn, the new bureau chief in New York, to ask him if he would break the news of Rose's death to Lillian in person rather than have her receive it by cable or trans-Pacific telephone call. Dobbyn was asleep at home in Forest Hills. Lillian wrote Moses an account of what happened:

Alan came down to tell me at midnight. I was at a jazz concert at the Museum of Modern Art. Apparently Jack was thoughtful enough to cable him at home and Alan came in and went to the museum looking for me. I was at home reading when the buzzer rang. I never ring back at that hour usually but I thought Oh-what-the-hell-they-can't-break-in and I was curious to see who it was who wouldn't phone first. I almost dropped dead when the voice on the other side of the door said it was Alan ... Then I thought something was wrong with Daphne [Dobbyn's wife], but when he said Jack had cabled I knew.

He came in and we sat until three just drinking and talking. He was simply marvellous. God help me if I'd heard in any other way any other time. I finally got to bed full of Scotch. I found it easier next day to be at work than not. At night I just sat very quietly with the flowers and just read some of my mother's letters and thought about her and the whole tragedy of her life. She could have been such a marvellous person and have had a good life. I think my sorrow was not so much for her death but for the waste of her life. I also thanked God I'd gone home this time and made some sort of peace with her and that I'd phoned a few weeks ago on her birthday.

Later Margaret Jones commented that she thought I would have been more upset. But I did what I usually do – hid feelings not under a cold mask like so many people do but under lots of distracting animation ...

The whole thing taught me several lessons. One is that human beings should prepare to face the fact of old age and helplessness and think beforehand what they'll do about it. It also taught me that closing yourself off from people as my mother did may protect you from temporary rebuffs and hurts, but that in the long run it's not living and that being open and vulnerable and alive is what makes the people who matter want to be with you. I am not going to become hard even if it means a few emotional grazed knees.

My mother's death has enormous implications for me. I think it will be the final step in my becoming an adult.

She was thirty-three. Her mother and Sope, two cardinal reference points of her life, were now dead. In another year Zell Rabin would be gone too. More than ever, she was alone and vulnerable. Out of the blue, as 1965 drew to a close, there came a morale-boosting letter from Jim Macdougall, a grand old man of Sydney journalism whose gossip column "Town Talk" in the *Daily Mirror* was read by everyone. He wrote to say how sorry he was to have missed her on his recent visit to Manhattan:

[B]ut it seemed sufficient to me to know that you are justifying all the good and promising things I had said to you when you first started in Journalism ... I think everybody needs encouragement for I am only too aware of my own young days in Journalism when a kind and encouraging word came too seldom. But you were slightly different. You had enormous drive and inventiveness and when I told you that you would go far I was merely backing a winner. Any girl who suddenly gathers her skirts and takes off for New York must have more than the average courage and ability ... I do not retract one word of what I said to you in 1956 for it has all been so beautifully justified.

Her sadness would soon be overtaken by excitement. The wheels of the sixties were turning very fast now, and in another year she would be swept up in their momentum.

Chapter 13 **Lillian and Linda**

Early in the New York summer of 1966, Brian Epstein, manager of the Beatles, called a press conference at a Manhattan hotel to introduce his new American band, the Cyrkle. The press turned out in force, but it was really Epstein they had come to see. The Cyrkle came and went after one hit. The Beatles by now were a phenomenon, and no journalist could ignore the bait of an audience with the man who controlled them. One young journalist in the room was Danny Fields, then managing editor of *Datebook*, an American teen magazine. Fields still remembers the press conference, not for the Cyrkle or Brian Epstein, but for one question that came amid a torpid series about record releases and tour dates.

"Mr Epstein, are you a millionaire?" The question came from a small woman with blonde hair whom Fields could barely detect among the other journalists, but who he soon discovered was Lillian Roxon. Her question may seem inconsequential today, when the record industry's size, power and wealth in the entertainment business is second only to Hollywood's. But rock music was still evolving then, and not taken terribly seriously by the mainstream press who preferred to see it as a passing fad of rebellious youth. To Fields, Lillian's question recognised that it was more than this, that rock was destined to become big business, which would influence or even transform almost every aspect of popular culture.

Reporting on the press conference for the *Sun-Herald* in Sydney, Lillian summed up her encounter with Epstein and his guarded response to her questions about making a fortune from rock: "The furniture salesman who originally wanted to be a dress designer and then an actor offers no explanation. Clearly he has the common self-made millionaire's occupational disease of restlessness and compulsive empire-building."

As the press conference broke up, Fields pushed his way through the departing journalists and introduced himself to Lillian. "I couldn't believe it," Fields says of that occasion:

I mean everybody was being so deferential and music-business oriented. And here was someone who asked the one question the answer to which people might want to know. It was the most shocking thing I'd ever heard. I didn't think people asked other people that kind of thing. That was my introduction to Australian journalism and tabloid journalism, which I suppose are synonymous.

I didn't know why she was there or what she was writing for or anything. But I just thought she was so funny and then we became instant friends. She was like a big sister to me and she later taught me a great deal about professionalism, how people should behave to each other and what people shouldn't do. She would always muse aloud, 'No, I don't think people should do that, Danny, do you? I think that's the wrong thing to do.' A lot of her conversation was about behaviour, usually of a press agent, and all from a professional point of view, except when it got personal. Because there were a few people she just despised and they could do no right whatsoever.

The rock revolution had really begun two years earlier with the so-called British invasion led by the Beatles, a band whose music, looks and manner changed everything, and who, as Lillian later wrote, "left all of us gaping in astonishment". By the mid-sixties America was fighting back with its own rock names, also destined to become classics: the Byrds, the Doors, the Beach Boys, the Grateful Dead, Jefferson Airplane, the Mamas and the Papas and the post-folk, electric blues Bob Dylan.

It was a tumultuous period when many things were simultaneously coming together and disintegrating, when no one could define exactly what was happening or where rock was going, except that the music and the lifestyles and mores that it engendered were turning the world upside down. In New York, nightclubs such as The Scene and Max's Kansas City became focal points for the performers, artists, writers, photographers and hangers-on that rock and roll spawned. Lillian and

Danny Fields emerged as influential figures at both venues: their opinions on who was hot among the up-and-coming talent of the rock scene carried weight. Fields moved on from *Datebook* to become a publicist for the Doors and the British group Cream, and then manager of the MC5, Iggy Pop and the Stooges, and the Ramones.

When Fields discovered Lillian in 1966, she was already making her own inroads into the rock scene. It was the phenomenon – and the changes it wrought – that intrigued her even more than the music. Around this time she wrote to a friend in Sydney trying to give a sense of it all:

I'm listening to WMCA to find out where it's at. "It's" at the Lovin' Spoonful and the Mamas and Papas, if you care. Being with it is a terrible strain. I'm also reading *Record Beat* and setting my hair for the Byrds' party at One Sheridan Square tonight. I've gone terribly pop at the moment mainly, I think, because I'm puzzled at what's going on. I understand what's happening everywhere else but the music thing is so big and so much more successful than anything else. It's like Red China. It's very big and it's there and you can't pretend it's not for much longer. The English, always much more with it, have handled the whole thing better in their press. Anyway, boy guitarists notwithstanding, I don't think I can stand the sight of another bloody electric guitar.

And if you think all this is anti-culture talk let me assure you Mr Allen Ginsberg himself was in the Byrds' dressing room at West Hempstead L.I. when they gave their concert. Not to mention that the whole thing was run by that dedicated folkie, Charles Rotschild, boy entrepreneur, international record carrier and now Mr Folk-Rock. I don't know *what* the world is coming to.

Having recovered from my National Book Week hangover, I am now trying to shake off the contact high I got in the dressing room when Ginsberg was turning the Byrds on, not to mention a nasty case of buzzing in the ears, the result of sitting in an auditorium with five thousand frenzied teenage girls. The Byrds, who are *all* very beautiful boy guitarists (though the most beautiful one is a boy drummer), are not just another rock and roll group. They sing Dylan. They turn on with Ginsberg. They teach the Beatles how to play the sitar and talk about ragas and Ravi Shankar and [John] Coltrane. They're very

California. When I was in Hollywood, I was unaware of all this and coldly ignored their and others' appearances at places called "It's Boss" and "The Trip" (wouldn't you?) – a big mistake. They're In. They don't like college audiences because they "intellectualise". Teenagers apparently don't. They just scream. You never get to hear the words.

It is without a doubt a number one status symbol in adult N.Y. to get done over by Dave Clark or any member of the Dave Clark Five. Mick Jagger of the Rolling Stones scores very high. The Little Rascals and the Turtles are also in demand. The most ravishing, ethereal little 19-year-old nymphets were all there in their expensive furs and Knack knees visiting the Byrds backstage. Clever teenage youths are growing their hair and dressing very English and finding themselves with a most definite improvement in their love lives. Even Barneys, the fat boys shop on Fifth Ave and 17th, has English mod clothes in large sizes, just to show you which way the wind is blowing and how a-changin' the times are. It's scary.

I'd love to be in Aussie for the Dylan visit. Here is a superscoop for you. Dylan is married, has a child. There have been printed column items about it which have been neither confirmed or denied which has sort of killed them. But it's troo. Auntie knows. I have other brilliant gossip such as that the Beatles were introduced to the evil weed by none other than the Minnesota poet, Mr Dylan Himself. Their last record album "Rubber Soul" was done entirely under its influence (wait till they discover LSD, as everyone else in California already has). Their next LP record is totally abstract and has no separate tracks or divisions. I know because I had dinner last night with a splendidly effete Englishman who spoke to one of the Beatles on the phone the other day. (I love the way Englishmen LOOK effete but aren't. It's the New Virility.)

Do you know about the camp (in the new sense) coffee house in the Village that plays only 1940 singles – The Shores of Tripoli, Don't Sit Under the Apple Tree etc? Rudi Komon and Cliff Pugh [an Australian art dealer and artist respectively] and I were in there the other night to be welcomed (just a coincidence) to the sound of Marjorie Lawrence singing Waltzing Matilda. We saw the only play in the world where the hero wears full drag but keeps his rather rich beard. Cliff and Rudi (whom I'd never known before though we have, of course, friends in common) are terribly nice and make me miss Sydney. I think I might try to organise my life so I can visit Sydney once every two years. I love and believe in it . I just don't have a place in it, or anywhere for that matter. (Lately I have dreams that Lyndon Johnson [then US President] is nice to me but speaks with an Australian accent, an indication I want America to accept me but let me retain my individuality.)

*

It was inevitable that Lillian would meet another woman who was also making her own way determinedly into the rock world. In early 1966, Linda Eastman was a 24-year-old junior fashion editor on *Town and Country*, a conservative magazine for rich people published by the Hearst Corporation. The job bored her to death. Linda had grown up in privileged circumstances in her parents' homes in Park Avenue, Scarsdale in upstate New York and in East Hampton. Her father, Lee Eastman, was a prominent New York lawyer in the entertainment business (not, as was often assumed, from the Eastman Kodak film empire). But she was something of a rebel: photography, art and horses captivated her more than her family's conservative, upper-crust world. When she was twenty-one her mother was killed in a plane crash. By then Linda had moved to Arizona where she married a geology student and gave birth to a daughter, Heather, in December 1962. The marriage did not last and in 1965 Linda moved back to New York with her baby and took the job with *Town and Country*.

When Lillian met her in early 1966, Linda was also mesmerised by the rock scene. They met at a press conference for the visiting British pop group the Dave Clark Five. Tall and well groomed in preppy clothes, with long slender legs and straight blonde hair, Linda cut a striking figure and caught Lillian's attention: "A society girl at a pop party! Wow, I thought, what next? I watched, fascinated." When he met her a few months later, Danny Fields was equally impressed: "Linda's bearing was classy, her smile atomic, her accent and her taste impeccable."

Lillian and Linda quickly identified their mutual interest in chronicling the rock scene, Lillian in a book, Linda with pictures. Perhaps they could collaborate. It was the start of a close friendship. Lillian also became Linda's confidante and supporter: she saw the younger woman as a female talent who deserved to be championed in a business dominated by men. The friendship was shattered three years later when Linda married the Beatle Paul McCartney and turned her back on Lillian and others in their tight New York rock circle. It is a story of the impact of fame on two women: one who crossed the line from being celebrity photographer to celebrity wife, the other who felt betrayed. Lillian never forgave Linda for closing the door on their friendship and later took her revenge.

Danny Fields met Linda shortly after he met Lillian. In June 1966, Lillian and Linda were in a press party that involved a Manhattan harbour cruise with the Rolling Stones on the *S.S. Sea Panther*. In this, the year of their *Aftermath* album, the Stones had become huge in America, second only to the Beatles in importance. After a foul-up with his photographer, Fields missed the cruise but waited on the wharf for it to return and was introduced to the disembarking Linda. She had struck up a friendship on board with Mick Jagger and had in her camera exclusive pictures of the Stones. With pictures from Linda and the story from Lillian, Fields was covered for *Datebook*. It was the start of a firm alliance between the three of them, one of the strongest in the New York rock world.

*

Lillian sometimes said that what sparked her interest in pop was not the Rolling Stones, the Byrds or even the Beatles, but Australia's first internationally successful group, the Easybeats. By 1966 the Easybeats had taken Australia by storm, as the first Australian group to top the charts with their own songs. They were a Sydney group of five young men who emulated the big British groups with their hair and clothes but had their own sound. Now they were ready to take on Britain and America.

In February 1966, Maggie Makeig, an old friend of Lillian's and editor of *Everybody's* – the magazine that evolved from *Weekend* – wrote to Lillian to introduce Mike Vaughan, manager of the Easybeats. He was about to arrive in New York to negotiate a US contract for the group. "I am doing more than sending you a letter," Maggie Makeig wrote. "I am sending you a man ... a real nice young man from the you beaut country who, by the time he finds you, will be sobbing for a touch of Australiana."

In New York Lillian was already known as one of Australia's great unofficial ambassadors. She seized on visitors from Australia, or at least those with talent whom she believed were going places, and proudly showed them her city, made a big fuss of them and took them to hip places such as Max's Kansas City where she hyped them to the New York rock music and art crowd as Australia's leading this or that. When Mike Vaughan arrived in New York, installed himself in the Hilton Hotel and contacted Lillian, she did her best to help him. They became good friends.

"Funnily enough it was he who turned me on to Pop," she later wrote to a friend. "I thought the group might come over some time and that it would be nice to have a few contacts for them. By the time I made them, I'd also made a lot of personal friends in the field and finally it became my scene."

As Vaughan got to work trying to sell his unknown group to America, Lillian wrote a progress report to Maggie Makeig:

The suspense is killing me. Will this simple unspoilt young man from Strathfield, New South Wales, swing the biggest deal in Australian show biz history and become the new Brian Epstein? Or will he return, as he so appropriately puts it, with egg on his face? Will the Easy Beats (Snowy, Little Stevie etc etc) show the US what music really is? Or will they fade away in obscurity in North Cunnamulla? Tensions run high on the 36th floor of the NY Hilton. Calls from Australia burn up the wires. A call from Mum means only bad news. The Yanks are wily operators out to exploit this baby digger with his innocent blue eyes and cynically curling lip. But they are not a match for good old fashioned Australian nous. Believe me. That boy has more good old fashioned Australian nous than my cat has kittens, as they say in Mildura. Well, Mag, I must say. I am steeped in gratitude. NY is never dull but it is certainly more lively for the presence of Mr Vaughan in person. He's probably one of THE great characters ever. I am filled with admiration for his sang froid, his savoir faire and his Zell-like Aussie disregard and contempt for phony gestures and wasted words.

The hard work paid off. The following year the Easybeats did crack the British and American charts with their hit "Friday on My Mind", written by two members of the group, Harry Vanda and George Young. With its success came a tour of America. Lillian covered part of the tour and got to know the band well. In New York she took Stevie Wright, the lead singer, to Max's Kansas City: "Andy Warhol was beside himself that he was there and so was everyone else and Stevie didn't even know who they were," she wrote to a friend.

It all happened when the Easybeats came to America to do their summer tour a few weeks ago. I got very turned on to, god help me, little Stevie who is really okay when he's not with other people and showing off. I really liked what was going on in his head and we became very close friends ... How's that for an old bat? (See what you can do when you lose 32 pounds and get a suntan and change your hairstyle?) I don't have to tell you that I considered it very seriously and since it was in my line of duty at work anyway, did go on the start of the tour. Some fink told him my age but he liked the idea I was two years younger than his mother better than anything. But of course you can't go on playing these sort of games ... and I cut out very fast back to the city. The situation is now as follows. Mike Vaughan the manager does not speak to me at all. Tony Cahill the drummer thinks I have been uncool and he's right so I'm on the outer with him. Little Stevie and I are barely civil. There was talk of getting back on the tour when things cooled down but I think not.

Lillian passed off the episode as one in which the rule of not becoming too closely involved with those you write about was broken: "I now know most of the groups fairly well, but think it's a mistake to know them too well. (It was probably a mistake with the Beats, whom I really love collectively anyway, but it was worth it.) The Bee Gees were here, rather guarded I thought. Lynne Randell I am very very pally with. She's touring with the Monkees and I met them all."

In the spirit of the times Lillian discovered *I Ching*, the ancient Chinese book of divination, and introduced it to Lynne Randell, an Australian singer, during the Monkees tour. "She in turn turned the Monkees on to it," Lillian wrote to a colleague. "I am always getting long distance calls from Monkee Peter Tork asking me to explain the true meaning of Hexagram 51 Inner Truth or something. It is an eery book, never wrong and cruelly truthful. It told me to get out of the swamps and lowlands the other day because the mud was getting a bit thick."

*

Thirty-five years old in 1967, Lillian was considerably older than many of those in the rock world she was starting to write about. Her maturity and her youthful looks gave her a distinct advantage. She sometimes called herself a groupie, but this was more for shock value. Groupiedom came in the wake of the rock scene, but Lillian did not need to behave as a groupie to find her way into the scene. She was a skilled journalist, a discerner of the new and the talented, and someone people liked to confide in; these abilities, combined with the authority of her extra years, gave her all the entrée she would need to depict the rock scene definitively in the *Rock Encyclopedia*.

Lillian devoted two entries to groupies in her *Rock Encyclopedia*, the *Washington Post* later taking her definition – "fans who have dared to break the barriers between the audience and the performer, fans with one thing to give, love, who want nothing in return but a name to drop" – as a point of departure for a lengthy article on the phenomenon, quoting rock stars, psychologists and groupies themselves.

Like Linda Eastman, Lillian was fascinated by the sexual power the new rock idols had over their audiences. Seeking access to these idols, both women constantly walked a line between chronicler and friend. And, in the pioneering days of rock, lines were sometimes blurred. Before she crossed the line and became Mrs Paul McCartney, Linda's status as a rock photographer gave her considerable personal freedom. In his biographical memoir of Linda in 2000, Danny Fields wrote: "I don't think anyone was keeping tabs on Linda, except perhaps the late Lillian Roxon, the great Australian journalist who became her confidante and closest friend. Lillian knew more about Linda's romantic escapades than any other single person, and probably more than all of Linda's friends put together; Linda told her everything, and Lillian repeated some of it, only some, to others in our little crowd when it suited her to do so."

But much as Lillian and Linda were in love with the same world, Lillian's maturity and her journalist's eye gave her insight into another side of that world: its brittleness, transparency and false hopes. "Life is better for the Doors being in town," Lillian wrote to a friend. "At The Scene they can be seen up close but sometimes they're not good. Sometimes they are. Jim Morrison is more of an actor than anything and exudes so much sexuality and menace on stage that dinner with him (and a bunch of others) last night at Max's at four was predictably anti-climactic. He's just one of the fellas. Linda was better off with one of the Tremeloes."

*

Lillian's excitement about the rock scene was shattered in late 1966 by news from Sydney. At the age of thirty-four Zell Rabin, Rupert Murdoch's great editor and Lillian's old flame, was dying. About eight years earlier in London, Rabin's first wife, Barbara, with whom he had briefly reunited, had noticed a mole on his back. It was diagnosed as a melanoma, a malignant form of skin cancer. It was treated but by mid-1966 the cancer had returned. Right up to his death, Rabin was unaware how serious it was. Only his sister Milly, her doctor husband, Peter Goldman, and Rupert Murdoch knew.

In June, five months before he died, Rabin wrote to Lillian from the Prince of Wales hospital in Sydney. He was irritated because "it appears my bleeding ulcer is a slow healer," but full of plans for the future: he wanted to write a book, to get married again and have children. He joked about his latest blood transfusions: "I'm sure I copped a Methodist in one of the bottles ... or worse a fucking Catholic. This accounts for my queer behaviour because aside from being under heavy sedation I'm certain a christian has got into me somewhere."

He probed Lillian about her love life: "Bloodless or not the first question I must ask you is whether your latest boy-companion is Jewish? If not, why? Someone has to mother you and I don't want to see you getting into trouble. I agree with you about the Sammy Glicks and smart-arsed broads from the Bronx but I don't want to lose you. For my money there are not enough Jews around and we can't afford to let a single one go, especially when they're as pretty as you."

He could at least pass on some triumphant news: after a three-year circulation war, the Sydney *Daily Mirror* had finally overtaken the *Sun* (and stayed ahead for the rest of both papers' lives). He signed off: "Meantime, I must cure my ulcer. Write to me, darling. Love – your, Zell."

There were operations but no cure. For the rest of 1966, when he was not in hospital, Rabin continued to put out the *Daily Mirror*. In early November he became too weak to carry on. Lillian wrote from New York to a friend:

Two days ago I heard the news that the ulcer Zell has been plagued by is in fact his old cancer back and that doctors at this moment are giving him less than a week to live. It's been very hard to accept. It's not (as people who couldn't know better thought) that I had a life-time thing about him, but there was one of those peculiar inter-twining of destinies that sometimes goes on even when two people don't get on especially well.

Some of the people here who are my best friends or who changed my life in some big way were people I met through Zell or through friends of his. Conversely, some of my friends are people whose lives Zell changed because they met him through me and so on. Some people when they die you can put aside neatly and forget, but this is just impossible. I really don't know what to do about it. I had yesterday off and just wept which was OK. But today I found I couldn't stand being alone. I filled the house with people, insisted on being taken for a drive, drank double Scotches, which I never do, and now here I am alone in the office and wondering how to distract my thoughts for the next eight hours ... Sydney will be full of women who importantly and overbearingly will Carry ON. I'd hate to be one of them. I was never in love with him except for about two weeks when I was 18, naive (and so was he) and had just met him.

At the *Mirror* office in Sydney there was a sense of impending doom. Elizabeth Riddell, a distinguished member of Rabin's staff, later wrote how the staff received the news: "There came a Friday afternoon when after lunch Murdoch called us into Zell's office, occupied by his deputy, and told us that Zell would probably die during the weekend. 'Go home,' he said. 'I'll call you when it happens.' About nine o'clock on that Sunday night it did happen, and he did telephone. After that, a lot of the heart went out of the *Mirror*."

Ruth Biegler wrote to Lillian from London on 25 November 1966:

The Zell news is awful. I understand exactly how you feel. Each time someone that has been close dies it's as if one sheds another fragment of one's own self. One death and then another and one wonders if there's going to be anything left after all the pieces have fallen away. All the memories and associations that are solidly and tangibly part of one's own foundations because they are tied up with his solid and tangible person suddenly with his death dissolve and disintegrate – and there one is, balancing precariously over a thin nothing. As the I Ching says, erosion and decay.

Rabin had made his son John David, then aged four, his sole beneficiary. After Rabin died on 13 November, Murdoch visited his parents and sat with them for several hours. It was said to be the only time people had seen Murdoch weep. He made only one request of Alex and Sonia Rabin. Jewish funerals are usually held in the morning. If Zell's followed tradition, Murdoch was worried that the *Mirror* office would empty and there would be no paper that day. They agreed to move the funeral to the afternoon of 15 November. Rabin was buried with Jewish rites at Rookwood Cemetery, Sydney – and the *Mirror* came out that day.

When he installed Rabin as editor, Murdoch owned only the two *Mirror* newspapers in Sydney and one in Adelaide. Since then News Corporation has grown into a multibillion dollar newspaper, television, magazine, film and publishing empire. Reflecting, at the age of seventy, on Rabin's place in his pantheon, Murdoch says: "He was critical to me. The turnaround of the *Mirror* under Zell was critical to the growth of this company. There have been many editors I've been very fond of, but none more so than Zell. When I think of those who've been really successful, who really were absolutely brilliant at what they did in different ways, there was Zell, Larry Lamb at the *Sun* in London …" He pauses for almost a minute but does not produce another name. "There were subsequent editors who fitted their time very well, but I can't say they ever had the attributes of great editors. They are far and few between. Zell Rabin in Sydney was an original. He had original ideas about editing, about the paper, about the country."

*

Three months after Rabin's death, Lillian flew to Mexico to do a story on quintuplets for *Woman's Day*. She returned through San Francisco where she spent a week with the hippies, the peace and love movement to which that city had given birth. "Both Mexico and San Francisco wrought major changes in me and I'm now sitting back nervously assessing the implications," she wrote to her brother Jack in Sydney. "I stayed for a while with Aaron Wildawski, a political science Fulbright you met in Brisbane I think a million years ago. He is now head of the political science department at Berkeley, very big time and terrific."

In Berkeley Joan Baez's sister Mimi, herself a folk singer, gave a party for her. Lillian's 3,000-word piece on hippies in the *Sydney Morning Herald* on 4 March 1967, just ahead of the so-called Summer of Love, was one of the first to look seriously at "flower power", even before the mainstream American press had started to make sense of it. She described the involvement of the San Francisco rock bands, Big Brother and the Holding Company, the Grateful Dead and Country Joe and the Fish in the rallies, protest marches and LSD happenings. Her Libertarian background allowed her to discern the valuable side of hippiedom – a capacity to embrace life – that set it apart from the Beatniks and the more earnest side of the Push that had left her cold:

> The shops cater to them or to those who come to see them with giant posters of such Hippie heroes, anti-heroes and martyrs as Peter Fonda, Lenny Bruce, Malcolm X, Timothy Leary, Mao Tse-tung, Trotsky and actor Ronald Reagan, now Governor of California (with the words "Thanks for da votes, sucker").
>
> The current big Hippie causes are best summed up by the three most frequently worn buttons. They are "Impeach Reagan", "Legalise Marijuana" and "I'm for Sexual Freedom". How long the Hippie craze will last and whether the way-out San Francisco variety of the cult will spread is still anyone's guess. Despite its bewildering (to "straights") aspects the movement seems to mark a final break with the hopelessness of the Beatniks. Hippies are not concerned about the Bomb. Despair isn't in their vocabulary. Maybe there is an overdue emphasis on sexual freedom and drug experimentation, but that is common to many adolescent groups. Essentially Hippies are joyful youngsters – they are embracing life not, as the Beatniks did, running away from it.

This, the year of psychedelia and the Summer of Love, was the last year of innocence before drugs, violence, business and mega-scale perform-ances transformed the rock scene. In February Mick Jagger and Keith Richards were arrested in London and later jailed for possession of mar-ihuana and pep pills, the penalty ludicrous even then. In August, while the Beatles were in Bangor, North Wales, turning on to meditation with the Maharishi Mahesh Yogi, Brian Epstein, the man who discovered and managed them to fame, died from an overdose of sleeping pills at the age of thirty-two.

*

After a holiday in London in May 1967, Lillian embarked on one of her periodic battles against her weight and triumphed. "My secret is lots of sleep, no grog, two hours whenever possible on Coney Island Beach and the Weight Watchers Cookbook," she wrote to a colleague in Sydney.

> There is no question of when the diet will end. I enjoy it so much that I fear I may waste away like the invisible shrinking man into a tiny creature scared by field mice ... I came back from London hating New York and loving all that London Oz-Manchester bricklayer-Chelsea dragqueen scene. But New York, as it always does, insinuated itself back into my good graces and now I love it all over again. My big dis-covery has been Coney Island Beach. Greasy it is, and full of cigarette butts in the sand, its Negroes are the worst and ladies in gold shoes play cards at tables set up near the kiosk, the Mafia dominates with Sicilian songs and Italian moms who flourish noisy castanets and tamborines, Spanish kids beg money, Jewish gents with careful tans and garment centre waistlines try to chat you up, the water is, as I've often said, Instant Hepatitis, but all the same, it's so American it's really got to me. I love that 45-minute subway ride and the wax museum and the big dipper and the yellow knishes I no longer eat and I go all the time. I took a Sydney girl there today and we had a frankfurter at Nathans Famous and I thought really happiness is now and then being able to touch America where it's real.

The Nathans frankfurter in the middle of a diet was an all-too-typical fall from grace. There was a constant flow of visitors from Australia, and just a few were admitted as house guests to the East 21st Street apartment. Some of her house guests embarked on New York adventures of their own. Of one Australian visitor, she reported in a letter to a mutual friend back home:

> Here she is the world's dowdiest woman (she knows —— so not a word, not that you would) with the world's hairiest legs and a bossy, critical, castrating personality and very definite about her own ideas etc and she has just got off with the eighteen feet tall, jet black, bearded, GORGEOUS (not my style but gorgeous nevertheless) doorman and bouncer at the Dom [an Andy Warhol-operated club] (he's also a jazz musician which makes it OK) who is constantly being pursued by hordes of women. She not only got off with him several times but she also came out on top because she decided he was no good and told him so, in no uncertain terms. "You have been a great disappointment to me," she said to him. And to me, "I think you should leave this country at once. Your sex life is in danger." The poor man is cowed and shrunk right down from his eighteen feet. She leaves today (and I must confess I'm rather sorry. It's been VERY funny) and he's actually going out to the airport to farewell her.

Lillian was sceptical about New York attitudes to personal intimacy. "It's considered very unchic in New York to feel and allow someone to get to your feelings, but the day that ends life won't be worth anything," she wrote. "So I'm going to continue to be unchic." She was a sensitive person, easily wounded, sometimes too easily, but also with a capacity to make fun out of situations in which her fearless approach to life sometimes left her stranded. In early 1968, she wrote to a friend in London to report that she was "in the throes of a major insane love affair":

> He is an embarrassingly pretty drummer and the scandal will kill me. He was supposed to be just for Xmas and to come down on twelfth night with the other decorations but he moved in the other day (without asking) and seems so comfortable I don't think he'll ever move. Every secret closet queen in town wants him and keeps ringing up offering him wealth untold or jobs or a future in Hollywood. Instant Brian Epstein, had dear old Bri lived. Not really a Lillian type, far too pretty, but as I said, we're into an addiction thing over each

other and no one can do any work, concentrate or anything. These
things CAN'T last in New York, but who knows? Anyway the age difference is very vast. (When I told him he said, not unkindly, I
THOUGHT you looked a bit worn for 20.) (He is also under the
impression that my advanced years account for my lack of condition.
I haven't the heart to say I am now "thin" Man, This *is* THIN for me.
I have to pretend I used to be thin and, well, I let myself go, man. You
get to say man a lot when there are babies around the house drumming along with Ginger Baker and reading Tolkien all the time.)

The drummer was David Wynne, who had gone to New York from
Montreal in August 1967 to cut an album with a Canadian blues, funk
and jazz band called Influence. The band moved into the Algonquin
Hotel while Valerie Reardon, the record company's publicist, and a
friend of Lillian's, introduced them to the New York rock scene.

Wynne met Lillian at a party at Linda Eastman's apartment on
Manhattan's west side. He was 19 to Lillian's 35. "I was still fairly shy
around New Yorkers," he recalls. "I must have been hanging on to
Valerie, not wanting to talk to anyone. She brought me to meet Lillian
who was sitting on a bed smoking and giving an I Ching reading. I
joined in and spent the rest of the evening talking, or more listening.
Then Lillian brought me home to East 21st Street."

Despite the "very vast" age difference, a relationship developed that
had a lasting impact on both of them. When it became clear they were
spending every night together, Wynne moved in ("not really unasked",
he says). The start of his relationship with Lillian was also the beginning of the end of his relationship with Influence. A disagreement with
the band over a proposal to re-record the album, and Wynne's living
away from the band with Lillian, had put him on the outside. He eventually parted ways with them. Lillian called it "internal strife syndrome". Wynne recalls of his life with Lillian:

Living with Lillian had a sort of dream-like, timeless quality, with no
defining schedules. The apartment was decorated in hippy
Marrakesh, lots of cushions, hangings, brass things and a makeshift
canopied bed with more cushions and hangings. We didn't go out as
a couple much, something I didn't question at the time. I spent days
at the New York chess club or just reading or walking the town. We

went to the Scene a few times and saw B.B. King at the Village Gate. Lillian was very good at compartmentalizing her relationships, which may have allowed her to live more lives more fully than most of us. In our compartment there were only the two of us, and it was mostly good talk and good sex.

After a few months, in early 1968, Wynne decided to return home to Canada to finish his education, which later took him into what he describes as a "very un-rock and roll life", first as a diplomat then as a businessman. "If I'd been perhaps even a couple of years older and wiser I would have tried to stay with Lillian," he says. "I certainly loved her, but it was clearly unequal. I knew I was privileged to be with someone very special, with a rare, rare nature. Things I learned from Lillian have stayed with me and influenced much of my life. Not only about love and sex, honesty and connecting—things where she was my first teacher, and a great one.

"She also woke me up to what it means to be on the cutting edge of something. I discovered through her the frightening capacity of New York to absorb *anything* and turn it to its own ends."

They stayed in touch, with Lillian writing frequently to Wynne giving gossip on the rock scene, accounts of her own life and a worldly woman's advice about how to handle human relationships. By now, in 1968, she was embarking on research for the *Rock Encyclopedia*. "Pop music has had it," she told him. "What I'm writing is history, the record of an era." Wynne sent her background material on Canadian bands, for an entry which she probably included as a tribute to him; the encyclopedia's Canada scene section as it appeared, he says, was "uniquely hers".

In April the research took her to London where she stayed with her old Sydney Push friend, Ruth Biegler, in Cromwell Crescent, before moving into the apartment of Richard Neville, the Australian editor of the London counterculture magazine, *Oz*. With Neville away in New York, Lillian threw a lunch party for 40 people. One visitor was Tim Buckley, the folk-rock musician who was very big on the New York scene, where he was briefly involved with Linda Eastman, and who later died of a heroin overdose. "Tim Buckley has been here which is a whole other story, burrowing into my lap, clinging to me like a baby, begging to be rescued from interviewers," Lillian wrote to Wynne.

A bunch of us went out to dinner and it did my image no end of good to have America's current sex symbol's curly little head collapsing all over me. But Buckley is not my sort of little boy and not my scene. The streets are full of prettier and less complex creatures. Without regret I turned down his offer to accompany them on their Scandinavian tour. I'd rather be chatted up by a cockney record salesman who looks like George Harrison on Earl's Court Road.

The London visit also opened up a chance for Lillian to put to rest the unresolved drama over her fling the previous summer with Stevie Wright, lead singer of the Easybeats, during the Australian band's tour of America. Three of the Easybeats were living near Cromwell Crescent, working on an album; Stevie Wright was living with a long-time girlfriend elsewhere. He and Lillian met. "I thought things would be very tense there," she reported to Wynne. "But the I Ching is right, once you're with someone it can't change, no matter what, and all the tension was gone."

There was a little romantic scene there. And then, in the middle of it, I happen to see a picture of his girl and I said I wanted to meet her. He was horrified and said I couldn't possibly meet her. But I insisted and it ended up with the three of us going out to dinner and Dave, I REALLY dug her, a lot, and vice versa. She's a really beautiful person, they've been together for years, and I felt the thing with me was quite wrong at every level though I really love him as a person. So anyway, we all went home and turned on and decided we all dug each other and now everyone is friends and it's got a happy ending.

Back in New York, Lillian reported to Wynne that she was mesmerised by someone even younger than him: a "16 year-old music freak who I have working for me". The teenager seems to have appealed to all her old fascinations with the freshness, sparkle and sex appeal of youth: "Very verbal. Talks more than I do. Very sophisticated. Rich kid. I go to dinner with grown men and they bore me and a 16 year-old kid can entertain me for eight hours, a living American novel. No I haven't and probably won't. I mean, one shouldn't. Should one? I can't see where it would go after the first couple of times. Still, it's very tempting and

there's lots of crackling electricity about. Don't write back patronis-
ingly and say I'm sick. I'm just touched by innocence."

As soon as the *Rock Encyclopedia* appeared the following year, 16
year-old Brian Cullman devoured it, then precociously sent several
pages of trainspotter's corrections to Lillian via her publisher. He
expected a brisk acknowledgement at best, but more likely to be
ignored. Instead, Lillian called him, asked how he knew so much about
music and whether he would like to work on the book's second edition
with her. "She was lovely and funny and made me feel fascinating,"
Cullman says. Why wouldn't I be smitten?"

Soon, the boy found himself being whisked to the epicentre of the
New York rock world, to Max's Kansas City and to Danny Fields's apartment in Greenwich Village, where musicians, pop stars like Jim
Morrison and Andy Warhol "superstars" like Nico were just some of
the guests. Cullman recalls:

> The second or third time I met her, I pulled out a guitar and played
> her some songs I'd written and asked if she thought they were any
> good. She said she wasn't sure but that her friend Danny would
> know, and next thing I knew we were in a taxi, hurtling down to
> Danny's place. It was dark, there were candles burning, various peo-
> ple were sitting around on the floor thumbing through magazines,
> Jim Morrison was passed out on the couch and Nico, I was told, had
> locked herself in the bedroom, to keep Morrison away. The phone
> kept ringing. Once it was Leonard Cohen, looking for Nico. For all I
> knew The Beatles were in the kitchen, fixing snacks. Lillian seemed
> to think this was all normal and encouraged me to play my songs,
> which I could feel wilting and shrinking by the second. I stumbled
> through part of a song. Maybe part of another one. Mercifully, no
> one was listening. Lillian rescued me by dragging me off to Max's
> Kansas City, where she held court and introduced me to everyone
> and filled the room with her wild laughter.

If Lillian, with her description of "crackling electricity", was giving
David Wynne a light-hearted account of her fantasy with her teenage
discovery, she saved her more serious comments for her friendship
with him. He was not to feel "displaced", she told him. Wynne had
called from Canada to discuss his own personal life. Lillian now wrote

back with an experienced, independent woman's guide to the universal problem of men handling their relationships with women.

> Look, Dave, women ARE demanding, and the more they care, the more they are, and you just have to work it out with each one of them, and try and get them into one other absorbing interest so the pressure comes off you now and then. Otherwise you are the focus not just for their love but also for the energies they should be pouring into some other things.
>
> I get a lot of reassurance and ego boost from work, which if I weren't working I'd expect to get from a man. Very womanly women are the worst - which is both what makes them so attractive and so exasperating. I am sure the high rise of homosexuality in New York is due to men getting exasperated by women's demands. (A man never makes all those emotional demands.) But I don't think men realise they can be dealt with, discussed and you can come to a truce and a compromise. It's like a big union situation. Negotiation.
>
> Listen to me, my life is a mess, and I presume to advise. Still, Dave, you know even from this distance, and after all this time, I hate to think of you having even one minute of unhappiness.

*

After almost four years of intense heat, the rock and roll pressure cooker started to cool in 1968. It was a big year for Lillian as she embarked on the daunting task of writing the world's first rock encyclopedia. Linda Eastman, too, was at the height of her career as a rock photographer. The friendship between the two women was at its strongest: they talked on the telephone several times a day and Linda wandered into the *Sydney Morning Herald* bureau to pass on photographs or sit on the edge of Lillian's desk and chat. At night they did the rounds of places like The Scene and the Fillmore East, the rock venue opened by Bill Graham, the West Coast promoter. Danny Fields later wrote: "In 1968, Linda and Lillian were so close that people suspected Something; Roxon boasted of her bisexuality and probably had a bit of a crush on Linda, but she was in fact a Mother Confessor and there was absolutely nothing physical between the two women."

Lillian was nine years older than Linda, and besides being mother confessor she was a combination of big sister, close friend and col-league who operated on the same wavelength; they were two ambi-tious, professional women who knew they were at the centre of a musical and cultural explosion and were determined to document it as contemporary history. Lillian was Linda's chief defender against those in the business, usually men, who belittled her work. "She worked day and night," Lillian wrote. "Turning out literally hundreds of pictures of every major group (and a lot of minor ones) working out of New York at that time."

By now Lillian and Linda were part of a small but influential crowd of writers and rock promoters that included Fields, Blair Sabol, a columnist and fashion writer at the *Village Voice*, and Robin Richmond, an editor at *Life*. Fields later wrote of Linda's inner circle: "Three women knew her best, and were her closest friends and confidantes – Lillian Roxon, Blair Sabol and Robin Richmond. All were formidable media dominatrices and easily among what Pete Townshend [of the Who] calls the 'thirty or so possible' people in New York at that time."

As 1968 unfolded, a recurring topic in Linda's intimate chats with Lillian was Paul McCartney. A certain mythology later developed that it was Lillian who introduced Linda to Paul, but nothing sug-gests that Lillian ever knew Paul McCartney, certainly not well enough to introduce him to her friend. Linda and Paul had first met on 15 May 1967 at a London club, the Bag o' Nails, where the British rhythm and blues group the Animals had taken Linda to see Georgie Fame and the Blue Flames perform. Paul introduced himself to Linda there and asked her to go on with him and his crowd to another club, the Speakeasy.

Linda was keen to meet and photograph the Beatles, and a few days later she talked her way into an exclusive press party at Brian Epstein's house in Belgravia to launch the Beatles' watershed album *Sergeant Pepper's Lonely Hearts Club Band*. At the party she chatted again to Paul and snapped pictures of him.

So began Linda's infatuation with Paul McCartney. Peter Brown, Epstein's assistant, reported in his book *The Love You Make*, co-written with Steven Gaines: "When Linda returned home to America, her close friend, Lillian Roxon, America's doyenne of rock critics, found a picture of Paul and Linda taken by another photographer at the party. She sent it to Linda, who blew the picture up big enough to cover her bathroom

door. She looked at it every day for two months, as if she could will
him back to her."

Then, in May 1968, a year after Linda and Paul's first meeting, Paul
and John Lennon arrived in New York to launch Apple Records in the
United States. On the strength of the *Rock Encyclopedia*, which Lillian
had now started to write, *Eye* magazine commissioned her to follow
Paul and John around New York for a story entitled "101 Hours with
the Beatles". This was probably how the story of Lillian's "introducing" Linda to Paul originated. Lillian chose Linda to take the pictures
for the "101 Hours" feature and arranged a press pass for her to the
Lennon–McCartney press conference at the Americana Hotel.

"We were ... sitting right in the front row," Lillian wrote. "Paul was
smiling at Linda but she, a true professional, kept snapping with her
camera. Next day she said, very casually, that Paul had phoned her.
Then she laughed and said, 'Now don't go around telling everyone.'
After that she became very silent and very cagy. The best word for her
mood would be thoughtful. I now realised she was doing some hard
thinking – like did she really love Paul? Even if she did, was she prepared to move into a scene that could be likened only to a loaded
minefield?"

Linda gave her own account of this press conference to Barry Miles
in *Many Years from Now*, his authorised biography of Paul McCartney:
"I was taking pictures and we started talking. He said, 'We're leaving,
give me your number,' and I remember writing it on a cheque. When
I got back to the apartment he'd rung."

Linda's caginess with Lillian, if that's what it was, did not last. After
Linda returned from another meeting with Paul in Los Angeles in June,
according to Danny Fields, "It didn't take long at all for Linda to phone
Lillian Roxon ... to tell her that she and Paul had entered into (hopefully, she said) a true sexual relationship. Lillian quickly made sure the
whole town knew about it as well, but Linda didn't mind."

The Linda and Paul story now gathered momentum. Linda told
both Lillian and Danny that she was thinking of going to London after
Paul had asked her to join him there. Lillian sensed something big was
about to happen: "I'd always thought her coolness with men had a lot
to do with the fact that American men weren't quite ready for the sort
of person she was. They took themselves too seriously."

So Linda flew to London in September 1968, and that was the last time Lillian Roxon saw or spoke to her. Danny Fields remembers post-cards coming from London at first, then stopping in the winter of 1968. "Have you heard from Linda?" he asked Lillian.

"No," she replied. "But she's going to marry him, you know."

"How do *you* know that? Have you talked to her?"

"I just know. A girl knows what her friends are going to do. She's going to marry him and that's why you and I haven't heard from her."

Fields says: "And sure enough, in March of 1969 we picked up the newspapers and they were married. Lillian predicted it."

Paul and Linda McCartney were married at the Marylebone Registry Office in London on 12 March 1969, surrounded by swarms of shouting fans and photographers. Before the marriage, in November 1968, Lillian received three cryptic postcards from Linda. The first had just a line drawing of a smiling man and woman with heart-shaped lips and was signed "Linda". The second, posted from Scotland, near Paul's remote farm a few miles north of the Mull of Kintyre, showed a bagpipe player walking down a highland track, and on the reverse side was written, "Watching away hay right wrong love song Linda Paul and Heather". The third card said: "Send me a copy of your book – and a letter – or just a letter will do – All is well xLinda".

On a fourth card the date is unclear, but the date is less important than the message. It reportedly made Lillian incandescent with rage. On the card is written: "Never believe the press. Blow your nose and keep quiet. Hello Lovey." Written vertically across the middle of the card, separately from the message, is: "From Linda Eastman".

Being told to keep quiet – after Linda had all but stopped communicating with her – was the last straw for Lillian. What did Linda mean? Was she having a joke? If so, she was taking a big gamble on Lillian's sense of humour. It looked to Lillian as if she was being told to draw a line under all those confidential talks they had once shared. Danny Fields says:

She stopped communicating with her closest friends in New York, me, Lillian, Blair, the journalist Howard Smith. We all just said, "Has she dropped us?" Lillian did not take that lying down. I think she thought, "That bitch. All those nights I sat and listened to her moan and complain and speculate. Now she marries a Beatle and I can't even get in touch with her."

Lillian carried the feeling of being dumped for the rest of her life and chose her moment to take revenge. Meanwhile Paul McCartney went through the legal, financial and personal trauma of the Beatles finally breaking up in 1970, while Linda learned to cope with being an unpopular wife – unpopular with British fans who resented this interloping, divorced American photographer taking "their" cute Beatle, and unpopular with fans everywhere who unjustly blamed Linda and Yoko Ono – John Lennon's new wife – for breaking up the Beatles.

In late 1971 Paul formed his own group, Wings. Its members were all unknown except for his wife, whom he put on keyboards. Linda had never been known to perform this role before, a fact many rock critics took cruel delight in pointing out. A postcard came from Linda, apparently the first in three years, that said: "Touring GB with our new group Wings – everything is lovely – hope you're well Love ZPLHMS Love to Danny."

In the lead-up to forming Wings, Paul and Linda visited New York in 1971. There, Linda called Danny Fields for the first time since her departure for London three years earlier. She took Paul to meet Fields, who suggested Linda should also contact Lillian. But Linda did not do this. "She knew she'd offended Lillian," Fields says. "She was afraid of confronting Lillian's anger, as anyone would be. She knew I was the only one of her old New York friends who wouldn't bark or bite."

Then out of the blue, almost two years later, Lillian received a Christmas card from the McCartneys, their family now having been augmented by two daughters, Mary and Stella. The photograph on the card showed Paul dressed as Santa Claus next to a Christmas tree, with Linda sitting on his lap dressed in a black sailor's suit with yellow and purple trims, a three-pointed hat pushed back jauntily on her head. An apparently handwritten message said: "Merry Christmas & many more good years Paul Linda Heather Mary Stella".

If this card was intended as a peace overture, it did not work. Or, with Wings due to make their first American tour early in 1973, was there more to it? In the wake of the success of her *Rock Encyclopedia*, Lillian now had a weekly column, "The Top of Pop", in the New York *Sunday News*. It confirmed her status as one of New York's most influential rock writers and gave her a platform to bestow her praise or declare her disdain before a readership of millions. Now she turned on the McCartneys publicly. In her column on 24 December 1972, headed "The Roxon Awards For 1972", Lillian wrote:

> You know the Grammy awards and how they never have anything to do with what's good or bad in music? (Well, not in the music *I* know.) I thought that since this was the time of sweetness and light and peace among men, I would announce some long-overdue awards of my own.
>
> Like the Blind Optimism Award has to go to Paul and Linda McCartney who have been calling their old New York pals like crazy now that it looks like their group, Wings, will come here in April. Just one thing, these are friends they have barely talked to in the last four years. The friendly overtures were *not* well received. (The McCartneys' Christmas card is a photo of Paul and Linda with Paul dressed as Santa Claus and Linda dressed, as far as I can make out, like the Statue of Liberty.)

But this was just a warm-up. Four months later Lillian wrote a devastating review in her *Sunday News* column when the documentary *James Paul McCartney* was shown on American television. This time she spared neither Linda nor Paul. "That was some pilot the McCartneys treated us to last Monday!" her piece began.

> Musically, the show was deadly dull. You couldn't exactly call Paul an example of high energy rock (though, heaven knows, at the end he *tried*). For a while it even seemed as if he were singing the same song over and over again.
>
> Did you see them in that pub scene? Paul as congenial and friendly as all get out, hugging dear old ladies straight out of British World War II movies. Linda positively catatonic with horror at having to mingle with ordinary people.
>
> I can tell you right now, she didn't marry a millionaire Beatle to end up in a Liverpool saloon singing "Pack Up Your Troubles in Your Old Kit Bag" with middle-aged women called Mildred. TV special or not, she didn't crack a smile once in that scene except for a little novocained grimace after, I suspect, Paul had given her a good hard shove in the ribs.
>
> For some months now, rock has been spreading over late night TV

like chocolate icing but, admit it, although it's been great to check up on the action without having to leave the living room, it's been just a little tedious to watch everyone do nothing but *play*. What kind of people are they up there on stage? Do they get on with their wives? Are they happy?

Not a soul I talked to afterwards could remember the names of most of the songs in "James Paul McCartney", but they certainly had names for Linda's varied hair arrangements – her Stevie Wonder multibraid, her Los Angeles groupie Moulin Rouge top knot, her modified Bette Midler '40s page boy, and her quite unforgettable David Bowie split-level crew-cut.

Visually, the show was pretty glamorous. It borrowed a great deal from the early Richard Lester films that helped to make the Beatles almost as successful on celluloid as they were on vinyl, but anything is better than one camera focused expressionlessly on a bunch of musicians plucking away at their guitar strings. I thought all the effects were terrific, the wall of video monitors, the chorus persons who were half boy–half girl (right down the middle), the lady in a babushka who sang "She Loves You, Yeah, Yeah, Yeah", Linda's Captain Marvel outfit and the scene where she snapped away at Paul with her Nikon, showing all the aspiring star-chasers of America that all you have to do to get musicians is to play David Hemmings to their Verushka.

But seriously, take away Linda's ringlets, her picture hats, her tambourine (very Major Barbara), and what are we left with? Sweaty, pudgy, slack-mouthed Paul McCartney trying too hard to get across what essentially turned out to be little more than bland easy listening Muzak.

Before I saw the show I thought that perhaps what it was intended to do was establish once and for all that Paul McCartney and Wings are a lot heavier than we ever gave them credit for. But they're not. They're so lightweight they make the new Seekers sound like Grand Funk. Paul, whose charm and talent shone through every minute of "Help!" like Elizabeth Taylor's diamond, revealed himself to be little more than an incredibly generous husband and a great piano player – *when* he could get the keyboard away from Linda.

The sight of him slumming it up with his old mates in his checked tartan woollen Jack Kerouac shirt while Linda looked merely disdainful, if not downright bored, gave some little clue as to why it isn't happening for him musically. He's no longer in touch with the kind of reality that made his music valid. "You are my sunshine", sang the people who gave the Beatles their original vitality, and Linda sat, her teeth relentlessly clamped in a Scarsdale lockjaw. I could have wept.

Lillian closed her review by unflatteringly contrasting Paul with Linda. The show, she wrote, revealed "that while Linda comes across as an incredibly cold and arrogant figure coming to life only when the TV cameras are focussed right on her, she is a great beauty and someone should forget about Paul and make a movie with her instead."

Lillian's review of *James Paul McCartney* appeared in the *Sunday News* on 22 April 1973, only four months before her sudden death. By then she had not seen or spoken to Linda for almost five years. Linda was cut by the piece when she learned of it. "How could she write that?" she asked Danny Fields. She appeared to be stung more for what it said about her husband than about her: that Paul should give up on his own career and focus on his wife's potential solo one. This was probably Lillian the feminist, the independent woman, speaking, but also the woman whose affection and respect for her old friend still lurked beneath the pain and bitterness of their estrangement.

For all its wounding words, Lillian's piece was mild compared with one that Blair Sabol, Linda's other close New York journalist friend, wrote two years later. Like Lillian, Sabol felt abandoned by Linda when she disappeared so suddenly from their lives. She was particularly upset, as were all Lillian's friends, that the torn friendship remained unmended when Lillian died. Sabol's platform was the *Village Voice*, where her sharp pieces on the world of celebrity brought her a solid readership.

On 14 April 1975, Sabol began a two-page article on the McCartneys:

On March 4 Linda McCartney was busted driving with Paul in West Los Angeles at 1 a.m. for carrying two scroungy joints at the bottom of her shoulder bag. On March 5 at 1 p.m. she called me for the first time in eight years. Did she need money ... no, she wanted to go shopping in Beverly Hills.

Now you must understand the last time I knew Linda was in her groping groupie days. I met her on an interview with Warren Beatty after his *Bonnie and Clyde* success when he was into giving nonverbal explanations and Linda was into photographing stars with little or no film in her camera. I remember how impressed I was with her come-on-hard-on talents as she sat in front of Mr B. in a mini skirt and her legs in a full wide-angle split for at least six rolls of Ectachrome. Warren ended up ushering me out of his Delmonico's suite within 30 minutes and kept Linda for two days.

Her pictures turned out to be mediocre to poor, but we became fast friends ... I was shocked at the disappearing act she pulled on all her New York City friends when she left for England in 1967 for the eventual McCartney score. The late beloved Rock Duchess and giant Linda supporter, Lillian Roxon, and I would spend endless hours discussing how she could pull such a brutal break with all of us. Didn't she think us worthy of her regal rock role? Why were we considered such cast-offs? Couldn't we keep good enough time? It was a puzzle that plagued us and crushed Lillian to her dying day.

Linda had once mixed on equal terms with Lillian, Blair and others as a media figure on the rock scene; then she had married one of its stars at the height of his fame. She had crossed into marriage, parenthood and celebrity status at a critical moment in her husband's life, when the press was obsessed with the demise of the most successful pop group ever, the group with which she was now intimately connected. Could old friendship and new celebrity co-exist? Danny Fields, who knew Lillian, Linda and Blair better than most, who was the only one who kept in touch with Linda and who wrote Linda's biography after her death, has suggested – and Linda indicated as much to him – that Paul's counsel could have played a part in Linda's break from Lillian. It is not unreasonable to imagine Paul advising his new wife: "Stay away from them, from journalists. They're looking for stuff about me. They're going to pump you for stuff about me. It's a critical time for both of us – better off to stay away."

For all that, there was nothing to stop Linda contacting her old friend later once the dust had settled. But she did not. Fields says: "One may say it was beneath Linda to have been so casual about the very close circle of very few friends she had in New York and who were very supportive of her. One could say it was thoughtless and insensitive to completely abandon them. She thought she had a good excuse, that she was totally occupied with this incredible role of being the most popular Beatle's hated wife. Things were thrown at her. Terrible things were said about her. During those very difficult first few years of her marriage to Paul you'd think she would turn to her friends in New York at the time, but she didn't. And knowing Lillian it would be easier to say 'I hate her' than 'I forgive her.'"

The longer the gulf persisted the harder it became to bridge, and then, suddenly, in August 1973, Lillian was dead. "Linda was heart-broken," Fields says. "She could not mention Lillian's name without feeling terrible that their relationship had deteriorated almost accidentally to the point that it did, that they let it get so far without making up and saying they were sorry. They loved each other very much. They had a real bond."

Linda survived the fame of her marriage to Paul, and the marriage survived the strains that accompany celebrity marriages. Linda went on to find a new role as a champion of animal welfare and vegetarianism. If she and Lillian had both lived longer perhaps their friendship would have revived too. As the years passed, some of Linda's detractors began to reassess. Twenty-five years after she flayed Linda in the *Village Voice*, Blair Sabol told Danny Fields that she had been "guilt-ridden" about her piece, a form of journalism she described as "kharmically hideous". At the time she had been getting even with Linda and striking a blow for Lillian, but later she came to understand Linda's position better: "She had to 'create' a world for herself that had little to do with people like Lillian who had been really supportive of her … Now I can't imagine Linda coming back to us after she married him. Once you've crossed that river, into that level of fame, it is levelling."

During research for this book, Linda McCartney agreed to break her silence and to talk for the first time about her friendship with Lillian. At the time she was suffering from the breast cancer that eventually killed her and had withdrawn for treatment, re-emerging briefly in April 1998 to attend the Paris showing of her daughter Stella's fashion designs. Soon afterwards, and before she was able to record the interview, Linda died. She was fifty-six. She once told Danny Fields, the surviving link between Lillian and her: "It's the one thing I'm sorriest about in the whole world, that Lillian and I never made up. I'm so sorry about it, about Lillian. God, I loved her, she must have thought I totally unfriended her. But I didn't know she was going to die! If she hadn't died, I'm sure we would have gotten together again, been friends again."

Chapter 14 *Rock Encyclopedia*

The year 1968 was an explosive mixture of politics, rock and revolution, the decade's three big driving forces of change. Robert Kennedy and Martin Luther King were assassinated. Andy Warhol was shot and almost killed by a man-hating woman, Valerie Solanas. Students in Paris and the United States rioted. Americans started turning against the war in Vietnam. Soviet tanks crushed the freedom movement of the Prague Spring. Richard Nixon was elected President of the United States. And Lillian Roxon wrote the world's first encyclopedia of rock music.

When it was published in late 1969, *Lillian Roxon's Rock Encyclopedia* had an instant impact. It was the first book of its kind to treat rock culture as a legitimate presence, something that would not fade away but was here to stay. It was also Lillian's announcement that a new breed of writer, the rock writer, was as much a star of the times as rock stars themselves. The encyclopedia established her own place in the pantheon: twenty-five years after its publication Steven Gaines, a leading authority on pop culture, wrote that Lillian was the "mother of rock and roll journalism".

If Lillian was the mother, then the father was not so much another person as a place. In New York City in the 1960s, there was really only one place for rock writers and their subjects to feel comfortable: Max's Kansas City, the restaurant, bar and nightclub where art, music, sex, drugs and rock and roll came together in an exciting, unstable mix. Jane Fonda, John Lennon, Yoko Ono, Janis Joplin, William Burroughs, Robert Mapplethorpe and Patti Smith were among its remarkable range of celebrity patrons.

Lillian later wrote that the *Rock Encyclopedia* "came out of all those nights at Max's and The Scene". The Scene was a performance club owned by Steve Paul, whom Lillian once described as the "new teenage Messiah, a phenomenon, a teenage idol who doesn't sing but talks, Bob Dylan without a guitar". Max's was the place where, as Andy Warhol described it, "Pop Art and Pop Life came together … everybody went to Max's and everything got homogenised there".

Max's opened in December 1965 on Park Avenue South and Seventeenth Street near Union Square, just a few blocks away from Lillian's home on East 21st Street. Mickey Ruskin, a Cornell law graduate and art lover, opened Max's initially as a restaurant, bar and exhibition space for artists. At the front was a bar and at the back was a large room, the famous back room. Warhol was among the first to go to Max's and to claim the back room and its round table as his nightly home. With Warhol came the Velvet Underground, the band he sponsored, its singers Lou Reed and Nico, and a stable of actresses, models, studs, transsexuals and drag queens, the "Superstars" of his films. Lillian knew Warhol from earlier times in New York; she had occasionally written about pop art before rock and roll began to consume her interests. "I went to another of those Warhol pictures and found myself next to Andy who had a pleasant chat to me about whippings," she wrote to a friend. "I am smiled on by Andy Warhol these days (known to his dear friends as Drella, but what else?)."

Soon after the Warhol crowd settled in, Danny Fields started bringing music people into the back room. Lillian held court in this circle of music writers, musicians, producers, photographers and publicists. She was at least ten years older than most of the Max's music crowd and did not take recreational drugs and rarely drank. Her age and experience allowed her to be an observer as well as a participant, and gave her an edge as well as an almost maternal authority. Danny Fields says: "She was like your mother in a way. She was older than all of us. You didn't expect her to get stoned and you didn't want her to and you were glad that she didn't. It just never came up."

Among this counterculture crowd a tolerant, democratic ethos prevailed. Lou Reed described it this way in *High on Rebellion*, a book about Max's Kansas City by Yvonne Sewall-Ruskin, Mickey Ruskin's former partner: "It was the most democratic meeting ground imaginable … It was a speedy world – New York – and revolutions were taking place in it – art, life and rock and roll. It was palpable and exciting. A young reckless nighttime bunch we were. The dark brigade who never saw the sun."

Lily Brett, an Australian writer whom Lillian introduced to her New York world in the sixties when Lily was writing on rock for the Australian magazine *Go Set*, recalls this democratic ethos and Lillian's place in it:

> At Max's Kansas City she was in the thick of it. There wasn't a table that ignored her. Everybody knew her, everybody was happy to see her, everybody greeted her warmly. Everybody went there. The feeling you got when you walked in was that this was the centre of the universe. It was a very cosy universe. Now everything would be segregated: behind a roped-off area there would be Madonna and whomever Madonna hangs out with. But at Max's the atmosphere was incredibly friendly. They were all very eminent people of the day. It was a very unguarded era of rock. You'd do an interview with Sonny and Cher and you'd be privy to their bickering with each other. Sonny's telling me this about Cher while Cher's in another room. John Phillips [of the Mamas and the Papas] did the same when Michelle Phillips walked out of the room.
>
> Now you wouldn't get close to anybody. But in the Max's era you actually got real people. They weren't coached, they weren't dressed, they weren't made up, they didn't have a stylist to tell them what to put on. Janis Joplin wasn't dressed by a team of 12 people, she didn't have four hair stylists on call to make sure her hair looked exactly as they wanted it to. It's totally detached now. Somebody's created it. Nobody created that era. It was the counterculture as it was unfolding and not produced by somebody. That's why it was so special.

Those who went to Max's were helping to create the counterculture, searching for a place in it or hoping to see it in action. Some became famous for being A-list personalities in the back room and nowhere else. Others started out as nobodies and ended up somebodies. Deborah Harry, a Max's waitress, later became lead singer of Blondie. And when Mickey Ruskin later opened a performance space upstairs at Max's, he helped to launch the careers of Bruce Springsteen, Bob Marley, Billy Joel and Alice Cooper.

One of the most colourful and outrageous characters among the Warhol crowd was Brigid Berlin, an artist, Warhol confidante and star of his film *Chelsea Girls*. The elder daughter of Richard Berlin, president of the Hearst Corporation, Brigid – like many of those at Max's – was on a personal journey out of the comfort zone of middle-class America. With the invention of cassettes in the sixties, she pioneered a fad to tape every one of her telephone conversations. Those who took up this fad maintained that nothing they or their brilliant friends said should go unrecorded now that the technology existed to preserve every word for evermore.

And it did not. Lillian Roxon, the compulsive telephone person, did not tape her own calls, but others taped her and each other and all their friends. Lillian is a leading character in the mountains of telephone tapes from that period that still exist in New York. In the 1972 book *Mug Shots*, which included her among the top 200 people in America's "alternate culture", Lillian remarked: "Everybody with their bloody tapes! I mean, people have been taping conversations for years. It's worse than *School for Scandal*. Somebody said they were going to make a Broadway musical from tapes of my telephone conversations, but I bet they don't give me any credit."

At Max's, Brigid Berlin also indulged in her notorious party trick of jabbing anyone who happened to be in range in the buttocks through their clothes with an amphetamine mixture, hoping that the resulting high would make their evening more enjoyable. This earned her an alternative name, Brigid Polk.

The personal freedoms that the sixties opened up were explored every night at Max's, and if you were shocked by people taking recreational drugs or sexually consummating their liaisons, then you were better off staying uptown. Leee Childers, a young photographer escaping from Kentucky, arrived in New York in 1969 on a mission to photograph drag queens: "I thought they were the most astounding people I'd ever seen in my life. Men dressed as women. Drag queens love to be photographed, so that wasn't a difficult task." Before too long he was among the Warhol crowd and at Max's, where he found a scene moving at a pace that was almost too fast for its own good:

First of all you had Brigid Polk sticking needles right through her blue jeans into her butt. And if you walked too slowly past the round table at Max's Kansas City, she'd stick them into you. It's a little depressing scene, but there's no other way to put it. It was pre-Aids. So sex was everywhere. The telephone booth at Max's Kansas City was not for making telephone calls. It was for blow jobs. If you wanted to make a phone call you went down to the corner and used the telephone booth on the street. It was really a rampant time. It was a very dangerous time. We didn't know how dangerous. Of course, none of us knew that a plague was lurking.

Sometimes it went too far. People who would be in the back room at Max's one night would be in the obituaries pages the next night. There was a good photographer. We all knew he was a little weird. I don't want to scare your tape recorder, but they found him with his ankles tied to his wrists tied to his neck, dead at the Chelsea Hotel. It was a sex crime. Of course, no one will ever know who did it. But he was there one night drinking wine and eating chickpeas with us and next day we opened the *Daily News* and he's dead.

But we just kept right on going because it was so much fun. In a way, we were bouncing off the walls. We were always on some kind of drug, always safe drugs, a little speed, a little acid. When you'd see Lillian in the back room at Max's it would be like, "Hi Mom, I'm really stoned." She never judged how crazy you were from one night to the next.

*

In January 1966 *Crawdaddy*, the first magazine devoted to rock and roll criticism, started publication. Its founder was Paul Williams, then a seventeen-year-old freshman at Swarthmore College, Pennsylvania and a fan of the new rock music who saw a gap in the market. "The *New York Times* wasn't going to take rock music seriously, yet wherever I went it was such a central part in people's lives," Williams says. "There needed to be a place where we could talk about why the Rolling Stones and the Byrds meant so much to us." His model was the self-published magazines that science fiction fans sent to each other. His magazine's title came about when he read that the Rolling Stones and the Yardbirds had started playing at the Crawdaddy Club in Richmond, near London. Crawdaddy, meaning crawfish, is a term associated with the American South. "So a piece of American culture came back to America via England."

Almost two years later, in October 1967, Jann Wenner, a former Berkeley student, launched the next serious rock publication, *Rolling*

Stone, in San Francisco. Later came *Fusion*, based in Boston, and *Creem* in Detroit. Lillian wrote, or was written about, in all these magazines. In the late sixties and early seventies several groups of rock writers became established in America, each of which approached the scene from a different angle. Some, such as Robert Christgau, Jon Landau and Ellen Willis, wrote quasi-scholarly, rather serious criticism of the music. Others like Richard Meltzer and Lester Bangs were wild cards, mavericks, "bad boys" who wrote in a style that was part underground, part new journalism but so idiosyncratic that they became cult figures themselves. Meltzer's opening to his 1985 piece "Rock-Crit Blood 'n' Guts (Part 1)" gives a sense of his approach: "Well, for starters, I invented this shit. Rock writing. I was first. Well maybe not *literal* first, just one of the first two-three-four, probably the first to take the ball and actually *run* with the fucker; certainly the sole early manjack you're still reading now. Before Lester Bangs was, I am (and he's dead)."

Lillian was the main figure among another group of writers for whom the aesthetics of the music was less important than the gossip and stories about the singers and bands who made it. With her background in journalism, her skill for placing herself in the story and her fascination for change and new popular movements, Lillian approached the rock scene from the point of view of a classic insider who was privy to the personal lives of the stars and their entourages and was always the first to predict who was destined to become the next hot thing. Jim DeRogatis, biographer of Lester Bangs, has described Lillian and her New York friend and colleague Lisa Robinson as the "Hedda Hoppers of rock, peddling salacious information about the stars".

Lillian first met Lisa Robinson in 1969, soon after the *Rock Encyclopedia*'s publication. She became good friends with her and her husband, Richard, already a disc jockey and columnist, and encouraged Lisa to establish her own career: Lisa later became a leading rock writer, columnist for the *New York Post* and contributing editor for *Vanity Fair*. Lisa says: "Lillian and I were much more aligned psychically. We thought rock and roll was supposed to be about sex and fun and cute boys and not about serious, pretentious criticism. Lillian was incredibly charismatic and all about the gossipy, fun side of the music. She was a real influence on me."

Lillian and Gloria Stavers, editor of the teen magazine *16*, were among the few women journalists on a scene dominated by what Lisa describes as a "boys club of rock critics". She says, "If I had any mentor whatsoever, it was Lillian or Gloria. Lillian totally helped my career. I owe her a lot."

Soon after she met Lillian, Lisa gathered a group of the most important rock writers together at the Robinsons' apartment on the Upper West Side for a series of soirées. The writers included Jon Landau, John Mendelssohn, Dave Marsh, Lenny Kaye, Lester Bangs, Richard Meltzer, Loraine Alterman, Henry Edwards, Vince Aletti and Jim Fouratt.

These parties have since been referred to as a "rock and roll salon" and as the "Collective Conscience", although Lisa disowns both terms. Lenny Kaye remembers Lillian's calming influence among all the egos: "There was a strong sensibility around these journalists. Lillian was very responsible for the good feelings within these meetings." Richard Meltzer recalls the parties sometimes having the sparks to be expected when so many clever people came together: "With the exception of a few early summer parties in 1970 that were fun because they were more free-form and new, Lisa's gatherings were much more like Collective Hell. Pecking orders were established and bringing along 'unwanted' friends was frowned upon. The only members of Lisa's inner circle who were generally tolerant and affable with a wide range of rockwrite folks, who were even willing to consider them 'colleagues', were Lillian and Lenny. And once Lillian was gone, the whole damn thing was over. It was clear she'd been the glue holding whatever it ever was even approximately together."

But for all this, Lillian championed the rock writers as a new breed, and these gatherings served to bring them together in what she described as a "unified force".

*

If the first encyclopedia of rock had been undertaken by anyone else in the club, it could well have been deadly serious, even academic in approach, as many of the guides and encyclopedias that followed it were: Rock Music as Art. In Lillian's hands it turned into a journalist's account of a phenomenon.

Although she was well placed to write the book, she was apparently not the first choice of the publishers, Grosset and Dunlap. According to her, they first approached a show business writer at *Eye*, a New York magazine where Lillian wrote a column called "Elevator" about people on the way up and on the way down; when the show business writer turned the project down, the editor of *Eye* recommended Lillian. Her advance for United States and Canadian rights was $2,500.

Writing the book started out as fun. She could draw on her intimate knowledge of rock and roll going back to her early days with Danny Fields and Linda Eastman, her journey through San Francisco in the Summer of Love and all those nights being confided in at The Scene and Max's Kansas City. "I'd known it and I'd lived it," she told the Australian writer Craig McGregor. But it soon grew beyond the projected paperback into a gargantuan hardcover that finally ran to 613 pages, listing more than 500 entries from Acid Rock to the Zombies, 1,202 rock stars and 22,000 song titles. An appendix of every Cashbox and Billboard top single from 1949 traced the transformation of popular music from "Goodnight Irene" by the Weavers and "Rudolph the Red Nosed Reindeer" by Gene Autry to "Hey Jude" by the Beatles and "I'm a Believer" by the Monkees.

She started writing it in May 1968 and finished the following January. Every album, every year, every member of every group had to be researched from scratch. The book took over her apartment and her life, and was to have disastrous consequences for her health.

Taking no time off from her staff job in the *Sydney Morning Herald* bureau made the task even more formidable, especially in a year as newsworthy as 1968. In August she was dispatched to Hyannis Port, Massachusetts to write about the Kennedy family, shattered by Robert Kennedy's assassination in Los Angeles two months earlier. In October she flew across America and back with the media contingent covering Richard Nixon's presidential campaign. Later, when promoting her book, she spoke of the "strong parallels between rock and politics. The charisma, the preparation, the publicity. Nixon's press secretary, Ron Ziegler, would make a terrific rock manager." The book had to be written at nights, on weekends, in hotel rooms, wherever and whenever she could grab the time. She wrote the Beatles section in a motel in Moline, Illinois while travelling on the Nixon campaign.

She called on helpers for the research. And, in the case of at least one entry, she called on helpers for the writing. When Lillian met him at Max's Kansas City, Donald Lyons was a classics teacher at New York University and the founding film critic for *Interview*, the magazine produced by Andy Warhol's Factory. He later became professor of English at Rutgers University and drama critic for the *Wall Street Journal*. Lillian and Max's seemed to Lyons a natural fit: "She was very funny, at once extremely droll and what you might call maternal, sweet and tolerant. Australians, of course, were a bit like Martians in those days. So it was just wonderful to have this extraordinarily attractive and warm and funny representative of this new place. And she knew everything and she knew everybody."

Lyons had written an article on the Beach Boys for *Rock Scene*, a magazine edited by the Robinsons. One night at Max's he said, "Lillian, I wrote this crap about the Beach Boys. You might as well read it."

So she read it. She said, "Oh this is divine. Why don't you write the Beach Boys segment?" Then we had Chinese dinner near her office in the *Sydney Morning Herald* bureau on Broadway in the old Paramount building, and afterwards we went up there and I just sat down and wrote it in the *Sydney Morning Herald* office. I'm sure she made adjustments. But I've always been very proud of it because Camille Paglia quotes Lillian on the Beach Boys – and they're my words.

(In her 1990 book *Sexual Personae: Art and Decadence from Nefertiti to Emily Dickinson*, Camille Paglia, the American academic and commentator, says that *Don Juan* and the Beach Boys both combine "youth, androgyny, aeration, and speed" and writes: "Lillian Roxon calls the Beach Boys' first album 'a celebration of airiness and speed, speed on the water or the road'.")

"The book became everybody's burden," says Danny Fields. "It was overwhelming. It didn't seem finishable. She was determined to finish it, we wondered if it would ever be finished. And then it was."

*

The encyclopedia sprang with Lillian's vivid approach. She set out to engage readers of all ages, reaching beyond the music to give a sense of what her subjects stood for (as this book's selection from the *Encyclopedia* shows). Of Little Richard, she wrote: "His pompadour was high and his hip action wicked when Elvis was still a pimply kid mowing lawns in Memphis ... Once you have seen Little Richard it is very difficult to take any other rocker seriously. He did it all first." Of the

Shangri-las: "From time immemorial the bitch goddess has haunted and fascinated man. And so, of course, has the girl next door. The Shangri-las were both, a real bargain for the boy who wanted everything in a girl and the girl who wanted to be that everything." Of the Rolling Stones: "The Beatles' songs had been rinsed and hung out to dry. The Stones had never seen soap and water."

At the time the roots of white rock and roll in black rhythm and blues music were still not widely acknowledged. Lillian told the *Washington Post* that the lack of information on black groups was one of the encyclopedia's shortcomings. It was easy to get information on Dylan, the Beatles and the Stones, but not on black performers. "But black artists have a tremendous impact on rock, and they're the best performers. If any white girl had one quarter of Tina Turner's talent she'd be a big star."

She told another interviewer that music was nothing without its audience, and that the same applied to the writing about it: never keep a distance between writer and reader. "Being a journalist I've always written for popular markets. I've always had in mind the average person that buys a publication. They read to be entertained and I've always tried to entertain them. That's what the book was supposed to be. Entertaining."

*

There was a launch party at Max's Kansas City. By May 1970, six months later, the hardcover had gone into its third printing, and the paperback soon followed. "It's the hottest property we've ever had," Peter Workman, the literary packager who sold the deal to Grosset and Dunlap, told the press. For her author's picture on the hardcover dustjacket, Lillian chose a shot by Linda Eastman. "Wonderful what makeup, retouching, fake hair and a friendly photographer will do!" she told Craig McGregor.

Up to 1969 there had been no books on the history of rock and nothing as comprehensive as the *Rock Encyclopedia* in pulling the whole scene together. The year was the beginning of what soon became an explosion in rock publishing. Two other books appeared the same year: *Pop from the Beginning* by the British writer Nik Cohn; and *The Story of Rock* by Carl Belz, an American art historian. Cohn's was a lively, though English-biased, survey of the whole scene; Belz's was an academic account of rock's place in folk, fine and popular art. The year also saw two collections of essays and articles: *Rock Will Stand* edited by Greil Marcus, and *The Age of Rock* edited by Jonathan Eisen.

In its review of these first rock books, the *New York Times Book Review* in February 1970 singled out *Lillian Roxon's Rock Encyclopedia* as "critically concise, extremely knowledgeable, marvellously readable and probably definitive". The *Montreal Star* said the Roxon book "remains the most satisfying of the rock books". The *Los Angeles Times* criticised it for being "too firmly rooted in the present to give her work lasting value and her style is cute to the point of being frequently cloying"; it was equally ungenerous to the other rock books. (See Roxon's own account of the response to the encyclopedia in this book's selection of her writing.)

The book made Lillian a media celebrity. She went on *The Tonight Show Starring Johnny Carson* ("the show was a disaster and I had neuralgia or something for days," she wrote to the Dobbyns), and the *New York Times* featured her in an article about rock fashions. The *New York Times* also ran a profile of her by Craig McGregor, who compared her to Oscar Wilde for her way with words, and to Mohammad Ali for her reflexes: "She is the mistress of the put-down and the send-up, the come-on and the come-uppance, the double-faced about-turn and the blunt, uncompromising insult. She blurts out what she thinks with impossible, calculating honesty, reels off aphorisms, bon mots and salacious insights like a virtuoso, and treats life as an exercise in instant improvised Drama, a hairy Happening."

John Sinclair, founder of the urban radical youth movement White Panthers (whose slogan was "revolution, dope and fucking in the streets"), and manager of the Detroit hard rock group the MC5, congratulated Lillian on the encyclopedia in a letter from his prison cell where he was serving a notorious ten-year prison sentence for the possession of two marihuana joints. In Sydney John Douglas Pringle, Lillian's editor at the *Sydney Morning Herald*, had grave misgivings about rock music's worth: "To me it was the great disaster of our time." Nevertheless he cabled her: "Congratulations on your brilliant success. Regards John Pringle". The New York bureau gave a combined launch party for Lillian's book and another by bureau chief Peter Michelmore, *The Swift Years*, about the nuclear physicist Robert Oppenheimer. The *Herald*'s evening stablemate, the *Sun* in Sydney, announced: "*Sun* girl is toast of New York".

She might have been, but soon after the book's publication Lillian was complaining to friends that her fame had brought her no fortune. She wrote to Richard Neville, editor of the London underground paper *Oz*, and his friend Louise Ferrier: "All anyone asks in Sydney, according to a friend who was just there, was not how I was but how much money I would make." Because the book had started out as a paperback project, she told them, she had negotiated a paperback contract, leaving smaller hardcover royalties. "Of course I had NO idea the hardcover would be so successful, so I have learned a bitter lesson the hard way."

To the Dobbyns in Sydney she wrote:

I'm continuing to find no pleasure whatsoever in my new status in this town. I STILL haven't seen the color of any money. They STILL haven't sold the book to England. I get a lot of exposure but nobody cares about that too much. Everyone is willing enough to talk about a new book, over a nice lunch, which I must say is pleasant, but nobody wants to pay anything. Like would I like to do the definitive book on the changes in medicine in the last five years for a $1000 advance? (They'll hire any unqualified hack if they think they can get a bargain and god knows I'm not qualified. This one came out of a suggestion of mine to do a small book on the new radical doctors.) The worst thing is my publishers want me to do a complete revision for them for NOTHING, a total updating …

The very heavy rock critics now idolise me, not for the book but because I have a collection of pictures taken of myself with Fabian, Ed "Kookie" Byrnes, Col Tom Parker (Elvis's manager) and others. The fifties are very in. Richard Meltzer, a brilliant young writer who just wrote "I was Charles Manson's bunkmate in Boystown" (Manson is furious), found the day he was *born* in my diary when I was 13, and can't get over it.

*

Meltzer had been kicked out of graduate philosophy studies at Yale for his propensity to turn in papers on rock music in response to topics such as "The Ethical Given in Kant's Second Critique". In 1967 Paul Williams took some of Meltzer's undergraduate writings and published them in *Crawdaddy* under the title "The Aesthetics of Rock"; a book of the same name followed three years later. Meltzer first saw Lillian at a Rolling Stones concert at Madison Square Garden in November 1969. She was with Viva (aka Susan Hoffman), a Warhol Superstar. He was indeed aged twenty-four to Lillian's thirty-seven. When they met later, Meltzer remembered Lillian from the concert. "She knew me from my writing and treated me like a celebrity, which was incredibly flattering."

To Lillian, the rock writers were the new celebrities of the age. Until now, the star-makers had been producers and money men like Colonel Tom Parker, George Martin and Phil Spector. But the times were changing yet again. The year of Lillian's encyclopedia was also the year of the Woodstock Festival, the biggest rock event yet, at which 400,000 people spent three days on a farm in upstate New York listening to some of the biggest rock performers of the era. A new consumer group was in the making, and promoters and businessmen took note. The change was reflected at Max's Kansas City too. "In both underground and high society, rock stars were replacing artists, writers and actors as the gods of the time," Yvonne Sewall-Ruskin wrote. "The new, young poets of the back room began to embrace rock as a vehicle for their words. Others were looking to the business side of it for a career. And still others were becoming 'groupies', a scandalous new term of the time."

Lillian argued that the new star-makers, those who had the power to connect the stars with their audience, were now the writers. In the *Rock Encyclopedia*, she acknowledged Gloria Stavers, Danny Fields, Linda Eastman, Richard and Judith Goldstein, Steve Paul, Maggie Makeig, Howard Smith and Jann Wenner "for being stars as well as star-makers". (There was special thanks to Mickey Ruskin and to the core of her Sydney Push friends, Ruth Biegler, Judy Smith, Aviva Layton, and to her brothers Jack and Milo; she dedicated the book to Margaret and Leon Fink.)

When the paperback edition followed in 1971, she went further by recording "one major event of 1970–71 – the emergence of the so-called underground rock press as a vibrant and unified force", and thanked her writing colleagues "for bringing so much vitality to the scene and making the words as magic as the music". When Lenny Kaye met Lillian in 1969 he was a 22-year-old rock writer, soon to make the transition to guitarist for the singer Patti Smith. Kaye says: "In the late sixties and early seventies rock journalism erased the difference between artist and writer. The writer saw himself more as an artist and the artist saw himself being taken seriously. It was a new, compact scene where there were no rules and everyone helped each other up the ladder. Now roles are cut and dried and somewhat predictable. Lillian and Danny Fields were my heavenly go-betweens. Neither wanted anything from me except my friendship and for me to know that what I was doing was worthwhile." Soon after she met him, Lillian filed a story to Australia mentioning Lenny Kaye and Danny Goldberg as two of the "new stars of America".

Danny Goldberg in the late sixties was a teenage writer for *Record World*. He later promoted the group Led Zeppelin and rose to become chairman and chief executive of Mercury Records. When he turned twenty-two, Lillian sent Goldberg a note which he kept years later in his New York office as a source of inspiration. She wrote: "Dear Danny, I was trying to think what else to give you for your birthday which was invaluable and I decided: advice! 1. I think it's important to get ahead and be a star but not if it ruins all the finesse and sensitivity which makes YOU special. It's much more important to be a fabulous human being. Especially if you were one to start off with. 2. If you're mostly with people you REALLY like, being terrific is much easier. I wish someone had told ME that at 22. 3. When the light is on inside you, you're VERY good looking. Better than the Hujar pictures." Goldberg says:

> She was an unbelievable source of strength and inspiration. She had this theory that the people writing about music were the most interesting people at that time. It was extremely intoxicating to be around her. She really changed people's lives. I always felt that Lillian's greatest contribution was what she did privately, that what she was able to do publicly as a journalist was the smaller part of her contribution. It almost diminished her accomplishment to see all the columns she wrote because she was the most incredible advocate for people she decided were special. She endlessly and selflessly promoted them and never wanted anything in return except the emotional rewards. Those people included artists like David Bowie, they included Germaine Greer and they included people like me.

They also included the rock photographers Leee Childers and Bob Gruen, both rookies in 1969, both of whom later credited Lillian with inspiring them to embark on careers that produced some of the most extensive archives in rock photography. She impressed on Gruen the importance of writing his own publicity to get himself known. "Advertise yourself!" she told him. Childers says: "Lillian was the Florence Nightingale of rock and roll. She took on people who she thought were afraid, were on the margin, the people who were trying. Her life was rock and roll, but like me I think it wasn't actually an intention. She fell into it. And once she was into it, she had the heart and the brains to say, 'OK, I'm in rock and roll now. So here I go.'"

But like Florence Nightingale, Lillian's disposition was not always benign. She could be self-confident yet insecure; and along with her outward selflessness towards others went a toughness that came from her determination to overcome obstacles and challenges at a time when the cards were still heavily stacked against professional women. Sometimes this toughness burst out unexpectedly, always against those she believed were giving her a hard time. Peter Coleman, a former Sydney colleague, remembers Lillian hurling a glass of beer at a man who was being obnoxious towards her on the Staten Island ferry. Mary Cantwell, her editor at *Mademoiselle* magazine, wrote of her slugging a woman who had gatecrashed a party. Steven Gaines, who gave Lillian the "mother of rock and roll journalism" title, also recorded her turning on a European female photographer who was rude to her with the response, "You have a face that looks like it's giving birth." Danny Fields puts it this way:

> We learned from Lillian a lot about being professional and getting what you want. And from Gloria Stavers as well. Those two women were the mentors to an entire generation of writers and journalists like me and Danny Goldberg and almost everyone else that came along. Certainly Gloria and Lillian were the most distinguished and had the seniority and experience and had beaten up a good many men in their lifetimes. Not literally. But they had had to face being a woman in a man's industry and had learned to be extremely tough. So they were both very, very important to all of us. And very influential each in her own sense.

After the *Rock Encyclopedia*, New York's *Sunday News* hired Lillian as a music columnist; she was the city's first female rock writer in a mainstream newspaper. Her column ran for two years until her death in

1973 and gave her a readership of millions beyond the confines of the rock press. But just how influential could a writer be in the world of popular journalism? Was Lillian's view of herself and her colleagues as star-makers realistic? At the time it probably was. Before rock videos and the dominance of the electronic media, and before producers and "image makers" became pre-eminent, newspapers were having their last hurrah as the principal communicators of pop and rock culture to a mass audience. Danny Goldberg believes Lillian was in the right place at the right time. "Newspaper journalism's being an influence in the rock scene was an anomaly anyway," he says:

> Radio is the dominant influence because music sells itself. But there was a period then when the commercial radio stations were out of synch with certain trends in popular taste. Newspaper journalism was better positioned to identify music before radio, and Lillian was part of that moment in time. By the mid-seventies radio, and later MTV, became the dominant thing and journalism declined in importance. She had this sense of herself as being larger than just a writer but as an arbiter of taste, and she did it with flair and intensity. Other people writing about music always knew what Lillian thought. She and Danny Fields often together would decide and their views would radiate out. It was a formidable combination. And I don't think there's been anyone like Lillian in newspaper journalism since then. You could be the greatest rock writer in the world today and not have the same influence because journalism itself is a secondary format compared to the electronic media.

Goldberg recalls his involvement as a press agent with the British group Led Zeppelin as a time when he looked to Lillian's influence as a rock writer. Formed in 1968, the group became enormously popular but eschewed contact with the press for several years after a series of poor reviews. "They were the populist favourite that didn't have the snob appeal to the sixties San Francisco-type writers," Goldberg says. "In part this was because their popularity was created by radio. They didn't need the press. So the press resented them for not having discovered them."

In 1973, Led Zeppelin decided to seek press recognition of their success and to talk to writers for the first time. As their press agent,

Goldberg chose Lillian as the first person to interview them: "It typified Lillian's role in the community of critics and writers that having her do it first was the way to start." In her *Sunday News* column on 13 May, Lillian hyped the band and its singer Robert Plant: "At the same time, and this is not a contradiction because, again, there's something innocent in this, too, Plant is inordinately sensitive to criticism of the band (not that he got it from me) and is very quick and very gleeful to point out that despite all the putdowns Led Zeppelin always gets from the intellectuals and the critics, the 'Houses of the Holy' LP took exactly three weeks to get to the number one spot on the charts."

Goldberg says: "What was important was not what she wrote but the fact that she wrote it. If other people saw that Lillian was taking them seriously then that would legitimise them in the eyes of other writers." It was one of the last favours Lillian would do for Goldberg; three months after her story appeared she was dead.

Jim Fouratt, a writer and political activist who knew Lillian from her earlier days in New York, gives her an even more elevated status: "If you asked me who was the world's first pop journalist, in the sense of translating sixties culture, art, fashion, music and politics in a popular way, Tom Wolfe got the credit but I think it was Lillian Roxon. The way she did it was to be in the scene yet objective about it, while Tom Wolfe was around the scene, and reported on it, but was never part of the scene like Lillian was. Lillian genuinely loved rock and roll, not just the music but the lifestyle."

Her love of rock and roll was what impressed Richard Meltzer. But it was a love that could be tempered by the unsparing side of Lillian which the McCartneys had encountered in print. "Compared to actual so-called gossip writers, when Lillian wrote 'scene pieces' she had a playfulness that was so much more authentic, and never nasty or ill-tempered in the slightest," says Meltzer. "She wrote from a state of genuine affection for probably a wider range of rock-roll characters than any other rockwriter I have any recollection of. The only exception I can think of was Carole King. She hated Carole King (but then so did most of her colleagues)."

In the early sixties King and her husband, Gerry Goffin, were a successful songwriting team working in New York's famous Brill Building, where some of the great pop hits of the pre-Beatles era were produced. That cut no ice with Lillian by the time Carole King sang her own way into the charts with "You've Got a Friend" a decade later. In her *Sunday News* column in June 1971 Lillian declared:

> Carole King may have a number one single and a number one album, but I find her as boring as my girlfriends who are always on the phone to me whining about the problems they have "communicating" and having "meaningful relationships". She is like every messed-up neurotic girl you ever had to confront in group therapy. Sincere, certainly, well-meaning, too – a nice girl, not bad looking, super-talented, but exasperating and totally unexciting. You know, of course, what her success means – that rock is going to go into a "Dark Shadows" period. Those moody broody songs about getting it all together and facing the world bravely are going to take over the airwaves, and then what are we going to dance to? The Pathetique Sonata? ... You can learn more about being a human being from Tina Turner's body language than from all of Carole's fortune cookie philosophising.

Richard Meltzer was always sceptical of the power and influence of his fellow rock writers. After the late sixties he became disillusioned with the rock scene and left New York in 1975. He says:

> As to influence, she probably had very little. There wasn't enough time for that, and the whole rock press degenerated very quickly into the garbage it is today. But to put it in perspective, hardly anybody from that era (up to the time of Lillian's death) had much "influence". Even Lester Bangs (in spite of the absurd claims of Cameron Crowe et al. that he influenced *them*) influenced virtually no one. Careerism came to the forefront by 1973–74. There was very little room any more for the nuances of voice and expression.

Lillian's dream of the rock writer as star and star-maker, as a figure at the centre of the culture, was a short-lived one. And, as she was living out this dream in the late sixties, a towering figure from Down Under arrived and departed from her life, providing Lillian with another colourful friendship and the New York crowd with much fascination.

Chapter 15 Lillian and Germaine

The revolutions in music and lifestyle were well advanced by August 1970 when another freedom movement opened up. At the height of that New York summer, 25,000 women marched down Fifth Avenue to mark the fiftieth anniversary of the day women won the right to vote. For many, this event symbolized the start of the women's liberation movement. Lillian Roxon filed a report on the march for the *Sydney Morning Herald* which turned into something of a landmark piece itself.

The *Herald* splashed her story on the front page on 28 August with a picture of the marching women beneath the headline "There Is a Tide in the Affairs of Women", followed by the dateline "New York, Thursday: Lillian Roxon cables a biased report". She opened her story: "This is the hardest piece I have ever had to write in my life. I am supposed to be telling what happened when 25,000 women marched down Fifth Avenue last night on the 50th anniversary of the day women won the right to vote. As is customary in my business I am supposed to be telling it briskly and factually and without bias. Fat chance. I'm so biased I can hardly think straight. My emotions are all in a turmoil and I don't know where to start." (Lillian's article is reproduced in full in this book's selection of her writing.)

For the *Herald* at the time, this was an unconventional, almost rebellious way of treating a front-page news story. The paper's management, under the chairmanship of Sir Warwick Fairfax, was conservative on two of the biggest issues of the day, the emerging voices of feminism and the rising tide of opposition to the Vietnam War. It was particularly strict about keeping news stories free from reporters' interpretations. Something of an undeclared war was being waged between news executives on the fifth floor and management on the fourteenth floor over the paper's treatment of the women's movement. Sir Warwick, who had access to all correspondence from the news editor's office, once rebuked a news executive for having addressed a letter to a reader as Ms. The honorific Ms was not *Herald* style, the chairman pointed out. The executive argued that, because the woman had signed her own name as Ms, he felt it was only courteous to reply in kind. To which Sir Warwick responded: "It was most discourteous of *her* to write to us and sign it that way."

So when Lillian's story landed off the teleprinter, Alan Dobbyn, standing in for David Bowman as news editor, decided to take a risk. "There was a conjunction of things," Dobbyn says. "There was Lillian's excellent report, there was a splendid picture and there was Doug Verity, who was an assistant to the news editor. Verity was greatly taken by the picture. He said, 'I know the heading: There is a Tide in the Affairs of Women.' All of these things came together to encourage us to do something adventurous. It was a bit out of character for the *Herald* at that time. But no thunderbolts descended on us. I thought it was a very effective front page."

When she saw it in New York, Lillian wrote her appreciation to Dobbyn, her former bureau chief there:

> Not a minute too soon to thank you for whatever you had to do to get my women's lib story on page one. It was really something. And I felt I simply had to counter the stand the blokes took here, especially Lea [Fitzgerald, the *Australian Financial Review* correspondent] who is very uneasy about it all. I don't know why they feel so threatened. As someone said recently, the only reason men don't want to see women free is because they're not free themselves. Come to think of it who said that was the big G, Germaine Greer in London, who has just written a book called *The Female Eunuch* with lots of four letter words. She is seven feet tall and a bully and about the only female I know who is NOT a eunuch. Good looking but. She dedicated the book to me and my cockroaches which I thought was kind of her. (Four other girls got a mention in what I thought was the all time weird dedication.)

*

The story behind this dedication began in late 1968 when Germaine Greer visited New York, a visit that tested the feisty friendship between these two formidable women. Germaine returned to London and wrote her great work *The Female Eunuch* – first published in October 1970 and never out of print since – that became the bible of feminism for a whole generation of women. It began with the following dedication:

> This book is dedicated to LILLIAN, who lives with nobody but a colony of New York roaches, whose energy has never failed despite her anxieties and her asthma and her overweight, who is always interested in everybody, often angry, sometimes bitchy, but always involved. Lillian the abundant, the golden, the eloquent, the well and badly loved; Lillian the beautiful who thinks she is ugly, Lillian the indefatigable who thinks she is always tired.

Shorter dedications to four other women followed. But none struck as many sparks as the one to Lillian. She always believed the cockroach image was a put down that overwhelmed whatever else Germaine wrote about her. There was something very Australian about the double-edged friendship of these two strong women who had come out of the same proving ground, the Sydney Push. As independent women who had broken free of a heavily male culture, they often seemed to others to be competitors more than compatriots. Germaine had her own connections in the British rock scene. And Lillian had already lived the life of a liberated women well before Germaine came along with her book on women's liberation.

The first Lillian heard of the dedication in *The Female Eunuch* was when Tony Delano, an Australian journalist working for the *Sunday Mirror* in London, rang to tell her about it. "He thought it was lovely. I thought it was simply horrible." Delano says: "I think Germaine probably made the dedication in commemoration of their times together in New York. It seemed to me that Germaine and Lillian did get on then. Germaine hadn't been to New York before. She relied on Lillian then: she chose Lillian as her guide to New York."

*

Germaine had come a long way since we last saw her arriving in Sydney from her home town of Melbourne in 1959, the year Lillian left for New York. Armed with a first-class Master of Arts degree in English from Sydney University and a Commonwealth scholarship, she left for Cambridge University in 1964, where she took her PhD three years later. By 1968 she was teaching at the University of Warwick. That year, too, saw her marriage to Paul du Feu, a hunky London construction site worker with a degree in literature himself. It lasted three weekends. Du Feu later told *Coronet*, an American women's magazine, that Germaine's "favoured method of conversation was to run both sides of the dialogue", while Germaine herself was quoted by the *New York Times* saying that du Feu had tried to "conquer" her in the "crudest form of colonisation". While at Warwick, Germaine also started appearing on *Nice Time*, a Granada Television program on which she grooved and jousted with rock stars, using the show as a launching pad for her later media stardom.

By the end of 1968 Germaine was finally ready, as she put it, to confront the New York scene. Up to then Lillian and Germaine appear to have met only in passing through mutual Push friends. Lillian first glimpsed her in Melbourne in 1959 when Germaine was working as a waitress while completing her English–French honours degree. The sighting was in the coffee shop where Fred Astaire, Anthony Perkins, Ava Gardner and others from *On the Beach* (then filming in Melbourne) hung out: "She had purple hair and was the first person in my life I had ever seen wear red stockings." Germaine later spoke of this period to Clyde Packer, the Australian media figure: "I was a waitress lots of times, but the best time was when Goldy [Brian Goldsmith] opened a restaurant in Toorak Road. By that time, I knew a lot of people in television and the media and I ran the backroom for him where all the television people used to come after hours ..." Germaine told Packer: "I believe in kicking ass and taking names, talking loud and drawing a crowd."

It was Christmas 1968 when Germaine landed in New York, preparing to call on their common Push background to stay with Lillian. She was not yet rich or famous. Lillian was already a star in the New York rock and underground scene centred on Max's Kansas City; if Germaine had designs on drawing a crowd there, Lillian was well placed to introduce her. The two women were a study in physical contrasts. Lillian was thirty-six, short, round, still a beauty with blonde, shoulder-length hair, but starting to suffer from the asthma that would eventually kill her.

Germaine was twenty-nine, tall, slender, striking, with dark hair. Lillian later described Germaine arriving in New York dressed like a counter-culture queen in "her embroidered satin antique jacket from the Chelsea Antique Market, her Bessarabian Princess's Defloration robe, a black net and silver belly dancer's vest and see-through chiffon velvet elephant pants".

What happened next did not conform to Germaine's expectations and appears to have endangered their friendship from the start. Lillian was writing the *Rock Encyclopedia* and fighting to meet her publisher's deadline. In these pre-computer days the book and its rising tide of research papers had swamped her small apartment on East 21st Street. She told Germaine she was in no position to put her up and had booked her instead into the Broadway Central Hotel, a budget hotel which, she believed, matched Germaine's financial circumstances. The Broadway Central had been one of nineteenth-century New York's grand hotels, known then as the Grand Central. By the late 1960s it had gone very far downhill. Lillian later wrote about this episode; but Germaine had never discussed it until, thirty years later, I approached her for the story behind the dedication to Lillian. She wrote back:

> My difficulty is that I did not know Lillian Roxon very well. By the time I came to Sydney she was in New York. I went to New York in 1968 thinking to stay with her but she would not let me. Instead she put me in the Broadway Central, a welfare hotel where people screamed and ran up and down stairs all night, from which I escaped the next day. I probably spent in all no more than five or six hours of quality time with Lillian after *The Female Eunuch* came out; of course she made it seem rather more.
>
> I admired her but she disliked me and did not bother to hide it.
>
> We could talk, I dare say, but I doubt if it's worth the trouble to you.

Germaine's letter raised more questions than it answered. Why had she dedicated one of the most influential books of the twentieth century to a woman who disliked her and had dumped her in a cheap hotel full of mad people? Was there more to it than this? If they had spent a mere six hours of quality time together after *The Female Eunuch*, what about before? Was Germaine simply showing her unpredictable side with this reply? Despite her apparent dismissal of Lillian, her last line left a door ajar.

*

She stood just inside the open door to her study at Newnham College, Cambridge, a tall figure in a long, billowing dress, the sunlight from the window at the other end of the room shining through her greying hair. At fifty-eight Germaine Greer had lost nothing of her commanding presence. She had six other substantial books under her belt now, but none as big a publishing phenomenon as *The Female Eunuch*. She looked up from an open book in her hands, glanced at me quizzically over the top of her spectacles and invited me to sit on one of her generous sofas, apologising for the way her students had tousled them. We chatted about the Cambridge gardens, then I asked her to recall thirty years into the past and her first meeting with Lillian Roxon. "I didn't have any money in 1968," she began.

Teaching at Warwick University I had a minute salary which barely paid to keep a roof over my head. But I was equipped with the Push addresses for people abroad. So it seemed the most natural thing in the world that, when I went to New York, I would look up Lillian. It was because of the way the Push did things it never occurred to me that I couldn't just doss on Lillian's floor. Enough people had dossed on my floor. We had the impression we knew each other because we knew so much about each other. Usually, contact between Australians abroad is very easy. People are very understanding and we all understand the way we're reacting to things because we all react in a predictable way.

And Lillian was a Libertarian, which was a plus and should have brought us closer together. But a lot of Libertarians will tell you that she really wasn't, that she really wanted to be mated and monogamous and have some kind of normal Jewish girl's life. That was always there somewhere. I arrived and she lived in a very over-heated flat opposite the police station. I was perfectly prepared to sleep on her floor and clean her flat and do all that stuff and sort her out a bit, but she didn't want that – at all. She just *did* not want me there.

The Broadway Central Hotel was located near Broadway and 3rd Street, about eighteen blocks south of Lillian's place. When Germaine arrived there during the day to check in, she was told her room would not be ready before midnight. "As I stood there all kinds of human flotsam and jetsam were creeping up to the desk, junkies and madmen. It wasn't that I was afraid. I was vulnerable. I just didn't know the score. It was like dropping someone into a snake pit." Germaine had academic friends to contact and went that evening to a party on Riverside Drive, near Columbia University. She met Andrew Sinclair, the English novelist and historian, who came to her aid.

He decided it was a *coup de foudre*, in his English-French, and that he wasn't going to let me out of his sight ever again. He forgot about this within 24 hours, but just right then it was a *coup de foudre*. He said to me "Where are you staying?" I said "the Broadway Central." He said, "What?" I said, "Well, my friend Lillian Roxon has booked me in and I really should go there because she's gone to the trouble." He said, "Well, I'm coming with you. You're not going there by yourself." So off I went with Andrew Sinclair to the Broadway Central. We couldn't go up in the lift to my room because there was someone being brought down who wasn't in a very fit state. The door opened and this person was pushed out in a wheelchair death rattling, with a cigarette stuffed in his face to make him look well.

Andrew said, "No – come on!" I said, "No, no." So we went upstairs and a drag queen, grotesquely made up with lipstick and five o'clock shadow everywhere, in a dress made of an Indian bedspread, came running down the stairs saying [mocking loud, distraught New York accent]: "Oh my God, the police are after me. I didn't pay my cab fare." I said, "How much is your cab fare?" [Loud, distraught:] "Ninety-five dollars." I said, "Where the fuck did you come from, Mexico City?" The police come thundering down after this guy. He runs screaming into the lobby in his platform soles. And we find my room, a corridor which had been partitioned off and the door didn't shut. But I still slept there. But, of course, I didn't sleep there again.

And I never understood why Lillian did that. Was she trying to teach me that life is real, life is earnest or something? Did my sort of convent girl thing annoy her or what? But she was Margaret [Fink]'s great, great friend and I just had to persevere and try to get her to like me. So I didn't say anything about the Broadway Central. I just moved out.

Next day Germaine moved to the apartment of other friends at 110th Street on the edge of Harlem, a long way from Lillian on 21st Street and the epicentre of New York's counterculture at Max's Kansas City.

Andrew Sinclair recalls meeting Germaine at the Algonquin Hotel before the Broadway Central drama unfolded:

> I met Germaine at the Algonquin, I think, at some literary party. She was terrified at returning to the Broadway Central Hotel. I offered her a couch at my New York publisher's. Bold girl, she elected to go back to her hotel. "Not without me," I said, tho' both of us were penniless. You must understand, I had always treated her as a Victorian lady, which she liked, and she had considered me as an "intellectual lumberjack", her terms.
>
> Arriving by underground, we found two members of the NYPD wheeling out a stiff on a wheelchair. "How do you know he is a stiff?" Germaine said. "Because they can't light the cigarette in his mouth." Going upstairs to G. G.'s hotel room, we encounter a young drag queen, mascara running from his eyes. "Give me twenty bucks," he says, "or they'll bust me." I take out my last two dollars and give it to him. "Best I can do," I say. He puts lipstick on my hand. At Germaine's cubby hole, I show her how to jam a chair and wardrobe behind her door handle to deter intruders. We do not even kiss goodnight, but we have continued to respect each other mightily – she's a fine woman.

Lillian's account of the visit appeared in *Woman's Day* in May 1971, soon after *The Female Eunuch* hit the international best-seller lists. The Australian magazine hoped to capitalise on their New York correspondent's being the dedicatee of this sensational book and asked Lillian to write about Germaine. In her article Lillian wrote:

> Just before she got the idea of writing *The Female Eunuch* Germaine, who had been living in England, came over to New York for a holiday. She had an open invitation to stay with me but, as luck would have it, she couldn't have chosen a worse time.

I had just finished covering a Presidential election, I was in the process of finishing my *Rock Encyclopedia*, I had just developed asthma and I had put on, in a matter of a few months, 30lb [13kg] I could definitely live without. My home was covered with news-papers and pages of my manuscript, New York was in the throes of a cockroach plague, I was exhausted and bad-tempered and definitely NOT in the mood to entertain anyone, let alone a lady larger than life and twice as clever.

I told her I was awfully sorry but I just had to be left to cope with my troubles alone. She said, without a trace of compassion, that it was all in my mind, and the love of a good man would solve every-thing, her usual solution, but that's small comfort when your breath comes whistling out like a tea kettle and your publisher wants your manuscript fast.

So I moved her into the only hotel she said she could afford. When I rang to ask how she liked it, she said in her best Cambridge Debating Society voice, "Listen, I don't mind the junkies. I don't mind the trans-vestites. I don't even mind the prostitutes. But I do object to riding down in a lift with corpses." I hadn't known that this particular hotel had the highest homicide rate in the world.

In its nineteenth-century heyday, the Broadway Central was the scene of an infamous assassination when Jim Fisk, a rogue tycoon, was shot dead on its staircase by an erstwhile business partner in 1872. Some things, it seemed, had not changed.

*

Despite this troubled start, Lillian and Germaine did get together dur-ing Germaine's visit. In Germaine's recollection their connection was clouded by Lillian's preoccupations with work and her asthma:

There was a lot of stuff going on and I think that was one of the things that annoyed her. I'd go and see her and she'd be doing her thing: "I'm really very busy, I've got to work." And I'd hear her on the phone becoming agitated. She'd be asking for a press pass or something and they'd be stonewalling her, and I could hear her hyperventilating. I could hear the asthma attack coming on. And all I could think was, "I mustn't play this asthma game because if you reward this phenomenon she'll do it more." And I could see it was killing her. She was short of breath, her heart was labouring, probably, already. I never knew how much she ate, and that might be one reason why she didn't want me there. Because I would have stopped her eating.

She interpreted my behaviour – which was to keep very calm when she was having an asthma attack, and to try to distract her – because I could see her working on it: "I can't breathe, I can't breathe." And I'm an asthmatic myself. She lived in this terribly dry environment. That flat was a tinder-box. I couldn't breathe in it. So I would try to be very cool with her. "Come on, let's go and get something to eat, let's go for a walk, let's get out of this apartment, let's get into some moist air." And she would think I was just being a cow, that I wasn't responding to her misery. I was her junior by miles, you know, in every way. She was a seasoned old hand and I was this convent school girl. So I tried that and it didn't work. She would get very, very angry with me and that would make the situation worse. So I couldn't intervene. But I tried.

At twenty-nine, already a woman of the world with self-confessed love affairs behind her, a TV persona and an authoritative book on the way about the history of women's sexual oppression, Germaine was hardly an innocent convent school girl. Her account reveals little sympathy for Lillian's need for solitude as a writer up against a publishing deadline, something Germaine as a brilliant academic, with three degrees to her name, must have understood. She never mentions the *Rock Encyclopedia*'s central role in Lillian's life at this time. Did she consider it unworthy? Or, at a time when Germaine had her own standing in the rock and roll community in Britain, was Lillian's forthcoming book a source of competitive friction between the two women?

Lillian's New York friends remember Germaine's visit through a somewhat different prism. They remember Lillian taking Germaine to Max's Kansas City and introducing her to the rock, art and Warhol crowd there. Donald Lyons, the academic and Beach Boys essayist for the *Rock Encyclopedia*, recalls having a spirited fight with Germaine at Max's one night over their differing interpretations of Shakespeare's *Antony and Cleopatra*. Danny Fields, rock manager, publicist and a central figure of Max's back room, says:

Germaine wasn't world-famous then. "My friend Germaine": she was a divine intellectual scholar friend of Lillian's. It seemed to me that Lillian invented Germaine. Lillian was always inventing people. Germaine hung out in Max's with the drag queens and the drug addicts all because of Lillian. Germaine got her taste of the real New York because of Lillian. Judy Collins and Lillian were friends and Leonard Cohen too. Lillian had great taste.

We would not have met this woman who was soon to become a world-famous feminist had it not been for Lillian, and Germaine would have missed something. She would have missed knowing Jackie Curtis [a drag queen and Warhol superstar] and the people in the back room at Max's who were wildly amusing and brilliant. Betty Friedan didn't hang out at Max's. Other great feminists didn't. Germaine, by doing that, became one of us. She wasn't writing from a distance or from afar or an isolated feminist position. We could talk to Germaine. We could talk to Germaine about fucking. We could talk to this distinguished author and intellectual about fucking.

Danny Goldberg remembers Lillian championing Germaine in the way she hyped other Australian visitors to her New York circle. But there was something ineluctably different about Germaine: none of the others ended up on the cover of *Life* magazine as Germaine would two years later. "It seemed to me that Lillian devoted [herself] full-time to publicising Germaine," says Goldberg.

They were together all the time before *The Female Eunuch*. In New York, they were inseparable for many, many weeks. Lillian was constantly having lunch with this one with Germaine or breakfast with that one with Germaine and taking Germaine to Max's or Germaine to this or Germaine to that. There is no way you could have paid anyone to do the PR that Lillian did out of her heart and out of her belief in her friend. I was there for that. I'm sure Germaine had other allies and had something to say that the world wanted to hear. But there is no question that Lillian was an extraordinary champion before most people in the US knew who Germaine was. Every day it was Germaine this and Germaine that. I believe later they had terrible fights.

One fight led to a severing of their relationship for more than a year. It happened one night in the back room at Max's Kansas City, although its origin and nature are unclear. Germaine gives a graphic account of it: "I came in and joined a party that Lillian was already in and she just ripped into me. She abused me up hill and down dale – everything about me. My face, my hands, my feet, my voice, my mind, my past, my future, my everything. The New Yorkers were just sort of sitting there as if this was some sort of mud wrestling contest and I was made to respond in kind. But there was no way I was going to do that. And besides, Lillian was too vulnerable. So I just sort of sat there with tears running down my face thinking, 'Why are you doing this? What have I done?' It was as if there was no need for it to be justified: 'I feel like giving you a pistol-whipping with my tongue and I'm doin' it and I'm doin' it good.' And I just couldn't believe the brutality of it. So I left."

It must have been one of the few times in her life when Germaine failed to respond to a verbal pistol-whipping, if that is what it was. How could a woman of her strength and verbal skills have remained so uncharacteristically passive? The survivors from that time at Max's have little recollection of this sensational incident, possibly because so many sensational things happened every night at Max's in 1968 and 1969. But happen it did, and it was possibly the culmination of an inner competitive tension between the two women that found its outlet in a public display.

Lillian was proprietorial about New York and enjoyed taking charge of visitors. Much as she might have needed Lillian to introduce her to the city's late sixties underground life, Germaine was not a person to be taken charge of. Germaine says: "I think what Lillian wanted, if she wanted to have anything to do with me at all, was to sort of be my agent in New York, that I would do what she said and I would meet the people she said. And she had a very odd way of doing that. She would say things like, 'Here is Germaine Greer, Miss Dover Heights 1956.' Gee, thanks." [Dover Heights was then on the edge of Sydney's most exclusive suburbs.]

It was almost as if the two women had too much in common: independence, drive, energy and an Australian background combined with a desire for stardom on a wider stage. New cultural frontiers were being explored and both of them wanted to lead the way. Their competitive edge was often apparent. Marion Hallwood, a Sydney friend then at

Columbia University, says: "Lillian would sometimes express political opinions. Lillian was having lots of direct encounters with politicians around that time, with the Nixon presidential campaign. She knew lots of details. But because Germaine had access to academics in New York she would score points. Germaine would say, 'Oh that's just gossip. All you know is gossip, Lillian.' That was one of her put down phrases."

Jim Fouratt says: "Lillian and Germaine had in common the fact that they gravitated towards intelligence. In some ways Lillian then was more successful than Germaine. Lillian Roxon was probably the warmest and nicest cultural mover and groover in New York at that time. It might have been because she was Australian: Australians are very direct and very kind. She didn't play games of the sort that occurred around the Warhol Factory. A lot of that was drug-induced. But Lillian always remembered what she'd said. Then there was a falling out between her and Germaine. There seems to be something about Australians criticising their own."

*

Germaine Greer returned to Britain in early 1969, ready to embark on the book that would make her famous. While writing *The Female Eunuch*, she also contributed to *Oz*, the London underground magazine edited by the Australian Richard Neville. (A few years earlier, Neville had helped to create the Sydney version of *Oz*, one of the first counterculture publications of the sixties.) In her work for *Oz*, Germaine wholeheartedly embraced the counterculture's demystification of sexual taboos. There, and later in *The Female Eunuch*, her approach to sexual liberation drew on the libertarian Push ethos she had brought with her from Sydney. Women, she argued, had been separated from their libidos, their faculty of desire, their sexuality. Like beasts on farms castrated in order to serve their master's ulterior motives, to be fattened and made docile, women had been cut off from their capacity for action.

Germaine's cover story for the February 1969 edition of *Oz* remains a landmark of counterculture journalism. "The Universal Tonguebath: A Groupie's Vision" was by-lined "DR G – the only groupie with a Ph.D in captivity". On the cover, in the elephant pants outfit Lillian later described, Germaine posed in three striking shots with Vivian Stanshall, singer of the Bonzo Dog Doo-Dah Band, a freaky English group: unzipping his fly, squatting behind him with breasts bared, and bowing in apparent homage at his feet. After the *Oz* piece appeared, Germaine described herself to the *New York Times* as not just a groupie but a super-groupie: "Supergroupies don't have to hang around hotel corridors. When you are one, as I have been, you get invited backstage." She told *Screw*, a New York sex paper: "My sisters ... get mad at me for calling myself superwhore, supergroupie and all that stuff."

"All that stuff" was partly about creating an extreme image that went with her clarion call to action. Lillian was happy enough to shock people by describing herself as a groupie, the groovy term born of the new rock culture; so was Germaine. Describing *yourself* was one thing, but in some of her writings Germaine described *others* in ways that shocked even the underground crowd. In 1969 Germaine became a co-founder of *Suck*, a sex paper based in Amsterdam where censorship was not the problem it was in Britain. It was launched soon after *Screw* started in New York, with two other founders, the Americans Jim Haynes and Bill Levy. *Suck* pushed the boundaries of pornography beyond a hetero-sexual focus on female bodies to include homosexual and lesbian sex and the fantasies of women. "Sex has no frontiers, no borders, no boundaries ... only pioneers of experience," it declared. Some of its "experiences", though, were decidedly shaky. One issue, the "special family issue", was devoted to the theme of sex with children under the heading "friendly families fuck together frequently".

In a column for *Suck* that Germaine herself wrote under the name Earth Rose, no one's privacy was considered sacred. Tom Wolfe, the American writer, later wrote of meeting Germaine and Jim Haynes at a restaurant in London in August 1969, soon after the first issue of *Suck* appeared. Germaine struck him as a "thin, hard-looking woman with a tremendous curly electric hairdo and the most outrageous Naugahyde mouth I had ever heard on a woman". She shocked him. They showed Wolfe their first issue and he started reading "Earth Rose's" gossip col-umn about people who, he assumed, were fictitious. Then he came across an item that said: "Anyone who wants group sex in New York and likes fat girls, contact Lillian Roxon."

Wolfe considered Lillian a friend. They had met and corresponded in New York, Wolfe having written to her once about an article she had proposed: "Needless to say I'll be anxious to see your article. I'll have it bound in kangaroo." Now – as he later recalled in his essay "The Me Decade and the Third Great Awakening" – he was confronted with her name in this newspaper full of "gaping thighs, moist lips, stiffened giblets, glistening nodules, dirty stories, dirty poems". Other friends of Germaine/Earth Rose's, some well known and all of them named, were similarly treated: one had "just recovered from a case of clap"; another "does not like giving head".

In New York, *Screw* picked up and republished Germaine's columns. The item on Lillian appeared within months of Germaine's visit to New York, and while she was researching and writing *The Female Eunuch*. It showed little sense of feminist solidarity towards a woman living alone in a big city. How could it be justified? Germaine later explained that her reason for joining the *Suck* editorial board "was that we needed an antidote to the exploitative pornography of papers like *Screw* and *Hustler*. I tried to insist on using male bodies as often as female, invading the privacy of the editors, naming names in sex news, and developing a new kind of erotic art, away from tits'n'ass and the peep-show syndrome." Her co-editors were "quite happy to let me expound my utopian sexual theories and utterly indifferent to them". What did any of this have to do with exposing people to risk?

Lillian received harassing telephone calls after Germaine's item appeared. She wrote to Richard Neville and his friend Louise Ferrier in London two months later, soon after the *Rock Encyclopedia* came out: "You can tell Germaine endless little men rang after *Screw* reprinted the *Suck* thing whatever it was, I never did see it. I wasn't feeling very well and all those calls were deeply depressing so she is to consider herself FULLY revenged and make her peace with me at once. I really have to get some sleep. I can't change my phone number at the moment for the fairly obvious reason that at this of all times I have to be continually accessible. Who knows when some Hollywood producer will want to do a film version?"

Louise Ferrier (who once found her own name in Earth Rose's column) recalls the reaction of Lillian's London friends: "We were outraged. Lillian seemed to throw it off, but I'm sure she was very hurt. I was surprised she didn't react more violently. But I think she understood Germaine better than Germaine understood her. I think Germaine saw Lillian as a rival, which was at the root of it all."

At the end of this electrically charged year there was a rapprochement. It seems to have been Lillian rather than Germaine who initiated it. At Christmas 1969, on the first anniversary of their fight in Max's back room, Lillian rang Germaine in London to tell her, "Enough is enough." Lillian wrote to Richard and Louise: "I made my peace with Germaine, rang her up. It was so boring fighting. As Richard says we really have to stick together." But the wounds never really healed.

Germaine Greer's recollections of Lillian Roxon thirty years after these events are overshadowed by dramas: the Broadway Central affair, the verbal pistol whipping in Max's back room, the introducing of Germaine as Miss Dover Heights. But there is also room for praise. "Even though my relationship with Lillian was such a mess," Germaine says, "I admired her."

> I thought she was very strong. She thought she was weak, but I could see that she was very strong. She was a mass of contradictions. And she had great physical presence, even though she was wearing outsize shapes of clothing. There are all sorts of things about Lillian that are so terrific. She is so good at telling stories against herself. I found in Lillian a very energetic, very engaged, passionate, receptive, democratic intelligence. I was interested in her as an independent woman. I'm interested in independent women who make independent lifestyles and who run their own sexual economies the way they'd never run them. Nowadays, of course, it's all proliferated way beyond our wildest dreams. You have people having their wombs cut out so they can be androgynous and all this kind of thing. Well, none of that was going on in those days. It was a much riskier business in many ways.

*

In the last two years of her life, Lillian had an influential platform in New York as a popular feminist as well as a rock expert. After the *Rock Encyclopedia*'s success, Mary Cantwell, then managing editor of *Mademoiselle*, a high-circulation women's magazine published by Condé Nast, hired Lillian to write a monthly column called "The Intelligent Woman's Guide to Sex". Every magazine seemed to be starting a sex column on the back of the sexual revolution and the women's liberation movement, but Cantwell instructed Lillian that hers was to be different. It started in March 1972 with Lillian's attack on sex manuals written by scientists and doctors and on pornography: both were part of a "male conspiracy to make sex a sensible and efficient physical operation with absolutely no regard for the spiritual and emotional forces which motivate it". Mary Cantwell says: "Lillian once told me she thought the best sex manual ever written for heterosexuals was one written for gay men: that the foreplay techniques discussed in that book were the best advice you could give to anyone."

In her *Mademoiselle* columns, Lillian married her discussions of sex with the rock world. "Why do Bob Dylan or the Grateful Dead or even, say, the Bee Gees have more to tell us about love and sex than Dr Reuben?" she asked. "It is time we created our own definitions of sexuality and got away from those imposed on us by people whose narrowness can only strangle whatever it is they have to say." In the last column before she died, she related a discussion of a book about Janis Joplin and her search for sexual fulfilment to the dangers of looking to sex as an easy solution to everyday problems. Sex, Lillian wrote,

> shouldn't be used just to calm you down, or to send you to sleep, or to put some distance between you and your problems. It shouldn't be used to give you control over another person. Or to make you feel you're good at something. It shouldn't be used for all those things – but it is. If someone could have persuaded Janis to find other ways to cope with loneliness and boredom, then she would have had narrower, more realistic motives for her sexual relationships. She would certainly have chosen better people, that is people who would have been more helpful to her as a suffering human being. There is, of course, a little of all of us in Janis.

The *Mademoiselle* columns spoke to her readers in a direct, motherly way and elicited considerable response from readers. When Lillian died, Mary Cantwell's instinct was to end the column. But the magazine commissioned work three months in advance, and the staff argued that Lillian's following among readers should not be wasted. So Lillian Roxon's by-line and column continued to appear in *Mademoiselle* in 1973 for three months after her death.

Lillian became firm friends with Mary Cantwell, who was divorced and raising two teenage daughters. She visited their house in Greenwich Village with gifts of a Tiffany's box inscribed "The Divine Miss C" and pencils inscribed "Big Time Editor" for Mary, and a lavender-painted box for her eldest daughter which Lillian told her was to hide her secrets in:

"Every child should have a place to hide their secrets from their mother." Cantwell met Lillian when her health was starting to suffer from asthma, her weight was increasing from the effects of the cortisone she took to fight it and her sartorial answer to it all was a "collection of strange floating robes".

Cantwell says: "She had a conservative streak that people didn't realise. That was why she liked coming to my house, with my two children. She kept saying, 'When I get it together'. I think she'd like to have lived that herself." Interviewed once by Louise Ferrier, her Australian friend from *Oz* magazine, Lillian said: "I'm very romantic about marriage. I think it's wonderful. How could you ever do away with it? But some married people think it's awful. I have friends who say to me, 'Oh to have the luxury of living alone.'"

Confronted with a conflict between these two states, Lillian's feminist instinct for women to live out their independence usually prevailed. One woman who experienced this was Lily Brett, then a young Australian journalist whom Lillian had befriended in New York in 1967. Impressed by her talent, and possibly seeing in Lily a reflection of her own earlier drive to establish herself as a writer, Lillian encouraged her to stay in New York and to pursue a writing career there. Lily had a boyfriend back in Australia and planned to return to marry him. "Lillian then suggested to me something that nobody else had ever suggested," Lily says.

> She suggested to me that there was a life to be had for women outside marriage, outside children. There are very few things one remembers in life for decades. This was 1967 when the goal of all women I knew in Australia was to get married, to land a boy, to land a man – especially if, like me, you came from Jewish parents. My parents would have been happy for me to get married at sixteen if anybody had wanted to marry me then. But Lillian said, "Don't. Don't get married. Come back to New York, you're so talented." Nobody had ever suggested to me that I was talented. I just thought that was the job I did. What Lillian said shocked me because everything to do with my own self-esteem and my own sense of failure or success was bound up in whether I got married or not. It was a feminist notion way before its time. I was twenty and she was saying don't get married. I thought about it for decades and I now feel I want to say it to all young

women, including my own daughters, don't marry young, have a life,
set up a life for yourself. Well, they're in no danger!

Lily Brett did return home and married. "I never heard from Lillian
again. I felt myself I had disappointed her." She had two children but
the marriage did not last. Later she remarried and returned to New York
where she settled with her second husband, the artist David Rankin,
and became a successful writer. She fulfilled the promise Lillian saw in
her, if by an indirect path.

Yet Lillian sometimes agonised about her own need for children.
When her elder brother Milo's second child, Penny, was born, Lillian
wrote to a friend: "For some reason (I heard this moment) this saddened me no end. This was made worse today by the arrival in NY of
a Sydney medical gentleman (he rang at 8 am to explain he was on a
world tour of morgues, which I took to be a joke played by a friend)
who flashed enchanting pictures of a thirteen-year-old daughter. Today
is one of those days when not being a mother seems the saddest thing
in the world ... I think I am probably now too old for squalling infants,
but still have fantasies of marrying a widower with several children of
suitable ages."

She made fusses of friends' children, wrote to them and sent them
gifts. She was torn, at least while her own mother was alive, between
the conflicts of finding the right man with whom to have children and
the demands and drives of pursuing an independent life. She once told
her mother she had not rushed into marriage because she did not see
it as a "cure-all" for every problem, an automatic happiness pill. At
the same time Lillian struck Lily Brett in New York as the first woman
she had met who did not talk about having children: "To me Lillian
wasn't looking to have children or to meet Mr Right. She was enjoy-
ing what she was doing."

Another woman who gave Lillian credit for helping her discover
her feminist voice was the singer Helen Reddy. Landing in New York
from Australia as an unknown in April 1966, Helen contacted Lillian,
whom she had never met, "and we were just mates from that moment
on". When Helen moved to California, Lillian sent her press cuttings
about the nascent women's movement and encouraged her to write
her own songs. "I don't think I'd have ever written a song if it weren't
for Lillian," Helen Reddy says. "I have to attribute to her my awareness

that it might be OK to write something and show it to someone and not be laughed off the planet." By the early seventies, Helen Reddy had made it big, with three number one hits in one year, and her signature song "I Am Woman" became an anthem for the women's movement.

As a feminist, Lillian did not achieve exposure on the spectacular scale of Germaine Greer. But her *Mademoiselle* column gave her significant influence as a commonsense populariser of feminist ideas for young readers. Most of the big name feminists, Gloria Steinem, Betty Friedan and others, wrote within an academic culture, but Lillian commanded a mass audience. Donald Lyons says:

> In many ways Lillian was the anti-Germaine Greer. She wasn't an ideologue. Lillian wrote about pop feminism. There was something indefinably modern about her, as there was about many of us in the sixties before these various liberations were codified, that you had to be a raging queer or a raging feminist. Lillian was sexually liberated, she was a brilliant career person, she didn't need a man. She just seemed to be an extraordinarily productive and professionally fulfilled human being. What better feminist is there than that?

*

Germaine Greer returned to New York in triumph in April 1971. *The Female Eunuch*, published in Britain the previous October, had become a publishing marvel and Germaine herself had been anointed by the press as the "high priestess" of feminism. *The Female Eunuch* arrived at exactly the right time and possessed what no other book on the subject had: a style that mixed earthiness, authority, personal experience, historical reference, literary allusion and a directness in its discussion of sex and sexuality that was still shocking in 1970. She made the idea of women's liberation accessible to thousands of ordinary people.

The book sold out its second printing in Britain within six months and had been translated into eight languages by the time Germaine arrived back in New York to promote the American edition. McGraw Hill, the US publishers, had paid, according to figures reported by Lillian Roxon, $30,000 for hardcover rights and $135,000 for paperback rights – a small fortune in 1971. Christopher Lehmann-Haupt's review in the *New York Times* called it "the best feminist book so far ...

a book with personality, a book that knows the distinction between the self and the other, a book that combines the best of masculinity *and* femininity".

Although the Max's Kansas City crowd did not see Germaine on this visit, Lillian did. A highlight of Germaine's frantic promotional schedule of interviews, television appearances and book signings was a debate in New York Town Hall on 30 April with Norman Mailer, the writer whom many feminists considered the embodiment of male chauvinism. Three other women were on stage with Mailer: Jacqueline Ceballos, president of the National Organization of Women, Jill Johnston, a radical feminist and *Village Voice* columnist, and Diana Trilling, an eminent critic. But such was Germaine's new stardom that it was she whom many in the capacity audience of 1,500 had come to see.

The *Sydney Morning Herald* assigned Lillian and Peter Michelmore, the New York bureau chief, to file reports on the event, which the paper set up as a stoush under the heading "Greer v Mailer/ Lillian Roxon v Peter Michelmore". Those hoping to witness the battle of the decade were disappointed. Germaine had flirted with Mailer in print before her arrival – "I'd really like to help that man" – and the pair flirted on stage. Lillian reported that Germaine "did a Dietrich in slinky black silk and a fluffy fur, making beautiful faces when things got dull, holding up her graceful hands in despair when they got hectic and patting her opponent maternally when he looked frightened". Michelmore wrote: "Mailer quite obviously was taken with Greer's body, for he caressed her arm a few times and quipped that she had failed 'manfully' to make her points." Germaine did launch an attack on the handicaps suffered by women artists down the ages, but both *Herald* writers concluded that the evening had ended in a draw.

Lillian captured the real tenor of the event when she wrote: "Sadly the only bitter contest of the night was not between Greer and Mailer but between Greer and the last speaker, noted critic Diana Trilling. They fought a surprisingly well-matched duel with razor-sharp words. True, as one person in the audience called out, Mrs Trilling's consciousness needed raising. Nevertheless women should have learned by now to present a united front in face of the 'enemy'." In a separate report for *Woman's Day*, Lillian took a swipe at Germaine's apparent smothering of her Australian accent, describing her as sounding like "a cross between Queen Elizabeth and Vanessa Redgrave": "Norman Mailer simply adored her and couldn't take his eyes off her. Everyone in that elegant audience (even Jean Kennedy Smith was there) kept joking how that would indeed be the romance of the year. 'Did you go home with Norman Mailer after the party?' I asked her kiddingly. 'Please,' she snorted. 'I got into the cab to leave and there at the wheel was the man of my dreams.'" Germaine herself, having later summarised the evening in an article for *Esquire* as "My Mailer Problem", appeared to find the discovery of the cab driver one of its highlights.

Apart from Lillian's reconciliatory telephone call a year after their fight at Max's, she and Germaine had barely spoken since the contretemps in New York at the end of 1968. Marion Hallwood told Lillian she should be charmed by Germaine's throwaway line dedicating the book partly to her cockroaches; but Lillian was not charmed.

Lillian later wrote: "When we made up, Germaine said it was never meant to be horrible. She was amused by the 'insect life' and exasperated by my unnecessary pessimism. And, she said, she was full of admiration for anyone who lived in New York alone for so long and survived. She had dedicated her book, she said, to 'five very strong women'. It was written only with love."

Now, despite past dramas and Germaine's hectic schedule on her 1971 visit, they seemed to have found an accommodation, if a brief one. This was the "six hours quality time" Germaine referred to in her letter to me. Germaine waved away her publishers' plan to put her up in the dignified Algonquin Hotel, where the top writers stayed, and moved instead to the more raunchy Chelsea Hotel, where the hip people stayed. Lillian went there one night so they could watch Germaine on the *David Frost Show*, the idea being that a British documentary crew could film their reactions. Lillian wrote in *Woman's Day*: "While we were there, Harry Benson, a famous *Life* photographer, came in to take pictures of the filming, whereupon the movie cameras turned on HIM photographing US watching HER on television. It was too much for me, all those lights and cameras, and I fled but not before she gave me a little Ali McGraw hat she made for me in the colours of marigolds, bluebells and cornflowers. She is an expert knitter and needlewoman with a spectacular eye for colour and people tend to overlook that homey little detail."

Around the time of this all-conquering visit to America, Lillian wrote three articles about Germaine. Each drew liberally on her friendship and each in its own way appeared to strike back at what Lillian saw as Germaine's slurs in *Suck* and the book dedication. In the event, the articles only drove a wedge further between the two women. The first piece on 15 May 1971 in *Nation*, a now defunct current affairs and literary magazine in Sydney, took the form of a lengthy letter responding to an article that the magazine had run about women journalists. Recounting her own career, Lillian described how being hired in New York by the *Sydney Morning Herald* had enabled her to upgrade her accommodation.

> I was then able to move into a place which was not used as a urinal by neighbouring drunks. It was used as a convention hall by cockroaches, hence Dr Greer's dedication. The week she came to stay they came from miles away to see this remarkable lady. Can you blame them?
>
> Since the dedication I have been forced to take steps to erase that little match girl image of me she insists on perpetuating. I hired a Mr Godowski from the Oriental Exterminating Company at $9 a month to come in and spray noxious fumes on my pets. I had the landlord come in and paint. I pay Mrs Kelley to shine the floors and, oh yes, I threw out a lot of papers. I now live alone with no colonies of roaches and one life size poster of Iggy Stooge mother naked to cheer me up.
>
> Germaine Greer and her double-edged dedication changed my life and is she ever proud of herself! She is by the way not a "rival" since no one can hold a candle to her particular brand of pizzazz but she is someone I have quarrelled with often enough to truly love. She's braver, crueller and bawdier than I'll ever be, also more generous and patient.

Nine days later came an article in *Woman's Day* in Australia, and six weeks after that another one in *Crawdaddy* in America (the latter reproduced in this book's selection of her writing). It was the *Woman's Day* piece that infuriated Germaine. She referred to it several times during our conversation in Cambridge. "It's extremely nasty," she said. It is hard to understand why this article got under her skin to such a degree. Worse things have been written about her. Lillian's piece did contain occasional barbs, such as Germaine's "Queen Elizabeth accent" one

minute and her "shouting like a fishwife" the next. And the observation: "You would never want to be Germaine's enemy for too long."
But there were generous references, too, giving credit for her "overwhelming frankness and honesty", her "systematic enslavement and
captivation of the great American public" and her being "enormously
dignified" and "gracious, articulate, ready to answer any question and
full of humour" on American television.

Almost thirty years later, Germaine says: "Lillian never said a good
thing about me ever. If she did, it was carefully modified so that it was
turned to my disadvantage."

Lillian and Germaine never saw each other again after Germaine's
1971 New York visit. Occasionally Lillian dropped a spicy reference to
Germaine into her articles. Her piece on the British group Led Zeppelin
in the New York *Sunday News* in May 1973, a few months before she
died, was an interview with Robert Plant, the band's singer, about their
triumphant American tour. Then out of the blue came: "Now what
about his famous date in Australia with feminist Germaine Greer?
'Who's Germaine Greer?' he says, vaguely, and he's not kidding. 'I don't
remember really. It's been a long time since I rocked and rolled, if you
get me. All I care about is getting back to my old lady.'"

Competitive as Lillian and Germaine were, it seems a pity that these
two great Australian women who were at the forefront of the social and
cultural upheavals of their time could not have, as Lillian put it, "presented a united front in face of the 'enemy'". They probably shared
more in common than either of them would have conceded: their
independent and pioneering lifestyles, their sense of historical mission,
their lifelong wars with their mothers, their unfulfilled wish to have
children of their own and their perception of men as lovable but somehow weaker creatures in need of help. Lillian once looked back from
New York on her adventurous love life and the men she had loved in
a piece of writing that might well have blended fact with fantasy. But
it showed her feminist side, her command of her own life and her own
"sexual economy", her wit and her capacity to tell a story against herself – all the qualities for which Germaine admired her:

> Next time you can't sleep at night, try counting old lovers. For mild
> insomnia, it's usually enough just to recite their names in chrono-
> logical order if possible. Part of the fun is finding yourself two or

three short at the end of the count. It's interesting to see which ones you keep forgetting. It's also useful to keep number thirteen indelibly printed in your mind as a sort of check on your count. Mine was an Irishman called — and it happened on Friday the 13th, but that's another story. For worse cases of insomnia you try grouping them by profession, let's say. It takes me hours to think of the ones who weren't architects or journalists. Or by names – a surprising number were called John. I had a Warren, Warwick and Walter in frighteningly close succession. More Peters than you might care to throw a stick at and an Irv, which is a terrible name to say in moments of passion. Then there's ages. The mean age, the median age and the average age. At one stage when I liked them young the average age was something like 19. A couple of seventeen year olds brought the score way down. Marriage – how many married ones? How many married now? Religion? Race? How many do you still know? How many do you still like? How many would you sleep with again gladly? Reluctantly? Never? How many did you drop? How many dropped you?

Chapter 16 Freedom's Trap

As the 1970s unfolded, Lillian Roxon's status in New York seemed secure. After the *Rock Encyclopedia*'s success, her column in the *Sunday News* made her the New York mainstream press's first woman rock writer. In 1972 a book called *Mug Shots* listed her among the 200 leading figures of America's "alternate culture": those who "propose to supplant – in one way or another – the existing way of life in America with a culture less rigid, less materialistic, less self-consuming". Its authors, Jay Acton, Alan le Mond and Parker Hodges, argued that society still regarded these top 200 as "social outlaws"; but they were also among America's "most creative, dedicated and humane people".

Lillian's fellow "outlaws" included Jane Fonda, Danny Fields, Allen Ginsberg, Abbie Hoffman, the Jefferson Airplane, Lenny Kaye, Ken Kesey, Timothy Leary, Herbert Marcuse, Marshall McLuhan, Richard Meltzer, Kate Millett, Lou Reed, Jerry Rubin, Mickey Ruskin and Andy Warhol. Lillian posed for her mug shot in a t-shirt that said "Pommy Bastards", a joke that was probably lost on the book's American readers. Her entry concluded: "And if you want to find out who went out with whom, who didn't do what, who did what, who's doing whom, who has a tape of who describing what they did to whom or what who did to them, and who's singing what or appearing where, just check with Lillian. She's bound to know. And though she might not tell you – she's carefully not cruel – she might just let you find out how to find out."

But beneath this confident surface bubbled a cauldron of insecurity. Changes were happening in the rock scene, in New York and in Lillian herself. The golden age of the great sixties bands had almost run itself dry. That pioneering era's innocence and romance, which had so captivated Lillian, was being replaced by a hard-nosed business approach to rock and roll in which artists and bands were regarded as products and record companies spent lavishly to promote and sell them. A turning point in this new approach came in early 1971 when Lillian and hundreds of other journalists were flown across America to attend a promotional party in California for Creedence Clearwater Revival, a seventies band that was making it big with a well-oiled sound which was both traditionalist and very commercial. The party cost Creedence Clearwater Revival $250,000. "These are super-efficient technicians and impressively well-functioning financial machines," Lillian wrote of the band (in an article reproduced in this book). It was a long way from the Mamas and the Papas and the Easybeats.

In New York record companies held promotional parties almost daily, with buffets of food that kept many of the rock writers alive. Why bother cooking at home when the record companies would feed you? "The glory days of Lillian Roxon were the glory days of the record companies," says Leee Childers, the rock photographer. He recalls one party where nothing but champagne and ice cream was served. "I was so sick I barely got home."

The drug-related deaths of Janis Joplin and Jimi Hendrix in 1970, and the death from a heart attack the following year of Jim Morrison, lead singer of the Doors, all at the age of twenty-seven, and all coming on top of the Rolling Stones' 1969 concert at Altamont, near San Francisco, where a Hells Angels "security" guard stabbed a fan to death, combined to bring a sinister foreboding to the scene. Lillian saw these events as symbols of a destructive side of rock and roll that many preferred not to confront. Jim Morrison, she wrote, had been and could have stayed the biggest rock idol in America.

When he died at the age of 27 last July he had already voluntarily dropped out from that particular scene, he had come to despise what being an idol and a sex symbol involved. He didn't care that he'd got fat, he loved it and he loved the big bushy beard he had grown, anything to escape from the unearthly beauty he had at the height of his glory, beauty he found he couldn't start to handle. He more than anyone brought home to me what a destructive thing it was for a musician to be subjected to adulation on that enormous scale.

It's not that they don't dig it but that it's hard to live up to 24 hours a day seven days a week. So you got a situation as Janis had just before she died – when people were complaining she wasn't as good as her last record or the one before that or some legendary night in which she'd been cosmic instead of merely very good. What Jim had started doing just before the end of his career was parodying himself, giving the crowd exactly what it wanted but with his tongue firmly in his cheek. He poked fun at his old sex idol image, exaggerated the sexuality of his movements. It was almost as though he wanted to get himself arrested so he could kill off the Lizard King and re-emerge as just another guy making films and writing music. He had gone to Paris to put some distance between himself and his musical past and get the new self together. The saddest thing about his death, and those of Jimmy and Janis, is that they came about just as they were entering a new, wiser phase of their lives.

Rock itself was entering a new phase, "glam rock", in which male rock stars wore make-up, glitter and high camp outfits modelled heavily on Hollywood's excesses, making the way they looked as much a focus of their performances as their music. Glam rock's most outrageous, inventive and brilliant exponent was David Bowie. He arrived in the back room at Max's Kansas City a few months after having been discovered in Britain, at least for the New York crowd, by Leee Childers. Childers and Cherry Vanilla, an actress, had met Bowie when they went to London in mid-1971 with an Andy Warhol play, *Pork* (said to be inspired by tapes of Warhol's and Brigid Berlin's telephone conversations). Bowie was then in the early stages of his career as a singer-songwriter-performer, appearing in dresses (which he described as "men's dresses") and Lauren Bacall hairdos. When Childers and Cherry Vanilla returned to New York, the people in the back room were mesmerised by their stories. "Lisa Robinson, Lillian Roxon, Gloria Stavers, Danny Fields and Danny Goldberg were all quite captivated by the pair's enthusiastic descriptions of Bowie's style, sexuality, wife (Angie) and guitarist (Mick Ronson)," wrote Yvonne Sewall-Ruskin. "And since these young movers and shakers were all sponges for new talent, and in the business of telling the world about it, they began touting Bowie as the Next Big Thing in rock."

Bowie found much inspiration in the America of Andy Warhol, the drag queens and actors of the Warhol Factory, the Velvet Underground and the singers Lou Reed and Iggy Pop – the "underbelly of American

culture" as Bowie called them – which he soaked up and then syn-
thesised into his first big commercial persona, the androgynous, extra-
terrestrial rock character Ziggy Stardust. When she first interviewed Bowie
in 1972, Lillian predicted in the *Sunday News* that he would become a
superstar "of such magnitude that I'll hold my horses", and described
him as "more beautiful than any girl". Childers was hired by Bowie's
manager, Tony DeFries, to help orchestrate Bowie's first American tour
that year. Bowie fraternised in the back room at Max's with Lou Reed
and Iggy Pop and later helped them to restart their own flagging
careers. Childers says: "Bowie had the last laugh because now he's the
richest rock and roll star of all. He was a smart marketing man. He
could get out to the public what Lou and Iggy couldn't."

Bowie also had a kind streak that reciprocated Lillian's support for
him in print. When Lillian's health started to deteriorate a short time
later and she was temporarily immobilised at home, Bowie sent her a
bunch of tulips with a get-well message, one of the few such gestures
she received. That was New York, a tough city where people were impatient with any sort of weakness.

Lillian's own relationship with New York was changing. She and the
city had been almost a perfect match. It had responded to what she
had to offer, and she had responded to the opportunities it gave her.
"New York is rough, competitive, cruel and hazardous, but it's a challenge that is rewarding to meet," she wrote to the Sydney writer Diane
Armstrong in late 1971. Hundreds of times she had talked of leaving it.
"Living in New York is like being married to a charming rogue," she
wrote in the *Sydney Morning Herald*.

> The roguishness almost outweighs the charm. But when you face up
> to this, and are ready to take your leave once and for all, because the
> balance is not in your favour, he begs you to stay, in a tone of such
> desperation that you cannot deny him. For it is only then that you
> realise he probably needs you more than you need him.
>
> New York is like that. It is brilliant and glittering and hard and
> ruthless, and a terrible cheat and a liar, but it is also full of tender
> little surprises, and when it's in a giving mood, it has a lot to give.
> If you play your cards right, and you sweat a lot, and you pay your
> dues, the rewards are not sometimes, but often, beyond your wildest
> dreams.

But as she approached the age of forty in early 1972, all the old conflicts and dilemmas started to crowd in: the conflict between being alone or mated, between the freedoms that independence gave and the need to take emotional and financial precautions to cover the future, between a world that gave an independent woman her head and a system that was prepared to take her only so seriously. "I am of course in deathly terror of being old and penniless," she wrote to her brother Jack in Sydney. And to a friend: "I don't ever again want to feel as trapped as I have here – trapped despite the fact that I have more freedom than anyone I know ... The worst thing about my own crises is that it's no longer about someone, it's about myself. I use negative experiences for positive good. I have a million names in my New York phone book of nice people. I quite like my work, or at least the challenge of turning it into something people on the street can understand. I am totally free to go anywhere I want to in the whole world. Yet it seems to me that if I live the rest of my life this way I may as well not bother to go on."

She talked to friends about moving to Italy, dividing her year between New York and London or returning to Australia and settling down – "before I have no eggs left" – with a nice, mythical man called Kevin. But New York had become an addiction she could never give up, even though it was starting to kill her.

*

Her biggest insecurity was now her health. While writing the *Rock Encyclopedia* during 1968 and 1969 she had developed asthma. She told Craig McGregor her first attack happened at four one morning when she was writing the entry for either the Supremes or Peter, Paul and Mary. "I was desperate for breath and I couldn't get a doctor to come. No one. So I rang a doctor in Australia. I mean, it was worth it. He calmed me down and told me to go to the emergency ward of the nearest hospital. I was there for nine hours with oxygen masks and bottles dripping away into my veins. It wouldn't have happened in Australia. Someone would have come."

The doctor was Julian Lee, a Sydney thoracic physician who had been a contemporary of Lillian's at the University of Sydney in the early fifties. They met again when Lillian visited Sydney in the late sixties and went to see him about the condition that was now starting to trouble her. Lee remembered her as a "bohemian" figure from the campus, although their student circles did not intersect, and by now he had started following her by-lines from New York. When Lillian returned to New York from this Sydney visit, she began a pattern of ringing Lee in Sydney for diagnosis, reassurance and advice as her asthmatic condition grew progressively worse.

No one can remember Lillian suffering from asthma before the *Rock Encyclopedia* or complaining about it. She told Diane Armstrong: "I was home briefly in 1969 but very sick with asthma, something I got writing that bloody book." Even less was known then about asthma and its management than now. Asthma is a narrowing of the airways triggered by allergy or infection, causing its sufferers to have trouble breathing. It can be inherited genetically or caused by exposure to chemicals and other environmental irritants. Most sufferers develop asthma in childhood, and it is unusual for people to get it out of the blue at the age of thirty-six, Lillian's age when she apparently had her first attack. Julian Lee believes it was possible she had had the condition in childhood, though not badly, and had recovered until it hit her again later.

Lillian was a physically small person living in a tiny apartment in a big city whose cycles of heat, humidity and pollution were a periodic test of endurance for even the most committed and healthy New Yorkers. It is possible that the stress brought on by writing the *Rock Encyclopedia* and keeping the rest of her intense working and social life running as well left her exposed in such an environment to whatever agents re-triggered her asthmatic condition. Lillian's New York friends said later that the book that made her famous also killed her. Initially Julian Lee prescribed two drugs that were not then available in the United States: Alupent, an inhaled medication, and Intal, a new anti-allergy drug designed to stabilise the airways. But as her asthma got worse and her lung function deteriorated, the only treatment that seemed to help her was the steroid cortisone.

Lee wrote to Lillian in New York in August 1969: "What bothers me most is the utter frustration when a nice girl like you gets in strife and I can't help you. What a lousy disease you have and what a way to learn about it." He prescribed Prednisone, a cortisone drug that was available in America and which had a good track record in relieving severe, even life-threatening attacks. Its downside was side effects that included weight gain and high blood pressure. Lee advised Lillian not to reduce her Prednisone dose below one-and-a-half to two tablets a day, "whilst remaining in your present environment". If this was a warning that New York was now a danger zone for a woman in her condition, it was one she could not, or would not, take.

When the *Rock Encyclopedia* came out two months later, Lillian inscribed a copy for Julian Lee – "who is not only a great doctor but also looks better than Rock Hudson" – his wife, Judy, whom she also knew from university, and their children. Lee says: "I told her she was always welcome to ring at any time of the day or night. She didn't abuse that. I used to joke that it was part of the after-sales service. She was grateful for it, too. So a lot of that medical care was provided by long distance telephone. She'd ring from New York and ask me to advise her what to do. I'd usually adjust her Prednisone dose and give her a regime to follow through. I'd ask her to take a deep breath in and blow out as hard as she could so I could time the expiratory phase of her respiration, which is a key to the amount of airways obstruction, the hallmark of asthma. I was trying to assess the severity of her condition in a way you couldn't do unless she was on the spot. Our ways of treating asthma were limited then."

Cortisone treatment was still mainly administered by pills or injection, making its effectiveness something of a hit-and-miss affair. Years later, with the widespread use of inhalers, low-dose treatments tended to maximise the benefits and minimise the side effects. But in the early seventies, the unavoidable side effect of piling on extra weight to carry was an enormous price to pay for a woman like Lillian, who had worried all her life about her fluctuating size. The cortisone blew her up, and this in turn created a vicious cycle, as overweight people run a higher risk of their asthma worsening.

*

As her asthma intensified, so did her workload. As well as writing for the Australian newspapers and magazines in the Fairfax stable, she churned out pieces for the New York rock press and almost any freelance assignment that came her way. In 1970, *Fusion*, whose contributors included such rock writer notables as Lenny Kaye and Richard Meltzer, commissioned her to write a column on food and health, a timely assignment as it turned out. Her first column in September announced that, in writing the *Rock Encyclopedia*, she had "lost that health no Australian should be without". She wrote of faddish things that have since been taken more seriously, such as giving up coffee, drinking herbal tea, switching to soy milk and eating organic food. She praised the Chinese for being the only people who had any idea how to cook vegetables. And, as with her sex column that soon followed in *Mademoiselle*, she married her subject with the rock world: "The first person to talk to me about health was Lou Reed of the Velvet Underground who introduced me to the ecstasies of Dr Bronner's nine-in-one Supermild Pure Castile Soap, not to mention chia seeds, ginseng, bio-strath and other legal ups."

In March 1971, she started writing and presenting a daily radio program on rock music called "Lillian Roxon's Discotique" which was syndicated to 250 stations across America. It was commissioned by a company called Syndicated Air Time which promoted her to the stations as "the famous young author of *The Rock Encyclopedia* ... one of the most informed authorities on today's music". The show ran to three series from March to October, for which she was paid more than $11,000. The stations gave the series good feedback to Syndicated Air Time, although some of their reports were mixed. One, in Claremont, California, liked Lillian's "great" insights into personalities but not her "Hedda Hopper style". A station in Denver, Colorado complained the series "comes off like a teeny-bop rock scandal", while to one in San Antonio, Texas it sounded "like it is produced for the over 40 audience". A station in Williamsburg, Virginia assumed Lillian was American: its listeners liked the show, but "some think her British accent is a put-on". In fact, she kept her Australian accent right to the end of her days.

Lillian's column in the Sunday edition of the New York *Daily News* started in May the same year. The *News* was a conservative newspaper that had largely ignored the advent of rock and pop music up to then, its male editors being convinced it was something that would not interest their readers. By 1971, when the *New York Times* had started to take rock seriously, and the lives and deaths of rock stars had become daily newspaper fodder, the *News* could ignore it no longer. "It was typical of the *News* that, having dithered, they then got someone who was entirely too hip for them," says one of the paper's journalists from that time. "Lillian knew everything, but it was incomprehensible to most of the editors and made them very nervous." One such case was an early column defending the Cockettes, the San Francisco troupe of performing drag queens who had (strangely) outraged some of their

New York audience. Lillian compared the scandal to that which had accompanied Elvis's first appearances fifteen years earlier. Both Elvis and the Cockettes, she argued, had made historic breakthroughs in rock and pop theatre.

At that time, the *Sunday News* claimed 4.5 million readers in New York City and its suburbs, New York's highest circulation. At first Lillian took second billing on a page dominated by Rex Reed, the veteran film critic. But as her column grew in popularity so did her space, until she was given a page almost entirely to herself. The column was still running when she died almost two years later.

*

Among the fans the column attracted was Kathy Miller, an eighteen-year-old high school senior from Queens who had designs to be a rock writer. Kathy read the big British music papers, *Melody Maker* and *New Musical Express*, and the underground American press. She became a devotee of Lillian's column: "She seemed subversive, especially being in a conservative, somewhat right-wing paper like the *Daily News*." One day Kathy wrote to Lillian at the paper and eventually received a reply answering her questions – in shorthand. Intrigued, she wrote back and, after two more exchanges, this time in longhand, Lillian gave Kathy her home telephone number and suggested she call her. "It took all my nerve, but I finally called her one evening. We gabbed for hours. It was like the big sister I'd never had. This older, sophisticated woman of the world mentoring this teenager."

Lillian invited Kathy to meet her at her apartment. She went there nervously, with the image of Linda Eastman's glamorous dustjacket picture of Lillian from the *Rock Encyclopedia* a slightly intimidating presence in her mind. "I was expecting this blonde goddess from the back cover of the *Rock Encyclopedia*. I was taken aback to meet this short, heavyset brunette. I was also overweight so this came as a relief for me." The same afternoon Blair Sabol, Lillian's friend from the *Village Voice*, and Paul du Feu, Germaine Greer's estranged husband, who was then being considered for the first male nude centrefold in *Cosmopolitan* magazine, also dropped by. "It was heady stuff for a nice Irish Catholic girl from Queens."

It was also the start of a career for Kathy Miller. Lillian began calling her regularly, sometimes late at night after she had finished writing, and encouraging her to submit work to the big rock newspapers, *Creem*, *Crawdaddy* and *Fusion*. Kathy was eventually published in all three. Lillian also encouraged her to write to her other rock writer idols, Lester Bangs and Richard Meltzer. Kathy ended up friends with both. "She had a way of making you feel you could do anything. She used herself as an example, how she'd been in Australia and decided to go to New York City. I think I might've reminded her of herself when she was my age. She became, very quickly, the most important and influential person in my life."

Lillian and Kathy eventually started going together to meetings of Weight Watchers, then a relatively new outfit with, as Kathy puts it, a "small group of chubby yentas". Lillian later sold an idea to *New York* magazine for a story on Weight Watchers, rating different group moderators. It was an unusual move for, whatever she was writing about, be it rock, health, sex or politics, she rarely, if ever, discussed her chief personal obsession: her weight. Yet it must have caused her constant anxiety in a world where glamour, body image and youthful beauty were held at such high premiums. In the rock world, Mama Cass was not the norm. Perhaps Kathy Miller was more than a surrogate younger sister: a fellow chubby yenta and reassuring shield.

Kathy went on to write on rock for several years and later moved to a senior management job with one of America's biggest health insurance companies. As a writer, she took Lillian's approach as her model. "Lillian was, first and foremost, a journalist," says Kathy.

> She was always on the hunt for what was new, what was coming down the pike, trends, stars, scenes. Rock writing was her passion, her first love. She would wholeheartedly refer to herself as a groupie. Back then, rock music and rock writing was very much a boys' club. Women were not taken seriously. I was once told by the publisher of a magazine I was writing for, after I refused to give him a blow job as a trade for an assignment covering the Who at an arena in Washington D.C., "What's the big deal? You're a groupie." I replied, "I'm a woman who writes about rock and roll." He answered, "Same difference."

*

In February 1971, Lillian managed to pull off the ultimate blending of her two cultural worlds, Australia and New York. The crowd at Max's Kansas City had grown used to Lillian bringing in Australian visitors to give them a frisson of underground New York. They obeyed her instructions to be nice, witty and outrageous to those she hyped to them as Australia's leading orthodontist/designer/town planner so the visitors would not go home disappointed. "Who's Lillian got on the griddle tonight?" the Max's crowd would ask.

Still in its infancy, the Australian Ballet was making its first big tour of the United States, with Margot Fonteyn and Rudolph Nureyev as its guest stars to give the company cachet with American audiences. Lillian threw a party for the ballet company's dancers and staff at Max's Kansas City to bring them together with the New York rock world. Among the 250 people who went were Lou Reed, Iggy Pop, Brigid Berlin, Holly Woodlawn and Jane Forth, both stars of the Andy Warhol film *Trash*, Eric Emerson and Taylor Mead, stars of the Warhol movie *Lonesome Cowboys*, the actress Sylvia Miles and Rio Rita, Vera Cruz and Penny Arcade, members of the Theatre of the Ridiculous. The Australian New Yorkers included Peter Allen, then estranged from Liza Minnelli and on his way up as a singer, Dennis Altman, the historian and academic, and Robert Hughes, art critic of *Time*. Hughes helped to create a giant map of Australia from oranges, apples and grapes ("Queensland kept collapsing," Lillian reported in *Woman's Day*). There was twenty gallons of Texan chili and cases of Spanish sangria.

*

By 1972, Lillian had been working in the *Sydney Morning Herald* bureau for almost ten years. The *Rock Encyclopedia* had made her a New York star, and she should have been a prized asset in any newspaper office. Instead it caused strains in the *Herald* bureau, although Peter Michelmore, bureau chief for much of Lillian's time there, shared some of her rebellious side. They both disagreed with the *Herald*'s editorial policy of supporting the Vietnam War and Australia's commitment to it. According to Gavin Souter, the paper's official historian, Michelmore clashed with management in Sydney when he argued in 1969 that the *Herald* should change its mind and declare in a front-page editorial that Australian troops should be withdrawn. John Pringle – the editor who himself was increasingly at odds with the Fairfax management's pro-Vietnam policy

– once wrote to Lillian to explain why he had rejected one of her anti-
Vietnam stories: "I think you are losing your cool!"

Derryn Hinch succeeded Michelmore as bureau chief in September
1972. If anything, he was less tolerant than Michelmore of Lillian's
eccentricities. Hinch had arrived in New York from Australia via Toronto
in 1966, when Lillian had already been ensconced there for seven years.
He was impressed by her generosity when she introduced him to the city
by taking him to lunch at Sardi's, restaurant of the stars, where Derryn
was intimidated by the waiters and the menu. Lillian cut the place down
to size and put her new colleague at ease by ordering scrambled eggs
on toast. Later, Hinch supported her in her fight with Germaine Greer
over the "cockroach" dedication in *The Female Eunuch*. "I thought it
was really cruel and I knew Lillian was hurt," Hinch says. "Lillian
Roxon in New York City was a much bigger Aussie than Germaine
Greer, and remained so."

But Hinch was also competitive. He had disagreed with Peter
Michelmore's assigning Lillian to cover the 1968 presidential campaign
across America, arguing that he was better qualified for the job. And
Lillian's New York star status following the *Rock Encyclopedia* was sometimes a source of disharmony. "An array of colourful musos, singers,
groupies and would-bes streamed through our office," Hinch later
wrote. "I would be at the next desk trying to write, while Lillian, the
phoneaholic with the loudest voice (she didn't really need a phone for
Sydney to hear), was handing on the latest gossip, describing the latest
love triangle or pleading for asthma drugs from Australia."

She faced a conflict between her commitments to the bureau and
demands for columns from American newspapers and magazines. A
solution came in the form of a contract from Sungravure, a subsidiary
of the *Herald*'s parent company, to work for *Woman's Day* and its other
magazines from her home, allowing her to freelance for the *Herald* and
others. In the process of cramming a home office into her apartment,
she was obliged, she wrote to a friend, to "bribe a chap with a John
Lennon album to tamper with my phone and turn the ring off so I
don't have to talk to press agents. My answering service deals with
their name and I answer about 1% of the calls." Tensions in the *Herald*
bureau had been partly about the deluge of her incoming calls.

But her new arrangement did little to ease the strain as she raced to
fulfil her other commitments to the *Sunday News, Mademoiselle, Fusion*

and the rest. In November, as Lillian prepared to leave for Britain to write about the Scottish glam rock group Slade, performing in Glasgow, Hinch wrote to her: "Since I took over two months ago I know there have been extenuating circumstances and you have been ill, but I really don't think you've been giving our publications a fair share of your concentration ... The fact that your retainer for all Sungravure magazines is only $200 a week probably comes into it, but you must know that's only a few dollars less than some journalists get working here full-time. Let's get together and talk it out when you get back from London."

Lillian complained to her New York Australian friend Marion Hallwood and others how tough it was for a woman to break the "glass ceiling" in journalism. Having served in the bureau for longer than anyone else, having covered everything from a presidential election for the *Herald* to the Burtons for *Woman's Day*, and having seen a succession of male bureau chiefs come and go, she felt she was as qualified as any man to be bureau chief herself. But no woman had ever held the job, certainly not one as overtly unconventional as Lillian. It would be at least another decade before women started moving into top jobs of this sort in journalism. Meanwhile the insecurities over her health, her looks, her age and her work mounted. "I was one of the safety valves to her," says Marion Hallwood.

> With all her friends at Max's she had to present herself as a successful, flourishing journalist who wasn't having fits of depression and mood swings. There were no holds barred when she talked to me because she knew I wasn't going to be anything other than support and certainly not a judge. I could tell her she was being foolish, and her feminism was such that it was excellent she was feeling that way, but it was causing her pain and misery. She really was not happy in the months before she died. Her illness was just called a neurosis by a lot of folk. She'd say they were putting her down and I'd try and reinterpret for her what they meant. But she felt there was a constant knife in her back.

*

In early 1973, Lillian left for what was to be her last visit to Australia, stopping for a rest in Tonga on the way. She started in Brisbane. Her old home town provided copy for two of her *Sunday News* columns: a concert by the group Black Sabbath and the premiere of the sixties rock musical *Hair*, which had finally made it to Brisbane in February 1973, four years after its Australian premiere in Sydney (the conservative state of Queensland had banned even the record of the show). Lillian reported to her American readers her reaction to *Hair*'s finale when the Brisbane audience jumped on stage and danced with the cast: "The men in the dark gray suits and short haircuts had never done anything this daring in their entire lives. Their wives, sitting back in their seats brushing the streamers out of their hair, watched them carry on up there with small, tight, grim smiles of disapproval. I can barely remember how long this show has been running, but I'm glad it still shocks somebody." She praised the production, directed by Jim Sharman, for being physical, fast and having the best dancing she had seen.

During her week in Brisbane Lillian looked up close friends from her school days, including the Gradwell family and Rhyl Sorensen. "We had a long talk," says Rhyl. "I didn't realise how ill she was. She told me, 'New York is killing me, but I can't live without it.'" June Gradwell's mother commented after Lillian's visit how it almost seemed as if Lillian knew that time was running out for her.

In Sydney in February she caught up again with both Slade and the Rolling Stones, the latter making their first Australian tour in seven years. The Stones stayed in the Kingsgate Hotel, then Sydney's newest, in Kings Cross. Mick Jagger was on the 33rd floor. Lillian checked in three floors down. She joked to Louise Ferrier that she wanted to be able to tell people that she'd slept under Mick Jagger. Richard Neville took Lillian up to meet Jagger. It was the first time they had met since the press cruise around Manhattan on the *S.S. Sea Panther* in 1966 when Jagger had caught the eye of Lillian's friend Linda Eastman. "God!" was all Lillian reported Jagger as saying, rolling his eyes to the ceiling, when she reminded him. Soon they were away:

He sits in his lime-green pants and a red T-shirt that shows his lean and very sexy midriff, and he gossips like a society matron, dishing friend and foe alike. A San Francisco reporter, who he claims misquoted him in a music paper recently, comes in for a terrible roasting. Warren Beatty is quickly put in his place.

Paul and Linda McCartney are referred to as "a lovely couple" with so much eye rolling and so many pregnant pauses you are left in no doubt whatsoever about their position on the Jagger Christmas card list. "I'd never let *my* old lady play piano," Mick mutters.

Would he let her make movies? I asked him about reports that Bianca will make a film for Andy Warhol. They are, after all, very close friends. "When girls get together," says Mick, and he knows *exactly* what he's saying, "there's a lot of talk but nothing ever gets done." That's funny, because he's very positive about his own projects with Andy – stage designs and a film from an André Gide book.

Lillian was in demand among her old Sydney Push friends. It was the last time most of them would see her. Margaret Fink threw a big party, one of several. Lillian wrote to Lisa Robinson in New York with her impressions of Sydney in the seventies: "Every single person I ever took to Max's has phoned. The millionaire with the strange habits is having a big party on Thursday, which is the night of my big party ... God it's weird here. Everyone knows everyone else, everyone has old houses redone, everyone is married with kids at good schools, everyone fucks around, or wants to, and despite wholesome hobbies like getting on to the national arts advisory boards, everyone is bored though busy (like us). Margaret looks at her stomach and says we must all diet. I keep being asked out to swank places for lunch. There is supposed to be a party for me that the prime minister [Gough Whitlam] and his wife have accepted invitations for, but then everybody claims to have the government's ear."

*

By March, back in New York, Lillian's asthma was worsening. Outwardly she appeared to her friends her usual energetic self; but she was living increasingly in a state of private alarm about her health. She avoided using the New York subway for fear of suffering an asthma attack on one of its stifling platforms or in a train. Then one day she fell, triggering a series of disasters that kept her immobilised for weeks. In April she wrote to Julian Lee and his wife, Judy, who had once considered writing a book on asthma:

You'd better write that book Judy. I need it. I'm SERIOUS. I was very well in Sydney but I fell off my wedgies and couldn't walk for a week, then my knee became abscessed and THEN they lowered my cortisone and I got HIDEOUS coughs. But HIDEOUS. And then (you'll love this) one morning at 6 a.m. I ran out of spray, used an old English spray and COLLAPSED. Came to some time later surrounded by blood (from a lip I cut when I fell). I crawled to a phone, rang an AMBULANCE and had an UNATTRACTIVE stay in COLUMBUS hospital (this on 6.5mg Prednisone!) Anyway I'm OK now but still shocked and terrified to go too far from home (like more than two blocks). I've been home EIGHT weeks almost, my leg still hasn't healed and I'm half asleep from the medication. SOMETHING HAS to be done. (Julian, the Dr here says the CORTISONE SPRAY is no good.) I don't know what to do. I do my work from home. I feel somewhat lacking in my usual ZIP. Hope the kids are well. I've sent them (sea mail, they'll take forever) some records. Love and x's Lillian

Around the same time she wrote an account of her predicament to Alan and Daphne Dobbyn in Sydney, adding that she had hired a four-teen-year-old schoolgirl, Lydia Laske, to do her errands: "I have decided from now on to buy my way out of problems in the US wherever possible. It ain't cheap but it's worth it."

They say Carmen Miranda was going to commit suicide by jumping off her wedgies, well I almost did. Okay, so I got one basket of tulips from David Bowie. (He said "I hope you can tiptoe through the tulips soon.") And one pint of hot chicken soup and one awful plant I had to throw out, and apart from that I never saw any of my friends so thank God for Lydia who brought mail, papers and carrots and cel-ery for the vegetable juice routine (I thought I might as well try to lose weight while at home, but I didn't). One reason [her leg] took so long to heal ... was the cortisone, so I am now on much less which is a blessing but means I wheeze like an engine again. Hopefully some of that cuddlesome fat will now come off a bit.

But it did not. And despite the stresses on her system, Lillian contin-ued to exhaust herself as soon as she was able to leave home. One Friday night in April, she went to a concert by her friend Helen Reddy at Carnegie Hall, then on to an after-party. At 2 a.m. she continued on to the Academy of Music for the night's second concert, by Slade.

This sort of schedule could only have compromised further her fragile health. Some of Lillian's friends noticed her moods becoming more volatile. She complained about perceived slights and had feuds with those who she believed had treated her badly, such as press agents and her answering service (before machines, this was a diversion service for which people like Lillian paid to have their calls answered). Her friends wondered if the asthma drugs were making her paranoid, as did Lillian at one point herself. "What they use to treat the asthma that came out of all this, the medicine, is almost worse than the disease," she wrote to a friend. "It is all this chemical that's making me crazy."

But she continued to churn out her *Sunday News* columns championing rock and roll, encouraging young people to start their own fanzines, calling for the establishment of a rock and roll museum (which later happened, in the form of the Rock and Roll Hall of Fame), demanding the making of more documentaries about rock music and more places in the management and promotion of the rock business for women. She also kept up her intensive networking. Richard Meltzer recalls:

> Lillian was so generous with her time and energy that she probably called every single person who meant anything to her 5–6–7 times a week, and encouraged them, nurtured and reassured them, told them they were the centre of not only her universe but THE universe. It was always a kick and a half to get these calls. Just doing this with such unstinting regularity must've taken its physical and emotional toll on her, but to the very end she kept it up … as if all of us really needed her love and support.
>
> During her last year or so I was kind of regarded as "rock's bad boy", and many of Lillian's New York friends wouldn't have wanted to be in the same room with me, and yet the nature of her direct connection to me changed not one iota. Given the cauldron of opportunism and deceit that the New York scene had already become by then, I find the continuity of her relationship to me absolutely amazing. She was a true, true friend to the end.

*

In July 1973, the wheels turned for three famous people whose lives had intersected with Lillian's. After a sixteen-day marital separation, Richard Burton and Elizabeth Taylor publicly reunited in a parking lot in Rome. "Miss Taylor arrived in Rome in a private jet after switching planes in London, where she was accompanied by her manager, two dogs and a cat," the *New York Times* reported. "When the plane landed in Rome, the doors did not open for 20 minutes while 100 newsmen and Mr Burton waited." At the same time, Germaine Greer was being sued for divorce by Paul du Feu. "She is not contesting the divorce," the *Times* reported.

The rock world, too, was changing yet again. Glam rock was giving way to the beginnings of punk rock with a new band, the New York Dolls, paving the way for the punk scene in New York. Max's Kansas City was approaching the end of its heyday under its founding owner, Mickey Ruskin. The performance spotlight would soon shift to a new club, CBGB, in the Bowery, for a new wave of bands such as Blondie, Talking Heads and the Ramones.

August 1973 opened with a performance at Max's by Iggy Pop and the Stooges, Iggy dressed for the night in a black bikini bottom studded with metal and rhinestones. Punk had not yet been defined, but Iggy Pop – "aggressive, pugnacious, throwing the songs at his audience as if he were throwing punches", as Lillian wrote of his performance that night – was showing which way it would go. Rock and roll was not dead, she declared, but only just beginning to happen in a new way, and Bowie, the New York Dolls and Iggy Pop were the harbingers of it. Symbolically the night was a curtain-raiser: she had been present for the stirrings of something new; but that would be as far as she would see.

*

During the days following Iggy Pop's performance at Max's, the chronology of events varies according to the recollections of the chief participants. Helen Reddy was performing in Central Park. Lillian, the woman who never missed a performance, especially by one of her friends, suddenly felt too ill to go. She called Derryn Hinch to offer him her tickets. Hinch swung by her apartment on East 21st Street to pick them up. He was struck by how unwell she looked. "We never realised how sick she was," Hinch says. "She complained a lot and we often thought she was crying wolf. But she was sick." They still managed to have a small argument. Hinch told her that, for the sake of her health, she should move to a bigger apartment with a proper air-conditioner; she "bitched about how she couldn't afford it because I didn't pay her enough"; he suggested, not unreasonably, that with her additional earnings from her *Sunday News, Mademoiselle* and other columns she could probably very well afford it. This, their last conversation, was about money and survival in New York City.

Lillian rang Marion Hallwood, whose mother was visiting from Australia. "We had a huge, long talk," Marion says. "She was complaining about her work, about friendships and loneliness. It was hard talking to her, reassuring her and trying to perk her up." Marion said she would call her again soon. When Lillian rang again next day, Marion's mother answered. "My mother gushed and told her she wanted her to know how she read every word she wrote. Lillian said, 'You've cheered me up. There were just a few things I wanted to run by Marion.' When I got home my mother said I had to phone Lillian. I said, 'Oh no, not now because it was such a long conversation before.' I just didn't call her back then."

At Max's Kansas City, Steve Lyons, a performer friend of Danny Fields, was giving a one-night show impersonating eggs frying in a pan to music. Fields urged Lillian, Lisa Robinson and others in their inner circle to go. Lillian complained that she felt too unwell but went reluctantly nevertheless. She appeared for what would be the last time at Max's in a long black dress and one of her flamboyant feather stoles, an Iggy Pop badge pinned to the centre of her bosom. Danny Fields took the last photograph of her that night, showing her eyes still sparkling under the strain of her illness.

The following night, Lisa was leaving home for a party when Lillian called her. She told Lillian she was running late and would call back later. When Lisa returned home at 11 p.m., she called Lillian and left a message with her answering service. Lillian did not return it. Next day Lisa left several messages with the answering service, none of which Lillian returned. By mid-afternoon Lisa was alarmed and called Danny Fields. "I haven't heard from Lillian all day," she told him. Knowing the unfailing regularity with which the two women spoke daily on the telephone, Fields replied in all seriousness: "If she hasn't called you she must be dead."

About four o'clock that afternoon, the answering service finally told Lisa that Lillian had not picked up any messages all day. Lisa summoned her husband and their friend, Danny Goldberg, and all three went straight to Lillian's apartment and banged on the door. There was no answer.

Danny Goldberg says: "So we went to the police station across the street and said, 'Look, a friend of ours who has asthma, we think she's sick. Could you go in?' The cop came back with us and went in first. He came out and said, 'You don't want to see this. She's dead.' Lisa said to him, 'Can't you pound on her chest or something, can't you do anything, isn't there anything anybody can do?' The cop said, 'She's dead.'"

*

When the police saw the state of Lillian's apartment, they told the Robinsons and Danny Goldberg they suspected it had been ransacked. There were papers, books, records and magazines scattered everywhere. They sealed off the apartment and took Lillian's body to the New York City morgue. In New York in the seventies, when crime rates were high, the sudden death of a 41-year-old woman alone in her apartment might have been calculated to raise suspicions. But there was no sign of forced entry, or of any other crime. Her friends told the police the apparent mess in her crammed apartment was how it always was. Lillian's death certificate confirms her cause of death was asthma – "status asthmaticus" – and that she died on 10 August 1973.

Her death was full of cruel ironies. The mother figure to many people died at a time when she needed mothering herself. The woman who moved in a scene where rock stars and those around them were starting to die of drink and drugs had fallen victim to a natural malady. Lillian sometimes joked that, if anything ever happened to her, people would assume it had been a drug overdose. And some people, on hearing of her death, did make that mistaken assumption. Her last hours alone in New York City can only be guessed at. But her death must indeed have been sudden. She was a compulsive telephone caller, and none of her closest friends had calls from her in a state of medical crisis pleading for help. Julian Lee, her doctor in Sydney, had not heard from her for some time. If she did try to call him at the end, it would have been fruitless: he was on vacation in Queensland and read about her death in the newspapers the following weekend.

From the other side of the world, he could only speculate on what might have happened. Fatal attacks of asthma are rare. When they happen, the airways gather secretions which so impair the functioning part of the lung that breathing becomes impossible. Lillian relied on a mixture of asthma drugs, some of which were not then available in America and had to be sent from Australia. It was a haphazard regime. Had she run low on them? Had she run out of them? Had she given up on them? "Maybe Lil got sick of taking the cortisone, got sick of being overweight," says Julian Lee. "I know she became increasingly depressed about her weight. It got to her. Although she wasn't a glamour puss, she had a body image like we all do."

Marion Hallwood learned of her friend's death when she returned Lillian's call the next day. A woman at the answering service said, "Lillian Roxon has passed away." Marion replied, "What do you mean, passed away? You don't mean she's dead!" "I'm afraid so," said the operator.

*

Derryn Hinch went to the New York City morgue to identify Lillian's body as the news ricocheted around the world. Margaret Fink, Lillian's closest friend from the Push, had just returned to Sydney from Europe with her husband Leon when they heard. Leon rang their old Push friends, Judy and Howard Smith, and asked them to come to the Finks' house in Woollahra: "Margaret is inconsolable."

Aviva Layton, in Greece with her husband, the Canadian poet Irving Layton, received the news in a letter from Ruth Biegler. Aviva could barely make out what Ruth had written: the words were in pale, yellow ink on white paper. "It was as if Ruth didn't want to commit the words to paper," Aviva says. She told her husband the news; there had always been wariness between Lillian and Irving. "Irving said, 'Mmm,' and walked away." Aviva was hurt at what she thought was his indifference, but soon afterwards Irving Layton came back with a poem he had just written for Lillian: "Death, the fathead, struck you when you were alone; / Stabbed that great heart of yours, sparing / The mediocrities and prudent losers you scorned." It ended: "My dear, incomparable Lilli, I find it strange to think / I shall never hear again your indecorous wit / Or see your wide luminous eyes glitter with humour / And affection. Unencumbered, now lighter than air / My fat companionable polevaulter, you leave the ground and soar." Aviva was moved.

In New York Richard Meltzer heard the news in a call from Susan Blond, a publicist and Max's Kansas City habitué. He dropped his plans for the day and, without thinking, walked to the Empire State Building with his girlfriend, Roni Hoffman. "Not paying any attention to the meter at the ground-floor elevator entrance that indicated a visibility of close to zero, we went up to the top floor, the observation deck, where the world was shrouded in smog. No other buildings could be seen in any direction. It just seemed so dismal a day in every way. It was only later that it became apparent that this atmospheric condition was precisely what triggered Lillian's death. I cried a lot that day."

At *Mademoiselle* magazine on Lexington Avenue, managing editor Mary Cantwell, who had become a good friend after recruiting Lillian as a columnist, was in her office preparing for an early morning meeting. Someone came in and told her Lillian was dead. "I just got up and left. I went home and sat in a corner of my living room and cried all day. I couldn't stop crying. I had my own wake with vodka. And I always felt my own life would have been simpler and easier in later years if Lillian had lived. She was such a prop and support, and so wise."

At the *Sunday News* office on West 33rd Street, there was confusion and concern when Lillian did not return editors' telephone calls. She had filed her last column, on the British glam-rock singer Marc Bolan, before she died. It went in the 12 August edition of the *Sunday News*, two days after her death, along with a short death notice that gave her age as five years younger than she was. But there was now a space to fill. The editor called in Stanley Mieses, the copy boy assigned to pick up Lillian's column each week from her apartment after she called to say it was ready. "How much do you know about rock music?" the editor asked. "Everything," Mieses replied. The young man took Lillian's place the following week with a column about Tim Buckley, the folk-rock singer he had seen at Max's Kansas City. It was a scenario straight from the musical *42nd Street*: the star meets with misadventure and the understudy is pushed on in her place. Mieses continued writing on rock music for twenty-six years.

*

The New York press was lavish with its obituaries. The *New York Times* ran a two-column article describing Lillian as "an authority on rock music and one of the leading chroniclers of its culture and personalities", and the *Encyclopedia* as "the most complete book on rock music and rock culture ever written". In a separate piece for the *Times* Richard Goldstein, a pioneer rock writer and critic for the *Village Voice*, wrote that Lillian had "reassured those of us who felt rock had become encumbered with ideas that it remained an emotional celebration of lust and pain ... Without Lillian, it will be that much harder to believe that there really is a New York style." *Rolling Stone's* tribute, by Loraine Alterman, ran almost to a full page. Leee Childers's picture of Lillian showed her smiling broadly, perhaps also having the last laugh. For, next to Alterman's piece was a news column announcing that the Broadway Central Hotel, a focus of her feud with Germaine Greer five years earlier, had "collapsed mysteriously in an apocalypse of falling beams, flying bricks and hydrogen mushroom plaster dust". An era indeed was turning.

By contrast with the American tributes the *Sydney Morning Herald*, the paper for which Lillian had written for most of her working life, ran a curmudgeonly four-paragraph announcement of her death. Derryn Hinch wrote a longer piece for the *Herald's* Sunday stablemate, the *Sun-Herald*. The Sydney radio commentator Brian White devoted an entire program on station 2GB to tributes to and reminiscences of Lillian. Sally Baker, her old friend and colleague from the early days in New York, wrote a warm personal tribute in *Woman's Day*. So did Helen Reddy, who farewelled Lillian with a letter that ended:

> Regrets? I don't think you would have any. You had a wonderful life. You travelled all over the world. Your peers were the most witty and intelligent of their generation. You saw a new art form arise and sailed at its masthead. You achieved success against discouraging odds and I think you were happy to go while you still looked so young and your bed was still warm. New York City has lost one of its legends and I don't want to walk into Max's Kansas City without seeing you holding court or having you clutch my hand and say "Darling, you *must* meet a fabulous person."

*

Jack Roxon arrived in New York two days after Lillian's death to find Lisa Robinson guiding the funeral preparations. It was a private funeral at the Universal Funeral Chapel in mid-town Manhattan. More than 250 people attended, including Judy Collins, rock managers Nat Weiss and Steve Paul, record company executives, members of Australia's diplomatic corps and Warhol superstars Brigid Berlin, Jackie Curtis and Candy Darling. It was fitting that the biggest contingent was the rock writers, to whom Lillian had been at once the midwife and the mother. One of them, Richard Goldstein, later wrote: "At her funeral, one saw the rock press in an unusual display of vulnerability, and one realised that we are all celebrants of lust and pain."

Epilogue

I have learned a lot, especially how right the *I Ching* and/or Chinese are about accepting good times and bad times as naturally as night and day, and accepting that when it is dark you lie low or venture out at your own risk. And that there is no such thing as bad things happening to you except your own reaction and that if you are able to understand the bad things then it doesn't matter.

– Lillian Roxon

While I was working on this book in 2001, I received an unsolicited email from Steven Ward in Baton Rouge, Louisiana. He had learned, somehow, on the internet that the book was in preparation. He told me he wrote for a webzine called Rockcritics.com and that in all his readings in the world of rock criticism Lillian Roxon's name kept coming up. He had recently discovered the *Rock Encyclopedia*: "Her personality – sly and witty but still knowledgeable and respectful – comes through strong." He wanted to put Lillian Roxon on the webzine site. Steven was thirty-three.

A few months later in March 2002, when I was working at the Varuna Writers' Centre in Katoomba, near Sydney, another resident writer, David Cohen from Perth, Western Australia, asked me who I was writing about. When I started to explain, he said: "I know who you're talking about. The *Rock Encyclopedia* introduced me to all kinds of bands and artists that I never heard on the radio (and still don't): Velvet Underground, Frank Zappa, Grateful Dead. Lillian's book opened up a new world of music for me." David was thirty-four. Almost thirty years after she died, it seemed Lillian Roxon had spanned the generations from the Beatles and Bowie to the cyber-age.

What makes a person a legend? Was it the force of her personality as a woman, a journalist, a promoter of talent, a seer of trends? Was it her capacity to take on a city and a cultural movement and make it her own? Was it her talent for inventing personalities and reinventing herself, and later for concealing her own fears and insecurities beneath her own myths? Perhaps it was all of these things, and the fact that she died suddenly and young, her death's bringing to a symbolic close the great era of sixties rock and roll. And her life and work brought her more than legendary status. Two years after she died the *Sydney Morning Herald* reported that Lillian left an estate valued at $44,378, a considerable sum at the time.

*

Three months after Lillian's death, Jack Roxon and a group of his sister's friends set up the Lillian Roxon Memorial Asthma Research Trust to help advance the understanding of asthma. The trust offers a fellowship for people involved in asthma research and still operates in Melbourne under the auspices of the Victorian Asthma Foundation. Asthma drugs have improved and death rates from asthma have fallen since it killed Lillian. But its prevalence has not. Thirty years later, the incidence of asthma among Australian adults has almost doubled to 10 per cent; it is higher among children aged under ten, about one-quarter of whom are expected to have an asthma attack during their lives. This upward trend is similar in America. Understanding asthma's causes, and how to control it, still has a long way to go.

*

On her last visit to Sydney with Slade and the Rolling Stones in early 1973, Lillian went back to the places where her adult life had begun almost twenty-five years earlier. Perhaps she knew this would be the last time she would see them. But most of them were no longer there to be seen. Most of the gathering places of Push life of the fifties had been swept away in a frenzy of development, and along with them the manners and mores of those earlier, more innocent times. Her old Push friends were still there, but the dividing line between them and the rest of Sydney had almost disappeared too. She started in Jamison Street.

I went to see the dusty house and it was pulled down, though they still sold hand-woven scarves at the Red Cross shop and khaki digger hats at the army disposals stores. I couldn't even find it on the old Sydney table mats.

The pubs now close at ten and you can get a drink at the all-night coffee shop if you don't mind it served in a coffee cup. The people in the book still play cards and the horses but some of them now own race horses and, unless it's a big race day, they do it all by phone sitting around in a nice green garden. The wives used to serve them very fancy luncheons until one of them rather shyly asked for meat pies, and now it's understood that's what you get – but good ones, from a good shop, no mice.

No one lives anywhere near a rat. They rent huge houses and live in communes. When I said things hadn't changed I didn't mean they still have abortions. I meant they still get pregnant during those steamy Christmas holidays but now they have the babies, often delivering them themselves.

No one goes to Repins any more. I don't even know if they have any poets left. All the poets who stayed alive became rich and famous. The man who dyed his ceiling black is a famous architect. Couples still fuck in the moonlight, but it's in Watson's Bay, Camp Cove or Lady Martins Beach because they're chic-er. The science fiction fans, who got so used to being sneered at they took on a grey-green coloration, now find themselves in the right on the subject of moon flights and they've had difficulty adjusting. One of them [Johnny Earls] went to Peru and lived among the Indians and taught them Australian folk songs, not the least being one called "The Bastard From the Bush".

The Hasty Tasty is done, but the sip and bite and the greasy spoon, also known as the stab and jab, survive. Australian men no longer think Hungarian food unmanly, and they even know about wines (they used to call them bombo and plonk and red ned). They've given up thinking sparkling burgundy is a good leg opener, and even concede there's something to be said for the fancy stuff.

The provincial city she had left in 1959 had grown up and was on its way to becoming a world city of the third millennium. Australia would produce many more rock bands, actors, writers and directors who would take on America the way the Easybeats had done. The family journey that began in Alassio in the thirties continues in Australia through Lillian's nieces, her brother Jack's daughters, Sally, Nicola and Annabelle, and Milo's children, Sue and Penny. And in New York the survivors of those nights at Max's Kansas City, performers and writers alike, still talk about her. Lenny Kaye, the rock writer who went on to become guitarist and musical collaborator with the poet and singer Patti Smith, says: "There isn't a moment when I don't wish Lillian could see me up on stage playing the guitar. In 1976 we played Central Park and I looked out and thought how Lillian would have loved to have seen me up there on the other side of the stage. She'd have been so overjoyed to see that one of her people had made it. And whenever we go to Australia now I always dedicate a song to Lillian Roxon from the stage in Sydney."

Donald Lyons, the writer, critic and helper on the *Rock Encyclopedia*, says: "She's somebody who stays with you over the years. The big Australian wave of cultural hits came after she was gone, particularly in cinema which happened from the middle seventies. Australia in general became what it is now. I think the whole notion of Australia as hot and sexy would have been magic to Lillian's ears.

"There was always a tinge of sadness whenever any of us reflected on or wrote about the extraordinary flowering of Australian culture. We would always think how Lillian deserved to be here for this. Above all for the rock culture. Yes, she was a rocker. Lillian was a rocker."

Notes on Sources

In writing about Lillian Roxon, I wanted to explore her role as one of
the groundbreaking chroniclers of an era, her life as an independent
woman and journalist before her time, and the story behind a
woman who remains a legend in two of the world's most dynamic
cities, Sydney and New York. Lillian Roxon inhabited many worlds,
and if people do not necessarily find "their" Lillian in these pages it
is probably because she was careful not to mix those worlds too
closely. As is usually the case, different people bring different recollections to the same events. Wherever there has been a conundrum
over a conflicting account, I have settled for Lillian Roxon's version
if it survives, or tried to leave readers to draw their own conclusions
if it does not.

My research was based primarily on interviews with Lillian's friends,
colleagues and contemporaries and on Lillian's own extensive material
in the "Lillian Roxon Papers 1945–1973" in the Mitchell Library,
Sydney. Lillian Roxon was one of the few women journalists to leave
such papers. They include copies of her letters, correspondence to her,
articles, memoranda, her essay on Sydney in the fifties written from
New York in the sixties and the manuscript of her unpublished novel.
Lillian was not only a compulsive telephone person but also possibly
one of the last great letter writers before the age of electronic mail. The
papers form the backbone of the narrative in the Sydney and New York
sections.

We owe a debt of gratitude to Lillian's younger brother, the late Jack
Roxon, for presenting the bulk of the papers to the Mitchell Library in
1973 and 1976, and to her friend Margaret Fink for adding to the collection in 1992. I am very grateful to Lesley Roxon, Lillian's sister-in-
law, for access to the papers and for her help. I am also grateful to
Barbara Roxon and Milo Roxon, to Lillian's nieces, Sally Roxon, Nicola
Roxon, Annabelle Roxon, Susan Roxon and Penny Roxon, and to Katie
Rich and Fred Roxon. Writing about Lillian's life inevitably meant writing about part of their lives, too, and I thank them for their tolerance
and forbearance.

I thank Ruth Biegler for permission to quote from her letters, Milly
Goldman for permission to quote from Zell Rabin's letters, Mary Hope
for permission to quote from Neil Hope's unpublished novel, Donald

Horne for permission to quote from his papers in the Mitchell Library
and Julie Moses for permission to quote from John Moses' letters.

My grateful thanks to the following people in Australia, the United
States and Britain who gave me their time for interviews and to help
me check material: Sally Baker, Michael Baume, Ruth Biegler, Barbara
Blackman, Karin Berg, Lily Brett, Mary Cantwell, Sophie Caplan, Rhyl
Cossins, Leee Childers, George Clarke, Peter Coleman, Roger Covell,
Robert Darroch, Tony Delano, Alan Dobbyn, Daphne Dobbyn, Peter
Edwards, Louise Ferrier, Danny Fields, Jim Fouratt, Phillip Frazer,
Margaret Fink, Grace Garlick, Danny Goldberg, Milly Goldman, Peter
Goldman, Myfanwy Gollan, Harry Gradwell, Louis Green, Germaine
Greer, Bob Gruen, Marion Hallwood, Glen Hamilton, Liz Hamilton,
Derryn Hinch, Mary Hope, Donald Horne, Sandra Jobson, Margaret
Jones, Lenny Kaye, Sylvia Lawson, Aviva Layton, Julian Lee, Donald
Lyons, Craig McGregor, David Malouf, Richard Meltzer, Kathy Miller,
Guy Morrison, Anna Muir, Don Munro, Rupert Murdoch, Gustav
Nossal, Charles Osborne, Ross Patrick, Ross Poole, the late John
Douglas Pringle, John Quinlem, Helen Reddy, Don Riseborough, Lisa
Robinson, Hope Ruff, Kay Russell, Suzanne Rutland, Roelof Smilde,
Judy Smith, Howard Smith, Peter Tranter, Judy Wallace, Paul
Williams.

My thanks also to the following for invaluable help with research:
Diane Armstrong, Nancy Austin, Ina Bade, Lesley Brydon, Jerry Capeci,
Terry Clune, Virginia Duigan, Konstanty Gebert, Peter Grose, Robert
Hurwitz, Brian Johns, Shelagh Jones, Clive Kessler, Rachel Knepfer,
Phillip Knightley, Yvonne Knightley, Valerie Lawson, Mary McCartney,
Paul McCartney, Anne Manson, Matthew Martin, Peter Michelmore,
Sue Milliken, Alex Mitchell, Richard Neville, Pat O'Haire, Jefferson
Penberthy, Victoria Roberts, Yvonne Sewall-Ruskin, Margaret Simons,
Andrew Sinclair, Michele Smart, Sasha Soldatow, Gavin Souter, Dimity
Torbett, Robert Treborlang, Christine Wallace, Steven Ward, the late
David White, Dot Wyndoe, Deane Zimmerman.

For background on the Sydney Libertarians and the group known as
the Push I am grateful to Anne Coombs' book *Sex and Anarchy*
(Penguin, 1996) and to Roelof Smilde, Judy Smith, Ruth Biegler, Ross
Poole and Margaret Fink. For background on Max's Kansas City I am
grateful to Yvonne Sewell-Ruskin's book *High on Rebellion* (Thunders's
Mouth Press, 1998) and to Danny Fields, Leee Childers, Donald Lyons

and other survivors of Max's. My thanks to Danny Fields for his help on the subjects of Lillian Roxon's friendship with Linda McCartney and Lillian's New York rock world in general. Danny Fields' book *Linda McCartney: The Biography* (Little, Brown, 2000) was also a valuable source.

The staff of the Mitchell Library and the State Library of New South Wales were unfailingly helpful and courteous, and I particularly thank Kerry Sullivan, Jennifer Broomhead and Rosemary Block as well as the document delivery staff for electronically transferring old photographs from Lillian's files to compact disc. My thanks also to the staffs of the New York Public Library, New York Historical Society and Fryer Library at the University of Queensland.

For access to archival material I thank the Australian Security Intelligence Organisation, Brisbane State High School, City of Alassio, Italy, City of Sydney Archives, Medical Board of Queensland, National Archives of Australia, Canberra, Powerhouse Museum, Sydney, St Hilda's School, Southport (Rosemary Hughes, St Hilda's Old Girls Association) and the Toowoomba Historical Society (John Larkin). Di Langmore and John Ritchie of the *Australian Dictionary of Biography* kindly gave me access to the dictionary's archival material on the Roxon and Rabin families.

My thanks to those people who took time to read sections of the manuscript and offered criticisms on shortcomings or pointed out errors. Any mistakes that have slipped through the checking process remain mine alone.

There would not have been a book without enthusiastic early support from my agent Lyn Tranter, of Australian Literary Management, Nadine Davidoff, then editor at Black Inc., and Morry Schwartz, publisher at Black Inc. I am enormously grateful to Nadine and to Chris Feik, her successor as editor at Black Inc., for their devoted work on the manuscript. No author could have asked for better. Sophy Williams, Silvia Kwon and Meredith Kelly at Black Inc. did an outstanding job in bringing the book together. Thomas Deverall provided an elegant design and careful typesetting.

I am grateful to the Literature Fund of the Australia Council for a grant that enabled me to complete much of the research. And I thank the Eleanor Dark Foundation for a fellowship that enabled me to focus on the writing as a resident at Varuna, the writers' house in Katoomba, near Sydney. Peter Bishop, the executive director, Inez Brewer, the administrator, and Sheila Atkinson, who kept me and my fellow writers-in-residence at Varuna superbly fed, were all great friends and supporters.

Select Bibliography

Aarons, Mark, *Sanctuary: Nazi Fugitives in Australia*, Mandarin Australia, 1990.

Belz, Carl, *The Story of Rock*, Oxford University Press, 1972.

Blackman, Barbara, *Glass After Glass*, Penguin Books, 1997.

Bockris, Victor, *Transformer: The Lou Reed Story*, Da Capo Press, 1997.

Brasch, R., *Australian Jews of Today*, Sydney, 1977.

Brett, Lily, *In Full View*, Picador, 1997.

Brown, Peter and Gaines, Steven, *The Love You Make: An Insider's Story of the Beatles*, Pan Books, 1984.

Cantwell, Mary, *Speaking with Strangers*, Houghton Mifflin Company, 1998.

Coleman, Peter, *Memoirs of a Slow Learner*, Angus and Robertson, 1994.

Cohn, Nik, *Pop from the Beginning*, Weidenfeld and Nicolson, 1969.

Coombs, Anne, *Sex and Anarchy: The Life and Death of the Sydney Push*, Penguin Books, 1996.

DeRogatis, Jim, *Let It Blurt: the Life and Times of Lester Bangs*, Bloomsbury, 2000.

Fields, Danny, *Linda McCartney: The Biography*, Little, Brown, 2000.

Fitzgerald, Ross, *A History of Queensland from 1915 to the 1980s*, University of Queensland Press, 1984.

Gilbert, Martin, *The Holocaust: The Jewish Tragedy*, Fontana Press, 1987.

Greer, Germaine, *The Female Eunuch*, Flamingo, 1993.

Greer, Germaine, *The Madwoman's Underclothes*, Picador, 1986.

Griffen-Foley, Bridget, *Sir Frank Packer: The Young Master*, HarperBusiness, 2000.

Griffen-Foley, Bridget, *The House of Packer*, Allen & Unwin, 2000.

Guralnick, Peter, *Last Train to Memphis: The Rise of Elvis Presley*, Little, Brown, 1994.

Haese, Richard, *Rebels and Precursors*, Allen Lane, 1981.

Halberstam, David, *The Fifties*, Villard Books, New York, 1993.

Homberger, Eric, *Historical Atlas of New York City*, Henry Holt and Company, 1994.

Horne, Donald, *Into the Open*, HarperCollins, 2000.

Horne, Donald, *Portrait of an Optimist*, Penguin Books Australia, 1988.

Jones, Margaret, "Travels With Myself" in *Inner Cities*, Drusilla Modjeska (ed.), Penguin Books, 1989.

Kahn, Ashley, George-Warren, Holly and Dahl, Shawn (eds.) *Rolling Stone: The Seventies*, Little, Brown, 1998.

Lawson, Valerie, *Connie Sweetheart*, William Heinemann Australia, 1990.

Malouf, David, *Johnno*, Penguin Books, 1975.

Meltzer, Richard, *A Whore Just Like the Rest*, Da Capo Press, 2000.

Miles, Barry, *Paul McCartney: Many Years from Now*, Secker and Warburg, 1997.

Murphy, John, *Imagining the Fifties*, University of New South Wales Press, 2000.

Munster, George, *A Paper Prince*, Viking, 1985.

Neville, Richard, *Hippie Hippie Shake*, Minerva, 1996.

Ogilvie, Judy, *The Push: An Impressionist Memoir*, Primavera Press, 1995.

Osborne, Charles, *Giving It Away*, Secker & Warburg, London, 1986.

Packer, Clyde, *No Return Ticket*, Angus & Robertson, 1984.

Paglia, Camille, *Sexual Personae: Art and Decadence from Nefertiti to Emily Dickinson*, Yale University Press, 1990.

Palmer, Robert, *Dancing in the Street: A Rock and Roll History*, BBC Books, 1996.

Pringle, John Douglas, *Have Pen, Will Travel*, Chatto & Windus, 1973.

Roxon, Lillian, *Lillian Roxon's Rock Encyclopedia*, Grosset & Dunlap, 1969.

Rutland, Suzanne D., *Edge of the Diaspora: Two Centuries of Jewish Settlement in Australia*, Brandl & Schlesinger, 1997.

Shawcross, William, *Rupert Murdoch*, Random House Australia, 1992.

Souter, Gavin, *Company of Heralds*, Melbourne University Press, 1981.

Thompson, Peter A. and Macklin, Robert, *The Battle of Brisbane: Australians and the Yanks at War*, ABC Books, Sydney, 2001.

Wallace, Christine, *Greer: Untamed Shrew*, Macmillan, 1997.

Watson, Steven, *The Birth of the Beat Generation: Visionaries, Rebels and Hipsters 1944–1960*, Pantheon Books, New York, 1998.

White, E. B., *Here Is New York*, Harper & Bros., 1949 (reprinted by the Little Bookroom, 2000).

Wolfe, Tom, *The Purple Decades*, Jonathan Cape, 1983.

Articles

Keavney, Kay, "The Liberating of Germaine Greer", *Australian Women's Weekly*, 2 February 1972.

Malouf, David, "My Kinda Town, Brisbane Is", *The Australian Magazine*, 12 December 1992.

Millis, Roger, "The Rosenbergs and American Justice", *Honi Soit*, 30 July 1953.

Porter, Peter, "Brisbane Comes Back", *Quadrant* (Sydney), September 1975.

Rutland, Suzanne D., "An Example of 'Intellectual Barbarism': The Story of 'Alien' Jewish Medical Practitioners in Australia, 1933–1956", Yad Vashem Studies, Volume XVIII, Jerusalem, 1987.

Sabol, Blair, "Linda: Who does she think she is? Mrs Paul McCartney?", *Village Voice*, 14 April 1975.

"Young Turks and Battle Lines – Barjai and Miya Studio", University of Queensland Art Museum.

Newspapers and Magazines

Bulletin (Sydney); *Crawdaddy* (New York); *Esquire* (New York); *Eye* (New York); *Fusion* (Boston); *Courier-Mail* (Brisbane); *Daily Mirror* (Sydney); *Daily News* (New York); *Honi Soit* (Sydney); *Mademoiselle* (New York); *Nation* (Sydney); *New York Times*; *New York Post*; *Pol* (Sydney); *Sun* (Sydney); *Sun-Herald* (Sydney); *Sydney Morning Herald*; *Woman's Day* (Sydney); *Semper Floreat* (Brisbane); *Washington Post*; *Weekend* (Sydney); *Observer* (Sydney); *Truth* (Sydney).

LILLIAN ROXON:
SELECTED WRITINGS

ACID ROCK/Originally, acid rock was music that tried to reproduce the distorted hearing of a person under the influence of lysergic acid diethylamide (LSD). The idea was to recreate for someone who was not drugged the illusion of an LSD experience through music (an illusion heightened by light shows designed to reproduce *visual* aspects of a trip).

LSD hit San Francisco in 1965 just a little before the big dance scene started to happen there, a scene touched off by the general exuberance of a community that had just discovered chemical ecstasy. All the music did was mirror that ecstasy. It was slower and more languid than hard rock, incorporating much of the Oriental music that was providing background sounds for the drug experiences of that period. Numbers tended to run on longer as though time as we normally know it had lost its meaning. Notes and phrasings lurched and warped in a way that had not, until then, been considered acceptable in rock. Lyrics conjured up images previously confined to the verses of poets like Samuel Taylor Coleridge and William Blake.

The acid rock and light shows of the San Francisco ballrooms did provide for many a joyous journey to the center of the mind without any of the inconvenient side effects, let alone the expense, of hallucinatory drugs. However, there is not much doubt that a sizable percentage of those 1966–67 audiences did not need musical help so much as sympathetic musical companionship for a voyage that had already been triggered with chemicals. Thus, the term acid rock could be taken to mean *enhancing* as well as *inducing* psychedelic transports.

Is acid rock written by someone under the influence of LSD or at least while his memories of its effect are still fresh? The original acid rock was. Later, when the sound hit national airwaves in 1967, there was a wave of ingenious reproductions which could have been composed after a trip to the nearest record shop. And today there are a few groups or even single performers untouched by the music that came out of San Francisco's discovery of hallucinogens.

FRANKIE AVALON was one of the boy wonders of pre-Beatle rock and roll. In 1955, when he was only thirteen, he was a precocious child trumpet player who wowed them at the Horn and Hardart's Children's Hour. But by 1959, aged seventeen, his song *Venus* was on the number one spot for five weeks and his career as a singer and teen idol seemed set forever, putting him up with names like Tommy Sands, Ricky Nelson, Paul Anka and Dion. *The Beatles buried him.* There were people who never got over it and still regard the Beatles as little more than beasts for what they "did" to the boys with the pompadours and the silk suits of the 1956–64 era. For others, Avalon is a symbol of the sort of adult-controlled teen love scene the Beatles *saved* us from. However, lately there has been a sentimental swing back to that era. And like quite a few former idols, Frankie does very nicely on the cabaret circuit, being an "adult" entertainer and bringing back nostalgic memories of a million senior proms in the early sixties.

JOAN BAEZ/There must have been better and sweeter voices than early Joan Baez (Isla Cameron in England was one), but no one can remember them. She arrived in 1960 in a folk scene where to be flat, nasal and otherwise out of tune was a mark of authenticity; and though she sang too well to sound authentic, there were people ready to forgive her that. Jack Elliott, for one, Rambling Jack Elliott, came away from one of her early appearances at Gerdes' Folk City with his head reeling. He later went around for weeks telling people she'd made the best first album he'd ever heard. As well as this, and it didn't seem possible, she had a whole look that matched that voice. Raven hair, olive skin, a white smile – a romantic figure born to be a heroine, voice or no voice. She had never studied singing, this girl who started off in the small clubs of Cambridge, Mass., but at the age of twenty she was already getting top marks from the critics for the classical musts: pitch and diction. When she started coming across as a bargain-basement Pete Seeger, urging singalongs, she captivated a whole new generation of Seeger fans and, much more important, won over all the people who had never even considered liking folk music before. She *must* have won them over, because by November 1962 she had three albums on the charts (more than Sinatra) and a *Time* cover.

She was not the first of the folk singers, of course, merely the first to make it nationally and internationally on a mass-market basis. It may have taken Peter, Paul and Mary to put folk *singles* on the charts, but "Joanie" (people really did call her that) was the first to put folk *albums* in among the best-sellers. She gave a young boy named Bob Dylan his start by dragging him on stage with her when he was still unknown. He would sing his strange songs and, because he laughed at her for singing her straight ones, the Childe Ballads and all that predictable folkie paraphernalia, she would sing his songs, and they knocked people out. There was one tentative move, in 1966, in the wake of Dylan, to go electric. A Baez rock album, produced by her brother-in-law Richard Farina, was reportedly recorded but never released.

Although a million girls with raven hair, white smiles and olive skins took up guitars almost immediately after Baez emerged singing *Donna Donna* and *Plaisir D'Amour* to all who would listen, her impact has always been more social than musical. Like many other folk singers, though she was among the first to do so, she moved out of her classical and lyrical stage into protest; but unlike others, she never did move out of protest, extending it instead to the non-singing part of her life: a school for non-violence, which by 1967 was taking up most of her time and energy, with concert appearances and records playing a much smaller role. In the South and in Washington, she marched and sang for civil rights. In Berkeley she marched and sang for student rights. She unfurled herself like a banner at the head of almost every big demonstration of the troubled sixties. She had taken the folk singer off the stage and into the theatre of the streets. Then, finally, when everyone else was marching, when everyone like her was holding back taxes so they would not contribute to the war in Vietnam, she retired to her school for non-violence, emerging only now and then to sing *Saigon Bride* or the Beatles' *Eleanor Rigby*. In 1968 there was an autobiography and an album of poems. She is obviously never destined to change the face of music again as she did when she first appeared with the perfect voice at the perfect moment. But she has made it clear she intends to change the face of society or die in the attempt.

BEACH BOYS/*Al Jardine, Bruce Johnston, Mike Love, Brian Wilson, Carl Wilson, Dennis Wilson.*
Southern California has the sweetest and highest lifestyle developed by the race. Its surface manifestations – riding in open cars, surfing, being in the sun, making love and watching TV – can be deceptive and puzzling, like Stonehenge and the Aztec temples. Pacific American civilization is a startling synthesis of opposites – sad rootlessness and

loving homeyness, crazy speed and narcotic calm, ugly plastic and the orange sun – the wise mindlessness of extreme America. The great musical poets of this land are the Beach Boys (perhaps along with the astral Byrds). They arose, high-school boys from Hawthorne, with Mike and Brian's idea for a song about surfing. That song, *Surfin'*, a local hit, was the theme of their first album, *SURFIN' SAFARI*, which was released in November 1962. A celebration of airiness and speed, speed on the water or on the road (as in *409*), perfectly realized in the energetic melodies, cheerful repetitions and magical harmonies masterminded by Brian Wilson, this music, beautiful in itself, beautifully captured the bright simplicity of the early sixties' California life. (Live, the group, attired in matching striped shirts, became a great youth attraction in the same bright simple way.) Their next twelve albums, vast hits with titles like *SURFER GIRL*, *LITTLE DEUCE COUPE* and *SUMMER DAYS*, worked this mindless joyfulness into exquisite songs, and the love songs, like *Wendy*, *In My Room*, *Barbara Ann* and, of course, *California Girls*, introduced a new softness and expressiveness.

The group produced a musical history of their place and time – summertime blues and chug-a-lug in 1962, noble surfers in 1963 (but also the getting away from the salty surf to the drama of black denim trousers and motorcycle boots. *Little Deuce Coupe* was immortalized as the contemporary gasoline-fed love goddess) and in 1964, when the Beatles were about to hit America, oblivious California was singing *Fun, Fun, Fun* and *This Car Of Mine*. At the same time, the classic rock songs of Chuck Berry had a place in the Beach Boys' repertoire (as they did in the repertoires of most other rock groups in the pre-Beatle period), and so even when Bob Dylan made his first surprising appearances on the charts, the Beach Boys were able to absorb that, too – and his *The Times They Are A-Changin'* turns up on their party record, a gracious acknowledgment that there was, from time to time, something happening in the "outside" world.

That was the way it was for the Beach Boys – glorious harmonious oblivion – until their thirteenth album, *PET SOUNDS*, released in May 1966. *PET SOUNDS* represents a curious moment in the astounding development of Beach Boys composer-producer Brian Wilson – and an equally curious moment in the history of southern California. The hot rods and the gremmies gave way to a more interior theme. No more celebrations of mechanical exaltations. What was happening to southern

California and to Wilson in 1966 was a more private matter, a thoughtful look inside the mind. For many in that sunny climate the new direction came through drugs and psychedelia via San Francisco. For others it came from religion or from a general contact high which became the occupational hazard of young Californians in the late sixties. Whatever it was for the Beach Boys, with the new private themes came a larger symphonic sound which suggested something of the expansions of Brian Wilson's musical and non-musical sound. Significantly, the new complex orchestrations in *PET SOUNDS* were as disciplined, as clean and as well organized as the earlier, simpler Beach Boys sounds. Nothing was lost in the change. (Other groups were changing too. The Beatles' *RUBBER SOUL* album had appeared, and the creative interrelationship of the great groups had begun.) *Wouldn't It Be Nice* and *God Only Knows* typify the mood of this album, which began to achieve for the Beach Boys a following among serious pop musicians previously put off by a theme and style that seemed too superficial and too commercial.

Suddenly more deeply involved in production and composition, Brian Wilson stopped performing with the group (to be replaced by Bruce Johnston). He withdrew to his mansion and entered into a curious, perhaps ill-advised and certainly ill-fated symbiosis with Van Dyke Parks. Their planned album, *SMILE*, never appeared, and the Beach Boys' next album, *SMILEY SMILE*, contained only one memorable Wilson/Parks collaboration, *Heroes And Villains*, and the Brian Wilson/Mike Long song, *Good Vibrations*, which is still their masterpiece. *FRIENDS*, a more recent album and a rather minor one except for a few charming songs, like the title one, is most notable for the song *Transcendental Meditation*, a reflection of their unsurprising involvement with the Maharishi Mahesh Yogi, who joined them on a tour he never completed. In general, the second phase of the Beach Boys' music, from *PET SOUNDS* onwards, did the same as the first phase – it mirrored the rising and falling fortunes of the southern California culture. Just as the cars and the surf and the simplicity of the early sixties was recorded in the Beach Boys' earlier works, so the arrival of hallucinogenic drugs and religious interiorization of the late sixties are reflected in their songs of that period. Miraculously, while some things changed (including the Beach Boys' uniform and appearance, from surfie to psychedelic to English mod), other things remained the same. The sun will always shine in California, drugs or not, the surf will always break, so the Beach Boys, though larger in their scope, have managed to retain their freshness.

THE BEATLES/*Paul McCartney (piano, fuzz bass, guitar, vocals), John Lennon (harmonica, guitar, piano, vocals), George Harrison (sitar, lead guitar), Ringo Starr (Richard Starkey) (drums, organ). Previous members: Peter Best (drums), Stu Sutcliffe.*

The day Paul McCartney was born, the number one song on the hit parade was *Sleepy Lagoon* played by Harry James. If it wasn't Harry James in those days, it was Glenn Miller, and if not Glenn Miller, Benny Goodman or Guy Lombardo or Woody Herman. Paul, John, George and Ringo were born in the forties, the era of the Big Bands. The world was at war and the songs were escapist – moonlight cocktails, sleepy lagoons and white Christmases. Bing Crosby didn't want to be fenced in, the Andrews Sisters drank rum and Coca Cola, and Perry Como was a prisoner of love when the Beatles were in their young boyhood. Later it was Peggy Lee, Nat King Cole, Dinah Shore and Frankie Laine who dominated the airwaves and the best-seller charts. Popular music was sung by adults for adults in the forties. Was there anyone else who mattered in the forties but adults? No one else was buying records, anyway, and that's what mattered.

It wasn't until the Beatles got into their teens, in the fifties, that something happened that was destined to change the face of popular music and to lay the groundwork for the revolution the Beatles themselves were to bring about in the sixties. That something was Bill Haley's *Rock Around The Clock*, a song that, while it was sung by an adult, was distinctly addressed to the younger generation. It had nothing to do with cocktails and moonlight and a lot to do with being young and rebellious. The Beatles were exactly the right age to be hit hard by that song when it came out in 1955. That was the year John, fifteen and still in school, started his own group, the Quarrymen. When the historic meeting between Quarryman Lennon and new friend Paul McCartney took place on June 15, 1956, Elvis Presley's first hit, *Heartbreak Hotel*, had been number one on the U.S. hit parade for eight consecutive weeks. One of the big attractions Paul, just fourteen, had for the worldly sixteen-year-old John, was that he looked a bit like Elvis. England was absolutely Elvis-happy at the time and, of course, rock-happy. Plastic

Elvises sprang up everywhere with Tommy Steele and Cliff Richard getting the same hysterical screaming adulation in England that Elvis had in the States. Paul joined the Quarrymen. He and John started writing songs together and, in 1957, when Elvis was singing *All Shook Up* and *Teddy Bear* and *Jailhouse Rock* and the Everly Brothers were singing *Wake Up Little Susie,* John and Paul wrote *Love Me Do,* which five years later in 1962 would be their first English (though not American) release.

In 1958 George Harrison, who wore tight pants and had a group called the Rebels, disbanded it to join the Quarrymen. In August of that year, when the group performed at the Casbah Club in Liverpool, the big hit was *Volare* and the latest plastic Elvis was Ricky Nelson. The Kingston Trio were about to put folk on the charts with *Tom Dooley,* beginning a folk revolution that would make Bob Dylan possible three years later in 1961. And a young man named Phil Spector in a group called the Teddy Bears had a number one record, *To Know Him Is To Love Him.* A lot of big things were starting to happen in 1958, but who could possibly know then that the Beatles were among them?

In 1959 the Quarrymen changed their name several times, ending up with the Silver Beatles. Out in the world Frankie Avalon was singing *Venus* and Elvis was still king with *Are You Lonesome Tonight?* 1960 was the year of Mark Dinning's *Teen Angel* and Ray Charles' *Georgia On My Mind.* The Silver Beatles went to Hamburg to back up a singer named Tony Sheridan. You can still buy the recordings they made there, just as a backup group. They did a sort of rock version of *My Bonnie* with Sheridan around that time. They were pretty terrible. Or, to be more generous, utterly undistinguished. People are fond of saying now that there were a hundred groups in Liverpool playing better music than the Beatles in those days. Let's hope so. It was only in Hamburg that they started to get themselves together as a group. George, Paul, John, Peter Best on drums, Stu Sutcliffe on guitar. Their image was very rough-trade rocker, all leather and menace, as opposed to the more established rocker look of another English group in Hamburg at that time, Rory Storme and the Hurricanes, who wore drape-shape suits with curved lapels and string ties. Their drummer, Ringo Starr, would eventually join the Beatles, but not before he learned to brush his hair forward instead of up and back in a greasy pompadour.

There were several Hamburg visits with increasingly triumphant returns to Liverpool. Then, just when kids were buying Ricky Nelson's *Travellin' Man*, in fact, the very week Dion's *Runaround Sue* was number one, someone asked Brian Epstein, a record salesman, for a record called *My Bonnie* by the Beatles. That was October 28, 1961, a big date, and if the rest isn't history, it ought to be. Epstein, made curious by this and other inquiries, tracked the group down to a place called the Cavern, where they were very popular. He became their manager and by the end of 1961 they were Liverpool's number one group – and the number one song was the Marvelettes' *Please Mr. Postman*. (Now you know why the Beatles recorded it.) In 1962 everything happened. Epstein, after an eternity of pushing and wheedling and a million rejections, got the group a record contract. Ringo shaved his beard, took the grease out of his hair, put away the drape-shape suit and joined the group, replacing Peter Best. John Lennon got married. The Twist was the only thing happening on a very stale scene, but a young kid named Bob Dylan had just made a folk record and a new American group called the Beach Boys had a single out called *Surfin' Safari*. The week the Beatles' first single, *Love Me Do*, was released in England, the number one record in America was the Four Seasons' *Sherry*, which shows exactly where America was at that time. *Love Me Do* made the top twenty in England (but was not a number one record). It was released in the U.S., where everyone was listening to the *Monster Mash* and *Big Girls Don't Cry*. In the four weeks it took their next single, *Please Please Me*, to rocket its way to number one in England, America listened to *Go Away Little Girl* and *Hey Paula*. America would not hear of the Beatles for another two years.

Now it was the beginning of 1963 and the year Beatlemania happened in England. The *Please Please Me* album was number one on the charts for six months. In 1963 the group also released *From Me To You*, but it was *She Loves You* that clinched it for them and *I Want To Hold Your Hand* that set the final seal on Beatlemania. In America, it was still Bobby Vinton singing *Blue Velvet*, but not for long. In a matter of weeks, at the beginning of 1964, the Beatles had displaced Vinton on the American hit parade with *I Want To Hold Your Hand*, number one for seven weeks (including the weeks the Beatles came to America, February 7 to February 21). *I Want To Hold Your Hand* was immediately followed by *She Loves You*, *Can't Buy Me Love* and *Love Me Do*, which meant that the Beatles were heading the U.S. charts from the beginning of February till the end of July, probably the biggest feat of its kind in history. When they finally were replaced, it was not by American groups but by other English groups, the Animals and Manfred Mann. The English invasion had started in earnest. The only American sound that was able to grow in influence during that British-dominated time was the Motown sound of the Supremes, which greatly influenced the Beatles and other English groups. Bob Dylan, at that time, was prophetically warning that *The Times They Are A-Changin'*, and in 1965 his prophecy came true. For the Beatles it was the end of being just another successful rock group and the beginning of serious musical maturity with *RUBBER SOUL* (in which the Beatles, for the first time, produced head music), an album very much influenced by Dylan, especially in Lennon and McCartney's lyrics. For Dylan it was another change: influenced by the Beatles – in *HIGHWAY 61 REVISITED* and *BRINGING IT ALL BACK HOME* – he went electric. As Dylan's folk went rock and the Beatles' rock went folk, 1965 was also the year of folk-rock and the Byrds (it was Byrd David Crosby who turned George Harrison on to the sitar).

The times continued to change. 1966 was the Beatles at their most Dylany with songs like the mocking *Nowhere Man*, a far cry from their early lyrics of teen love (Lennon directly, and frequently, credits Dylan for the change). And if the Beatles had changed, it was nothing to what was happening to the Beach Boys – and there were others. All of a sudden, in 1966: Simon and Garfunkel, the Mamas and the Papas, the Lovin' Spoonful, Donovan, the Stones – all coming out with something more than music had been till then. And to top it all, Dylan's *BLONDE ON BLONDE*. (Dylan, as usual, always a jump ahead.) By 1967 the Beatles were into the electronic intricacies of *SERGEANT PEPPER* (anything to top the Beach Boys' *PET SOUNDS*, *Good Vibrations* and a work in progress, *SMILE*, reportedly the greatest thing that had happened in rock to date). The Bee Gees and the Monkees dutifully stepped into the shoes the Beatles had by now outworn. Eventually *SMILE* didn't happen, Dylan was silenced by a motorcycle accident and the Beatles just about had the year to themselves, except for the emerging San Francisco scene. By 1968 Dylan was back, topping the elaborate *SERGEANT PEPPER* with an artfully simple *JOHN WESLEY HARDING*; the Beach Boys, cowed by the disaster of *SMILE*, were no longer, for the moment, a force to be reckoned with; but Cream and the Jimi Hendrix Experience and the San Francisco groups captured the popular imagination. Privately, it was a torturous time for the Beatles. Nevertheless (the Dylan influence again), they closed the year not with a new *PEPPER* but with a double album of great simplicity, a nostalgic look at rock styles.

The simplicity was misleading since, away from the studio, Beatle lives were increasingly complex. John divorced and married Japanese filmmaker Yoko Ono (with a lie-in here and a peace crusade there), Paul married American photographer Linda Eastman, George and his wife were busted, and Ringo landed in the movies. Their enthusiasm for Indian religion turned to an enthusiasm for big business, with the group starting their own record company, Apple. On the Apple label, Paul presented Mary Hopkin; George presented Jackie Lomax; John presented Yoko Ono, the pair of them sweetly naked on the record's cover; Ringo stayed in the movies.

BEE GEES/*Barry Gibb (vocals), Maurice Gibb (bass), Robin Gibb (vocals, piano), Vince Melouney (guitar), Colin Petersen (drums).*
The Bee Gees first appeared in 1967 with a gimmick so brazen it just about took the public's breath away. They came on like the Beatles. Imagine that, people had been coming on like the Beatles since the Fabulous Four first made it outside Liverpool, and here was this new group, years later, doing it again, and what's more, doing it with a fan-fare of trumpets. Why did they get away with it? Because they did it well. They did it so well in their startling first single, *New York Mining Disaster*, that it was like having a wonderful new Beatle single out on the market. For those who were bewailing the loss of the comparatively uncompli-cated pre-*SERGEANT PEPPER* Beatles, the Bee Gees were a godsend and their first album a delight. The thing is that they sounded more like the Beatles than the Beatles ever did and that they wrote songs considerably better than the Beatles had done that early in their career. (An unfair comparison, though, that last, since once the Beatles had done it, it became easier for everyone else.)

The Bee Gees' defense was this: the three Gibb Brothers, nucleus of the group, were born in Manchester, not far from the Beatles' Liverpool, and subject to much the same musical influences. They were perform-ing in public before the age of ten (they even preceded the Everly Brothers), and therefore claim that their so-called Beatle sound was the Bee Gee sound before the Beatles were ever heard of. In 1958 the family migrated to Australia, and the boys, still very young, made quite a name for themselves as performers there. They grew up in the middle of a very busy and very competitive rock scene in Australia. But they were *not*, as has been claimed (not by them), Australia's number one supergroup. In fact, it was a great source of distress, and later of great bitterness, to them that although they were good and they knew it, they were never fully appreciated by rock critics or played enough by disc jockeys. (Ironically, the Easybeats, the real number one group in Australia then, later moved to England where they watched the "lesser" group produce hit after hit and rake in a fortune, while they themselves battled for airplay.) After a while, the frustration of not being able to break into the Australian scene (they were constantly told they were too much like the Beatles) led them to decide to try London. On arrival there they were immediately signed up by another Australian, Robert Stigwood, who in partnership with the late Brian Epstein groomed them for stardom. No expense was spared in arrangements, production, studio time or publicity.

It was clear that Robin Gibb's heartrending vocal quaver, which became the one thing most closely identified with the Bee Gees' sound, was entirely his own. So were the lush orchestral backgrounds – and therein lay a huge problem. Without a sixty-piece orchestra, the Bee Gees live did not sound like the Bee Gees on record. So although there were some appearances outside England (and one rather unfortunate concert at Saville) the Bee Gees did not face an English audience properly till one year after their first single was released. But when they did it, they did it in style. The Royal Albert Hall and a sixty-piece orchestra (some of those first violins are still recovering from the teenyboppers, who rushed the stage). There was more – a forty-voice choir, for only one number (*Birdie Told Me*), and even more, a whole Royal Air Force Apprentice Band. It was the most spectacular concert in rock history. A few months later they did the whole thing again without the choir but with a sixty-piece band at Forest Hills Stadium in New York. It was impressive but it was no way to make a profit.

Illness stopped the rest of the tour and after that it was one problem after another for the group. First, lead singer Barry Gibb announced he was leaving to be A Star. Then guitarist Vince Melouney left to start his own group. Finally, just as Barry had been persuaded to stay and temporarily postpone his personal ambitions, younger brother Robin did leave to pursue a solo career. The future of the group as a performing unit may still be in doubt, but there is nothing dubious about their future as songwriters. Except for the Beatles, no other group has had as many of its songs recorded as successfully by top name stars as the Bee Gees.

CHUCK BERRY may be the single most important name in the history of rock. There is not a rock musician working today who has not consciously or unconsciously borrowed from his sound, the sound which was to become the definitive sound of fifties rock. The Beach Boys made their national reputation with a Chuck Berry song, *Surfin' U.S.A.* And both the Beatles and Stones started off in the sixties by "reviving" Chuck Berry's fifties material, songs that were enormously popular at the height of the rock and roll era, only to be forgotten as the hard-rock sound became more and more watered down. Like Elvis, Jerry Lee Lewis and other giants of rock, Berry was a raver. When the raving quietened down, it was supposedly a sign that rock was growing up. What, in fact, rock was doing was becoming very dull. And the reason the Beatles (and the Stones) had so much impact in 1963 and 1964 was that they brought the raving back. Both groups had grown up to the sound of Chuck Berry and Bill Haley and the old-guard rockers, only to see the sound disappear prematurely. Both worked tirelessly to bring it back; and every now and then when it seems in danger of losing its basic punch, back they go, the Stones and the Beatles, for new inspiration to the sounds of Chuck Berry and hard rock.

Like Presley, Berry was half into rhythm and blues and half into country and western and, again like Presley, what he came up with, having combined the two, was what we now know as rock and roll. His lyrics were for teenagers, but always wry, not vapid. His music was intended to accompany the rolling of an automobile on a highway, but not until nearly fifteen years later did the songs come through as the major rock classics they always were. Despite all this and the awesome reputation Berry has with the rock cognoscenti, he never had anything like the professional success his imitators had. Part of the reason was some trouble he had with the law at the height of his career. The rest, many believe, had to do with his color. He emerged at a time when the black entertainer was still confined to the rhythm and blues charts and white talent dominated. Later, when acceptance came to black artists, it was apparently too late. Critic John Gabree is one of many who feel that Berry, had be been white, would have had as big a career as Presley. Meanwhile, it is interesting to note that the absence of black faces at concerts given by Beatles and other white rock groups is due, in no small part, to the resentment black Americans feel at having their own music played back at them by white musicians from the other side of the Atlantic.

BIG BROTHER AND THE HOLDING COMPANY/*Janis Joplin (lead vocals), Peter Albin (bass, vocals), Sam Andrew (lead and rhythm guitar, vocals), James Gurley (lead and rhythm guitar, vocals), David Getz (drums, vocals).*

Cameras play over those rugged features of hers as if she were an incredible beauty and, in her very own way, she is. Men's eyes go glassy as they think about her. Writers rape her with words as if there weren't any other way to deal with her. No one had gotten as excited about anyone in years as people did about Janis Joplin. She was a whole new experience for everyone. People had to readjust their thinking because of her. Her voice, for instance. Chicks are not supposed to sing that way, all hoarse and insistent and footstamping. They're not supposed to sound as if they're shrieking for delivery from some terrible, urgent, but not entirely unpleasant, physical pain. For one thing, it is the age of cool (give or take Aretha and Levi Stubbs, and they're black and Janis is white). Janis has redefined the whole concept of the female vocalist. She's so beautiful it takes your breath away, and nothing makes you change that opinion – certainly not the knowledge that at any other time you'd have had to say the girl was homely. She lopes about, dressed like a dockside tart, funny little feathered hats, ankle bracelets, sleazy satins. Her hooker clothes, she calls them with a hooker laugh. And she drinks. Drinks – think of that – in a drug generation. She drinks Southern Comfort: a 24-year-old chick singer with the habits of another decade.

Big Brother and the Holding Company existed before Janis. They were a San Francisco group that used to jam around Chet Helms, head administrator of the Family Dog, a group designed to organize the musical community there. Janis was a Texan and so was Chet and it was he who thought Big Brother, one of the better bands of the many that had sprung up there, might use a girl singer. She'd sung country music and blues with a bluegrass band but she'd never had to sing as loud as she had to with Big Brother and that battery of amplifiers; and with all that rhythm going she found herself moving and dancing like another rhythm instrument. It was June 1966. She was a mean blues singer and she looked it, with her trailing draperies and tangled hair. San Francisco fell in love with her as if she were the first woman on earth. One year later, at the Monterey Pop Festival of 1967, everyone else did too. The press, the big music names from New York, everyone. The word was out: Janis Joplin is it. Albert Grossman, dean of the rock managers, with Dylan, Peter, Paul and Mary, and other major talent in his stable, snapped her and the band up on the spot. New York saw her finally at the Anderson Theatre and couldn't believe the voice actually carried all the way across Second Avenue to Ratner's Restaurant. Also unbelievable, the way she controlled the entire audience with her body, her hair, her stamping feet, her jewels, and breasts that were like something out of an erotic novel.

What a Jimi Hendrix or a Mick Jagger did to fainting girls, Janis did to fainting men – made her whole performance a frantic, sweating, passionate, demanding sexual act. Women watched for pointers through narrowed eyes. It was all very overwhelming for everyone: for Janis who couldn't believe she was a star until she saw it in *Time* magazine; for the media who hadn't heard anything like this since Tallulah Bankhead was a girl; for Big Brother, a good band that was nevertheless having difficulty keeping up. But all this abundance had to be captured on acetate, and their first album, which included *Down On Me*, got nowhere near it. A second album, done under the best circumstances possible, also got nowhere near it. When the news broke that Janis and the band would go their separate ways by the end of 1968, there was a general burst of anxiety that no matter what Big Brother's limitations Janis would lose whatever it was she had. Every time she sang, it seemed as if this was the time that rough, overworked whiskey voice would finally give. "I'd rather not sing than sing quiet," she said and she's right, the frenzy that's in her feet and hips is also in her throat. No wonder, after all that, there are times when she looks old and used. But there are times when she looks young and vulnerable and the transition takes place sometimes in the matter of a minute. They're both there, those two extremes, and everything in between.

Janis's new band (still nameless) is into a big band-soul sound complete with horn section. Sam Andrews, former guitarist with Big Brother, has stayed with her. The band is not yet as tight as it could be and Janis's sound suffers for it. She seems to be leaving raunch and moving toward slick sounds. Whether she will maintain her vast popularity now remains to be seen.

PAT BOONE/Whether anyone wants to admit it or not, Pat Boone did much to popularize early rock and roll songs with a large segment of the public that might otherwise never have heard them or bought them. Songs that were totally unacceptable to cautious parents when sung by big, black, raunchy, rhythm and blues type singers somehow seemed safe emerging from the clean-cut, white, thoroughly wholesome and very happily married (with several kids) Pat Boone. Like many other white singers of the fifties and early sixties, he listened to the all-black rhythm and blues hits which were played only on black stations, took what he liked and cut his own version. This practice, which was widely accepted and still is and is perfectly legal, was regarded with great bitterness by the original singers, who would see some other version of their song hit the number one spot and make a fortune and a reputation for someone else while the original version never got a hearing. Few white rock and roll stations gave black artists airplay then, though over the years this was to change considerably. Boone was often insipid, commercial and namby-pamby, but he *was* the answer to those who found it impossible to identify with a motorcycle hood like Elvis.

JAMES BROWN/The first time James Brown played white New York (he had played in Harlem's Apollo theatre before that) it was in 1966 at the old Madison Square Garden. It was at a time when American music was busy finding itself again after the English invasion of 1964–65, and whites were starting to take a closer look at all the Isley-Brothers-black-soul the Beatles and others were bringing back over. There on stage was soul brother number one, Mister Dynamite. A big, black, beautiful, shouting, raving, screaming presence in the good old-fashioned tradition of showmanship – buckets of perspiration, grimaces of unendurable pain, blaring brass, writhing girl dancers and a smooth, sleek male chorus. Although that sort of thing had been around the southern soul circuit for years, for the whites, those who had never ventured as far uptown as the Apollo, it was a penetrating experience. The concentration of it all. Cufflinks hurled into the audience. The long, gasping collapse at the end. The colleagues running forward protectively with a brightly colored cape. Then, with a superhuman effort (a black Houdini), the struggle to throw off the cape and the protective arms. And again on stage for another sweating, agonized encore. Then, inevitably, another collapse and another race with the cloak, and the knees giving way and – oh, what's this? – muscles straining dreadfully, the whole body trembling in deathlike throes and, this time, more dead than alive, a return to the stage to thunderous applause.

He does it performance after performance, time after time, each cloak a different color to underline that – look folks – it's only a *performance*, but no one believes, no one wants to believe. Everything in the James Brown show is staged and contrived – the oohing and aahing, the little shuffles of everyone on stage, every rivulet of perspiration. It's the biggest show on earth, played for every possible angle, and James Brown does it 364 days a year, or something like that, in every town that will take him. They flock to see him (mostly black and sometimes white), and that keeps him in white shirts and shiny shoes and cufflinks and Cadillacs and great personal splendor. The man's rich, and he works for every penny. There must be better performers (there are) who sing better, look better, but James Brown gives the best show, the best value for money, and he's king. Others aspire, all the time, to his title, but somehow his act never palls. Once, during a riot season, he was put on television and everyone forgot the riot and stayed home to watch the king.

BYRDS/*Roger McGuinn (guitar, lead vocals), Jay York (bass), Clarence White (guitar), Gene Parsons (drums). Previous Members: Gene Clark, David Crosby, Mike Clarke, Gram Parsons, Chris Hillman.*
Until the Byrds, the very notion of a group of folk singers strengthening their sound with rock devices was unthinkable. Folk was high-minded, pure and untouched by sordid commercial values. Rock was something you played for a quick buck. The most important thing the Byrds ever did was to recognize that rock could revitalize folk – with a finished product that was considerably more than the sum of its parts. Folk rock was officially born with the Byrds' early 1965 version of Dylan's *Mr. Tambourine Man*, the classic model for ten thousand imitations that year as folk rock swept the West and then the East.

The Byrds were the first of the *thinking* musicians. And they were articulate (at least Crosby and McGuinn were) at a time when the best that the Beatles could do was whip off a string of funny but not necessarily deep one-liners. The Byrds were the best innovators around. Folk and rock! It changed the face of American music and put them on the charts in a way no one in the business believed possible. At an early 1966 concert in New York, they were as mobbed and screamed over as the Beatles.

After the Byrds, it no longer became amazing to find someone like poet Allen Ginsberg backstage at a rock concert, or when they opened at the Village Gate a little later, Norman Mailer and Timothy Leary among the ringsiders. For the Byrds were not only musical but political and mystical. Later, acid rock would become commonplace. But the Byrds were the first acid rockers, the first head rockers, the first message rockers and, of course, the first outer space rockers. It's no wonder then that by the time everyone else caught up with it all, they lapsed happily back into the country sound that had been in their music all along, in with everything else they offered. Right from the start, the quality that had marked the Byrds as quite, quite different from the Beatles' imitators was a twangy, uniquely American country harmony. No one since has ever been able to capture that sound any more than they could capture the distinctive jangle of McGuinn's electric twelve-string Rickenbacker.

Everyone knew they had to be the greatest group alive – everyone from the Beatles on down – but destiny was to plague them with a series of personnel changes that would weaken the group almost beyond repair. For a while they were a fixture at Ciros on Hollywood's Sunset Strip and the nucleus of all the good things that would be coming out of Los Angeles. They were five until Gene Clark, now of Dillard and Clark, left. Early in 1966 the remaining four came to New York with a sound that was newer than folk – raga rock (they cringed at the name) or rock with sitar, a David Crosby innovation that touched off a whole sitar craze. Their sitar song *Eight Miles High* was banned on some radio stations on the grounds that it glorified drugs. It was, however, like so many of their songs of that period, a song about jet airplanes, which they used to watch from airport observation towers. At the Village Gate they used a light show, the first in New York. The audience complained that it was distracting. By March 1967, the American music scene was jumping and in some ways the Byrds were being left behind. Their songs looked back in some anger, *"So You Want To Be A Rock and Roll Star?"* asked one a little bitterly.

During the 1967–68 period when the first wave of success had receded, the group began having internal problems. Drummer Mike Clarke left, and so did David Crosby. Hillman and McGuinn kept going, though, and did an album, *THE NOTORIOUS BYRD BROTHERS*, with a little help from some friends. By the time they made *SWEETHEART OF THE RODEO* they had a strong new member, Gram Parsons, who brought out the country mood that had been there all along. However, neither it nor the next LP, *DR. BYRDS AND MR. HYDE*, had anything like their initial chart successes although they were albums everyone listened to and took note of. On *DR. BYRDS AND MR. HYDE* the only original Byrd left was McGuinn (Hillman and Parsons were in the Flying Burrito Brothers and Crosby had started his own group with the Hollies' Graham Nash and the Buffalo Springfield's Steve Stills.) Nevertheless, that strange mixture of country music and outer space that had always marked the Byrds remained. And the irony is that in sticking with what had always, more or less, been there, they still managed to produce an album that seemed fresh and timely.

JOHNNY CASH/One of the few country singers who has managed to transcend the narrowness of that classification, Johnny Cash came on the scene a little after Elvis first appeared on the country music circuit (and just before Elvis became a rock and roll star). By late 1955 he was recording for the same label Elvis started with, Sun records. Jerry Lee Lewis and Carl Perkins, also on that label, went on to Elvis-like rock 'n' roll fame (but when that ended, finished up back in the lucrative country field). Cash never climbed the big rock bandwagon in quite that way, but with songs like *I Walk The Line*, *Folsom Prison Blues* and *Ballad Of A Teenage Queen*, established himself as a big seller and has continued to make the charts with his own songs, regardless of whatever fad was current. Interestingly enough, by 1968 music started moving into exactly the area Cash had been in right from the start: the records that made the most impact – Bob Dylan's *JOHN WESLEY HARDING*, the Band's *MUSIC FROM BIG PINK*, the Byrds' *SWEETHEART OF THE RODEO* – all had turned away from hard rock, psychedelics and electronic trickery to the purity and simplicity of the country rock Cash had been singing all along. He has never been anything but a big star and a big seller, and was always revered as much by folk and pop people as by country people, but the 1968 swing back to country might very well give him superstar instead of merely star stature. The fact that he has teamed up with Bob Dylan in an album hasn't hurt.

LEONARD COHEN/It has been fashionable to say, for some time now, that the young men writing and singing rock today are the same young men who in some past time might have been novelists and poets. Leonard Cohen, who is writing and singing for rock audiences today, *is* a novelist and poet. His reputation as a poet extends back more than ten years, especially in Canada where he comes from, but in America and England too. His reputation as a novelist extends back almost that far and both his novels, *The Favorite Game* and *Beautiful Losers*, have been more than well received, especially the last, which came out in 1966. So, it might be asked, what on earth would induce a man with that behind him to go into the business, at the age of thirty-three, not only of writing songs (both words and music) but also of performing them? Add to that question the additional caution that the man has no great voice to speak of. Cohen, who is dark and brooding and made to be a poet and a novelist, will tell you quickly that he started as a musician – a guitarist and singer of folk songs with his own square-dance group – and that that never died. Then came the heady example of Dylan, whose words splashed out of every jukebox. Poets have such small audiences, but songwriters ...

Judy Collins was the first to record a Cohen song, *Suzanne*, on her *IN MY LIFE* album in 1966. In the summer of 1967, when she did a concert in New York's Central Park, she brought him up on the stage with her. He was diffident, handsome, very vulnerable – and his voice was thin. But when his album came out in 1968 every one of those qualities worked for him. His face stared out compellingly in a picture he'd taken himself in a picture machine. His thin and diffident voice made for a realism that seemed to bring him right into the room with the listener. The songs are exactly in the mood of his novels and poems – and his life. The lyrics are always a poet's lyrics. You'd never say the tunes were *funky*, but there is a hypnotic repetitiousness that makes the album a calm antidote for loneliness. It's very easy to see how the whole album might not have worked. The fact that it does work might very well be merely a happy accident of fortune, but it still remains one of the most remarkable first albums ever. His second album is a gentle continuation of the first.

JUDY COLLINS started in the days when what a girl needed most was a trusty guitar, a soulful expression, a formidable repertoire of songs from other times and other places, and a fine clear voice to sing them in. There were a lot of them around in the folk boom of the late fifties and early sixties – soulful ladies singing *John Riley* and *I Know Where I'm Going* – but Judy was one of the few to survive that whole sweet, sad, gentle and unrealistic period. Who could mourn one long-lost love in 1963 when a whole world looked as if it were about to go up in flames? Once the gentle maid from Denver heard what Bob Dylan, Phil Ochs and Tom Paxton sang and wrote about the troubled, changing times, she knew that for her, anyway, there would be no more *John Rileys*. This was the beginning of her Stage Two, and if it seemed then, on *JUDY COLLINS NO. 3*, that she was just about the first to sing those songs of protest, it was because she was one of the first to sing them with conviction. When others saw that protest folk worked musically and aesthetically, as well as socially, they followed, and soon so many folk and pop-folk albums had their mandatory track of angry Dylan or ironic Ochs that it was easy to forget that Judy Collins had been one of those who made it possible.

With her point made, she was now able to move into Stage Three and return to lyricism and romance. On her last two albums she introduced the new lyricism of Leonard Cohen, Joni Mitchell, Donovan, Randy Newman and even of the wildly romantic songs she is now writing herself. Within this framework she has done a lot of moving: classical musicians on stage with her for some concerts; the songs from *Marat/Sade*; a hard-rocking single that was in the jukebox at Berkeley's Blue Cue for a whole summer; her own three electric musicians travelling with her; a huge international hit with *Both Sides Now*; and even, in 1969, a budding career in the theatre as Peer Gynt's Solveig.

CREAM/*Eric Clapton (lead guitar), Ginger Baker (drums), Jack Bruce (bass, harmonica, vocals).*
Cream was the first of the superblues groups. Born of the musician's perennial dream of bringing together the cream of the current musical

crop into one mind-boggling all-star group, Cream brought together Ginger Baker, master drummer, Eric Clapton, king of the English blues guitarists, and Jack Bruce, superbass. This was early 1967, when those who had outgrown early Beatles and early Beatles imitators were ready to get their teeth into some adult and substantial music, so their timing was perfect.

With Cream rock finally grew up, and Eric Clapton became the all-time rock hero, edging Lennon and Jagger from their pedestals. Although there's been plenty of blues playing around, it took Cream to fully tune a whole new generation in to that kind of music. Cream was almost entirely responsible for the blues revival of 1968 and for the great interest in the roots of the new blues-rock. Clapton and Mike Bloomfield (of the Paul Butterfield Blues Band and the Electric Flag) continually gave credit where it was due, talking of roots and sources, bringing up the names of blues originals like B.B. King, Muddy Waters and Howlin' Wolf. It worked two ways for them, for once some of the more astute heard the originals they were less impressed by what Cream and the Bloomfield bands were doing. But that was irrelevant because Cream conquered like no other band did, so that by the end of 1968, when they called it quits, they were able to sell out New York's enormous Madison Square Garden weeks before their "farewell" concert.

To hear them was to be left stoned and stunned. No one had quite seen anything like the way Cream worked – not as an uninspired background for a brilliant soloist, but three major musicians giving it everything from start to finish. In spite of Clapton, there were no stars, just the music. There had been several seasons of delicate imagery, Donovan and the other poets; Cream gave it out hot and heavy and very physical, which is not to say there was no delicate imagery. Martin Sharp's lyrics for *Tales Of Brave Ulysses* are among the most beautiful in the new rock. Clapton's guitar (you knew he had listened to and played with every blues record ever made, all the way back to the Mississippi Delta) was as lean and melancholy as his face. Jack Bruce – who could believe he had played on Manfred Mann's hit *Pretty Flamingo* – was the embodiment of music: instrumentalist, vocalist and composer. Ginger Baker was the devil with drumsticks. Each gave the others a run for their money, frantically competing for attention, though never at the cost of what they were playing. In any case, all of them were always winning, which was what made the music so heavy and rich.

Cream's music was essentially interpretative blues and rock, with all kinds of personal versatility but very little cheap flash, and no help from musical friends, except on their last album, in which they did use sidemen. The group always came off better live than on album, and when *WHEELS OF FIRE* was made, as a two-record set, one record was live. There were criticisms of the albums (after all, the standards set by Cream were high) and there were personal problems (Clapton, particularly, seemed unable to cope with the lack of time and thinking space), but all the same, it came as a great shock, just when they could be said to be the number one group in America, to hear their announcement that they would disband. The only possible consolation at that time was the thought that out of the break could come, after some cunning contractual reshuffling in other circles, not one supergroup like Cream, but three, with Bruce, Baker and Clapton each heading one.

And where was Cream when all the other English groups were happening, from 1964 on? Bruce, who started off singing Scots folk songs, was in the Graham Bond Organization, an organ group with jazz and blues influences with which jazz-oriented Ginger Baker also played. Bruce also played with the highly commercial Manfred Mann group for a while, and with the blues-oriented John Mayall Bluesbreakers, the group Eric Clapton went to after starting with the Yardbirds. You can hear echoes of all these groups in a Cream performance, for they all had a lot to teach a young musician, but the format had always been too rigid. Cream represented unheard-of freedom for the three, at first anyway. Now that the band is finished, its legacy is everywhere. Until Cream, few groups thought of having solos; now even Ginger Baker's drum solo *Toad* is widely imitated. Other groups, seeing Cream's huge success with albums rather than "commercial" singles, finally dared to move out of pop back into music – and record companies approved. There is a lot to thank Cream for: the new enthusiasm for blues, the new enthusiasm for rock generally.

DETROIT SOUND/A few years ago the Detroit sound was the sound of revving motors, the city being the automobile capital of the world. Today the sound of Detroit is the sound of Motown, the first Negro owned and operated record company in America, and one of the most successful enterprises in music today. The company was started by Berry Gordy Jr., a part-time songwriter who worked on a Ford assembly line at $85 a week. Gordy went into the music business in 1957, and by 1960 he had his own label. His first million seller was *Shop Around* by the Miracles, his second million-dollar seller was *Please Mr. Postman* by the Marvelettes – and from then on Motown was bound for glory. Their secret formula was no secret: always a very danceable lead, James Jameson's incredible bass lines, and a sort of watering down of soul for the white pop market (some rhythm and blues people did not quite approve of it, but it sold). The formula worked, so it was always strictly adhered to. One of the big criticisms of the Motown-Detroit sound was that there was no room for spontaneity. The Four Tops, however, one of Motown's biggest sellers, managed to work passion and frenzy within that controlled framework. But the Supremes, who really established Motown as major hitmakers, were perfect examples of how discipline could work *for* music as well as *against* it.

Motown also had its own writers (Holland/Dozier/Holland) and its own producers. It worked out its artists' choreography, stage routines and arrangements, and also taught them dancing, grooming, dressing and even manners. Gordy's ambition was to see every one of his acts headlining at the Copacabana, and he has just about realized that. One of his biggest assets is Smokey Robinson, a best-selling artist with his group the Miracles, a brilliant songwriter and an even more brilliant producer. The Detroit sound stands for a sophisticated black sound. One of its biggest drawbacks is that of late it's become just a little too commercial and predictable. Later, however, Mitch Ryder, the MC5, the Stooges and other artists from that city emerged to show that there's more to the Detroit sound than just Motown.

DISCOTHEQUE/By 1961 music had the most kinetic beat since tom-toms. In France, clubs found they didn't need live musicians to get people to dance – just a disquaire who "programmed" dance records and moods for the evening. Such a place had a name too, a discotheque. The first one in New York, a private club called Le Club, was a raging success. Dozens and then thousands followed in the wake of the biggest dance craze of the decade, the twist. By 1964–65 there were 5,000 in America alone. Although many of these stick to the original formula of recorded music, others, including famous ones like Arthur, Cheetah, The Electric Circus, Trude Heller's, The Scene, Ondine, Salvation, also use live bands. Many big rock groups got a more than flying start in a discotheque (the Rascals in The Barge in Southampton, the Doors at the Whisky A-Go-Go in Los Angeles). Discotheques in America and in London, places like The Scene in New York and London's Speakeasy, are also meeting places of off-duty performers. On a good night you can also see just about anyone you've ever wanted to see. If you can find them in the dark, that is.

FATS DOMINO (Antoine Domino)/The undisputed emperor of the pre-Elvis rock and roll scene. But, as he kept insisting, he'd never played anything else that he could remember; he'd just always known it as rhythm and blues. He played a honky-tonk piano, singing in a grating voice that almost every post-Elvis rock and roll pianist-singer tried to imitate. In one of those curious cycles that are now happening in the new rock, Fats was in the odd position of recording, on a 1968 album, the Beatles' *Lady Madonna*, a 1968 single born out of nostalgia for the Domino sound. (But something was lost in translation: Domino's imitation of the Beatles imitating Domino somehow doesn't work.) When people get nostalgic for the mid-fifties rock period, it's Domino they think of. He broke all records at the Brooklyn Paramount in those days. And in the summer of 1968, when everyone started getting very serious about the new rock and its historical roots, it was the Brooklyn Paramount all over again in Central Park, with Fats making a triumphant reappearance in New York after all those years.

DONOVAN (Donovan Leitch)/Imitation is not just the most sincere form of flattery, it's a very good way to get a moving start in just about any of the creative arts. So it was not really the worst thing in the world that Donovan in 1965 came on like twelve million other Dylan freaks (after all, Dylan in *his* time came on like twelve million other Guthrie freaks). It didn't matter in the long run, but in the short run it was very sad when Scotsman Donovan came to America for the first time in February 1966 to play to a two-thirds empty Carnegie Hall and to be put down for presuming to do a Dylan on Dylan's own home ground (he even *looked* like Dylan). It was a disaster, and a pity because even then he'd done *Catch The Wind*, which was not only a beautiful love song but also a beautiful love poem.

He went back to England and went through a lot of the changes that produced, among other things, *SUNSHINE SUPERMAN* and *MELLOW*

YELLOW, which were nothing like Dylan. Coming out as they did, when everyone's head was buzzing with talk of grass, trips, highs and turn-ons, they seemed to be telling Young America that here was a new Donovan and now his head was where theirs was, with the flowers flying and the bells ringing and the incense burning and the colors swirling in the air around him. Which was not exactly where Dylan was then. So this time, when Donovan arrived for his second visit, there was no empty Carnegie Hall with its handful of earnest folk and protest fans. This time there was the Philharmonic Hall at Lincoln Center, packed with the entire flower and feather population of greater New York City (and Westchester, New Jersey, and some of Connecticut), all under twenty or at least looking it, all dripping more love and beauty and tranquillity than had been seen in Fun City since the first Easter Be-In. Brooklyn girls in panniered antique skirts, Bronx boys in ruffles and velvets.

And Donovan did it. Not the Beatles, not Elvis, not Dylan. Donovan. Nor did he let them down, this Sunshine Superman. No Dylan caps this time. Instead, in a piece of showmanship worthy of the Maharishi, Donovan stepped out on stage into a sea of massed flowers, feathered boas and burning incense, looking, in his floor-length white robe, like an escapee from the Last Supper (and, for one chilly moment, not entirely unlike its Guest of Honor). Perhaps one group too many had come out in love beads and Carnaby frills. Perhaps it was just the luxury of not having the eardrums damaged for once. But whatever it was, and though it must have all been very contrived (he did the same things at every concert), it was a heady night. Donovan sang, the incense burned and no one could stop hallucinating. Later, away from his sweetness and intoxicating presence, a Donovan backlash started. Yes, the showmanship and the musicianship was superb, but wasn't his public renunciation of drugs smug and pompous, considering? If America didn't take to Stage One Donovan, the folk minstrel, it certainly took to Stage Two Donovan, the musical trips man. About Stage Three Donovan, a product of success, the Maharishi, and Mickie Most, no one is yet decided. One thing is sure: he has written some of the most beautiful songs in the new rock.

THE DOORS/*Jim Morrison (vocals), Ray Manzarek (organ), Robbie Krieger (guitar), John Densmore (drums).*
More gloppy, pretentious, pseudo-surrealistic, hyper-literary, quasi-mystical prose has been written about the Doors than about any rock

group ever. Whenever the Doors are mentioned in print, the similes fly like shrapnel in an air raid. They are unendurable pleasure indefinitely prolonged, they are the messengers of the devil, they are the patricide kids, the Los Angeles branch of the Oedipus Association, the boys next door (if you live next door to a penitentiary, a lunatic asylum or a leather shop). So say the metaphor makers anyway. The Doors seeped in through the underground early in 1967, a time when no one could possibly have predicted that a group that sang about the evil and the reptilian and the bloody was about to become not just the number one group in America, but the number one *teenybopper* group in America, which just shows what secret dreams of mayhem and vengeance and violent sexuality all those dear little suburban nymphets were harboring in the infant hearts beating under all those pre-teen bras.

Initially there was an album, *THE DOORS*, a growing reputation on the West Coast, and a ferocious single, *Break On Through*, that defined their sound and image perfectly but got nowhere. The album, on the other hand, scored up the biggest underground following any local group had ever had – there was an organ *before* Procul Harum, images more grimly surreal than Dylan's; there was poetry, violence, mystery, suspense and terror. Wow, they were saying in those days when the Doors first came in from the West, this is *adult* rock, and the adults of the underground settled down smugly to keep this group to itself. At Ondine and then Steve Paul's The Scene, it became clear that theatre was a very important part of what the Doors were doing: Ray Manzarek played the organ as if he were on leave from a black mass engagement. In person, singer Jim Morrison was cold, insolent, evil, slightly mad and seemed to be in some sort of drugged or hypnotic trance. His shrieks as he killed that imaginary father in *The End* (which is an eleven-and-one-half minute piece) were straight out of Truman Capote's *In Cold Blood*. At that stage it was probably one of the most exciting rock performances ever.

Then several things happened. The second single, *Light My Fire*, got on the charts and, as fire after fire was lit all over America, rocketed to number one. From that day on Morrison was lost to the underground forever. It's one thing to lick your lips and strain and sneer at Steve Paul's The Scene to a roomful of cognoscenti. It's another thing to do your thing, every nuance of it, not even bothering to change the order of each gesture, in front of five thousand screaming little girls. Jim Morrison's grimaces, Robbie Krieger's peasant-boy bewilderment, Ray Manzarek's satanic sweetness, John Densmore's wild drumming – they were all public property. As triumph piled on triumph for the Doors – packed auditoriums, television appearances, riots, hit after hit, albums in the top hundred, fees soaring and soaring – the underground drew back first in dismay, then in disgust. Incredible, incredible, the Doors, of all people, had sold out. First they sold out to *Sixteen* magazine, where Morrison allowed himself to be molded into a teeny idol. Then they sold out in performance by stereotyping all those seemingly spontaneous movements that had originally whacked half the underground out of its collective skull. It got so you couldn't go to a Doors concert because you'd seen it all before. An earth-shaking second album might have saved the scene and allowed the Doors to win friends in both camps. But the second album was a repeat, a lesser repeat, of the first. And the third album, *WAITING FOR THE SUN*, strengthened dreadful suspicion that the Doors were in it just for the money (as did a single, *Hello I Love You*, that seemed to be a straight cop from an early Kinks hit). Then a magical thing happened to the Doors, the big beautiful bust in New Haven, which to this day has not been matched for theatre and excitement. Morrison in tight leather pants or less embracing a beautiful young girl in the dressing room. Enter police. Morrison makes one violent movement and is Maced on the spot. He is allowed to go on stage and perform, but the "performance" is a monologue telling what has just happened. Police rush on, and there, in front of the paying customers, looking for all the world like a crucified angel or Saint Sebastian, Morrison is dragged off. It is no accident that the picture blown up to monster size now graces the walls of his recording company. Millions wouldn't have bought publicity like that. Later, Morrison made national headlines again when Miami, Florida police issued six warrants for his arrest on charges involving, "lewd and lascivious behavior in public by exposing his private parts and by simulating masturbation and oral copulation" and for alleged public profanity and drunkenness during a March 2, 1969 concert in Miami.

Things are looking up for the Doors. One more bust and they'll be back in favor with the underground.

BOB DYLAN (Robert Zimmerman)/The moment of truth. Bob Dylan is a book, at the least. At the most he is a continuing autobiography of this country – its music, its confusions, the failure of its dream.

Charting his course is the simplest and perhaps the most complete statement one can make at this time.

Fall 1960. Dylan arrives in New York from Hibbing, Minnesota, to visit the ailing Woody Guthrie, his idol. He hangs out in Greenwich Village – Gerde's Folk City, the Gaslight, Izzy Young's Folklore Center – and sings like Guthrie, but he soon discovers that that's not what is making money in the winter of 1960.

1961. Dylan survives the winter. He is writing a lot of songs. Robert Shelton hears him at Folk City and on September 29 writes in the *New York Times* that this boy who looks like "a cross between the choirboy and a beatnik" is "bursting with talent". John Hammond, Sr., producer, signs the young (twenty-year-old) unknown up on the spot. He cuts his first album, *BOB DYLAN*, and gives his first concert in Carnegie Recital Hall – to fifty-three people.

1962. The first album is released. Dylan writes more songs – among them *Blowin' In The Wind*, which becomes the unofficial anthem of the Civil Rights Movement. (Eventually something like sixty people make records of that song – not just Peter, Paul and Mary who make it a number one record, but unlikely people like Sam Cooke, Marlene Dietrich, Duke Ellington, Percy Faith and the New Christy Minstrels.)

1963. Dylan's first solo concert at Town Hall, April 12, makes him a star. *FREEWHEELIN' BOB DYLAN* is released. He's invited on the Ed Sullivan Show, May 12, but CBS bans his *Talking John Birch Society Blues* and he refuses. He meets Joan Baez at the Monterey Folk Festival. That summer Baez and Dylan are the stars of the Newport Folk Festival. Peter, Paul and Mary have a hit with *Blowin' In The Wind*.

1964. *The Times They Are A-Changin'* is the song of 1964. Dylan is in *Life* and *Newsweek*. Dylan, whose songs have made a whole generation political (*A Hard Rain's A-Gonna Fall, Masters of War, Talking World War III Blues*) is slowly starting to move out of politics. *ANOTHER SIDE OF BOB DYLAN*, out that summer, seems like a betrayal to the protest movement. The Beatles and the Rolling Stones come to America.

1965. Dylan uses electric instruments in *BRINGING IT ALL BACK HOME*, released in March. He and Baez do a successful tour of London. In America, the Byrds do *Mr. Tambourine Man* with electric guitars and amplifiers and folk-rock is born. On July 25, Dylan appears on stage in Newport with an electric guitar on hand. He is booed and hissed. He loses many of the folk people, but already there is a rock generation growing up who understands him. *HIGHWAY 61 REVISITED* reaches them, reaches more people than any other Dylan record yet. Forest Hills Stadium, August 28: thousands find the new Dylan unbearable; millions have a new hero. Elsewhere, especially in California, folk-rock takes over and wins over some of Dylan's harshest critics (some are never won over).

1966. The furor has settled down. Rock is respectable. *BLONDE ON BLONDE* is released and is superb. Everyone is playing Dylan and singing him *(Don't Think Twice, It's Alright* from the second album is eventually recorded by more than thirty people including, of all people, Lawrence Welk). The 25-year-old troubador is now writing a novel, called *Tarantula*.

1967. The motorcycle accident. How bad was it really? More rumors. Was he crippled? disfigured? a mindless vegetable? or hurt just enough to have an excuse to take some time off? He hides out in Woodstock with wife, one, two or three children, depending what story you're hearing. The novel is dropped. *BOB DYLAN'S GREATEST HITS* comes out, but no new album. Nor will there be one for eighteen months.

1968. JOHN WESLEY HARDING gives some clues as to what happened in Woodstock, reflecting its (and perhaps Dylan's) rustic calm. He appears at a Memorial to Woody Guthrie in Carnegie Hall. He sings (with The Band) rockabilly. The acid generation is somewhat disappointed by *JOHN WESLEY HARDING*, but there are plenty more who welcome the new tranquillity. After *JWH*, both the Beatles and the Rolling Stones put out albums that are significantly simple. Later in the year Dylan turns up at a Johnny Cash concert.

1969. NASHVILLE SKYLINE is released early in the year, and all the people who had acquired a taste for that harsh Dylan voice now have to get used to the new voice. The album is very country and a continuation of the direction he took in JWH, only warmer and more personal. Almost sexy. Even so, the change costs him a few friends. He appears on the Johnny Cash TV show, singing with him *Girl From the North Country*. He makes a surprise appearance in St. Louis at a concert for The Band (is introduced as Elmer Johnson) and sings four songs. As usual, he speaks best to his audience through his work. They love him.

THE EASYBEATS/*Little Stevie Wright (lead vocals), Dick Diamonde (bass), Tony Cahill (replaced Snowy Fleet) (drums), George Young (rhythm guitar, vocals), Harry Vanda (lead guitar, vocals).*

They seemed to come out of nowhere with *Friday On My Mind*, one of the best songs and biggest sellers of 1966, but they had paid their dues by starving for years before. They started off like a million other groups, playing for fun, then for parties and dances, until they were discovered by a shrewd manager who made them Australia's number one rock group. It was the Beatle thing all over again – weeping fans, torn shirts, mob scenes. Finally, when it seemed they could go no further in Australia, they went to England and again did the same starvation route they thought they'd left behind forever as they battled for an English hit. *Friday On My Mind*, their first try, was it, and they toured America in the summer of 1967 on the strength of it. But after that, nothing took off in England and when it didn't take off there, no one in the States wanted to know about it. It's a pity, because *Falling Off The Edge Of The World*, written by the *Friday* team, Harry Vanda and George Young, in 1967, was one of the great rock songs; so was *Come In Or You'll Get Pneumonia*, which was never released in the U.S., and *Hello How Are You*, which was a hit only in England. The Lemon Pipers, Buckinghams, Music Explosion and Los Bravos have recorded some of the constant stream of new Easybeats material and the proceeds keep them going.

Their technique is the quiet start, slowly and systematically working its way to a frenzy (often with a Kink-like crescendo chorus). Musicians like them a lot and a 1969 change of label with a new single, *St. Louis*, could finally swing a change of fortune for them.

FOLK ROCK/Marrying rock to folk, blues, gospel, raga, Bach or anything else you can think of is so much the thing to do that it is difficult to recall those weeks in August and September of 1965 when the idea of giving a folk song a rock beat seemed blasphemous. Folk was integrity, purity, the people. Rock was Tin Pan Alley, corruption, payola, the Establishment. Who could have foretold then that the two would meet? When Dylan sang with electricity for the first time at the Newport Folk Festival and Forest Hills, it seemed like a major sell-out. There are still people who feel that way. Actually, like everyone else, he was moving with the changin' times. Before the Byrds came up with the first of the folk-rock hits, *Mr. Tambourine Man*, rocking Dylan was as unlikely, as unsavory and easily as sacrilegious as producing a Hard Rain's Gonna Fall Cha-Cha, a Masters of War Twist or a Girl from the North Country Bossa Nova. But the Byrds were different. The Byrds were mystic and holy. The Byrds could do no wrong. And the rock they played wasn't Tin Pan Alley but music from another planet. They could have rocked the Bible and gotten away with it (and they did). *Newsweek* called them Dylanized Beatles when the whole point was they were Beatlized Dylans. In any case, the Byrds were the first with the new sound in March of 1965 when Dylan had already recorded an electrical *Subterranean Homesick Blues* on *BRINGING IT ALL BACK HOME*. After that, the folk rockers came in droves. Sonny and Cher with nice imitation Dylan-like *I Got You Babe*, Donovan, more Byrds, Barry McGuire's *Eve Of Destruction* (rock protest), the Turtles' *It Ain't Me Babe*.

1965 was the year of the folk rocker, the year when 1963–64 protest went pop and made the top of the charts. The two biggest things in music in those years – the Beatles and Dylan – had come together in an absolutely foolproof formula. By the end of 1965, everyone who had been into folk was ready to go electric. By 1966, two new groups, the Lovin' Spoonful and the Mamas and the Papas, had absorbed the new form so completely, had built their sound so much on its premise, that folk rock was taken for granted. Even to use the word was passé. The new sound had arrived. It was ready to move on to other things.

THE FOUR TOPS/*Levi Stubbs Jr. (lead vocals), Renaldo "Obie" Benson (vocals), Abdul "Duke" Fakir (vocals), Lawrence Payton (vocals).*
In the fierce battle for supremacy between the Memphis sound of Stax and the Detroit sound of Motown, the Four Tops are Motown's biggest asset. When the pro-Memphis faction accuses Motown of producing "black muzak," computerized, slick, pre-planned, predictable, commercialized emotion (as opposed to Memphis where it's all just allowed to happen), all the Detroit people have to do in return is point to the Four Tops. Certainly everything *around* the Four Tops is pre-planned and blueprinted, but all this does is give the group a stable framework to work *against*. The resulting stress, as critic Jon Landau has pointed out, is what gives the Four Tops' work its excitement. They are like swimmers battling their way upstream against the current – and winning. In the beginning they must have been like a thousand other singing groups. They got together at high school in 1954 and battled for professional work until 1964, when the Motown "machine" gave them the backing and polish and purpose they needed. Their first release that year, *Baby I Need Your Loving*, was an immediate hit, all passions

unleashed, a frantic cry for love (as are all their songs), and all the more so for being played against the restrained background of impeccable Motown arrangements.

And the Four Tops play it sophisticated, never stooping to cheap trickery, flashy costuming or any other distracting trappings. They come on stage beautifully rehearsed and disciplined and looking for all the world like a team of British bankers in their white shirts and well-cut suits. Then, when they *do* start flipping out (these seemingly sleek and polished entertainers), it comes with double the shock. You expect mad ravings from Little Richard and James Brown, but Levi Stubbs Jr.? Hardly. The Four Tops, more than anyone in rock, soul or whatever you want to call it today, have managed to find the perfect ratio of abandon and restraint. It transforms just about any song they care to pick up – *Standing In The Shadows Of Love, Shake Me, Wake Me, Bernadette, It's The Same Old Song* and, of course, their classic *Reach Out*, which, no matter where they sing it, has every hand in the audience reaching out for them in one great involuntary reflex. Just as Motown helped to establish the Four Tops, the Four Tops helped to establish Motown. They had an especially strong influence in London, and it was their enormous success with the English (everyone from the Beatles on) that, once and for all, turned younger American fans on to them. For every black musician who thinks the Tops and Motown have sold out to commercial values, there is a white fan for whom the Tops have opened up the door into the whole new rich world of black music. Their backings and arrangements alone are a musical education for anyone who has listened to little more than top-forty rock.

ARETHA FRANKLIN/That she's America's best-selling female singer is not as important as why. In an age of cool, Aretha has made it cool to be hot. Musically, she's the epitome of unleashed female passion. She's what female singers have been trying for from time immemorial, but if you don't have it you can't sing it. And even if you do have it you can't always sing it. Aretha must have had it for the six years she was with Columbia, but she didn't sing it. She came on like a road-company Nancy Wilson, said Pete Hamill – all polish, no feeling. She moved to Atlantic, where her producer, Jerry Wexler, had cut his teeth on Ray Charles for six years and all that Charles passion – physical, moral and spiritual – is in there in Aretha, Lady Soul. In 1968 Aretha was only twenty-six when it was all unleashed. She does gospel shouts that are holy, then her voice husks up and she bashes you with it. *Respect, You Make Me Feel Like A Natural Woman, Satisfaction* – they are all a great big raucous shout for women's rights, looking for love, getting it and suffering when you lose it, but always how good it is when you've got it. The suffering is important. At twenty-seven she's paid her dues.

FUTURE ROCK/Some people believe that by 2001 rock will be entirely machine-made. Machines will be programmed so that combinations of different sounds will be left to chance. At-home listeners will have controls that will make it possible for them to "produce" a record – speed it up, slow it down, make it louder and softer, and separate the tracks, adding, subtracting, overdubbing – to create their own version of a hit. There will be no live performances, no stages. Music will be heard with a small circle of friends, not with a group of strangers. The sound will possibly be closest to that of the United States of America, an electronic-rock group. So many groups of the sixties have gone after a future-rock sound, however (the Byrds in their explorations of jets and space; the Jefferson Airplane in its explorations of the mind), that 2001 may very well bring a reaction against these "prophetic" sounds and move into something quite different, perhaps more along the line of Oriental music. Already the sitar, which was regarded as "boring" by musically uneducated westerners, has been taken up – and discarded. Thousands of fads are sure to come and go before 2001. There will probably be no more records, just tapes sold in combinations that can be mixed and mingled. And there will be Sunday producers (like Sunday painters) playing with sounds on their home sets. Then it will be possible to have the Byrds and Beatles singing together with the New York Philharmonic. Or Aretha Franklin and Donovan and the New Lost City Ramblers. The sort of thing that has been happening informally in jam sessions, and more formally on the *SUPER SESSION* albums, the mixing of performers who don't usually play together, will be taken for granted on tape.

LESLEY GORE/In her day (1963) she was the reigning queen of teen-suffering then so musically fashionable (and commercially successful) on Tin Pan Alley. For a whole summer she bleated *It's My Pa-a-arty And I'll Cry If I Want To* and the song shot to the top of the charts as a million or so teen buyers empathized with the plight of being dumped on. The rule then for female singers was for the voice to be insistently high, penetrating and shrewish (a steal, consciously or otherwise, from country and western music in which the women sing darkly of sin and retribution in a voice that cuts right into the male conscience). You could savor every bitchy second of Lesley's triumph with her sequel *Judy's Turn to Cry*. It took the Beatles to put a finish to shrill female nastiness. And from 1964 on, there was a long period of reaction against almost any female singer who was noisy about it. As America grew out of that sort of thing, so did Lesley Gore, who took herself off to college for a little educational, emotional and presumably musical gentling.

THE GRATEFUL DEAD/*Jerry Garcia (lead guitar), Phil Lesh (bass), Ron "Pig Pen" McKernan (conga drums, harp), Bob Weir (rhythm guitar), Mikey Hart (replaced Bill Sommers)(drums), Bill Kruetzmann (drums), Tom Constanten (organ).*

They were not so much a band as a social institution. It would be impossible to tell the story of the Grateful Dead without telling the story of what happened when love hit San Francisco in 1966, just as it would be impossible to talk about that period of San Francisco without talking about the Dead. The two were inextricably intertwined. Most bands tend to live an existence somewhat removed from their fans. The Dead lived right in Haight-Ashbury where it all started. They were an integral part of the community.

They didn't, as might be expected, play what we now call acid or psychedelic rock but instead produced fine, strong, straightforward traditional blues. (Much of the San Francisco music of that period came out of blues, but because of the whole psychedelic coloring of that culture, moved out of blues into the wilder realms of acid rock.) Nevertheless, their *ANTHEM OF THE SUN* album is said to be a good companion for an acid trip. They were a performing rather than a recording band and are still uneasy in a studio setting. Their contribution to the free society of San Francisco was the free concert. They must have given more free concerts than any band in the history of music. For this, and all sorts of other non-musical reasons, they were San Francisco heroes. And their unwillingness to play the rock game with a record company (which earned them the name inside the business of the Ungrateful Dead) endeared them even further to their anti-Establishment fans. San Francisco is prouder of them than of the scores of other local groups that are considered to have sold out in one way or another. As for their influence, it could be said that just about every band that has ever given a free concert, and certainly every *name* that has, has been influenced directly by the Dead.

GROUPIES/The concept of the groupie is not new but the term is. An extension of the wartime "camp followers", groupies are girls whose sexual favors extend exclusively to rock musicians. The term came into use late in 1965 or early 1966 with the emergence of local rock bands. Those fans who were turning out to meet and greet visiting English players now found that with the flood of local bands and their increased availability, being a fan could be a fuller occupation than merely shrieking outside the stage door. (It wasn't easy to get to the Rolling Stones or the Yardbirds and the competition was heavy, but the local groups were friendlier and there were more of them.) Thus, a girl could confine her activities to rock musicians and shut any other sort of person out of her romantic life. There are many kinds of groupies: sad groupies who never get further than screaming and wishful thinking; apprentice groupies who cut their teeth on the local high school band; compromise groupies who are prepared to settle for the road manager or even his friend; daring groupies who bravely scale walls or dangle from helicopters to get their prey; bold groupies who ride up and down hotel elevators until one of "them" gets in and then minces no words in propositioning him. There are expert groupies who can get to anyone, who have guards bribed, hotel managers snowed, desk clerks distracted and bell boys and house maids on their payroll. There are socialite groupies who give big dances and have the singer later. The most clever groupies get jobs in the industry and often persuade themselves they aren't groupies at all. Finally there are groupies who just don't kid themselves: they know what they are; they know what they want.

Groupies can be high class and rich, they can be gentle confidantes, they can be ribald courtesans or ugly desperate children that English stars contemptuously call "scrubbers" or "band molls". But they are what give rock its sex appeal and its magic. They are fans who have dared to break the barriers between the audience and the performer, fans with one thing to give, love, who want nothing in return but a name to drop.

GROUPIES (Male)/Not all groupies are female. Male stars have male groupies who envy them and want to identify with them, run errands for them, breathe in the golden air around them (and perhaps even pick up a female groupie on the side). There are also discreetly homosexual male groupies, many of them sublimating it all by finding themselves jobs in the business side of rock – management, etc. Male groupies for female performers are less common, female performers on the road being, on the whole, less available than male ones. Janis Joplin was one of the few female performers to bewail the shortage of male groupies. The truth is, female performers are groupies of the very worst kind, eternally forming alliances with the most starstudded of their colleagues. They would never be seen with a male groupie.

WOODY GUTHRIE/Once Arlo was known as Woody's son, now inevitably Woody has to be described as Arlo's father. Folk singer, folk poet, writer, rambler, chronicler of the thirties and forties, he was a friend of Leadbelly, Pete Seeger, Ramblin' Jack Elliott, Cisco Houston and, later, Bob Dylan. Dylan came to New York from Minnesota in 1960 just to visit Woody, and if he sang a lot like Woody in those days, well, that's all right, so did a lot of kids. Woody is the man you sang like in the early sixties. Woody wrote hundreds of songs – talking blues, protest songs, ballads – which went on to form a large part of the repertoire of every folk singer of the fifties. By then Woody lay in a hospital with the illness that would finally kill him in 1968. Woody was the father of the folk revival, the father of protest, the father, as it happens, of country-folk. After all these years you can hear him most in Dylan's *JOHN WESLEY HARDING*.

BILL HALEY AND THE COMETS/His band was originally a country band and later what must have been the first white instrumental rhythm and blues band. Bill Haley himself was probably the first white face on what was still, in 1954, a basically black rock and roll scene. He wrote and recorded *Rock Around The Clock* in 1954, but the record never took and everyone wrote it off then as a very small-time hit. Then, a whole year later, it turned up again as the theme song of the film *Blackboard Jungle*, and that was another story. In the context of that film of teenage rebellion, the song took on a whole new meaning. It became the first song to have a special secret defiant meaning for teenagers only. It was the first inkling teenagers had that they might be a force to be reckoned with, in numbers alone. If there could be one song, there could be others; there could be a whole world of songs, and then, a whole world. Unwittingly, Bill Haley, basically a very square man, had opened up a Pandora's box of teenage emotions. He had done so unwittingly because he was not *for* what he started. And he was always apologizing for the monster he created. Musically he was proud though. Proud that as far back as 1951 he was combining Dixie, rhythm and blues, country and western, and pop in what was to become one of the basic rock and roll sounds. He always said that he had developed rock and roll, while Alan Freed, the disc jockey, had only *named* it and *exploited* it. Well, to say *Rock Around The Clock* was a sensation is a gross understatement. It was the *Marseillaise* of the teenage revolution. Later he followed up with his own version of Joe Turner's rhythm and blues hit *Shake Rattle and Roll*. And there were a lot of other hits. Haley was enormously successful, not just in America but all over the world. Wherever he went there were riots, and years after the rock and roll craze had abated in the United States, it still went on dizzily in other countries. When the boom died down, he never did stop working. During England's rock revival of 1968 Bill was back there, with scores of old rockers at the airport to greet him, all drape-shape suits and boot-lace ties, obviously dying to tear up more seats and wreck more cinemas. Oh, how they had been waiting for this day!

Historically, Haley had the first international rock hit. He gave teenagers the first heady taste of a music of their own. But while he was moving into that sound, so, in other places, were others. Fats Domino. Jerry Lee Lewis. Buddy Holly. Little Richard. Elvis. It wasn't that Haley happened and everyone else copied so much as that some of the country people were casting an interested eye at rhythm and blues and arriving at much the same thing independently. What Haley did with rock and roll, or whatever it was in those early days, was to make it a commercial proposition for the charts. When *Rock Around The Clock* worked for him, a score of others said, "Why, that's exactly the sort of music I'm playing," and moved in. Others still simply imitated. It was a fad. It was an explosion. It was a revolution. After that, a million things became possible. Black rock like Fats Domino. Black country rock like Chuck Berry. Elvis. Polite white rock like Pat Boone. And eventually a teenage scene so mewling and insipid that only the Beatles could save it.

HEAD MUSIC/In its most common use, head music can be defined as music that enhances the marijuana experience – gentle, soothing, calm, but at the same time with enough happening to engage heightened perceptions. (Marijuana is said to increase the awareness of instrumental passages often "lost" in the overall sound when heard under normal conditions.) Some music is more appropriate to certain chemical states than to others. There is music that doesn't even start to make sense, say drug aficionados, until the mind has been suitably altered or bent to receive it. Ravi Shankar's sitar music, not entirely to his pleasure, is highly regarded head music, as are Shankar-influenced tracks like the Beatles' *Norwegian Wood*, the Byrd's *Eight Miles High* and the Stones' *Paint It Black*, all of which have sitar sounds. There are people who claim you can't possibly know what's going on in Van Dyke Parks's album *SONG CYCLE* if you are listening to it straight. *Day In The Life*, from the Beatles' *SERGEANT PEPPER*, is the ultimate in head music with sound effects that are guaranteed to turn on a little old lady from Dubuque with not as much as an aspirin to help. But no "head" would dream of listening to it unaided. The Beach Boys' *Good Vibrations* with its screaming theremin and its unearthly harmonies is such a good piece of head music that it could be a million dollar seller if it were expanded into an album or, better, an hour-long tape.

THE JIMI HENDRIX EXPERIENCE/*Jimi Hendrix (guitar), Mitch Mitchell (drums), Noel Redding (bass).*
Jimi Hendrix was one of the experiences of 1968 – or 1967, if you were on the ball and found him early. An unlikely hybrid, the Seattle-born Negro with years of orthodox rhythm and blues tours behind him was snatched from a New York discotheque, where he was playing brilliant back-up guitar, zipped over to England by trans-Atlantic jet and exposed to a London in the most extreme throes of freaked-out frilled-out flower power, lace power and velvet power. And then when the time was ripe and this escapee from the southern music trap was considered sufficiently Anglicized, he was zipped right back across the Atlantic with his ruffles, his velvet hat, his guitar and his two English sidemen. It was the summer of 1967 and the Monkees tour, and no mother who had taken her apple-cheeked little daughter to shriek over Peter, Mike, Mickey and Davy was ready for what Hendrix got into that hot night out at the Forest Hills stadium. Lynne Randell, who was little

and blonde and wholesome, had just sung her numbers in her sequined jump suit. It was a bit daring, *Going Out Of My Head*, and Mom got very protective about that. But wait. That was nothing. On stage now with that insolent saunter came the Jimi Hendrix Experience. Three huge frizzy dandelion heads. Three decadent Regency rakes. Amplifiers turned up to infinity. And now the star, like Christ between his two thieves, black hair flying from his head in electric fright, doing things to his guitar so passionate, so concentrated and so intense that anyone with halfway decent manners had to look away. And that was the way the act began, not ended. By the time it was over he had lapped and nuzzled his guitar with his lips and tongue, caressed it with his inner thighs, jabbed at it with a series of powerful pelvic thrusts. Even the little girls who'd come to see the Monkees understood what this was about. What Mick Jagger and the early rockers had so saucily promised and hinted at, Jimi Hendrix delivered. And was there ever a row! The Mothers of American Girl Monkee Watchers or some such association had him taken off the tour at once. (Exactly what his gleeful manager had hoped would happen. The publicity was perfect.) After that they could hardly go wrong. Nothing changed except the guitar-nuzzling was even more intimate, the caresses more intense and the thrusts so furious that from time to time the guitar at the end of it all would burst into flames and no one would seem the least surprised. Jimi Hendrix was hotter and sexier and more explicit than Jim Morrison, the Rolling Stones, the Beatles, Mae West and a battalion of strippers. And though there had been some pretty acrobatic bumping and grinding along the rhythm and blues route and up at Harlem's Apollo, this was not one of your come-back-to-Africa performances in shiny suit and processed hair. This was the Wild Man of Borneo, all right, but crossed with all the languid, silken, jewelled elegance of a Carnaby Street fop. It was a very erotic combination, and no doubt a shrewdly calculated one. First layer: noble savage. Second layer: San Francisco acid freak. Third layer: swinging London dandy. How *could* he lose?

Chas Chandler found him in a New York club, playing backings as he had always done (but not without hopes and dreams and a million jam sessions all over America). Chandler, an ex-Animal, who knew audiences, knew that Hendrix had it and that England was ready for a black superhero. Hendrix was a fantastic success in England, which could have been predicted, but Chandler couldn't wait to play his hunches in America. He had done everything right first, like getting Mitch Mitchell, a pale frail drummer who played faster than the speed of light, and Noel Redding, a pale frail bass player. The whole notion of a rock trio then was very new (though Cream, which emerged about the same time, was to make it a very popular form). When the excitement died down it became apparent that there was music there. Hendrix was, for one thing, a very good writer. Much of the material was his own. He also did Dylan material and took it one step further (his interpretation of *All Along The Watchtower* was masterful). His guitar playing was admired by the one man whose opinion counted, Cream guitarist Eric Clapton, who warned that you have to be there when Hendrix is really trying, and that Hendrix only tries when he has to. If he can get away with theatre and pyrotechnics, he will do so. But if it's music people want, and he senses it, he gives the pelvic girdle a rest and no longer feels compelled to roar out his words like a randy lion. Instead he settles down to some very serious blues guitar work, the kind that makes other musicians' voices drop with respect when they mention his name.

BUDDY HOLLY (Charles Hardin Holly)/He was one of the giants of early rock, a figure so important in the history of popular music that it is impossible to hear a song on the charts today that does not owe something to the tall, slim, bespectacled boy from Lubbock, Texas. He started off in 1956, as so many of those early rock figures did, as a country singer, but from the summer of 1957 until his death in February 1959 he recorded scores of rock songs – the great classic *Peggy Sue*, *That'll Be The Day*, *Maybe Baby* (with the Crickets), *Oh Boy*, *Early In The Morning*. Just how prolific he was in a career that was only a matter of months came to light recently in England during the great rock revival of 1968 when four albums (47 titles) of his were released under the title *THE IMMORTAL BUDDY HOLLY*. More than any other singer of that era, he brings back a time when music was fun, when rock was fun, when no one was trying to push it as an art form and when sheer animal exuberance was what counted. As well as his own material (co-written with manager Norman Petty), he did all the standards of the day: *Shake Rattle And Roll*, *Blue Suede Shoes*, *Rip It Up*. Like a lot of country boys of that time who automatically headed for country music, he was sidetracked by the success other country musicians were having in the new field of rock –

Elvis Presley, Bill Haley, Johnny Cash, Jerry Lee Lewis, Carl Perkins. Once he got going, he became one of the big hitmakers of rock. You only have to listen to those hits to know where a lot of the early Beach Boys and Beatles come from, not to mention the hundreds of groups that literally wouldn't have been possible without him. At the time, of course, there was no such thing as the serious rock appreciation that sprang up in 1967 and 1968. People didn't know much about music, they just knew what they liked. Adults put him down with the rest of the Presley era as shock rock. Kids just remembered it was impossible not to dance, not to groove, while he sang. Most of the giants of ten years later, of the booming rock scene of the late sixties, were teenagers when Holly was king and their music reflects it. Looking back from the twin peaks of psychedelia and electronic gadgetry, he comes through fresher than ever. It would be nice to speculate where Buddy Holly would be today if he had lived. But he didn't. He died with two others who were just beginning to make their names in rock, Richie Valens and Big Bopper, in a plane crash in Mason City, Iowa, on February 3, 1959. There are people who still weep at the thought of the talent that went down that day.

JANIS IAN/This prodigious child was singing and writing songs at fifteen. By the time she was sixteen she had an album out. Her single, *Society's Girl* (white-girl-meets-black-boy, girl-loses-boy, girl-blames-society) was not the sort of song the disc jockeys were accustomed to playing, and they obviously would never have done so but for the intervention of Leonard Bernstein, conductor of the New York Philharmonic, who in a TV special on rock made a point of featuring the diminutive Miss Ian (four foot seven) and her ballad of miscegenation. That was it. The record took off and so did Janis. Her songs are concerned with the hypocrisies of modern society. She has clearly been influenced by Bob Dylan, Joan Baez and Tim Buckley, but her style is her own and her following, especially among earnest middle-class sixteen-year old girls who are also concerned with the hypocrisies of modern society, is enormous.

JEFFERSON AIRPLANE/*Jorma Kaukonen (lead guitar), Jack Casady (bass), Spencer Dryden (replaced Skip Spence) (drums), Paul Kantner (rhythm guitar), Marty Balin (vocals), Grace Slick (replaced Signe Andersen)(bass & rhythm guitar, vocals).*

Jefferson Airplane was the first of the big San Francisco bands to make it, the first to snap up a big contract, the first to get big national promotion, the first with a big national hit (*Somebody To Love* in 1967). The implications of that are enormous. Until then, in spite of the minor eccentricities of the Byrds and the Lovin' Spoonful, the national rock scene was reasonably sedate. A Beatles cut here, a touch of Carnaby Street there, but little that was really freaky. The arrival of the Jefferson Airplane changed all that forever. Even the New York hippies had to do some serious readjusting when the Airplane first arrived (their first piece of promotion was the first of the psychedelic hippie-nouveau San Francisco style posters most New Yorkers had never seen). This was early 1967, when San Francisco and Haight-Ashbury and Flower Power were in full bloom, and the Airplane breezed into New York to plant those first seeds of love power in the East. Initially, the nation as a whole was a little suspicious, a little afraid of being taken in by a San Francisco hype. But you only had to hear Grace Slick and Marty Balin sing and Casady on bass and those incredible songs that told you, between the lines, swirling tales of chemical journeys and wondrous discoveries – and you knew it was real. After all those years of Frankie Avalon and Pat Boone, it was startling to hear Gracie singing about acid and drugs and pills on your friendly neighborhood station.

The commercial (as well as the artistic) success of the Airplane was immediate and enormous. Record companies rushed to sign up every other San Francisco band (after having completely ignored them). None ever equaled the Airplane in draw power, though Big Brother and the Holding Company, thanks only to Janis Joplin, was to get a number one album. In any case, we now had on a national level what San Francisco had had all along since the golden days of the fall of 1965 – the San Francisco sound. Apart from the goodtimey noises of the Spoonful and the Mamas and Papas, the San Francisco sound was the first original sound the United States had since the English invasion of 1964. (And the English loved it too.) It was a time of be-ins and bells and flowers and incense, and the oriental undertones of the San Francisco sound were the right background music for it all. There were bands that played good music and bands that were a total environment happening. The Jefferson Airplane hit you from all sides. They had Grace Slick, the first girl singer with a big band (she had, however, replaced another girl singer). Grace was an ex-model, a great beauty with a piercing voice. And though she tended to dominate, the band also had Marty Balin, one of the great singers of love songs in modern rock. They sang around each other and around the music like dancers.

The Airplane has a very wide musical range. In the beginning, when they were playing for dances at the Fillmore in San Francisco – where, if the participants weren't exactly zonked out of their minds, they at least wanted to feel that way – anything went. They could freak out all over the stage; they could get into jazz improvisations, into folk, into blues, into anything. There was no form in the usual rigid sense. There was no "audience" sitting rigidly with rigid expectations. Everything was flowing and free form, with just one important discipline, the usual one: give the customers what they came for. In this case, the customers came to be made one with the music. So there would be long instrumental passages, when everyone wanted to move and dance, and then the voices confirming for them what they knew already. *Triad* is about three people who all love one another, or at least, that's the only way out for them. *White Rabbit* reminds you that *Alice In Wonderland* was probably about drugs. In *Ulysses* you realize that James Joyce was ahead of his time and belongs to the age of McLuhan after all. And so on.

Away from the hot, heavy, sensual atmosphere of the San Francisco Fillmore (and do they ever miss it), the Jefferson Airplane has to come on like any other band. In a recording studio it was hard for them, since so much of their act was dependent upon their contact with their fans. And even in a concert hall without the feedback of that glazed, stoned Fillmore audience, without patterns and images swirling around them, it's very hard. Whenever possible they take Glenn McKay's Headlights with them, a light show that produces visually what the Airplane does with music. (Or is it the other way around?) But when they play, something does happen, even if it's not always their best. And Donovan sings *Fly Jefferson Airplane*, not just because the band has the right name but because it is one of those bands you fly with. That's the whole thing about acid rock. Having experienced, as most San Francisco bands did (as most young San Francisco people did), the sometimes frightening, sometimes ecstatic but always overwhelming effects of lysergic acid diethylamide, the Airplane could not conceive of music in any other way. The group grew with San Francisco, with Timothy Leary's drug revolution, with everything that followed.

In 1965 Grace was with another group, the Great Society, which often appeared on the same bill as the Airplane. When the Airplane's girl singer left and the Great Society split, Grace moved in with the Airplane, taking a lot of her songs with her. (Grace says it was the Airplane that inspired her and her husband and brother-in-law to start their own group.) Since then a lot has happened. The magic went out of San Francisco. The San Francisco sound was imitated, cheapened and weakened, so that by 1968 it was stale. And the Airplane became America's top group anyway. This should have meant the kiss of death for the group – the usual death from over-work, over-promotion and too much money – and it's true that the hard core is unhappy about the Airplane's playing class gigs like the Whitney Museum and the Waldorf on New Year's Eve. Nevertheless, that mixture of jazz, folk, blues and surrealistic electronic tinkering works, and even when they're not performing well they never sound uptight. Years, or maybe centuries from now, someone will discover that there really was a music of the spheres, and it will sound not unlike the music the Airplane plays in the moments of its highest flight.

B.B. KING/He was playing the blues before Eric Clapton was born – but not too many people knew about it. Not too many people knew too much about B.B. King except that Clapton (and other blues guitarists like Mike Bloomfield) kept mentioning him in interviews, and that when he did his voice turned pale with respect. That was it until one night early in 1968 at the Café Au Go Go in New York. The Cream were at the top, then, and Eric Clapton, their guitarist, was going to be jamming there that night. Also due to play were Elvin Bishop (lead guitarist for Paul Butterfield) and B.B. King. B.B. King?

So now we are inside and the stage lights are on and there's Clapton, decked out from head to foot in psychedelia, complete with flaming painted guitar and Afro-fuzz hair. And Elvin Bishop, more Afro-fuzz, funky as all get-out, and chewing away on a toothpick. And beside him – now, just a moment, hold it, what? – sittin' back, relaxin' on a stool in a corner, is this middle-aged spade, shiny suit, slicked-down hair, smoking a Tiparillo while his candy apple Guild just rests on his lap. The show starts. Everybody gets together for basic blues number one – bass player, drummer, everyone's sort of struggling to hang on in there. Elvin steps forward, intent, toothpick clamped down hard between his teeth. Solo.

A few complicated blues riffs, nothing too flashy, but you know it's good 'cause it just looks so hard. And now it's Eric's turn. Swaying, moccasined foot stomping the floor. Flash, flash. Such dexterity. The crowd is wild, and Eric's done it again. The solo ends. And now, oh yeah, the chubby spade in the corner. Well, for a start, old B. doesn't even stand up. He doesn't have to. He just sits back in his chair, still relaxin', smilin' a little and smokin' his Tiparillo, and suddenly he just lets go a little pure and ever-so-simple soul. Like he's been doin' this for a long time. No fancy playing now, just a couple of strokes, and – well, the whole room is wiped out. A great collective gasp. It goes on just long enough to prove his point.

The point: contemporary white guitarists learned the blues from B.B. King. His slow, easy style of playing and singing has long made him a hit artist on the rhythm and blues charts. But it wasn't until recently, until people like Clapton talked about their sources, that he came to the attention of the vast white audience that knew the blues only as interpreted by other whites. Once they heard him play, and others like him, it was all different, because you couldn't see B. at work without thinking of how many other unknown masters were still lurking behind the scene, undiscovered by a whole generation. It was probably because of B.B. King that the 1968 audiences suddenly became interested in musical roots and the men who had influenced the music they were buying up in such huge quantities. And it's one of the great ironies in music today that American kids had to learn about one of their own big blues men from a bunch of English kids (the Rolling Stones, Cream) who, as always, had had much more respect for America's black heritage than most people in America. In any case, success or no success, B.B. King has been around for years and is likely to continue to be. That kind of musician doesn't ever stop playing.

THE KINKS/*Peter Quaife (bass guitar, vocals), Mick Avory (drums), Ray Davies (harmonica, rhythm guitar, vocals), Dave Davies (vocals, lead guitar).* The Kinks are probably the one group most admired by other musicians and certainly the one invariably held up as an example when someone is trying to prove that the Beatles aren't all that good and there are groups that were doing cleverer things earlier. *You Really Got Me*, the first of their singles to be released in the States, came out in August 1964 – a time when music, even the Beatles' music, was fairly simple – yet it was an incredibly complex number with the voices doing all sorts of elaborate things, things most other groups wouldn't even try (although the Beach Boys did eventually, months later). The Kinks instinctively anticipated all the complexities of post-*Good Vibrations* and post-*SERGEANT PEPPER* music, but intricate as their vocal harmonies were, the sound was never anything but delicate and subtle. *All Day And All Of The Night* in 1965 was another single no one dared imitate, until 1968 when the Doors did *Hello I Love You*, a song so similar the Kinks thought of suing. Ray Davies, Kink leader and writer, had already established himself as a composer and lyricist equaled only by Bob Dylan and the Beatles. *A Well Respected Man* and *Dedicated Follower Of Fashion* showed the particular gift for light, wry satire that put him up there with the masters. *Well Respected Man*, a put-down of the English middle-class, was done at the end of 1965, scarcely a breath behind the Beatles' first *real* album, *RUBBER SOUL*. All this time one thing was apparent to Kinks fans (many in London, a loyal few in America, and every musician of note in either place), and that was that the Kinks were suffering commercially because of all sorts of basic problems – no image, not enough hard sell. In places like New York, they never got anything like the major airplay they should have gotten. In cities where they did, they were right on top of the charts, but no one seemed to learn that lesson. They never had the big ballyhooed tours lesser groups had. None of the usual big-group apparatus was used to help them along. Yet every single and every album was masterly. *Dandy*, sung sweetly by the Hermits, was another Davies put-down when sung by the Kinks. *Sunny Afternoon* was one of the beautiful songs of rock. So was *Dead End Street*. Soon it became obvious that so much of Ray Davies' energy was going into writing and recording that little was left over to promote the group as a live performing unit. People have written a lot about the Kinks, but there is little to say because there is no spectacle, no drama, no intrigue – just that music.

LEADBELLY (Huddie Ledbetter)/By the time he died in 1949, aged sixty-one, Leadbelly had influenced most of the folksingers of the '40s, especially Pete Seeger and Woody Guthrie, who in turn gave so much to the folk people of the '50s and early '60s. There are people around today who think they're singing like Bob Dylan when they're actually singing like Bob Dylan singing like Woody Guthrie singing like Leadbelly.

One of the first folk songs ever to make the hit parade, and it was number one for thirteen weeks in 1950, was *Goodnight Irene*, written by Leadbelly and sung by the Weavers.

JERRY LEE LEWIS/It was the golden age of rock, that period from 1956 to 1960, but scarcely anyone in it – except Elvis – was destined to come out of it unscathed by scandal, or in some cases, even alive. Jerry Lee Lewis, the boy from Louisiana who sang such all-time classic rock hits as *Great Balls Of Fire* and *Whole Lotta Shakin' Going On* in 1957, was no exception. He was Elvis's contemporary, worked out of the same Memphis studio that gave Elvis his big start, and went in for the same hillbilly rave-up performances that characterized early rock, only his freaking was done at the keyboard and he belted the piano with all madness, energy, fists, feet and elbows. He was twenty-two, married to the daughter of his bass player – she was thirteen (and his cousin, some say). It was one of those young marriages not unusual in the South. And as Lewis said himself, "I know lots of people married to thirteen-year-olds." And she said, "I'd marry him a million times," and that was nice. But on his May 1957 English tour the hotel asked him to leave. The twenty-seven shows that were booked were canceled. Silence greeted his first appearance. "I sho' hope yawl ain't half as dead as you sound," said Jerry Lee. "Go home, crumb, baby snatcher," was the answer. "It's just jealousy," said young wife Myra. But there it was. The ball was over. The fire had gone out. Jerry Lee faded away but, like some others of that time, was able to keep going on a local, if no longer national or international, level. In 1968 Jack Good produced a rhythm and blues version of *Othello* starring Lewis as Iago. It was very well received. In the same year he also began a highly successful comeback in the country and western field.

LITTLE RICHARD/His pompadour was high and his hip action wicked when Elvis was still a pimply kid mowing lawns in Memphis. He was the model for 99 per cent of the screaming, jet-propelled pelvic freak-outs of the post-Elvis early rock era, down to the shiny suits, lurid showmanship and acrobatic piano-playing. Little Richard was wildly frantic and intense, all urgency and fervor, given to wild falsetto shrieks and a lot of showy costuming. He was the reason that much later everyone realized there wasn't one thing in those feverish rock years that wasn't copped straight from what was then known as "race" music (black rhythm and blues). Pat Boone rode to fame on his songs and the Beatles took a lot from his style. Mick Jagger and James Brown have never stopped doing the raving Little Richard thing. Richard Penniman had fought hard, though, but when he finally came into his own, he decided to leave rock for religion. Happily he did come back. Once you have seen Little Richard it is very difficult to take any other rocker seriously. He did it all first.

LOVIN' SPOONFUL/*Steve Boone (bass), John Sebastian (harmonica, autoharp, lead vocals), Jerry Yester (replaced Zal Yanovsky)(lead guitar), Joe Butler (drums).*
For a lot of people in America, the Lovin' Spoonful was Liverpool – in Manhattan. Our own little moptops, born, bred and raised right here in the streets we walked each day, hanging around outside the coffee shops, playing in the basket houses, making a nuisance of themselves in Izzy Young's Folklore Centre. Scores of kids must have gone the Lovin' Spoonful route at the same time as the Spoonful, but John Sebastian, son of a great musician, had talent. And when all his folky friends started making it before he did, he was only playing harp on their albums. Before the Spoonful there was a strong, very creative folk scene which had already spawned Dylan, among others. There was a country scene down in Nashville that wasn't really being felt in New York – except by Sebastian, who had been in a jug band, and by the Spoonful's producer, Erik Jacobsen, who had played banjo in a country string group. And there were a lot of leftovers from pre-Beatles hard rock, tough commercial little groups playing at dances. And in California there was a burgeoning folk-rock scene with the Byrds and Sonny and Cher. And then, of course, there were the English groups – no American group had anything like their stature in America or out of it.

There had been an attempt to change all this but they had failed. And the Spoonful, with all their talent, weren't that good, weren't clicking or jelling. The story goes – and it's such a legend now that everyone has forgotten what's true – that they were at the Night Owl and terrible, and that Joe Marra, the owner, told them to go away and practise. Zally and Joe had a room at the Albert Hotel then, mainly to store equipment. When they rehearsed there, there were complaints. So Miss Feldman, the assistant manager, suggested the basement. And that was it. The group made it. The basement became a shrine; and no musician feels he's a musician unless he's stayed at the Albert and rehearsed among the pools of water and the cockroaches. The Albert became *the* hotel and the Spoonful became *the* group that eventually turned the hurricane eye of rock away from Liverpool and London to New York and Los Angeles (and later San Francisco). The tide had turned. *Daydream*, written and sung by Sebastian, was the big hit of early '66 along with the Mamas and the Papas' *California Dreamin'*, a beautiful coincidence, since the two groups were friends. It was winter and both songs were about good times and good climes. Later, much later, people were to say that the Spoonful never developed, that the songs after a while were all the same, that there was never anything like the maturing of the Beatles or Stones, or even the Byrds or the Rascals. But at the time it seemed like one perfect hit followed another and that each had the happiness of jug-band music and country strings and some of the sweetness of folk, with all the punch of rock.

Off stage and on, the Spoonful were such *characters*. John had sidies and steel glasses when both were new. Zally wore a cowboy hat all the time and sometimes great bear-like furs. None of the four ever dressed mod-English as other groups did but from the start wore the striped shirts and vests that were the uniform of every Village kid. American kids couldn't believe their luck, that they had their own group. On tour, to Americans the Spoonful seemed so real and human. And when they visited England they wowed them. (They even made friends with the Beatles.) Joe got some of the most English gear in creation but he still looked, in his undertaker's coat, like a Greenwich Village kid playing Carnaby Street. Even if the songs weren't developing, and they were no longer America's only moptops, things looked like they might remain rosy forever. Then, and this was before rock busts were a frequent occurrence, there was a bust in San Francisco. It was revealed later that huge pressures were put on Zally, who could easily have been deported. All anyone knew was that Zally and Steve had fingered their source, and that they were free but the source wasn't. In San Francisco in 1967 their name was mud, their albums were used a doormats, groupies were urged not to ball them. Later, Ralph Gleason said for heaven's sake, forgive and forget, remember what Lenny Bruce said about how easy it is to blurt out everything when the hot lead is on its way to your interior. But later was too late. Zally left to go solo and was replaced by Jerry Yester.

Yester was a fine musician, but already it wasn't the same. Sebastian left to go into other ventures, a musical, a solo album. And Zally, who hadn't done too well solo, returned. But it was over. The group split. They had done what they had set out to do, and on the way changed the whole musical scene.

MAMAS AND THE PAPAS/*Denny Doherty (vocals), Cass Elliot (vocals), John Phillips (vocals, guitar), Michelle Phillips (vocals).*

The Mamas and the Papas were the royal family of American rock – not because their music keeps growing and progressing to plateau after plateau of greatness (it doesn't), but because they were the first, with the Spoonful, of the *big* American groups, the first, that is, since the Beatles. Besides, they look regal. John Phillips, tall and stately, looks like Everyking, Cass Elliot, majestic earth mother, like Everyqueen, and Michelle and Denny the essence of princehood and princesshood. They came to us, that dreary winter of 1965–66, singing that all the leaves were brown and the sky was grey and that it was a good time to dream of California. Until then, everything new and interesting and commercially successful (all those things *can* go hand in hand) was English and had been since 1964 and the Beatles. Now, with the Mamas and the Papas, the spotlight that had been fixed so firmly on Liverpool and London suddenly swiveled over to America (and caught the Spoonful's *Daydream* as well). America had had Dylan, of course, but not a group scene with any sort of style, and nothing like those first three singles the Mamas and the Papas brought out in less than a year.

The story of the group was new then, though by 1968 there must have been a thousand groups that told variants of it. They came out of the Village folk scene that had developed around Dylan and those who followed him. Cass had been with groups before (the Mugwumps and the Big Three), but these were not particularly successful. As the Mamas and the Papas tell it, the four met in the Virgin Islands, where there was not too much more to do than sing, but still the blend was not quite perfect till a piece of piping fell on Cass and changed her voice. Back in California the sound impressed people in the business who, having made one adjustment already to English moptops, found it difficult to readjust their vision to this motley quartet. The word "hippie" was not then in common use, but the concept existed. Groups in beards and boots and funny hats and strange drag were still new at the end of 1966 and not the cliché they became in 1968. The way this group looked, once the music business got over the shock of it all, was a novelty and very promotable. And the Mamas and the Papas were a sensation musically, visually and commercially. And what was really exciting was that they managed to establish the fact that there *was* an American scene. This was America's answer to the British invasion. Because of all this, it's quite incidental that the Mamas and the Papas never did live up to the glorious promise of their first year and that although every album they did sold, by the time they got to their fourth, in 1967, they just couldn't do it, couldn't put out another bland, predictable, salable, repetitive product. So in the middle of it all, in the middle of the taping, they just cut out, splitting to England and Europe to clear their heads, rethink their music and their lives, and give themselves a rest. It was a case of too much too soon – too much work, too much touring, too much freshness expected of them and too much to think about. No one really minded. Everyone understood. By 1968 Cass decided she wanted to sing solo. They had never intended to stay together any longer anyway, they all said. John Phillips, particularly, wanted to be not so much a performer as a writer, producer and discoverer of talent. Always there was much more to say about the Mamas and the Papas than the sweet-sad harmonies and the number one hits. They really *were* the first hippies to make it big and strike it rich, living in luxury in Bel Air and setting a bad example for the neighbors. Later, when other hippie groups made it, it no longer seemed unusual. But it was the Mamas and the Papas who established the precedent.

MEMPHIS SOUND/The first "sound" to come out of Memphis was Elvis. Elvis and Carl Perkins and Jerry Lee Lewis and Roy Orbison, all of whom started their careers with a small recording company in Memphis called Sun Records. Before long, the company, and the town, became famous for that blend of country-and-western and rhythm-and-blues that music people named rock and roll. That was Memphis in the early fifties, and the success of those early names lured scores of others over to try their luck with the new sound. When rock and roll fizzled out in the late fifties, so did Memphis, as a recording center. By the middle sixties Memphis was a name to be reckoned with again. What was coming out of Memphis now was not the old style rock and roll anymore, but the sound of blues, rhythm and blues, and soul, a sound familiar enough to black Americans but quite new and wonderfully exciting to the white buyers who were first discovering it. It took some of the English groups (they had always been big rhythm and blues freaks over there) to tell white Americans about their own sounds.

Now what was happening in Memphis was Carla Thomas, Sam and Dave, the late Otis Redding, Booker T and the MG's – some of the best music in the country. It wasn't the Memphis air, but Stax, a recording company with its own house group of seven hand-picked studio musicians who played on all the records in almost telepathic accord not only with each other but with every artist they backed. The seven were Booker T and the MG's (on organ, guitar, bass and drums, plus three horn players collectively known as the Mar-keys). No one else gets to play on Stax records, and no one outside the company gets to use the studio, let alone its musicians (despite constant and heartfelt pleadings from everyone from the Rolling Stones down). It's a very personal freewheeling sound and they themselves say that the difference between Memphis sound and Motown's Detroit sound is that the Memphis people play what they feel and the Detroit people play what they're told to. Another big studio is a mere hour's drive from Memphis at Muscle Shoals, Alabama. This is where Aretha Franklin, Wilson Pickett and Percy Sledge recorded their biggest hits in 1967. Muscle Shoals is said to be a little more country than the already countrified Stax studio, with an emphasis on a gospel sound. The Boxtops live and record in Memphis, which explains why they sound so black and soulful. Albert King records in Memphis too. It's important to note that the original country and rock sound that put Memphis on the map still creeps into the recordings there, giving them that special little extra something that other studios have found completely impossible to duplicate.

MRS. ELVA MILLER/She couldn't carry a tune. She was no beauty. But in 1966 this middle-aged lady was one of the great hit-making phenomena of rock. Mrs. Miller's gimmick: a non-voice. Listening to her struggling and screeching her way through the top forty was one of the funniest experiences in years. Like so many *in* things of that trendy year, it was high camp. And high camp made funnier by the fact that Mrs. Miller honestly believed people liked her voice. Or at least she was shrewd enough to let people think so. It seems that she had always fancied herself a singer and had often made, at her own expense, records of herself singing sacred and inspirational tunes. The pianist and organist who accompanied her for these private recordings thought it might be "interesting" to hear her on more contemporary material. He got her to do four sides and took them along to a friend who was a producer. The result, in April 1966, was *MRS. MILLER'S GREATEST HITS*. They had her making personal appearances in Hawaii, on the Ed Sullivan show, and at the Royal Tahitian Hotel in Ontario. She had a marvelous time but faded out after about a year. By 1968 someone came along who did Mrs. Miller's high-camp thing bigger and better: Tiny Tim. Even Mrs. Miller couldn't beat that one.

JONI MITCHELL/Tall, pale, slim, frail, the very model of a lady folk singer, Joni didn't emerge as a personality until 1968 with an album and some delicate personal appearances. But she was a name to be reckoned with from the moments some big names – Judy Collins, Buffy Sainte-Marie, Tom Rush and Dave Van Ronk – started doing her material a year before. Her *Both Sides Now* is one of the most beautiful songs of this decade, whether it's rasped out by Dave Van Ronk or honeyed out by Miss Collins, with tinkling bells in the background. *Urge For Going* is what Mitchell audiences scream for. She's probably the most talented lady songwriter about, though not quite as big a singer as a writer.

THE MONKEES/*Mickey Dolenz (guitar, lead vocals, drums), Davy Jones (vocals, tambourine), Michael Nesmith (bass). Previous Member: Peter Tork (guitar).*
The cynicism with which it was done was incredible and created a lot of resentment. Four boys would be cast in Beatle-like roles, and each installment in the fall 1966 TV series would be done as much like *A Hard Day's Night* as humanly possible. Nobody really minded that the Monkees, as this new group was called, were manufactured entirely in cold blood and for bluntly commercial reasons. But when, never having played together before, their records hit the top of the charts on the strength of what seemed like nothing more than TV exposure and a good sound financial push, the bitterness from other struggling groups was overwhelming. The story went that they were being told what to play note by note, that it had all been worked out for them, and that

half the time on the records *they* weren't playing but the Candy Store Prophets, experienced musicians (with Bobby Hart of the Hart and Boyce team which produced and wrote many of the Monkees' early hits), were. Today, merely to mention this possibility brings on the wrath of several million Monkee fans who regard even the suggestion as treason. But it really no longer matters whether the Monkees did play every note themselves on those early singles or not.

The four boys were brought together one way or another (the story that they all answered an ad in *Variety* is sometimes contradicted) and told they would star in a weekly TV series about a rock group. It was one of the Beatles who pointed out that just getting out that weekly episode was a full-time job and that it wasn't fair to expect the group to be monster musicians as well. And they said it too, that they were hired as *actors*, actors who would portray musicians, and that musical background would help but that that wasn't what it was about. So then why put out singles if they weren't musicians? The answer to that is why not? The public bought, didn't they? And in the beginning it was like that. The Monkees were treated as one big hype. It was very hard on the boys. Not so much on Davy, who was basically an actor (he'd been very big on Broadway as the Artful Dodger in *Oliver*). Not so much on Mickey, who also was a former child actor and had starred in the *Circus Boy* TV series. But on Mike Nesmith and Peter Tork, who had paid a few dues in the music scene, it was rough. The point was in the beginning, with the series and the publicity, there hadn't been *time* to get together musically. But there was pressure to get a single out, so everyone did the best he could, and if that involved a little help from professional musicians, it wasn't the first time or the last time it had happened and with much more established groups than the poor old Monkees. Still, there was no doubt, and they were the first to admit it at the start, that they weren't four musical geniuses.

Mickey Dolenz had been a lead singer with a group called the Missing Links and he could play guitar and had started to play drums before he became a Monkee but, well, he was no Ginger Baker. Davy Jones played a little guitar and he'd sung in *Oliver* and Screen Gems had tried unsuccessfully to make him a solo singer before the Monkees. Peter Tork did that whole Greenwich Village coffeehouse circuit and had a lot of musical know-how. And Mike Nesmith was also performing professionally before the Monkees. After a while it got to be a matter of pride for the Monkees to master their own instruments, so when things were a little settled in the summer of 1967 they got together a live "act" with which they toured the country proving they could provide a pleasant evening's entertainment as well as anyone. The tour won them a lot of respect from people who had previously dismissed them as a nongroup. It was not that they were so fantastic, though they certainly were entertaining and competent, but that they were willing to face an audience and be judged like any other group was to their credit. Somewhere in all this they got away from their plastic image into something a bit earthier. Individual personalities started to emerge. Nesmith's stint as a folk singer and comedian at Los Angeles' Troubadour stood him in good stead. (Later, when the Monkees were established, he wrote, produced and conducted an instrumental album of serious music, THE WICHITA TRAIN WHISTLE.) Dolenz did his James Brown imitation. Jones has Broadway ambitions. Tork is all gentleness and peace. It was the music people who first discovered that the Monkees were good guys. Everyone else followed. By 1968 it was distinctly *not done* to put down the Monkees. And to top things, they did a rather nice album that suggested there was more than TV exposure selling their singles for them. The end of 1968 saw their film *Head*, which finally established them as, if not exactly underground heroes, then underground pets. Early in 1969 Peter Tork left the group, but the Monkees decided to continue as a trio. Their latest album, *INSTANT REPLAY*, was recorded without Tork, and the group is supposedly much tighter now. Only time will tell if a barrel of three Monkees is as much fun as a barrel of four.

NASHVILLE SOUND/In Nashville they say there's no such thing as a "Nashville sound", which is odd, because the musicians and recording engineers down there are making a comfortable living providing it. They say there's no Nashville sound, just the happy, easy rapport of men who have worked together so long that communication is perfect and spontaneous. But that's not entirely right, for when those same men are flown to other places to play for recording sessions, it's just not the same. Oh, but that's because they're at their best when they're on their own comfortable home ground, they explain. So all right, it's not just something in the air, as some English musicians found when they went to record there with their own musicians. Those who come from far away to get the Nashville sound say it is a combination of three factors: the studio musicians, the relaxed atmosphere of the southern capital, and the cheerful mixture of homespun rawness and sheer professionalism of Nashville's country musicians.

Nashville has three lives. First and foremost it's the capital of country music with hundreds of recording and publishing companies and Grand Ole Opry every Friday and Saturday night. Secondly, long before the current country boom in rock, Nashville became a center for ailing singers, a place where they could go to bring a new fresh sound to their albums. Finally there is the Nashville where Buffy Sainte-Marie, Leonard Cohen, Joan Baez, Nancy Sinatra, Ian and Sylvia, and the Union Gap among others have gone to make albums. This new wave was started by Bob Dylan, who was persuaded by his producer, an old Nashville man named Bob Johnston, to cut some albums there – with great success. It was Dylan and the Byrds who brought a Nashville feel into rock – Dylan with *JOHN WESLEY HARDING* and his latest *NASHVILLE SKYLINE*, and the Byrds with *SWEETHEART OF THE RODEO*.

The Nashville sound uses light, feathery-textured drums, the sounds of banjos and fiddles and dobros (steel guitars) found in traditional country music, and the ching-ching-ching of guitars; and the musicians are always open to innovations within this framework. There are fine studio musicians at the Motown studios of Detroit and the Stax studios of Memphis, all with their own sound, but nowhere are there as many good session musicians in one place working better together than in Nashville.

ROY ORBISON/What is the secret of Roy Orbison's success? He's not beautiful or even grotesquely arresting. His stage act is non-existent. When singers all went hairy, Texas-born Orbison stayed pompadoured. A lone cowboy dressed in black with a pale face and perennial shades, he had an air that managed to be both sinister and old-fashioned. Yet he's constantly touring; he has the most fantastic fan clubs in England and Australia; and even in America, where he doesn't have major hits anymore, he still has an impressive following.

Orbison started in 1956 in the Elvis days and never really outgrew them. He's the last person anyone would think of trying to make a star and yet his sweet-sad songs attract not just record buyers, but other singers, especially, during the early rock boom, people like the late Buddy Holly, Jerry Lee Lewis and the Everly Brothers. He toured with the Beatles when he was big and they weren't. He toured with Elvis when Elvis was still a country singer, not a rock star. Nashville claims Orbison as a country singer, but he has to this day a lot of the mood of early rock. There must have been a million country singers trying to make it in rock after Elvis. Orbison, in his puzzling way, was one of the few who actually did.

PETER, PAUL AND MARY/*Peter Yarrow (tenor vocals), Paul Stookey (baritone vocals), Mary Travers (female vocals).*
In the summer of 1961 Fred Weintraub had opened a new place in the Village, the Bitter End, and he'd taken all these advertisements to say that the trio he had there, Peter, Paul and Mary, were the greatest thing that had happened in years. Who really believes that sort of talk from a guy who owns the place? Besides, the real folk action was all up at Gerdes' Folk City and Izzy Young's Folklore Centre, and the few folk people who did venture over to the Bitter End didn't think the two bearded guys and the blonde Villagey looking chick were very *authentic*. A small circle of friends hung around, of course, the still undiscovered Dylan among them. But this was 1962, and folk music wasn't where it was happening as far as money went. What was happening on the uptown music charts was the twist, Neil Sedaka and the Monster Mash.

The story of Peter, Paul and Mary begins with Albert Grossman, today the formidable manager of Dylan, Janis Joplin, the Band, Richie Havens, Butterfield, and Odetta, but previously known mainly for running the early Newport Folk Festivals. Folk performers had gotten into the charts from time to time, but only because of one good song, not as a consistent pattern. One big exception was the Kingston Trio, whose success made it clear that there was room at the top for a certain sort of processed pop folk. It was Grossman's inspiration to improve on the all-male Kingston Trio formula by teaming up two men and one girl, matching them carefully, visually as well as vocally. That was when Joan Baez was starting to move and Mary, blonde, long-haired gypsy that she was, was cast in the same mold. And there are people who say that if they didn't know better they'd suspect the Machiavellian Grossman arranged for facial surgery to heighten the resemblance between Peter and Paul. As for the names, could a man hope for better? Would they have had a chance as Marvin, Seymour and Shirley?

The rest is history. The PPM sound was a huge commercial success, and every single a hit. There were mutterings among the folk purists that they had sold out musically, but what the purists didn't know then was that Peter, Paul and Mary's success would open the doors for a massive folk take-over and, later, for Dylan, folk rock and a whole new American music scene that wasn't dominated by Tin Pan Alley. Their first big hit was a song by Pete Seeger that folk people had known for years (*If I Had A Hammer*). And now here were busboys whistling it and jukeboxes blaring it. And when Bob Dylan happened in a small way, Peter, Paul and Mary, now thoroughly established, were able to make him happen in a *big* way by making *Blowin' In The Wind* one of the top ten songs in the nation. They did a lot of other things that opened up a lot of other doors, directly and indirectly, including making it possible for a lot of folk people to make comfortable livings by letting the American public at large know folk was good entertainment.

Musically, the trio stuck to a predictable but very smooth and professional formula. From time to time they did introduce a new writer as they had Dylan. (One of their newest finds is the gifted Gary Shearston, who wrote *Sometime Lovin'*, which in fact he sings best himself.) The other interesting role Peter, Paul and Mary played was a political one. Generally, singers at the top of the charts had previously stayed out of politics. Peter, Paul and Mary sang at rallies and marches, in the good old folk tradition, but with the additional advantage of a huge public following. They did have a hammer, they had a bell, they had a song to sing, and they sang it where it counted.

WILSON PICKETT/One of the big soul kings of music, he started as a gospel man and singer of spirituals, first solo, then with the Falcons, one of Detroit's top groups. Then he discovered he had a talent for writing rhythm and blues songs – and for singing them. His first single after he went solo again in 1963, one of his own songs, *If You Need Me*, was a hit at once and still is a classic. It has been recorded by everyone from the Stones to Tom Jones. Since then, nearly all the singles he has done (many of them his own compositions) have become not just hits but all-time rock classics. Among the most notable are *In The Midnight Hour, Mustang Sally, Land Of 1,000 Dances, Ninety-Nine And A Half* and *I'm A Midnight Mover*. There isn't a rock group with soul leanings that hasn't performed these songs and borrowed more than a little from Pickett. He's probably solely responsible for the 1967–69 "soulization" of literally thousands of young white rock groups that a few years ago wouldn"t even have known what the word meant – and possibly still don't.

PINK FLOYD/*Rick Wright (organ, piano, cello, fiddle), Nick Mason (drums), Roger Waters (bass guitar, piano, beat frequency oscillator), Dave Gilmour (replaced Syd Barrett)(lead guitar), Mick Lowe (lights).*
Pink Floyd caused much excitement in England early in 1967 by being the first English rock group to come on stage with a light show. They were also one of the first English groups to play San Francisco style psychedelic rock. Since then, trying to understand the music of the Pink Floyd has become a sort of underground hobby in England. As with most experimental groups, it was difficult to decide what was sheer lack of control and what was courageous dabbling in the music of the future. They have been highly praised by some big names in music and dismissed as psychedelic muzak by others. In America, where psychedelic music and light shows started, the Pink Floyd never had quite the impact they had in England. Their experiments involve pure electronic sound, freaky electrical piano and an ethereal organ.

ELVIS PRESLEY/The Elvis Presley story has been told so often that it is sometimes difficult to remember that he is alive and well and thriving in Hollywood making film after film after film. Perhaps the reason most of what is written about him has that flat, dead quality of a past event is that Elvis in a sense "died" when he withdrew from the live concert circuit. And both his record releases and films, of which there are many, have a posthumous quality, as have the nostalgic pieces that are written about him from time to time. One of those nostalgic biographers, Kurt Von Meier, pointed out that Elvis was most alive in his immediate pre-stardom period. It started with the release, in 1954, of *Mystery Train* coupled with *I Forgot To Remember To Forget* on the Sun label in Memphis. The disc made the top of the local country charts and Elvis went on tour on the country circuit as a promising newcomer. Within a year he headed his own country and western shows and might very well have gone on to be a major country and western star had not the major companies started to take an interest in him.

He went of course to the highest bidder, RCA Victor, which had taken note that Elvis' abilities were not confined to country and western but included rhythm and blues and general pop potential (most of his singles were backed by lively rhythm and blues numbers, a not too usual procedure in the country field). Early in 1956 RCA released *Heartbreak Hotel* – and pop, rhythm and blues, and country and western customers rushed to buy it. It was, at this stage, just about unheard-of to crack three such different markets – perhaps one or the other and pop, but not all three. (Ironically, one other singer achieved the same feat at the same time, Carl Perkins, with a song he had written himself, *Blue Suede Shoes*, and if anything less sensational than *Heartbreak Hotel* had been around, the Perkins song might have made it. Instead, it had its big success only when Presley recorded it himself some months later.)

So he'd gotten the music down. Then there was the show. According to Bo Diddley, who was a rock and roll star when Elvis was still an electrician, Presley was out front at the Apollo night after night watching him and the rest of the show – and everyone knows that the gyrations at the Apollo are something to behold. Elvis learned a lot from those performers and quickly assimilated their movements. Perhaps for the public there was some sort of surprise in seeing a white man move the way black men had been moving for years. Whatever it was, Elvis's bumps and grinds were new to the teen audiences of the time, and wildly erotic. Mothers were horrified to see those frankly copulatory demonstrations right there on the home television screens. All the adult uneasiness that had been accumulating, as earthy "race" music spilled out into the teen market, finally had a focus. Elvis and his obscene hips would have to go. Well, of course it never was that way. The hips stayed and so did he. And so did his music.

PRODUCERS/Record production, which once was a mere technician's job, somewhere in the late sixties became an art form. Records came out, like the Beach Boys' *Good Vibrations* late in 1966, with arrangements that were difficult if not impossible to do in live performance. And inevitably the question was raised: did a performer have the right to put on record a sound he could not reproduce in person? And if so, who was the star – the performer or the producer and engineer? Or both? The Beatles, typically, provided one answer when, after they came out with *SERGEANT PEPPER*, a masterpiece of electronic art, they announced they would no longer appear in person. It's still being argued how much of the Beatles' art is theirs and how much credit is due their producer, George Martin. He is jokingly but accurately referred to as the Fifth Beatle. *SERGEANT PEPPER*, which wouldn't have been possible without him, is a catalog of the hundreds of possibilities that have remained untapped in the recording studio.

So fascinating is the work of the producer that serious rock musicians have moved into the field. Harry Nilsson and Lee Michaels not only perform but also produce their own material. The Who's Peter Townshend has had a recording studio built into his home so he can, at his leisure, go into the further potentials of tape, amplification, double tracking, etc. The Beach Boys' Brian Wilson's real genius lies in production. And Jimi Hendrix is also a very talented producer. Producers like Bob Crewe (the Four Seasons), Felix Pappalardi (Cream, Youngbloods), Jimmy Miller (Rolling Stones, Traffic), Paul Rothchild (the Doors), Tom Wilson (Simon and Garfunkel), and Bob Johnson (Bob Dylan) are stars in their own right. Fans recognize them, magazines write about them, they actively influence the direction music is moving in. Country-oriented Bob Johnson persuaded Dylan to record in Nashville; Jerry Wexler brought out the "real" Aretha. The producer, as much as the star, decides when double tracking (or triple tracking or quadruple tracking) will work and when it won't; when trickery is too much trickery; what changes have to be made in the layer after layer of sound that goes into the making of even the simplest single these days; what sidemen to use; what arranger to use; whether the sound should be clean or muddy.

Experts say they can detect when certain producers have been at work – like Mickie Most, for example. Most has a distinctly *clean* commercial sound, and he has a lot to do with what material is recorded and how it's done (he works with Herman, Donovan and recently Lulu). The king of all producers however is Phil Spector, who did twenty-eight records between 1962 and 1966, eighteen of which sold more than a million copies. His records were so commercially successful that not everyone was able to see the amount of artistry Spector was putting into them. He was the first to put elaborate walls of sound behind vocals. More goes on in his records than in anybody else's, and although just about everyone who followed him tried to copy him no one really succeeded. The Beatles are as indebted to his ideas as anyone.

The roles of producer and arranger, producer and manager, performer and producer, often overlap though as music becomes more and more intricate in the studio. The producer will suggest to the arranger that there should be a little more noise in one spot, a little less in another, and what sort of noise it should be. He can make things louder, softer, faster, slower, closer, more distant. In a way he is the conductor of the symphony of studio sound. Meanwhile, there are groups who manage to reproduce in person what they do in the studio (United States of America brought elaborate recording equipment on stage for just this purpose). Others, like the Moody Blues, who play many instruments on their albums, find this impractical live, so they work at getting a similar sound, as close as they can come, with available instruments.

There are groups however with an uncanny knack for reproducing live what other groups can do only in a studio. One of these is the much underrated Candymen, who astonished audiences in The Scene in the summer of 1967 by reproducing the Beatles' *Day In The Life* and the Beach Boys' *Good Vibrations* with every effect as easily as if they were bellowing out *Louie Louie* or *Gloria*. But few groups can do this. As rock becomes more complicated, producers' roles grow more important. A day could well come when the producer will be not just the *real* but the *only* star of the performance, twiddling knobs and mixing sounds.

OTIS REDDING/When they buried him, he was only twenty-six. It was the end of 1967, and everyone knew, and had known for some time, that 1968 was going to be his year, the year he really got there – and stayed there. Because there was something else everyone knew by then, that there was no topping him. Otis Redding was born in Dawson, Georgia, in 1941, but while still young he moved to Macon, the home of Little Richard. And it was Little Richard's success that encouraged him. It all began in 1962, when Otis was driving someone else to a recording session and just happened to mention that he sang too. He cut some things right at the end of the session and although they liked him they thought he was a bit too country for a rhythm and blues man. The song he had just tossed off in twenty minutes was *These Arms Of Mine*.

Little Richard and Sam Cooke were Otis's boyhood idols. On his first album, he came on a bit like Little Richard. And he liked to do intense

Sam Cooke numbers, especially the unforgettable *Shake*, the perform- ance of which is still with anyone who saw him do it at the 1967 Monterey Pop Festival.

They had to take over the Macon City Auditorium to find a place for all the people at Otis Redding's funeral. James Brown. Joe Tex. Sam and Dave. Wilson Pickett. Four thousand five hundred men and women weeping inside the auditorium and who knows how many waiting in the streets. Booker T played the organ and Johnny Taylor sang. Musicians used to love to work with Otis. He was the king at the Stax- Volt studios in Memphis. One reason there are still so many tracks of his in the can is that he loved to work and cut what he could when- ever he had time. Among his earliest fans and promoters were the Rolling Stones, who turned people on to him who might never have encountered him otherwise. The Stones did a lot of his songs, and he did one of theirs, *Satisfaction*, in a way that made people wonder whether it mightn't have been his song all along. The story was told that the Stones had "bought" *Satisfaction* from Otis. But Steve Cropper of the MGs with whom Otis worked so harmoniously, told Jann Wenner of *Rolling Stone* magazine that the story was "completely false". He said they all sat around and listened to the Stones version for five minutes, then cut their own. That was all there was. Never mind the compliment paid to Otis; it was an even greater compliment to the Stones.

Soul moved out of the rhythm and blues charts into the pop and rock charts in 1965. Otis was working hard then but it took Aretha Franklin to open things up properly in 1967 and really take over. Otis had released his own brilliantly aggressive version of his song *Respect* in mid-1965, but the general white public (apart from the soul freaks) didn't get to hear it till 1967, when Aretha had a million seller with it. And Arthur Conley, his protégé, made it to number one with another Otis song, *Sweet Soul Music*. In 1967 England's *Melody Maker*, which had voted Elvis Presley top male vocalist for eight straight years, named Otis number one. It was obvious that rhythm and blues, soul, or any other bag was too small to hold him. He was just getting started. And even without his singles and other people's versions of them, there were the albums, the definitive one being a *DICTIONARY OF SOUL*. But the others had titles that, in the light of that plane crash in 1967, the crash of that new private plane that plunged Otis and five of the Bar-Kays into the icy waters of Lake Pomona that December, well, they were titles that would make a strong man weep looking back. *HISTORY OF OTIS REDDING. THE IMMORTAL OTIS REDDING.*

Owning that private plane of his – a symbol that showed he'd made it and didn't have to tour in a bus – was a big triumph and just a small sign of what was ahead for him, and this was his first tour in it. He was just leaving a concert at Madison, Wisconsin, and heading for Cleveland, Ohio, when it went down only four miles from the Madison Municipal Airport on Sunday, December 10. Four thousand five hundred people were at the funeral. Sugar Pie Desanto and Percy Sledge and Gene Chandler and Mabel John. Otis had a plan to bring back Fats Domino and Little Richard and Big Joe Turner and Clyde McPhatter, to get them out of their 1950s thinking into a 1960s groove and watch them take over the charts again. Most of his songs were about chicks and missing them. But his last song, *Dock Of The Bay* (ironically the only one that sold a million) was personal, introspective and, perhaps because it was posthumous, the one for which he'll be remembered.

RHYTHM AND BLUES was a nice way of saying "race music", which was what black popular music was called for a long time. It grew up out of jazz, gospel and the blues and was a far, far cry from the pop songs that dominated the pre-Elvis white charts. Rock and roll was born only when whites became intrigued with black music and sought out recordings of it. Soon white artists, noting the sharp rise in sales of those records, took to studying black charts to see what they could find. Elvis was among the first to combine sounds from the black charts with his own country-music background. That was rock and roll. Others followed and before long hundreds of white artists were "covering" songs from the black rhythm and blues charts. Once in a while the original record would hit the white charts, but very rarely. Eventually more and more black artists started crossing into white charts, but there is still an active rhythm and blues chart which features many names barely known to the white public. Once in a while, but very rarely, a white performer makes it on those rhythm and blues charts.

ROCK MANAGERS/You could put Colonel Tom Parker up on a stage, let him talk, charge admission and you'd have a big star. Or you could put Albert Grossman in a film and he would upstage the leading man. Brian Epstein was a shy man, they say, but when he forgot that and was feeling self-assured and a little arrogant, he too could go in for some delicious bits of stage business.

Perhaps not all managers have a star inside them clamoring to get out, perhaps there are some good ones who are small, drab, uninteresting businessmen, but few spring to mind immediately. The great managers of great acts are almost invariably great acts themselves. It is a pity they have to stay behind the scenes, at least as far as audiences are concerned. Elvis Presley's manager, Colonel Tom Parker, is more than a shrewd financial adviser and tactician. He has never lost the air of carnival barker, which is how he started out. Albert Grossman made Bob Dylan a star (not to mention, Peter, Paul and Mary and a bunch of others), but in *Don't Look Back* he almost steals the limelight from his client. His wheelings and dealings are as much a part of the Dylan story as the lyrics of *Positively Fourth Street*. As for Brian Epstein, the Beatles' biography makes clear what a major role his faith, persistence and levelheadedness played in their success.

And yet: Grossman, successful as he is, never did find another Dylan; Parker never found another Elvis (though he has been reported casting covetous eyes at England's hip-swivelling Tom Jones); Epstein searched and searched but none of his groups got anywhere near the Beatles; Andrew Oldham, who managed the Stones to fame and fortune, had smaller successes with smaller groups but never repeated the Stones coup. What does all this mean? That any good manager has only one good star in him? That the Presleys and Dylans would have made it regardless?

Was it the Beatles or Epstein? Dylan or Grossman? Presley or Parker? The answer is – it must be – that it takes two to create that rare chemistry that makes a great match. The star has to have it, but the manager has to *know* it. The manager has to have the same sort of instinctive sense of timing *off* stage that the star has *on* stage.

The relationship between manager and star is not an easy one. Some stars in the end have preferred to manage themselves. The Beatles did after Epstein died. The Stones now work without the man who got them together. Jefferson Airplane, once managed by Fillmore impresario Bill Graham, now look after themselves. Others thrive on a relationship where one man takes care of all sordid business details, money matters, tax payments, everything that takes away much needed energy from performing.

Tim Buckley could not hope to function without Herbie Cohn, who also manages the Mothers. Harold Leventhal has Judy Collins, Arlo Guthrie and Pete Seeger in his stable, among others. Kit Lambert and Chris Stamp had the vision to pilot the Who to glory. Ex-Animals Chas Chandler and Mike Jeffrey saw the potential in Jimi Hendrix when he was an unknown guitarist. Steve Paul carried his discovery, Johnny Winter, financially until he got him his half a million dollar record contract. And if in all these men there is a personal flamboyance, well, so there should be. Presenting an act or a performer to the public is as flamboyant an act as getting up on a stage and singing. Not many make it in that perfect combination but those who do are probably as much the real stars of rock as the people they represent.

ROLLING STONES/*Mick Jagger (lead vocals, harmonica), Keith Richard (lead guitar, vocals), Brian Jones (rhythm guitar, harmonica, sitar), Charlie Watts (drums), Bill Wyman (bass guitar).*
When the Beatles were still four sweet little moptop dolls in 1964, and we didn't know then that they were going to grow into more than faces on a Woolworth's charm bracelet, the Stones did not come on, as almost everyone else on the English scene did, as moptop imitations. Even at that early, early stage they did their own thing. And their thing was the full slummy English lout barrow-boy gutter-rat routine. Mean, moody and magnificent (as was once said about Jane Russell).

While the 1964 Beatles looked as if they had been personally scrubbed down by Brian Epstein himself, the 1964 Rolling Stones looked as if they had been sent to bed every night for a week with the same clothes on and no supper. By the time they hit Beatle-sated, Hermit-sated America, they looked different, not to say positively menacing. This immediately established them as personalities at a time when so many hairy groups had come through that they had all eventually become faceless. Their music had much the same impact. The Beatles' songs had been rinsed and hung out to dry. The Stones had never seen soap and water. And where the adorable little wind-up Beatle moptops wanted no more than to hold a hand, the hateful rasping Stones were bent on rape, pillage and plunder. Well, at least satisfaction. At that stage, both the Beatles and the Stones were doing English imitations of American music (there certainly

wasn't any English music worth imitating then), but the Stones were bas-
ing their music on an earlier, earthier and less polished period than the
period the Beatles were concentrating on.

English groups were into raunchy American blues before the Stones
(there was a long tradition of that), but they had always done it in a very
removed way – a little too earnest, a little too intent and reverent. Not
Jagger. No one had ever seen a white man move on stage the way Jagger
moved. Later, like Elvis, whom he completely overshadowed, he was to
become the prototype for stage sexuality, the most imitated singer in
rock. Right from the start he parodied himself completely, but that
worked *for* him, not against him. His lips and no-hips drove every rele-
vant point home; a not-so-distant relative of the Shangri-las' Leader of
the Pack, he laid it all on the line.

Most of the girls who watched had never before had the word put
on them quite so explicitly. It was heady stuff for fourteen-year-old virgins, and others besides. And the publicity played it up, although it is
hard to say where manager Andrew Oldham's shrewdness left off and
the Stones' own natural boorishness began. In any case, they were
never photographed to look pretty; they seemed under orders not to
smile and their music was full of disdain for women, morals, parents
and under-assistant West Coast promotion men.

What started off as a series of straight pinches from a variety of black
blues musicians of the past eventually came out as the Stones sound.
Even in the first three albums, where they were simply searching for a
musical identity in their vast repertoire of soul music, rhythm and
blues, and Chicago blues, they were producing what was then the
heaviest music to come out of England in that 1964–early 1965 period.
They started to find themselves in mid-1965 in their fourth album *OUT
OF OUR HEADS* (stopping only to pay tribute to some heroes, Sam
Cooke and Otis Redding), continuing the process with *DECEMBER'S
CHILDREN*, where it was clear from the growing number of Mick
Jagger/Keith Richard compositions that a Stones "personality" was
emerging in unambiguous lyrics and music. *BIG HITS (HIGH TIDE AND
GREEN GRASS)* in the spring of 1966 was the wrap-up of that time,
their sort of farewell to that first golden era.

AFTERMATH, that summer, saw something quite new. The Stones
had made every point they needed to make. Now they could relax.
Some of the brute force was gone now, to be replaced by tenderness,

impatience and more than a touch of the sardonic. Guitarist Brian Jones played dulcimer and, in *Paint It Black*, sitar, which had hardly been used then in rock except by the Beatles and Byrds. There was early fuzztone in *Think* and a most un-Stones-like Elizabethan mood prevailed, just mocking enough to make it believable. A live album followed and *BETWEEN THE BUTTONS*, where the Stones told it all (*Let's Spend The Night Together* and *Something Happened To Me Yesterday*), then *FLOWERS* in the summer of 1967, a farewell to the second golden era.

The second golden era was marked by the highly publicized 1967 bust, the first *big* drug bust in English rock. They didn't have the sort of public image that a bust would hurt and the uncharitable never stopped insisting that manager Oldham had engineered it all, but the bust *was* a jolt to them, and two further busts of Brian Jones were harrowing, to say the least. Out of all this private confusion emerged the Stones' answer to the Beatles *SERGEANT PEPPER* album – *THEIR SATANIC MAJESTIES REQUEST*, an album that induced more visions than anything coming out of San Francisco in the height of the psychedelic revolution. The album was not entirely a critical success and the two hard-rock singles that followed suggested a possible return to their earlier styles.

Their new album, *BEGGAR'S BANQUET*, bears this out. It is a comeback, a great rock and roll album with no pretenses, Dylanesque lyrics, and a country and western mood. For the big people in rock, 1968 was the year for a return to simplicity, and that seems to be what happened with the Rolling Stones. For a while, all seemed well. Then in June 1969, a shock: Brian Jones left to do his own music. His replacement was Mick Taylor, formerly of John Mayall's Bluesbreakers. A few weeks later Brian was found dead in his swimming pool.

The group is still strong and together. Jagger is becoming a film star (*Performance* and *Ned Kelly*). But nothing is the same. How could it be?

RONETTES/There are two kinds of lady singers – the angels and the devils. The angels sing ethereal songs in ethereal voices and wear long, loose gowns. The devils sing earthy songs in earthy voices and their gowns fit where gowns should fit. The Ronettes were every teenage boy's dream of a teenage devil in triplicate. Brazen, shapely and without any illusions about men and sex. They were like girlie magazines come alive and set to music. Their song *Do I Love You* made the boys feel like men. Nothing psychedelic there, just straight from the hip or wherever.

The Ronettes were Phil Spector creations, and Phil Spector knew, better than anyone, what made a record sell, what popular music was all about. The Beatles adored them and had them on their 1966 tour – more, one suspects, because *they* wanted to hear them sing than because they thought their audiences wanted to.

DIANA ROSS AND THE SUPREMES (formerly THE SUPREMES)/*Diana Ross, Mary Wilson, Cindy Birdsong (replaced Florence Ballard).*
You always get the feeling when you read newspaper interviews with the Supremes, the world's most famous and highest-paid female trio, that they are keeping a secret. The talk is always about clothes and wigs and families. Never about their music or their feelings. They are not, as someone described them, Aretha in triplicate. They're too slim and chic for that and it comes out in their voices. If they must be compared with anyone, they're like three black Marlene Dietrichs. Diana Ross is Supervamp, all soft purring, but with claws.

When Diana and the Supremes move it's in the beautiful but predictable steps they have choreographed inside their minds. And yet it's that very timing and planning that makes them exciting, like a woman who has planned every detail of what she'll wear, and she knows you know, but you are flattered that she has gone to that trouble for you. Audiences are flattered by the obvious hours, days of rehearsals that lie behind every Supremes appearance. Every single sells, every album sells. The Supremes epitomize the machine-like precision of the Motown sound. Everything is worked out for them and they don't buck the system.

Although they didn't give the Motown writing team of Holland/Dozier/Holland their first hit (Martha and the Vandellas did that), the two teams have worked together in perfect harmony. Holland/Dozier/Holland have a formula. Ross/Wilson/Birdsong sing to that formula.

In the part of Detroit Diana and Mary came from (Cindy is from New Jersey) a lot of girls were harmonizing, in church, for fun, for amateur contests. They were in their senior year at high school just when Berry Gordy was getting the whole Motown operation underway in 1960, and they auditioned for him then. When they finished school (he wouldn't take them until they had), he let them sing background. He had other fine female trios but this was the one with the magic.

They fit perfectly into the Motown image of sophisticated soul – everything very cool, very clear, no last-minute deviations in the recording studios.

It was all very assembly line, like the job former Motown head Gordy had had in an auto plant (and there was always cracks made about that). But there are people who have to be told what to do and people who are best left to themselves. The Supremes need to be told, but give them their thing to do and they'll do it with flawless perfection, though not without a certain sharp bitchy passion.

Then Stax in Memphis came out with a rival sound that was earthier, fiercer and more erotic. The Supremes had provided the only black sound the mass public was ready for in 1964–66, the sophisticated, commercialized, polished-down sound. It took rock musicians' interest in funkier black music (an interest that was there in 1964 and 1965, but only started emerging publicly in interviews when these musicians were more securely established in 1966, 1967 and 1968) to ready the field for the less sophisticated, gustier sound of Memphis. By 1968 there was a feeling that Motown was too predictable and commercial and watered down, and slowly but surely the interest started to swing back to Memphis. It won't put Motown or the Supremes out of business, but it will be interesting to see if the Motown machine learns anything from Memphis soul.

BUFFY SAINTE-MARIE/Although she insists only five per cent of the songs she sings are protesting anything, Buffy Sainte-Marie, a Cree Indian, sings one of the most bitter protest songs ever: *My Country 'Tis Of Thy People You're Dying*, which tells of the atrocities American Indians suffered at the hands of the white man. Her anti-war song *Universal Soldier* is a classic and much recorded. She can sing an old folk standard like *Sir Patrick Spens* and then move into a contemporary song like Joni Mitchell's *Circle Game*. *I'M GONNA BE A COUNTRY GIRL AGAIN* was made in April 1968 in Nashville. Buffy, who grew up in Maine, moved into the folk places of New York in 1963. She is now one of the giants of the contemporary folk circuit.

PETE SEEGER/Someone said he was born too early. If Pete Seeger had been twenty instead of fifty during the sixties' folk boom he might be a multi-millionaire now. But without Seeger there would probably not have *been* a folk boom. We'd still be singing about teenage love. Seeger was not too early, he was just in time. Already it's difficult for a new generation to realize that there was a time when folk music was an "inside", small-circle thing, with people swapping songs and turning each other on to whatever new finds they had just collected. Pete Seeger was one of the people who kept that feeling going all those years. (There were others who did the same thing in their own way – John Jacob Niles, Woody Guthrie, Leadbelly, Alan Lomax – but Seeger, the most active, combined the lot.)

Seeger set the stage for the early folk boom of 1956 when companies like the now powerful Elektra were just getting started and the Clancy Brothers and Odetta, to their amazement, found that folk music paid. Pete Seeger was the big daddy of the hootenanny, of the popularity of folk in colleges, of everything that was happening around the fountain in Washington Square Park. When the folk boom grew, Seeger was left behind. The reason: his left-wing political views got him blacklisted from TV. Meanwhile the tide was changing – Kingston Trio, Joan Baez, Peter, Paul and Mary, Dylan, Judy Collins – Seeger's children were coming into their own (Joanie turning the masses on to folk by using many Seeger techniques).

For a multitude of reasons Seeger was never destined to make one of his own songs a hit, and he himself never made the charts, though he must have sold millions of albums. It was Peter, Paul and Mary who made his song *If I Had A Hammer* famous around the world, and so many of his songs are sung so often it's difficult to remember they originally came from him. He is part of anyone who ever picked up a guitar and even some who didn't (Marlene Dietrich sang his *Where Have All The Flowers Gone*). He sowed the seed for protest songs.

Nothing demonstrated more dramatically than the 1968 Woody Guthrie Memorial Concert how very much did spring from Seeger (who was himself influenced by Leadbelly and Guthrie). And there are enough people carrying on the tradition. When Baez at the Fillmore or Guthrie at Forest Hills urges you to sing along, it's Seeger's ghost overseeing the concert – and the nice part of it is Seeger still lives to enjoy it.

THE SEEKERS/*Judith Durham, Athol Guy, Keith Potger, Bruce Woodley.*
If there hadn't been the Seekers some shrewd manager would have invented them. One cuddly girl-next-door type (complete with

nose-crinkling smile) and three sober cats who looked like bank tellers. They came from Australia, singing nice harmonies for their supper on a boat bound for England. The English squares liked them immediately because they represented something they could understand and feel secure with. As for the rest, well, it was a good clean sound and the tunes were catchy.

Their sound was, for lack of a better name, pop-folk with the strong and vibrant voice of Judith Durham giving it definition and added distinction. They didn't really click in America until *Georgy Girl* (done for the film in 1966), which went on to become a White Rock radio commercial. After that there was success wherever you looked: back in Australia, where they visited in triumph, in England, with TV show after TV show, and in America. By the summer of 1968, inexplicably, they were tired of it all. They had never meant to stay together, they said. Durham of the exceptional voice says she'll sing solo. Bruce Woodley, who wrote *Red Rubber Ball* with Paul Simon, will probably come to America to write songs. Their last hit in England was called *The Carnival Is Over*, and it was.

THE SHANGRI-LAS/From time immemorial the bitch goddess has haunted and fascinated man. And so, of course, has the girl next door. The Shangri-las were both, a real bargain for the boy who wanted everything in a girl and the girl who wanted to be that everything. They played it soft and tough at the same time. Their toughest song was *Leader Of The Pack*. (He was the head of the motorcycle gang and she was his tough mama. Then he dies. Tough mama goes soft, but not for long. You know whoever gets to be the next leader gets her too. Teased hair, doe eyes, ankle bracelet and all.) It was the necrophilia of it all that shocked the adults, not the funkiness of three bitchy white girls who told it straight out that in motor-bike gangs you don't just hold hands. The Shangri-las were akin to Clyde Barrow's Bonnie, in a reversal of the proverbial image, the velvet hands in the iron gloves.

SIMON AND GARFUNKEL (Paul Simon and Art Garfunkel)/Everybody loves a Cinderella story and Simon and Garfunkel are it. In 1957, when everything in rock is Elvis, these two precocious sixteen-year-old schoolboys in Queens, New York, come up with a hit, *Hey Schoolgirl*. They have flattop haircuts and call themselves Tom and Jerry. They get to play on the Dick Clark show. But they turn out to be more or less a one-hit wonder, and within a year they're has-beens. Weep for their disappointment. Years later, now it's the sixties folk boom and Bob Dylan has just made *Blowin' in the Wind* and *The Times They Are A-changin'*, the two boys, now calling themselves Simon and Garfunkel, make a folk album with Dylan songs and some Simon songs. They call it WEDNESDAY MORNING, 3 A.M. Well, no one's heard of Simon and Garfunkel and late in 1964 everyone and his brother is recording Dylan, so nothing happens with the album. Simon splits for England where American folk singers at least have novelty value. But meanwhile, the Cinderella story. (Do things *really* happen like this?)

A disc jockey has fallen in love with one cut on *WEDNESDAY MORN-ING* and keeps playing it. Tom Wilson, a producer at Columbia who's nobody's fool, has watched the folk-rock explosion of 1965 and sees his chance. He gets the gentle folky single *Sounds Of Silence* and adds the standard rock backing of drums, bass and electric guitar. And before you can say Simon and Garfunkel, it's a hit record, a number one hit. What happens is that the folkies buy because it's one of theirs and the rockers think they're buying a new kind of rock, which it is. Now that the market has been opened up for that fetching little combination, there's no stopping Simon and Garfunkel. (In a way, it's the success of the Kingston Trio all over again, folk pop, folk made acceptable by nice tuneful harmonizing.)

Paul Simon writes some of the loveliest melodies around, and his *Feelin' Groovy (59th Street Bridge Song)* is one of the best songs ever. And not *all* the lyrics sound as if they came out of a college yearbook, though their cleverness is often exasperating. The big point is the records sell. The two boys with a bomb on their hands in 1964 are selling records by the millions and picking up as much as $50,000 a concert. They are asked to do the sound track for a Mike Nichols film, *The Graduate*. They are growing moustaches. They're very American college student and American college students can identify with them. The criticisms have been that they're too bland, too sophomoric, too commercial, too safe, that they don't have and never will have the magic of a Bob Dylan. Unfair. They made a whole new gentle thing in rock possible, opened up the doors for a whole lot of melodic sounds, and are heading for interesting places.

NANCY SINATRA/Until her boots took to walking sadistically all over gentlemen, no one wanted to know anything about Frank Sinatra's little girl. She was Nancy with the smiling face and she would have stayed that way forever but for the inspiration of one Lee Hazlewood who in 1966 thought it was about time Nancy let some of her bitterness (one divorce and five years of trying to make the charts and a lot of hassles) come through in her voice. His instructions were to let it all hang out. The result was a new growly-voiced Nancy, full of rage and fury and a growly Duane Eddy guitar in the background confirming she meant it when she sang that her boots were made for walking and they'd walk right over you. (The song was in the best country tradition of women who had had it up to here with their men.) Every woman identified, every man dug her spirit. Nothing the new Nancy did after that quite lived up to *Boots*, but she was mean and wasted and deliciously disillusioned in *Sugar Town* and a few others. Hazlewood stuck with her as producer, writer, arranger and singing partner, and kept her in the same gutsy groove.

SONNY & CHER/A husband and wife duo as teenage idols? Unthinkable. Sonny and Cher Bono pulled off this unlikely coup in 1965 by suddenly making marriage seem like the grooviest thing possible. To adults, all that conjugal bliss on display on stage veered close to the distasteful. To the young, it was frankly beautiful – and contagious. To watch Sonny and Cher love each other was to feel loved by them and indeed they always encouraged flesh contact with their fans. The other thing about Sonny and Cher was that they were not just an ordinary husband and wife, but a *rebel* pair, constantly being asked to leave restaurants and hotels because of their appearance – he in long hair, bell bottom pants and furry vests; she also in bell bottoms which went on to set a whole teen and then pre-teen style (in fact, when the first of the genus teenybopper stepped out in 1965, she was wearing "Cher pants" and they have been a teeny uniform ever since).

Socially, then, Sonny and Cher, working out of Los Angeles, were a massive influence: kids identified with them, tried to look like them and relished the financial success that enabled them to thumb their noses at hotel managers and head-waiters. Musically, what got them moving was that new combination of folk and rock that the Byrds and the Turtles were pioneering in Los Angeles. But while these two groups were doing it by rocking folk material like Dylan, Sonny and Cher did it with their own material. To some, *I Got You, Babe* seemed like an obvious imitation of Dylan folk rock. Never mind, it was a huge hit and well timed.

Gradually it became apparent that the voice of the team was not Sonny but Cher. Cher worked increasingly as a solo singer, with no apparent dismay on the part of Sonny, who continued to write songs for her, to conduct the business of being a star duo, and to play straight man on stage, lending his voice when the occasion called for it. When the union of folk and rock became something to be taken so much for granted that the term folk rock dropped out of popular use, Sonny and Cher still sold records.

By the time the other rich freaks happened in Los Angeles (the Mamas and the Papas, the Doors and others), they simply settled back to being an essential part of a very lively music scene where the people in the long hair and the bell bottoms had completely taken over. When celebrities like the Bee Gees or Twiggy and Justin visited, it was Sonny and Cher who would host the star-studded parties. Gradually the eccentric costuming of the pair began to seem less eccentric, partly because everyone was wearing it by then and partly because with success, everything they owned became so much more lush and luxurious that even *Vogue* took to featuring them on its pages.

Sonny and Cher (who had once recorded as Caesar and Cleo) no longer are quite what they were in the early days; too many other people are being rebels both socially and musically. But they're still immensely popular, and exactly who they were was revealed at the huge soul-together in the summer of 1968 when Cher, in evening dress (she'd always worn pants in the old days), and Sonny, in exquisite silk Nehru jacket, announced they were going to become parents – to 40,000 fans. It seemed only right that that announcement should have been made from the stage of Madison Square Garden to an audience of 40,000. (Sadly, Cher lost the expected heir – she had lost a child in 1967 too – but you can bet that when the next one's along, the announcement will be made at the very least from the Hollywood Bowl).

DUSTY SPRINGFIELD (Mary O'Brien)/Dusty Springfield is one of the very few English girl singers to have made the international big time. She used to be a country and western girl, in gingham and frilled

316   LILLIAN ROXON: MOTHER OF ROCK

petticoats, singing with a family group, but she went solo and fell under the spell of Motown at a time when all of England (and really the world) was dazzled by Motown. In fact, she was one of the people who turned the English public and many of its musicians on to what was coming out of Detroit. Her first big international hit, *You Don't Have To Say You Love Me*, reflected her growing soulfulness. In 1967–68 she went all out on the glamour bandwagon with a new image (fantastic blonde wigs and eye makeup that reportedly took three hours to put on). She then broke ties with her English manager and announced that America was where it was at. Once England's top girl singer, she's now working at being the same in America, busily recording in Memphis with Aretha's producer – and doing well.

SURFING MUSIC/Someone once defined surf music as wet rock and roll. Surf music was born in California with the Beach Boys in 1962. Everyone knows the story. The Wilson brothers and assorted friends and relatives, not a group then, got together, wrote a song about surf-ing, sang it, recorded it, had a small local hit with it and went on to make three huge consecutive national hits on the same theme. The ball the Beach Boys got rolling with *Surfin' Safari* (a Brian Wilson/Mike Love 1962 composition) and *Surfin' USA* (written by Chuck Berry in 1963) was quickly picked up by Jan and Dean, whose *Surf City* in 1963 was the first of a long line of Jan and Dean surf hits. When people talked about California sound in those days they didn't mean acid rock, they meant the Beach Boys' *Fun, Fun, Fun*, the Surfaris' *Wipe Out* and Jan and Dean covering the world of surf and drag racing. The songs were about beach dollies and ho-daddies and marked the first time in music history that a sport actually had its own music. Surf music had a nice summer sound and was a good beat to drive to. It had the kind of high, summery harmonies that the Beach Boys used, and the thing to do, of course, was to sound as if the sound had just happened on a sandy beach. It grew and grew so that at one stage even Chubby Checker had a surf record out. A comedy album, *MY SON THE SURF NUT*, had num-bers like *The Teenage Surfing Vampire* and *Some Gremmie Stole My Hair Bleach*. By 1964, when the novelty wore off, hot-rod music took over, but California lost its supremacy with the arrival of the Beatles and the new sound of folk rock in 1965. Jan and Dean turned to something called folk 'n' roll; the Beach Boys went sophisticated and even the

Surfaris recorded an album called *IT AIN'T ME BABE*. But surfing music comes back every year with each new batch of summer rock; its tingling harmonies live on in the Mamas and the Papas, the Fifth Dimension, the Cowsills.

TINY TIM (Herbert Khaury)/Financially, 1968 was the year of Tiny Tim, with $50,000-a-week engagements at Las Vegas, a best-selling album, English concerts, adulation, world fame, the whole long, glittering, predictable star trip. But Tiny Tim had been performing for years before that in Greenwich Village clubs like the Fat Black Pussycat and the Page Three, and his act then was much as it is now. First Tiny himself: tall, thin, hawk-nosed, with hair well down below his shoulders (this as far back as 1962, when the only people who wore long hair were girls). His face powdered into a pearly pallor, a delicate pastel circle of coral rouge on each cheek. His grin huge and disarming, as the falsetto notes of a long-forgotten soprano and a long-forgotten song trilled from his throat. Even in the early days, it was impossible to think he was not a put-on. But as the years wore on it became obvious that Tiny was not a comedian, or a joke. He was a living archive of songs of a period that had fallen into oblivion, a human jukebox of the songs of the twenties to the fifties, and even earlier – and not only the songs, but the style in which they were sung.

Since he had a rich and flexible baritone as well as a pure (if occasionally comic) soprano, he was able to sing not just male and female voices separately but also duets. The Jeanette MacDonald/Nelson Eddy duet was a standard in his repertoire. He loved duets that showed off his versatility, so Sonny and Cher and Paul and Paula imitations were among his favorites, with the two voices often seeming to blend. Such virtuosity could not fail to bring applause, and when it did, which was often, Tiny would respond with a Shirley Temple gesturette, fingers delicately touching lips as though to blow the babiest of kisses. Offstage too everyone was called Mister or Miss, no coarseness of any sort was indulged in, and the word "dear" recurred constantly, gentling and sweetening his every pronouncement.

For years Tiny Tim had his following, but it was a small, loyal ingroup, not the world. One day he stumbled into Steve Paul's club, The Scene, where he so enchanted the clientele that he was booked on the spot for 365 days a year. The fee was modest, though more than he'd received in the past, but the exposure was fantastic. Every rock musician in the world makes the scene at The Scene. And Tiny's fan club grew. Peter Townshend of the Who decided to record him in London. Others had similar plans. Then it happened. Tiny Tim, who had made records under other names, got a serious, big-company record contract.

To promote his album he was put on several national television shows. Now a nation was seeing him. Old ladies fainted at hearing those songs again. Little children shrieked with delight at the sight of him. Trendy young executives pronounced him camp. Flower people said he was a beautiful person. Here and there were people who thought he couldn't be for real, that the whole thing was a brilliant invention – as though any mere writer or idea man could have dreamed up Tiny Tim's dialogue, or his pumpkin-seed habit, or his deliciously dated gallantry and romantic worship of the fair sex, or his perpetual showering, or anything.

Musically, Tiny's range is wide, enabling him to sing to *Mister* Dylan one of his own songs sung in the style of *Mister* Rudy Vallee, and then one of *Mister* Vallee's songs sung in the style of *Mister* Dylan. He has a perfect sense of showmanship, of comedy, of timing. And somewhere in Queens is a mother who for years had to explain her son to the neighbors ("How come, if he's so good, he ain't rich?"). Tiny's success vindicated all that. You make fifty thousand a week, it's okay if you wear your hair long.

TRAFFIC/*Stevie Winwood (piano, organ, auto-organ), Chris Wood (flute, tenor, alto and soprano sax), Jim Capaldi (drums, piano), Dave Mason (bass guitar, sitar).*
Someone once asked Jerry Wexler, who produces Aretha and is therefore in a position to know *something* about soul, what he had to say about white soul and he said two words: Stevie Winwood. The voice, guitar, organ and piano of Traffic, Stevie is white, frail, English and one of the Renaissance men of rock – writer, arranger, performer.

The Traffic story starts with the Spencer Davis story. Davis started a group in 1963 with three others, two of whom were brothers already playing together. One of those brothers was Stevie, aged fifteen. Like the Beatles, he came out of the skiffle craze of 1959 (though he was only eleven when he was in a skiffle band). He had lived and breathed American blues from the start, learned from the record collection of friends. It was Stevie's voice, his songs, his organ and piano work that made Spencer Davis's band. *I'm A Man* and *Gimme Some Loving*, two of Stevie's songs done under the Davis umbrella, were so black and strong it took a lot of adjusting to get used to the fact that they were coming from a seventeen-year-old English kid from Birmingham. In 1967 Stevie decided to leave Davis (life on the road was bringing him down) and start his own group.

With maturity and wisdom you don't find even in older musicians, Stevie took himself and his new musicians off to a quiet country cottage in Berkshire to work and get themselves together as people, as a band, as musicians. Photographers were barred. Reporters were barred. Under assistant promotion men were barred. It was all peace and quiet there, with green grass, and roaring logs on the fire at night. An idyllic setting that was immediately reflected in the first Traffic singles, *Paper Sun* and *Hole In My Shoe* and in everything else that followed. You could see it in the way Stevie smiled, a smile with no tensions, or with the way his group moved physically on stage. They worked together so perfectly with so much telepathy and trust that sometimes the audience felt a little left out.

For a long time Traffic looked like it would be a great band, a nicely balanced blend of three or four good musicians (depending on whether Dave Mason was in or out that week). Winwood's voice was strong; Capaldi's drums were strong; Chris Wood on flute, Mason on sitar and Winwood on organ were gentle and peaceful. Traffic was in the process of changing the whole mood of popular music when Mason left, leaving a trio that worked well only when it was the then unusual organ-drums-flute combination. In the traditional guitar-bass-drums grouping it was invariably too thin. When Mason returned, all seemed to be saved and the group never seemed happier. They started to get away from the blues that had put them on the map with Spencer Davis. But Traffic wasn't to last and at the height of their popularity, to everyone's surprise, the group split, Winwood to join Clapton and Baker in Blind Faith, the other three to try and work out a combination of their own.

IKE AND TINA TURNER/Although they are American, Ike and Tina Turner are much bigger names in England than at home, partly because their sensational 1966 single, *River Deep, Mountain High*, took off there as it never did in the United States. Some say it is the most passionate performance ever to be put on record until Aretha came along. While much of the credit has to go to producer Phil Spector, whose great triumph it was, one has only to see Tina Turner in live performance to see what raw material Spector was lucky enough to have to start with. The easiest way to describe Tina Turner is to say that she doubles in intensity whatever any other singer is capable of – her screams and wails are faster and more uninhibited, her boogaloos are double the speed.

Ike is an integral part of the act, not just because he plays guitar (and how) and sings (less, lately), but because the whole performance is *for* him. Tina, all skintight glitter and sequins and long hair whipping about in primitive frenzy, is making the definitive statement about what it means to be a woman. Behind her are the Ikettes, purring and sophisticated. While recordings released in America have simply not done Ike and Tina justice, in England and Europe they are superstars.

RITCHIE VALENS (Richard Valenzuela)/When Ritchie Valens died in the 1959 plane crash that killed Buddy Holly and Big Bopper, he was only nineteen – but he was already one of the legends of the golden age of rock. His father had been a Latin guitar player. While he was still a schoolboy, his widowed mother put up her mortgage money to rent a hall for a dance at which Ritchie would provide the music. When the dance made a profit he started having them three times a month and was so good he was signed up by Bob Keene, a veteran bandleader with his own record company. Keene still remembers how his song *Come On, Let's Go* typified his impatience and energy. *La Bamba*, which Valens also wrote and which made Trini Lopez a star, is still a rock standard and is one of the few examples of Latin rock. Even when rock got sophisticated, you could still hear echoes of Ritchie Valens.

VELVET UNDERGROUND/*Lou Reed (lead guitar, vocals), Sterling Morrison (bass & rhythm guitar), Maureen Tucker (percussion), Doug Yule (guitar, organ, vocals). Previous Members: Nico (vocal), John Cale (piano, bass, electric viola).*
It takes some of the magic away when you realize that when Andy Warhol found them in 1965 they were called the Falling Spikes, and before that the Warlocks. And certainly it seemed at that time as though Warhol, anxious to get into everything while his name was red-hot and flashing, had picked up just any group, given them a fancy name with a double meaning (*Velvet Underground* was the title of a bizarre,

sado-masochistic book) and told them to get out there and freak out the paying customers. That's how it seemed but it really wasn't that way at all.

After you heard them you knew it was they who enhanced Warhol's image and not necessarily the other way around (though his famous name did help). They were ever so much more than their master's voice. First of all, most of their good songs were written *before* they met Warhol, not at all under his influence. Secondly, they had a whole long history of good musicianship, longer than most other American groups. Lou Reed had been studying piano seriously since the age of five. John Cale was a child prodigy in England, doing his own compositions for the BBC at the age of eight and classically trained from an even earlier age. Sterling Morrison played classical trumpet from the age of ten. Maureen Tucker, one of the very few girl drummers in rock and the only one in a top group, got her training in an all-girl rock band. So if they were overshadowed at first by Warhol, and then by the tall blonde dream-like Nico, that was misleading.

Their role in the beginning was to tour in Warhol's portable total environment show, *The Exploding Plastic Inevitable*. This was the first show to incorporate music, dancers, films, lights, projection, environment and *people* (there was no audience, the people were part of the show). When everyone else got their discotheques tuned in to all that action and the multi-media experience stopped being new, Warhol lost interest. But the band continued. Their first album came out with a Warhol banana on the cover; the second cover looked all black (but held in certain light a skull becomes visible). Everything else was pure Velvet.

The important thing about the Velvet Underground was that in 1966 and 1967 they were as far away as a group could possibly be from the world of incense and peppermints and lollipops and even earnest teenage protest. Theirs was the dim underworld of drugs and sexual perversion, of heroin addiction and the desperate loss of hope that goes with it. Their concern was with death and violence. They were singing about a world that exists and that they knew. *Venus In Furs* was about sado-masochism. *Heroin* didn't have to code words to get its meaning across. Musically they were very advanced, using sounds and voices in a way most groups didn't start using till 1968. They were using whips on stage before the Nice and Dave Dee, and with far more sinister intent. Oozing evil and lubricity, they made every other group look like kid stuff, and they made a lot of people nervous. Their records were never played on commercial stations. There is no word for their sound but sometimes it seems as if a *presence* has taken it over, perhaps even His Satanic Majesty himself. You can easily imagine someone performing black masses with the Velvet Underground's albums. Not for the kiddies.

MUDDY WATERS (McKinley Morganfield)/One of the Rolling Stones' earliest singles was an old Muddy Waters' song, *I Just Want To Make Love To You* (written by Willie Dixon). Someone should issue a single with Mick Jagger's version on one side and Muddy's on the other and let them fight it out, because in those two cuts is the whole story of how the young English musicians of 1962, 1963 and 1964 took the American sound of the Mississippi Delta over to England and then sent it back across the Atlantic with love and admiration. And a whole generation grew up believing that that was the *English* sound. By 1968, after Jagger, Eric Clapton, Mike Bloomfield and others had talked freely and, yes, worshipfully, of their roots and influences, Muddy Waters's name, already revered in blues circles, started to become known to the general public.

A singer, guitarist and songwriter now in his fifties, Muddy appeared in 1968 at Steve Paul's The Scene, at the Café Au Go Go, at the Schaefer Festival in Central Park, establishing where that sound had come from in the first place – from the flat Mississippi cotton country where he grew up, and later from Chicago, where he sang to the homesick Mississippians who had migrated there. In the Delta he'd learned to play guitar with the distinctive whining sound that the Stones used in *Little Rooster* and that so many others have copied since (many of them imagining it was the Stones they were copying). And Cream did his *Rollin And Tumblin'* on *FRESH CREAM*. The debt blues-rock owes Muddy Waters is massive.

THE WEAVERS/Looking back now, it is obvious that from a mass-market point of view the Weavers happened too early. Their version of Leadbelly's 1931 song *Goodnight Irene* was number one for thirteen weeks in 1950, a particularly amazing achievement when you consider the 1950 charts were dominated by Patti Page, Mario Lanza, Doris Day,

Bing Crosby, Perry Como, the Andrews Sisters and Eddie Fisher. (It was the year of *Rudolph The Red-Nosed Reindeer* and *Mona Lisa*.) They also managed to make the charts with Woody Guthrie's *So Long It's Been Good To Know You* and *On Top Of Old Smokey* and they were the first *big* folk group to sell well outside folk circles. Nevertheless it was too soon, for one reason or another, for the overwhelming success that was to meet the Kingston Trio a decade or so later. But the Weavers did set the stage for scores of other folk groups that made it commercially as the folk revival gathered momentum from 1956 onward; and just about everything that happened in the first half of the sixties (when folk took over completely) – everything from Joan Baez, Dylan, protest folk rock and the Byrds – came from the Seeger-influenced Weavers of the fifties.

MAE WEST/She is better known as an actress, comedienne and sort of souped-up sexpot from way back, when saying "Come up and see me some time, tall, dark and handsome" was terribly naughty. That Mae West would do a rock and roll record at the age of seventy-five came as a surprise to some, and that it wasn't an aging freak thing came as an even greater surprise to most. But there it is. At seventy-five she sings Dylan and Lennon/McCartney as well as anyone. The lady has always been one of the better blues singers about (only her undulating figure and flashing innuendos distracted from her voice). Now she's discovered that all you have to do to sing rock and roll is double the blues beat. The Beatles' *Day Tripper*, which she sings, is about exactly the sort of shady lady Mae knows better than anyone. And Dylan's *If You Gotta Go*, another of the star tracks on her album, tells of a situation that existed long before the composer was born. When you compare Miss West's wiser, sadder versions to the originals, you know what people mean about older women. She could read a telephone book and make it sound like a list of her lovers.

THE WHO/*Peter Townshend (guitar), John Entwistle (bass), Keith Moon (drums), Roger Daltrey (lead vocals).*
The Who are so English it's difficult to imagine them the essentially American stars they have now become. You can't even start to understand the Who unless you lived in the England they came from. They're summer dances in Brighton, and whole weekends of mod-rocker riots,

and all those old rock and roll Eddie Cochran songs like *Summertime Blues* that were always more popular there than here. There was Roger Daltrey, always more mannequin than singer, throwing the mike around his head so the mods could see every line of that new jacket. Who could understand that without understanding England's mod revolution and the glorious faddish tyranny of clothes that overtook the British working boy? And Keith Moon, the mad drummer? Listen, it's one thing to kick over the drums in America, just to be different, just to have a gimmick, because there's plenty of bread here to buy more. But in England, where forty dollars a week is not a bad wage at all, the violence and madness have to be for real. And Entwhistle the bass man, isn't he perhaps a little *too* sane?

At the helm, controlling the whole Who sound and playing the Fourth Stooge, Peter Townshend and the meanest-looking guitar in all of rock. The great hand is poised high, as high as it will go, only so it can swoop down on the strings like an angry hawk, ready to snatch its prey. The great face, that can be gentle and whimsical or haughtily aristocratic, grimaces horribly. The guitar is put through such terrors that when in the end it's smashed to bits by its enraged tormentor, you heave a sigh of relief for the suffering that is finally over. Ho, ho, says Peter Townshend about all that, it's simply brilliant showmanship. In the days when he felt he couldn't measure up, he covered his deficiencies with an extravagance of gesture that, he says modestly, has fooled everyone ever since. You really don't ever realize how well he's playing because his performances are so visually seductive. So are Roger Daltrey's, a singer in the best mincing, primping, foppish Mick Jagger tradition. And though the Who sound pretty good on record, you still feel you are missing something because they are rock theatre first, and that's how it should be.

They were originally called the Highnumbers, and they came out in 1963, a little after the Yardbirds and the Stones. Chris Stamp (who is actor Terence's brother) and Kit Lambert were two boys in search of a group, their heads full of Brian Epstein fantasies, when they first clapped eyes on the scruffy Highnumbers. First they changed the name. The Who, how could you ever go wrong with that? (Who? The Who.) The group's distinctive mark then was Townshend's jacket, made from the English flag, the Union Jack. Now those were the days when a new band had to fight for recognition, and while clothes were already pretty interesting and Roger Daltry's florals and ruffles were giving the fans more than their money's worth, there had to be more than that. (No one else, it must be remembered, at that time had anything made from the Union Jack – no ashtrays, no wastepaper baskets, no shopping bags, no whole shops of Union Jack merchandise in London as there are now. No, that was what Peter Townshend's jacket started.) But with the emergence of pop art at that time, Peter's Union Jack jacket was a sensation. And one of the saddest moments ever came at Murray the K's Easter Show, during the Who's brief first U.S. season, when a Who fan sat in the front row in a Union Jack red-white-and-blue shirt, and Peter Townshend, in velvet or something, just *looked* at him. By then Townshend was sick to death of the flag, but to the fan it was as shocking as if Townshend had come on stage without his famous nose.

In any case, with the ready-made audience of mods waiting for them in England, the Who clicked. *My Generation* became the national anthem of the under-twenty-fives in England and a number one record there. But in 1966, when Lambert and Stamp came over to sell their boys to America, all anyone was getting excited about over here was Herman's Hermits. When the Who did play Murray the K's Easter Show a year later, it was on a sort of guest basis – they got to do two numbers. No one knew them in the U.S., so their records, including *My Generation*, got no airplay, which in turn meant that no one got a chance to know them. They started to make their name after the Monterey Pop Festival later in 1967, when their guitar-smashing and smoke-amplifier act went over almost as well as the ritual burning of Jimi Hendrix's guitar. *Happy Jack*, a nicely characteristic single, all wry humor and perky tune, quickly established them as a group to be taken seriously musically as well as theatrically.

Since then, Who singles have continued to be wry and perky, Townshend's lyrics almost always telling a little story with a beginning, a middle and an end. They were the first of the now popular three-instrument groups (drums, bass and lead guitar) and the first to popularize the creative use of feedback (though whether they were the first to use it is still being argued out with the Yardbirds). The big thing was the orgy of destruction at the end – drums kicked, guitars smashed, amplifiers and microphones wrenched from their places and ominously smoking and sputtering electric leads. Once in a while Townshend wouldn't break his guitar totally (he claims the whole thing started accidentally, because he felt like smashing a guitar, and that to this day he doesn't smash unless he wants to) and now and then a smoke bomb was planted to add to the fun, but the rock and wreck part of the act was always a refreshing change from the blandness of the Dave Clark Five and Herman's Hermits.

By 1968 the Who were stars. The gimmickry never blinded anyone to the true talent of the Who. The singles were making it, the albums were selling. *A Quick One While He's Away* was a very complicated twelve-minute rock opera. A whole album was done as a BBC radio show with commercials. *TOMMY*, a rock opera, is about a deaf and blind boy who's seduced by his uncle, but because Townshend wrote it and the boy is deaf and blind, the seduction becomes just another interesting experience. Townshend is one of the great musicians of the new music, not of the blues or some other era's music like most of the greats, but of rock and pop itself and all of its future possibilities.

HANK WILLIAMS/In 1968 there was suddenly a lot of talk in rock circles about country music, and the term country rock was used about some of the best albums to come out that year. Suddenly a lot of people who had never thought one way or another about country music started digging into its albums to see what it was about. One of the best examples of what country music is about is Hank Williams, who died in 1953 at the age of twenty-nine. Country-music fans have not recovered to this day, and when you hear his songs or read his story it's easy to see why. He was an Alabama farm boy who sang in the church choir and got turned on to music at the age of eight, when someone gave him a guitar. By the time he was fourteen he had gotten together a group, was playing at dances and was a regular on radio. From there he went on to Nashville's famous Grand Ole Opry, which was broadcast nationally every Saturday night. Hank was a star.

He was tall, dark and good-looking, a beautiful, gentle singer. And he wrote literally hundreds of hits. At first for others who were more well known in the world of popular music, hits like *Hey Good Lookin'* and *Your Cheatin' Heart*, but eventually for himself, getting himself as high on the pop charts as he had been on the country and western. Then his marriage fell apart and so did he. There was talk of alcohol and drugs, and to this day no one is sure if they were what killed him, but it really doesn't matter.

Today you hear echoes of Hank Williams in so many singers, often in Tim Hardin, who has the same gentle voice overlaid with unexpressed pain. Sometimes you hear him for a moment in the work of the Spoonful or the Buffalo Springfield, and in fact in all the groups where the early influences were country. His songs were enormously popular with everyone from Louis Armstrong, Fats Domino and Teresa Brewer to Jerry Lee Lewis and Elvis Presley. *Your Cheatin' Heart* has been recorded by at least fifty people. *Cold, Cold Heart, Jambalaya* and *Ramblin' Man* were among the biggest of his hits. He was very hardworking and productive and it's almost impossible to comprehend, looking at the long list of his albums (some released after his death) and hearing the legends about his life, that he was so young when he died.

JOHNNY WINTER/Somewhere in the deep heart of America at this very moment is a man or woman, black, white or brindle, who, if properly promoted, properly packaged, properly booked and handled, could be bigger than Elvis and the Beatles put together. The question is where? Or, if you like, who? When the December 1968 issue of *Rolling Stone* mentioned almost in passing, in an article on the Texas scene, a totally unknown cross-eyed albino who played Delta blues, New York club owner Steve Paul snapped like a divining rod that had at last found water. He left on the first plane to Texas and didn't return until he'd tracked down the pale thin cowboy with the pale white hair and the black, black voice.

Johnny Winter may not be exactly the legendary unknown destined to reign as the greatest song hero since Bob Dylan, but he was an exciting discovery to make early in 1969 when everyone had seen everything except a cross-eyed albino who could sing. Columbia Records believed in him to the extent of a six figure contract and his lean white presence and silky hair brought an unexpected new twist to a musical scene already heavily dominated by a Black is Beautiful philosophy.

Once the first flurry of excitement was over, however, the big question that needed to be raised was, could Johnny Winter have made it if he'd been, say, Jewish and from Chicago, like Mike Bloomfield? Yes, said the ecstatic *New York Times*. Well ...? said the doubters. All in all, it became one of the most pleasant subjects to argue about in that drab winter.

America's first albino bluesman learned his sound from the black radio stations he listened to as a child. When he first became a professional entertainer in Texas (Johnny Winter and the Black Plague, he called himself and his group – later renamed It and Them with his brother Edgar) he played little blues, just hits of the time, rhythm and blues and soul material. Nobody played blues for fun or profit in the rock and roll decade (1956–66). Then the blues revival of 1967–68 got underway and when Steve Paul, entrepreneur extraordinaire of the New York music scene, met the albino boy wonder of the Lone Star State, his big selling point was that Johnny had a right to sing the blues, just like anyone else.

By mid-1969 Winter's vintage blues had clicked with most of the insiders and tastemakers, barring the one or two who always dissent fashionably. Then the mass media moved in and billed him, to everyone's astonishment, as the most talented and irresistible freak since Tiny Tim. If the pitch didn't show where he was at musically, it at least sold a lot of records and nobody, but nobody (not Dylan, not the Beatles, not anyone) is ever likely to knock *that*.

YARDBIRDS/*Jimmy Page (replaced Jeff Beck who replaced Eric Clapton)(lead guitar), John Paul Jones (replaced Paul "Sam" Samwell-Smith)(bass, organ), Robert Plant (replaced Keith Relf)(vocals), John Bonham (replaced Jim McCarty)(drums). Previous Member: Chris Dreja (rhythm guitar).*
In late 1963–early 1964 when the English "scene" was having its birth pangs, the Yardbirds followed the Rolling Stones into the Crawdaddy Club (by day the somewhat staid Richmond Cricket Club) as house band. Like the early Stones, they used standard material – Bo Diddley, Isley Brothers, Muddy Waters, Sonny Boy Williamson – always remaining more faithful to the original than the improvisation/variation-prone Stones. This was important at a time when the concept of original material was not as overworked as it was to become in 1967–69. Also, man for man, the Yardbirds were better instrumentalists than the Stones were then.

The original Yardbirds came out of a parent group called the Metropolis Blues Quartet, which featured Chris Dreja on rhythm guitar, Paul "Sam" Samwell-Smith on bass, Jim McCarty on drums, and Keith Relf doing vocals. They were joined by a very straight-looking crew-cut Eric Clapton who played lead guitar, and they became the Yardbirds. Now of course what the Stones had over them, even then, was the charisma of their lead singer, Mick Jagger. And although the Yardbirds were better musicians in 1963–64, the Stones were better performers, and their rival factions used to fight it out rather bitterly at times.

By 1964 the Beatles had hit America, the Rolling Stones had hit America, everyone English and his brother had hit America (including some of the worst groups in England) and the Yardbirds, like some other good, even great groups, found themselves lost in the shuffle. A lot of things went wrong. Their first British album was recorded live at the famous Marquee Club where they used to play every Sunday night. The ten tracks were fine, but to fit them all on the album they had to be speeded up, only a little, but enough to make the music almost unrecognizable to hard-core Yardbird fans. And the tragedy was that the album *was* the Yardbirds – *Five Long Years, Louise, Smokestack Lightning, I'm A Man.*

During that time the Yardbirds happened on to what they called a rave-up, a long wild instrumental break, sometimes as long as thirty minutes, during which all the attention was focused on guitarist Clapton (for a change, since singer Relf was the natural star of the group). The rave-ups were Eric's big chance. He took off and the audience flew with him. His whole personality changed during these breaks, and because they weren't ever as long and as frequent as he wanted them (or needed them) to be, he eventually left – for John Mayall's group, which was even more tradition-oriented than the Yardbirds. Later, when he formed Cream, it was obvious that Eric was a breaker of new ground, and the Yardbirds merely excellent tillers of already-cultivated soil.

The tradition of the rave-up stayed with the Yardbirds. Much, much later the long instrumental breaks started to be associated with the dance scene of San Francisco and as a result were given the name of psychedelic. By 1968 people were saying with admiration that the Yardbirds had been the first to get into a psychedelic "bag". Clapton was replaced by Jeff Beck, another guitarist extraordinaire, who was eventually to leave, too, and start his own group. He was succeeded by Jimmy Page, one of the best session men in England (who is said to be on anywhere from fifty to ninety per cent of the records released in England in the 1963–65 days).

In America the Yardbirds were never as lucky as other, often lesser, groups. Their first album here, *FOR YOUR LOVE*, was full of material they thought (or were made to think) was most suitable for American audiences. The material was more modern than material they had done in England. The second American album seemed to be designed to correct this, with new material on one side (the *Evil Hearted You* side), but with older material – Muddy Waters and Bo Diddley tracks from their first English album – on the other (this time they were presented at their normal speed). Because they were recorded when Clapton was still with the group he is, naturally, featured on them, even though he had left by the time the album was released. The problem, was, though, that this material was wildly exciting in England where no one had access to the originals. Americans seemed to prefer the "modern" Yardbirds. (With the 1968 blues revival this was to change, but too late for the old Yardbirds.)

In 1968 the Yardbirds announced they were splitting. One of the best groups to come out of England, one of the most concerned with music, they influenced the development of every group that came out of the English scene from the Beatles to the Who.

Will Success Spoil Lillian Roxon?

Part 1: How Rock Encyclopedia *came to be written, a necessary explanation.*

There is nothing worse than a New York summer. It is mid-winter as I write this, so I can hardly remember exactly what it is that makes the summer here unbearable. In any case, there are only three ways to cope with it. You can leave town, you can lie about in a state of enervated limbo waiting for steamy July and August to turn into September, or you can switch the thermostat of a $200 air conditioner all the way up to seven until you start to shiver and have to huddle under a blanket.

On the whole, summer in New York is not a time when anything much gets done. But of course, it's not always like that. There are nights in early summer when you almost think you can hear cicadas, nights so balmy they smell of frangipani and lantana. And when the breezes come in from Central Park or the river, the leaves of the few sad trees around the city actually rustle.

On nights like this, even the most sensible human beings get into trouble. The summer of 1967 was one of the few summers when every night had that quality. Mischief hung about in the air like a spicy perfume. If you weren't going to live that summer, you never would. I think everybody knew that. That was the summer, they still talk about it now, when everyone became nineteen.

Now I know that, in Australia, summers are such that a lot of people are nineteen a lot of the time. But in New York it's not like that. Giddiness is not the hallmark of the New Yorker at any time of the year. He is cautious, guarded, highly suspicious. Romantic encounters, not that you would *ever* call them that, tend to be perfunctory though wordy. Everybody does whatever has to be done, but carefully, so that not more than is absolutely necessary of the body is involved, and the head and heart are not touched at all. The New Yorker does not like involvement. But the summer of 1967 was the summer that everyone got involved.

If I'm going to talk about success, whatever that is, a funny word with malicious sibilants, and how I came to write about rock which, for the lack of a better definition, is the bigger and better music that came out of rock and roll, then I certainly have to talk about that summer.

There had been very little rain and everyone was deeply tanned, which is unusual for New York. I was working, for the *Sydney Morning Herald*, on a strange shift, five in the afternoon till one in the morning. It was a beautiful shift, I loved it. I could lie all day in the sun on the damp grey sands of Coney Island beach, go to work at five feeling healthy and athletic, and finish at one positively electric with energy.

I don't suppose I would have ever got interested in rock music, though I had been watching developments in that field for about a year because I could see how overwhelming a force it was going to be, but there were only two places to go at one in the morning.

One was a restaurant near my home called Max's Kansas City, a place rock groups found comfortable, glamorous and convenient for late-night meals. Another was a small club only a few minutes' walk from work called The Scene where groups played nightly and musicians hung out if they were lonely, bored or simply needing one familiar spot to focus on in a large, cold and often unfamiliar city.

Among my papers the other day I found an old advertisement for The Scene. It captures just a little of the excitement of those nights. Listen to this: "We got together last night TRAFFIC played. They were great. You could have come. The JIMI HENDRIX EXPERIENCE, FAT FRANKIE, THE JEFFERSON AIRPLANE, TINKER BELL, FRANK ZAPPA, THE YARDBIRDS, TAYLOR MEAD, SPADE PIXIE, THE RASCALS, THE McCOYS, JOE BOYD, CATHY S.F., DEVON, FRAN & WINONA, EMERETTA, CHAS CHANDLER, SUSAN'S DAVID, SPENCER DAVIS, PATRICK SKY, LARISSA & MARCIA, SLY AND THE FAMILY STONE, ARTHUR GORSON, THE VAGRANTS, IRON BUTTERFLY, EIRE APPARENT, FRANTICS, JESSE'S CARNIVAL, THREE OF MAX'S BACK TABLES, LITTLE FREDDY AND PETITE PATTY, DEERING AND BRADLEY, TERRY FRAMIS-SHED, TOMMY BOYCE & BOBBY HART, MURRAY ROMAN, MICHAEL GOLDSTEIN AND DOMINIC SICILIA, VALERIE & KEITH, and even I managed to come. DANNY FIELDS AND NICO were out of town. Together. Sorry you couldn't make it. We're getting together again tonight. Call JU2-5760."

I still don't know half those people but you had to be a real fuddy-duddy to resist *that* invitation. It was sort of junior Damon Runyon. *Guys and Dolls* with everyone well under twenty.

I suppose people think I researched my book in some library, and maybe I should have, and my employers must be wondering to this day how I could do a 611-page book and not encroach on their time, but there it is. *Rock Encyclopedia* came out of those nights at Max's and The Scene. In a way, it's an autobiography of that summer, especially if you read between the lines. And don't think most people haven't.

You see New York has all this spare energy, though usually only in its crisp autumns. And it has to settle somewhere. The year I first got here it was the coffee shop folk scene that saw the birth of Bob Dylan. A few years later its hurricane eye shifted to Mississippi and the Freedom Marches. Then it was the underground cinema when everyone conveniently forgot the Deep South and its miseries and turned to hand-held cameras and 16 mm masterpieces. Pop art had its year and so did experimental theatre. In 1967, it was rock music and I can remember when it didn't surprise me one bit to see Norman Mailer, Timothy Leary and Allen Ginsberg all sitting raptly at ringside the night the Byrds first played New York. (By 1968 and 1969 rock began to give way to politics but that's someone else's book.)

If it had been the usual New York summer, there would have been no energy. Everyone would have gone home to their air conditioners. But this was a sort of extended spring and there was a great restlessness and recklessness in the air. The Scene was filled with the strangest people – society ladies who really should have known better, high school girls, teenyboppers who could teach me a thing or two, little gilded things from Connecticut, girls from the Bronx trying to look like King's Road Chelsea, wonderful creatures from Harlem that you could describe as escapees from the cast of *Hair* only *Hair* hadn't happened yet. In fact when *Hair* was looking for its cast, the first place the producers looked was in The Scene and in the back room of Max's.

Heaven knows what those ladies with late spring fever were looking for but here's what they found. Drummers from Manchester with accents so thick you couldn't understand them and never tried. Bass players from Newcastle or East London. Organists from Glasgow, or Toronto, or Memphis, Tennessee. Heartbreakingly lonely little groups from Denver, Colorado. Giant redneck groups from Alabama. And mystic mysterious beaded young guru groups from San Francisco. Not to mention their agents, managers, chauffeurs, photographers, equipment carriers, press agents, connections and impresarios. It looked pretty sleazy, at least it would have to an outsider, but in that crowded cellar any night there was more money and power than in the rest of Tin Pan Alley put together. The limousines lined the shabby streets outside for blocks and you always knew when Nat Weiss, the Beatles' American manager was there, because you'd see the psychedelic painted Rolls he'd borrowed from John Lennon parked in the place of honour just outside the door. I think Nat Weiss is in his middle thirties but even he was nineteen in June of 1967.

One night Paul Newman, the actor, came in with the Mamas and Papas' press agent John Kurland. John was in a white Cardin suit looking so beautiful it took your breath away. No one looked at Newman. Several summers later I discovered John hadn't been nineteen at all that summer, and he discovered the same about me, but by heavens, with our tans and the rest of the magic, you'd never have known it.

I'm not going to be prissy and pretend that all those lovely ladies and all those lonely musicians did nothing but sit and listen to music. If you were a beautiful girl, and as I keep saying everyone was beautiful, when The Scene eventually closed at four, the limousines would whisk you off to the city's great hotels, the Hilton, the Plaza, the Americana, the Regency, and you could sit around and listen to more music, have breakfast, watch the late movies on television, talk, rest or simply fall in love for twelve hours or twenty-four or forty-eight depending on who was going where next day. Much later, I think, all these things became very sordid, because the boys from Newcastle and and Manchester and Leeds got used to the money and the fame and were spoiled rotten with too much attention. But then it all had a very innocent quality, something like wartime, when every man is a soldier about to leave for the front, and the least a decent woman can do is see that on the last few days of his leave he is shielded from everything unpleasant and painful.

No one had invented the word "groupie" then. The word is supposed to mean something like a stage door Jenny and god knows there were plenty of those. But the girls at The Scene and at Max's were witty and pretty companions who never saw themselves as anything but ministering angels. It was, after all, the summer of love and flower power.

Naturally it didn't last. By September everyone had become a little corrupt. The frightened little Cockney barrow boys came back from their tours around Illinois, Louisiana, Texas and Nevada, jaunty and just a little jaded and hard. The girls became competitive, bickering over whether the favours of a Byrd rated higher than those of a Candyman, and was an Animal rated lower than a Stone? They, too, grew jaded and hard and none of them looked nineteen for much longer, not even the seventeen-year-olds.

As the weather turned cold, and the tans faded, the whole thing soured. On the juke-boxes, the songs of the summer took on a shrill tone, as though they knew their days were numbered. I woke up one morning and discovered I wasn't nineteen any more but, well, I didn't know, thirty or something, and it was too cold for the beach and the night shift was a drag and life was humdrum again. When someone sent me a Canadian drummer "for Christmas", I didn't know what to do with him and sent him home to his mother in Montreal on a Greyhound bus. He was twenty-two, and very pretty, but he was six months too late for everything and I didn't know how to tell him that, with the snow falling outside and ice forming on the footpaths.

The winter was long and cold. I went to London in the spring for a holiday and comforted myself with daffodils and crocuses but when I got back, and another summer was starting, it was obvious this was not going to be one with frangipani in the air, but another of those gritty oppressive humid ones that sapped strength and spirit.

I was honestly afraid of what was ahead, and when someone recommended me to a publisher as the "perfect" person to write a brief encyclopedia of rock, it seemed like an ideal way to fill the spare hours of the three hot months ahead.

Also, it sounded like fun. Eventually the book took not three months to write but seven. And naturally when you are writing a book, you have to work twice as hard at your ordinary work to prove to your boss you're not slacking. I wasn't. I did my best work during those dreadful months.

What was to be a small unpretentious paperback grew into a huge volume. A month before it was finished I developed severe asthma, so that when the last page was done in the middle of a blizzard, I headed straight for Sydney, wheezing and coughing and whistling all the way across the Pacific.

After four months of sunshine and fresh pawpaws and twilights when the light hung around like a lingering kiss, my health improved and my spirits revived. Back in New York, though, things were terrible. A new ugly summer was beginning. Everyone at Max's back room and The Scene looked a hundred including me. The book was still being edited. I looked at every change they made and changed it back. The publishers told me that in order to get the book out in time for

Christmas, corrections would have to be kept down to a minimum. And the unpretentious little paperback, the one that had become an unpretentious big paperback, was now to be an enormous hardcover book. I said I thought it was a little eccentric and a little too personal to be a ten dollar hardcover, but my publisher said what the world needed now more than anything was an eccentric encyclopedia.

After Sydney, New York was especially grim. It had never been aromatic like Sydney, though it had seemed so, but now it smelled of car fumes and factory smoke and even if there had been a breeze, the leaves couldn't have rustled because they were already dead from lack of oxygen. I felt exactly like those leaves, suffocated by concrete and the wastes of civilisation.

Part II: What happens to the author of a "Rock Encyclopedia" or what success is really like, close up, though, of course, it all depends on what you call success. As far as I'm concerned, you're not successful until you sell it to the movies.

In November, the book came out. It weighed in at nearly three pounds, and it sure looked nice. Howard Smith, a columnist on the very influential *Village Voice*, had read in *Publisher's Weekly* that it was "terrific". So he rang and asked me to have dinner with him in a soul food restaurant and tell him all about it.

When his column came out, it said the book was a "pleasure trip from A to Zombies". Alex Bennet who has a rock talk show at WMCA rang and asked me if I could come in after work and do a show with David Peel of David Peel and the Lower East Side. David's biggest hit is called "Have a Marijuana", cops love it, you can imagine the sort of character he is. I didn't have to talk much but Alex mentioned my book eight times or more in four hours. In prime time.

Then *Newsweek* rang and asked if I would mind going down to the Fillmore one evening and having my photo taken with "Legs" Larry Smith, drummer of the Bonzo Dog Doo-Dah Band. They cut "Legs" out of the picture, which is a pity because he's very picturesque, leaving only a very unflattering picture of me. Their review was wonderful, though.

Goodness knows what happens in Australia but in America a book has to be promoted. While *Vogue* was recommending it as a Christmas present and the *Wall Street Journal* was calling it "delightful" I had to go on the Casper Citron show in my lunch hour and talk about where rock was heading. On the show with me was Allen Hughes, classical music critic for the *New York Times*. I was the quiet staid one. He was the outrageous one who kept saying how great rock was and how important the book was.

Now the music papers gave their verdict. *Cashbox* thought it was magnificent, *Billboard* sold it by mail to its show business readers, *Variety* thought it was hip and *Record World* said I was a star. Only one music paper hated it and I would be ungenerous to suggest that was because that particular critic had just brought out a rock book, but not a 611-page encyclopedia, himself.

On the Jack O'Brian show taped at an unearthly time of the morning, the thesis I was presented with was that rock stars had dirty hair. Obviously Mr. O'Brian had never been to the Americana hotel to do an interview with a rock group or he would know that you can hardly hear yourself speak for the noise of the hair dryers. If anything, I told him, there was too much, not too little, shampooing in that world.

Now it was the *New York Times* quoting freely from the book and the *New York Times* asked me to give them the latest on rock fashions. I put on all my silk shawls from Kaleidoscope in Woollahra, the ones with the rosella parrots hand embroidered on them, and made an appearance on its stately pages looking as much like a rock encyclopedist as anyone could desire. Very nice, except they ran the piece on Boxing Day.

Next came the hippie press. The *East Village Other* after some grumbling conceded it was the "perfect" reference work; *Fusion* made it its book offer of the month; *Rat* the revolutionary magazine called me "incredible"; *Changes* said I was "gentle and unassuming" and so was the book.

Later came the out of town critics. The *Los Angeles Times* hated it. The *Los Angeles Herald Examiner* liked it. The *San Francisco Chronicle* found it eccentric but pronounced it the most useful book in rock. The *Chicago News* liked it, as did the *Washington Post*, the *Washington News*, the *Montreal Star*, the *St Louis Post Dispatch* and papers in New Jersey, Massachusetts and Tennessee. The London *Record Mirror* found it entertaining but a small rock magazine called *Action World* found it boring.

The promotion continued. I did the Mike Klein show in Long Island (100,000 listeners) from eleven to one, one night. Next day Voice of

America did a lunch interview in a cafeteria, the BBC came round for dinner, 2GB rang from Australia at eight, and Richard Robinson, one of my closest friends, did a broadcast that will go to 400 stations all over America.

In Washington on a brief holiday I did twelve interviews in two days, one hour on television all by myself, a 45-minute radio show shared with a makeup genius. Breakfast with the *Washington Post* resulted in spectacular, two-inch high, fourteen-inch wide headlines "ROCK KEEPS CHANGING. CHRONICLER LILLIAN ROXON REPORTS".

Afternoon tea with the *Washington News* got me a column in its political page. On an open end radio show I had to cope with a lot of questions the answers to most of which were "Elvis is King". The Washington visit was rated a huge success and book re-orders were so big that it was decided to go into a third printing, especially as word came from the Book Find Club they would take ten thousand for starters, and from the New York Public Library that the book had been selected as one of the best reference works of 1969.

By now the *Saturday Review* had it on its reference list too. *Status* magazine pronounced it as a status symbol, *Sixteen* magazine recommended it, *Glamor* magazine recommended it, *Charlie* magazine recommended it, *Cavalier* magazine recommended it. So did *Screw*, a pornographic magazine, which meant 100 phone calls I left to an answering service to cope with.

I forgot to mention some Israeli paper that sent me its clipping in Hebrew; the David Frost show (he didn't mention the book); the Mike Wallace show where you never meet Mr. Wallace, he tapes his voice in afterwards; Charles Woods who does book reviews for every ABC station in America; Murray the K the disc jockey whose show goes on the NBC Monitor network; Mike Jahn, rock critic of the *New York Times* who called me the most sensible person in rock; the lady at Associated Press who talked to me for two hours; *Time* magazine who bought me a Chinese meal but I think they were just picking my brains; *Student Voice* who was for me, *University Review* who was undecided.

The London *Sunday Mirror* wanted to know what I thought about the seventies ("marijuana biscuits and unabashed nudity"), *Cosmopolitan* wanted to know what I thought about brassieres ("unfriendly"), *Hit Parader* and *Circus* rang to say they were doing good reviews. Bob Christgau, the best rock writer in America, gave the book his seal of approval and another very critical rock writer Juan Sodriguez said, "It needs no apologies." The London *Evening Standard* bought the serial rights – for too little. I was asked to teach a course in the history of rock at the New York School for the Visual Arts.

[Recently I heard that Jack Kroll at *Newsweek* is using the book to teach his writers to write concisely, informatively and entertainingly, which is flattering, but also ironic, since my wages are almost $100 less a week than those of the lowest paid junior reporter on *Newsweek*.]

I've deliberately gone into this long recital because I know that it sounds impressive, in a way. And yet, I don't know. I've only "done" two towns and not to saturation. *Playboy, Esquire,* the *New Yorker, Mademoiselle, Ingenue* and *Look* among others apparently don't know the book exists. The *New York Times* flatly refuses to review it on the grounds it's done its rock book for the year. A big record company asked me if I'd do a record, choose tracks to go with the book, but there would be no royalties and I'd have to pay half the advertising myself.

True I've been offered ten books but they're all dreadful. The worst is called "Under Thirty" which I'm no longer qualified to write. What I would like to do is finish my novel about Sydney but American publishers are not enthusiastic about that.

I'm not exactly disenchanted but I didn't ever imagine success would mean continuing to work twice as hard to show that my heart is with my job and that I don't harbour secret hopes of becoming a professional encyclopedist. Nobody told me writing a book, a first book anyway, ages you ten years and it's a good idea to recover from that before taking on the next one. And nobody told me till it was too late that the only people who ever make money out of books are those who sell them to the movies. I offered to tell the real story of that marvellous summer but Mike Jahn of the *New York Times* beat me to it. He was around then, being nineteen, too, like all of us. He's writing it for Bernard Geis which did Jacqueline Susann's incredibly successful *Valley of the Dolls*. He's calling it, but of course, "The Scene" and from what I hear it tells all the raunchy things they wouldn't let me put in the *Encyclopedia*.

He's going to sell it to the movies!

Quadrant, January–February 1971

There is a Tide in the Affairs of Women

New York, 28 August 1970

This is the hardest piece I have ever had to write in my life.

I am supposed to be telling what happened when 25,000 women marched down Fifth Avenue last night on the 50th anniversary of the day women won the right to vote. As is customary in my business I am supposed to be telling it briskly and factually and without bias.

Fat chance. I'm so biased, I can hardly think straight.

My emotions are all in a turmoil, and I don't know where to start.

I might start, for instance, with my own cowardice. We were all supposed to go on strike yesterday, it was to be a national women's strike for equality, and in our hearts we all knew it was deadly serious.

But we didn't, of course. Some of us were afraid to lose our jobs. Some of us let our bosses charm us into turning up for work because, of course, none of this had made us less susceptible to men – yet. Some of us pretended it didn't really matter, though we looked at each other a little shamefacedly in buses and lifts.

We all had our little excuses ready to salve our consciences but it is more important for me to admit right here that I know I did wrong than it is for me to tell you who carried what funny slogans on the march.

Another emotion I hardly know how to cope with because it's so unfamiliar is rage – against men who have been making a big joke of this all day.

Someone just phoned me long distance to interview me live for Australian radio. He treated the whole thing as a delightful lark – and I let him. My cowardice appals me far more than his well-intentioned levity.

He could laugh at the demand for free abortions but anyone who saw the tragic condition of ghetto women seeking help at hospitals wouldn't laugh quite so much.

Everyone thought it was terribly funny that marriage manuals were ritually burnt at the big rally last night. The manuals are almost always written entirely from a man's point of view. The women's liberation ladies have on the whole been a bit too delicate to bring that subject up just now, but they're going to. It upsets me that even as I write this

I know that the men editors and sub-editors handling this story will probably choose to delete this particular paragraph.

One of the saddest aspects of the march last night was the jeering reaction of some of the women spectators – their universal theme, expressed one way or another, was: "We're happy being slaves."

Girls carrying pink placards that read "M-O-M" for "Men Our Masters" actually scuffled with their marching sisters. That distressed me far more than the many predictable accusations from male hecklers that we were nothing but a bunch of deviates

I must confess there were many aspects of last night's demonstration that I found melodramatic and silly. I think, for instance, that when we women get whatever we want it won't be because we burnt our brassieres.

Part of my confusion and everyone else's is that we still don't know exactly what it is we want. Like the Negroes in America's Deep South, we are so used to our inferior roles we get nervous when we consider anything else.

There are splits inside the women's liberation movement reflecting varying degrees of timidity and courage. I, for instance, plan to work with Anne-Marie Micklo and Karin Berg, two young feminists, in a series of health workshops for women, but only because I'm too scared to fight.

There is no question of giving up men or, as men have been saying, "girl-cotting" them. In fact many men are enormously sympathetic and more than a little anxious to make up for past sins. The idea is, after all, to liberate everyone – not just women.

As for the others, they'll just have to change. Because, you see, whatever you may read, this isn't a fad like the hula hoop, this is for real. The strike may not have been successful in itself but the attention it got in the world press more than made up for it.

The grievances are too many to list here. And too complex. But everyone knows what they are. Mainly, I think, what women want is to be taken seriously. Being a woman has always been a bit of a joke. Women don't even take one another seriously.

If the idea of change makes you uncomfortable, don't worry. You're not alone. All of us ladies agree that this time getting there is not going to be half the fun. But being there is going to be an important part of a brave new world.

It had to start sometime, somewhere. It started last night on New York's Fifth Avenue. It disturbed me and confused me but I'm glad I was there when it happened.

Sydney Morning Herald, 28 August 1970

The *Other* Germaine Greer: A Manicured Hand on the Zipper

Germaine Greer is faster than a speeding bullet, taller than the Eiffel Tower and more complicated than Einstein's theory of relativity. *Life, Newsweek, Time* and *Vogue* had a hard time getting her down on paper and I'm not sure if I can or want to.

But I do think that the media, from Johnny Carson down, made a severe mistake when they allowed themselves to be intimidated by the lady just because she had a Cambridge doctorate, a best-selling book and a rather scary repertoire of scholarly put downs.

Because, you see, you can take all that away and you're still left with this great belle who is just as campy and grand as Jackie Curtis, just as innocently outrageous as Viva and just as bawdy and nosy and gossipy as Brigit Polk. Great lady? The author of *The Female Eunuch* is a dozen such ladies rolled into one.

Let me take you back to the summer of 1959 in Melbourne, Australia, when Stanley Kramer was down there making *On The Beach*. She was twenty at the time and working as a waitress in one of those elegant late-night coffee shops where all the Kramer people were hanging out – Tony Perkins, Fred Astaire, Ava and that lot. She had purple hair and was the first person in my life I had ever seen wear red stockings. I didn't know then that she was going to end up on the cover of *Life* and photographed by Tony Armstrong Jones and autographing books in Bloomingdales, let alone in Town Hall debating Norman Mailer, but I did know that she was a Presence.

Whip forward now to the spring of 1968 and swinging London and the Notting Hill flat of *Performance* and *Walkabout* cameraman Mike Molloy, and suddenly there is Germaine in a pastel angora sweater, tweed skirt and leather rocker jacket. Too much. She has just got that intimidating doctorate and is teaching English at the University of Warwick. We are watching the Miss England contest and the men are making the usual crude jokes about which contestant they'd like to ball and who has the best legs and tits. "Gawd," said Germaine, stifling a yawn, "I haven't seen a decent Mons Veneris all night." And as a matter of fact, we hadn't.

Talk turns to one of her great idols, Viv Stanshall of the Bonzo Dog Doo-Dah Band. I tell her I had just spent the most delightful of evenings with "Legs" Larry Smith, the Bonzo drummer, and how the best thing about him was the way he had someone spell out his name, "Legs", in studs on the back of his jacket. Next time I see her the rocker jacket has an addition. When she turns around, on the back of it, in the most florid of scripts, someone has taken silver studs and spelled out her name, "Dr Greer". Well, it's one way to celebrate a PhD.

Now it's December of the same year. The lady has an open invitation to come visit in New York and here she is in time for Christmas with her embroidered satin antique jacket from the Chelsea Antique Market, her Bessarabian Princess's Defloration robe, a black net and silver belly dancer's vest and see-through chiffon velvet elephant pants. All I have is asthma, cockroaches and a manuscript to finish.

When she approaches, the cockroaches scatter in fright. Love, she says cheerfully, will kill the bugs, clear my lungs and put pep into my typewriter. She offers me Paul Krassner. I don't believe he will solve my problems so I move her to the Broadway Central. She is on the phone two hours later. "Look here," she says in that Vanessa Redgrave voice that rang out so inspiringly when she took on Mailer at the Town Hall. "I don't mind the whores and the drag queens and the junkies but I won't ride up and down the elevator with a corpse."

Fortunately, we are able to distract her with a big romance. The MC5 are in town. She offered me Krassner, I gave her Rob Tyner. Fair swap for The Five are then at the height of their glory. When she goes to dinner with William Styron and Norman Podhoretz she wears Rob's White Panther button as proudly as if it were his fraternity pin which, of course, it is. Later she wonders if she should write a piece called "Why I won't make it with Norman Podhoretz". Eventually she spares him that.

But she goes back to London disappointed by my hospitality. We don't speak for a year until I ring her in London on Christmas Eve, 1969 to tell her, on the first anniversary of our fight in Max's back room, that enough is enough. By then she's writing her book and her house is overrun by black widow spiders. So now she understands.

Our next meeting is in London in May 1969. She has just been on the cover of Oz, the English underground paper, in the see-through elephant pants and the net and silver vest and a great deal of rather comely bare tit. What she is doing on the cover is unzipping Viv ("Bonzo") Stanshall's fly. Oh, well. When I see her on Carnaby Street she is wearing six-inch clogs. She's in a crepe suit from the forties, all bias cut and peplums, and Beverly Robin who is with me and from New York doesn't believe what she's seeing. But she can't stop to talk except to tell me that she wants to call her women's lib book *The Clitoris Hits Back*.

Next day at the offices of *Oz* she sits planning a special women's lib issue. As she talks, she sits and embroiders a belt for her old man, making up the design in petit point as she goes along. Clouds, flowers, butterflies, words too. I peek to see what they are. "Cunt power," she smiles prettily at me. "He should wear it in good health."

Later when *Oz* comes out, it features a piece by "our needlework correspondent" with instructions for a "cock sock" ("Begin with a fine crochet hook, working a chain of five and adjoining with slip stitch ... continue until you have handsome accommodation for the knob ... leave room to expand"). I detect madam's fine hand. There is also a most unusually embroidered pantie ("you will need about seven hanks of cotton depending on the luxuriance of the pelt ... the labia minora in a more visceral shade ... later catch up every stitch around the labia crocheting a chain of three stitches in between"). As I said, a GREAT lady.

Just as congenially genital was her gossip column in *Suck*, the European sex paper. Crabs, non-specific urethritis, latent homosexuality. If you had it, it was in *Suck* for the world to read. What she wrote about me got me 125 telephone calls. I wish David Frost had asked her about THAT. "Well," she said, "it was all true, wasn't it?"

After that, I honestly thought she might be the first person to say "vulva" on *Johnny Carson* or even show it. But she didn't, she didn't even unzip Ed McMahon's fly which was very much what all of us old friends expected. When she went out with Peter Gimbel, the shark expert and department store heir who was on the show with her that night, all she did was take him off to see James Brown at Cheetah. And when she did say she'd never have a child to anyone but a black man it was on Kup's show in Chicago and would have gone unnoticed if *Jet* hadn't picked it up.

You have all read about the Town Hall debate and there's not much I can add to that except that she looked stunning and made mincemeat not of Norman Mailer which would have made it a wonderful night for everyone, and she could have done it too, but of Diana Trilling, whom she must have seen as her true adversary. It would have been nice to report she went home with Norman Mailer that night or even Jill Johnston (after all, she did wear a Gay Power button for her *Vogue* photo session with Lord Snowdon) but no, she got into a cab "and there at the wheel was the man of my dreams". A moonlighting rock photographer of unearthly beauty, the kind of boy who is used to rich and famous people falling in love with him. She will impress him but not intimidate him. He'll find her, as the drummer of the Easybeats did, softer and bouncier than a water bed; or as the manager of Family did, brisk, practical and domestic; or as Ginger Baker did, tender and melancholy.

Should I have talked about her money and what it feels like to sell a book to America alone for $165,000, and I'm not counting serial rights and book clubs let alone those sales to the other countries? Well, she's learning to handle that, she always thought big. Or should I talk about her marriage to one of the few men who was probably ever her match? It didn't last three weeks as the reports say but three weekends and she's never divorced him. And they like each other a lot these days.

Should I talk about the significance of her book? You can read the reviews for that. Like all authors, she's already well beyond what she wrote nearly two years ago. But for all the women, especially the older ones and the straighter ones, who are only JUST coming around to women's liberation, it's timely and presents its case well. It may very well change the face of female upper middle America, if you get me. Her dignity and scholarship gets to them.

All the same I wish they could get a glimpse of the other Germaine with the see-through elephant pants and the bare breasts and the manicured hand on the Stanshall zipper. "Listen," she rang frantically the other day, "McGraw Hill says you're going to write about me for *Screw*." "No, no," I said, "*Crawdaddy, Crawdaddy*." "Oh," she said and sounded relieved. Relieved? The Real Germaine would have been disappointed.

Crawdaddy, 4 July 1971

Creedence Clearwater Revival – The Band That Means Business

You've read what John Lennon is saying these days, that the party is over. I think, although he has his own good reasons for saying it, that he's being unfair. As far as music is concerned, it's only the honeymoon that's over. The serious part of the business is only just getting under way.

If you want the word "serious" to read, "without the first, giddy magic that happened at the beginning", fine. Let me show you how the scene is now.

A couple of weeks ago I was astonished to find in the mail a letter inviting me to a party for a group called Creedence Clearwater Revival – 3000 miles away in California. Where, asked the letter, would I like to have my plane ticket sent?

Where indeed? Out at Kennedy Airport for this weekend jaunt were some of the most important reporters on the music scene in America: Albert Goldman of *Life*, Don Heckman of the *New York Times*, Alfred Aronewitz of the *New York Post*, Ernest Dunbar of *Look*, Stephen Oberbeck of *Newsweek*. Also, representatives of *Saturday Review*, *Glamour*, *Jazz and Pop*, *Gentleman's Quarterly* and just about every other top-circulation publication you can think of.

All being flown at the expense of a rock and roll group across America and back for a party. Not bad for a scene John Lennon insists is dying.

Inside the plane things were pretty lively. A spry girl from a nationally circulated intellectual weekly leapt up the minute we were off the ground and passed around a tin of homemade chocolate biscuits. To this day I could not tell you what was in those biscuits, but a state of great exhilaration hit the assembled company like a sudden ray of bright sunshine. The middle-aged men from the important magazines looked as if they suspected they had been fed something slightly illegal, but weren't about to complain.

In California we were met by limousines and whisked off to one of the great hotels of Berkeley, the Claremont, all towers and colonnades and an air of refreshingly decadent luxury. (Modern hotels are SO wholesome.)

By this time there were close to a thousand of us. Flown in or bussed in from places like Toronto, Denver and Chicago, Los Angeles and nearby San Francisco. The party was costing at least one quarter of a million dollars!

What kind of a rock and roll band shells out that sort of money? And why?

Ah, yes, this is my answer to Mr Lennon and his death cries: A band that means business.

Like a couple of other big bands who are around today, Creedence Clearwater is not peddling magic, it's peddling music. It's not pretending it's 1966, which, alas, we'll never get back. It's facing up to the hard-fisted demands of 1971. Of course, it was better the other way, but if you agreed with Bob Dylan that the times they were a-changing back in 1963, then you really have to concede they are changing again, even if not perhaps the way you might like.

So here is Creedence Clearwater, the quintessential group of the seventies, practical, hard-working, hard-headed and supremely businesslike and materialistic. Don't knock it, that's the way the whole rock scene is heading.

Rock is no longer "Lucy in the sky with diamonds", it's Lucy in the bank with billions. The reason Creedence Clearwater threw the party was to dramatise an important point: the group has sold something like $82 million worth of records. It has had seven straight $1 million singles, and four of its five albums have passed the $2 million sales mark. When it makes a live appearance, it is usually not in a normal concert hall but in a huge arena where its night's share of the profits will bring in $40,000 or $50,000.

You may well ask why, with this incredible financial success behind it, Creedence would need to spend $250,000 to get a little attention and media space.

Well, the hard truth is that the big magazines and the little ones, too, are living in the past. It took them a long time to wake up to the Beatles and the huge changes the emergence of that particular group brought about. It is now taking them an equally long time to realise that that dream is now over and that music is moving on to other things.

I must confess that I am one of the worst offenders. I loved what happened to music in the middle sixties. I loved the hysterics and the carry-on, the girls in tears backstage and all that strutting and hip-waving up front. I hated it when the Beatles started coming apart at the seams. I hated it when the Stones threw a free concert and it ended in death and disaster. I hated it most of all when a man called Robert Weiner made a film called *Groupies* and showed us no magic at all, just a lot of sleazy, greedy, sad girls debasing themselves for a lot of smug, spotty-faced musicians.

"It's not like that at all," I complained to Weiner, and he said: "You know how it is with cinema verite: You only photograph what's there." He didn't make it up, he said, and I had no answer to that except to say that I didn't feel like having my illusion shattered.

But the truth is, and I find it hard to face, that all that is over and the music scene is different and it was kind of brave of Creedence to get us all together and confront us with it.

The band, quite rightly, considers itself the most successful band in America today. What it was asking with its huge gesture was that the media finally acknowledge this.

Why should Jefferson Airplane be on the cover of *Life* or the Band on the cover of *Time* when Creedence Clearwater was really in terms of money and fans what was happening?

Well, there's an answer to that. Jefferson Airplane still carries with it all the glitter of its San Francisco, Haight-Ashbury, flower-power, summer-of-love origins. The band hangs heavy with its associations with Bob Dylan and the Woodstock crowd. Creedence Clearwater has everything – except romance.

They have about as much romance between the four of them as four young executives from General Motors or Minneapolis Mining or something, which is not surprising when you consider that they are four of the most successful young businessmen of our time.

One of them has a beard, one has a moustache and steel-rimmed glasses just like John Lennon, they all have long hair, but don't let them fool you. These are super-efficient technicians and impressively well-functioning financial machines.

"I would like to think I run my business the way they run theirs," said Bill Graham, owner of the two Fillmore theatres and one of rock's top businessmen and entrepreneurs. I think other companies would agree. In the old days the one distinguishing mark of a group was how unbusiness-like they were. That is the thing that's changing.

It would be wrong to give the impression at this stage that Creedence Clearwater Revival is some sort of computerised operation and that their music is produced to some sort of formula.

They started off playing good, strong, middle-fifties rock when they were still at high school, perfecting it at every playing, always bringing it up to date by deftly adding whatever else was happening in music as the years progressed.

Creedence Clearwater's present sound, a sort of middle-fifties Little Richard hard rock brought up to date with a touch of country rock, has worked successfully for the group for the past three years.

It's good to listen to and dance to, but it has been around too long to be the beginning of something new in music.

If groups are influenced at all by Creedence, it will be Creedence's hard-nosed practicality and business sense that is doing it, not its sound.

Their songs like "Up Around the Bend", "Down on the Corner" and "Bad Moon Rising" are hits because in their way they are perfect songs. And Creedence works as hard at that perfection as they do at running their business properly.

It was worth $250,000 to them to get that point across, not just to the underground and music magazines, but to *Life*, *Look* and *Newsweek*.

So there we all were eating crab pancakes and banana cake, and learning that we should stop taking Creedence and its excellence for granted. In a big Berkeley theatre, not far from where students had rioted so historically in past years, we saw an hour-long television special the group had just made which was as good as anything I've ever seen on the music scene anywhere.

Then more food and pampering in the big warehouse and factory Creedence calls home. Over creamed chicken and chocolate fudge pie and little petits fours with red icing we heard the new album, written, produced and put together by the group that books its own concerts, carries its own sound system and generally takes care of business in a way that just couldn't have happened in rock a few years ago.

Some of the writers helping themselves to the second slice of the lemon cream pastry started feeling a little bought. "How can I ever say anything bad about them now?" complained one New York writer.

"What do you have to say that's bad?" I asked.

"Nothing," he confessed, "but who'll ever believe that?"

If that $82 million group had been any less lavish in its hospitality the same writer would have complained about the niggardly treatment. Some people simply don't know how to conduct themselves in the presence of millionaires – especially millionaires who are turning it on. They start feeling guilty.

I don't feel guilty about praising Creedence. I never loved them but I always liked them. I did take them for granted, and I know now that's unrealistic thinking – like putting down Blood Sweat and Tears for being a success and playing Las Vegas and being professional and business-like and frankly interested in making a fortune. Or like putting down Led Zeppelin or Grand Funk Railroad because they play the sort of music that sells out every concert.

I'm in the old school that loves a group when it's down and out and battling and torn with strife and conflicts and emotional drama. I keep thinking that "commercial", when teamed up with rock music, is an ugly word. That, I'm afraid, is very sixties thinking.

The seventies are here and that's not the way it is any more. Rock is big business and that's that. I may not like it, but I can't change it any more than I can get the Beatles together again.

Creedence Clearwater, you complained no one respects you. I want you to know I respect you like crazy. I'll remember your crab pancakes and your fudge pies as the moment when the seventies really happened. Whether I'm ready for the seventies is something else again.

Sydney Morning Herald, 23 January 1971

Picture Acknowledgements

Lillian Roxon aged five. (Roxon family)
Lillian with her mother Rose and brothers Milo and baby Jack. (Roxon family)
Lillian on the beach in Alassio. (Roxon family)
On holiday with Rose and Milo at Zakopane. (Roxon family)
On the deck of the *S.S. Tyndareus*. (Roxon family)
Isadore Roxon-Ropschitz. (Roxon family)
Rose Roxon. (Roxon family)
Lillian aged thirteen with prize cups. (Roxon family)
Lillian aged seventeen visiting the campus of the University of Queensland. (Rhyl Cossins)
Lillian with friends. (Roxon family)
Lillian in Sydney, mid-1950s. (Mary Hope)
Windsor House. (Clem Seale, *Sydney Morning Herald*)
Neil C. Hope (Sope). (Mary Hope)
Lillian with her Push friends. (Jack Roxon)
Farewelling Isadore on the *Himalaya*. (Roxon family)
Lillian and Ross Poole. (Lillian Roxon papers, Mitchell Library, NSW)
Interview with Colonel Tom Parker and Lee Gordon. (*Weekend*)
Interview with Rock Hudson. (*Weekend*)
Interview with Peter Finch. (*Woman's Day*)
Interview with Richard Burton, 1963. (*Woman's Day*)
Zell Rabin, Rupert Murdoch and President Kennedy. (*Daily Mirror*)
Lillian, Don Riseborough and Margaret Jones. (*Sydney Morning Herald*)
The Easybeats. (Lillian Roxon papers, Mitchell Library, NSW)
'There is a Tide in the Affairs of Women.' (*Sydney Morning Herald*)
Germaine Greer as "Earth Rose". (*Suck*)
The apartment building at 221 East 21st Street. (Robert Milliken)
Lillian's photograph for *Mug Shots*. (Raeanne Rubenstein)
Lillian Roxon with Lester Bangs. (Lillian Roxon papers, Mitchell Library, NSW)
Paul and Linda McCartney. (Lillian Roxon Papers, Mitchell Library, NSW)
Lillian with Danny Goldberg, Richard and Lisa Robinson, Richard Neville and Cherry Vanilla. (Leee Childers)
Lillian with Lenny Kaye and Lisa Robinson. (Bob Gruen)

Max's Kansas City bar and restaurant. (Chris Shawn)
Lillian launching the *Rock Encyclopedia*. (Lillian Roxon papers,
   Mitchell Library, NSW)
Cover image of the first edition of *Lillian Roxon's Rock Encyclopedia*
   (Grosset and Dunlap, 1969).
Danny Fields, Lou Reed and Jim Jacobs. (Anton Perich)
Lillian outside the Fillmore East. (Lillian Roxon papers, Mitchell
   Library)
'Lillian Roxon's Diskotique' poster. (Lillian Roxon papers, Mitchell
   Library)
Lillian at Max's Kansas City. (Danny Fields)
Rolling Stone's tribute photograph. (Leee Childers)

Index

Note: In subheadings Lillian Roxon is abbreviated as LR. In the names of rock groups the initial article has been omitted, for example Beatles *not* "The Beatles" *nor* "Beatles, The".